Russia after the cold war

Pearson Education

We work with leading authors to develop the strongest educational materials in International Studies, bringing cutting edge thinking and best learning practice to a global market.

Under a range of well-known imprints, including Longman, we craft high quality print and electronic publications which help readers to understand and apply their content, whether studying or at work.

To find out about the complete range of our publishing please visit us on the World Wide Web at:

www.pearsoned-ema.com

Russia after the cold war

Mike Bowker and
Cameron Ross (Editors)

LONGMAN

an imprint of **Pearson Education**

Harlow, England ■ London ■ New York

Reading, Massachusetts ■ San Francisco ■ Toronto

Don Mills, Ontario ■ Sydney ■ Tokyo ■ Singapore

Hong Kong ■ Seoul ■ Taipei ■ Cape Town ■ Madrid

Mexico City ■ Amsterdam ■ Munich ■ Paris ■ Milan

Pearson Education Limited
Edinburgh Gate
Harlow
Essex CM20 2JE
England

and Associated Companies throughout the World.

Visit us on the World Wide Web at:
www.pearsoned-ema.com

First published 2000

© Pearson Education Limited 2000

ISBN 0-582-36815-4

British Library Cataloguing-in-Publication Data
A catalogue record for this book is available from the British Library

Library of Congress Cataloging-in-Publication Data
Russia after the Cold War / Mike Bowker and Cameron Ross, eds.
     p. cm.
   Includes bibliographical references and index.
   ISBN 0-582-36815-4 (alk. paper)
   1. Russia (Federation) – Politics and government – 1991–
I. Bowker, Mike.   II. Ross, Cameron, 1951–
DK510.763.R857   1999   99–10634
947.086–dc21   CIP

10 9 8 7 6 5 4 3 2 1
05 04 03 02 01 00

Typeset in 10/12 New Baskerville by 35
Produced by Addison Wesley Longman Singapore (Pte) Ltd., Printed in Singapore

Contents

PART II
Economics, culture and social policy *119*

CHAPTER 6
The political economy of Russia: transition or condition? *121*

Anthony Phillips

CHAPTER 7
Crime, corruption and the law *135*

Mark Galeotti

CHAPTER 8
Social policy after the cold war: paying the social costs *151*

Nick Manning and Nadia Davidova

Editors

Mike Bowker, Lecturer in Politics at the University of East Anglia, Norwich. He has written on Russian foreign policy and the cold war. His publications include *Superpower Detente: A Reappraisal*, with Phil Williams (Sage, 1988) and *Russian Foreign Policy and the End of the Cold War* (Dartmouth, 1997). (Introduction.)

Cameron Ross, Lecturer in Russian and East European Politics at the University of Dundee. He has published widely in the field of Russian politics, his most recent publication (co-authored with David Lane) is *The Transition from Communism to Capitalism: Ruling Elites from Gorbachev to Yeltsin* (St Martin's Press, 1998). He is currently working on a book on regional politics in Russia. (Chapter 4.)

Contributors

Alexei Avtonomov, a leading researcher in Moscow at both the Institute of State and Law and the Foundation for the Development of Parliamentarianism in Russia. He has also been a member of the Russian Political Association since 1985. He has written many articles, books and pamphlets over the years, mainly on political parties and parliamentarianism in Russia and around the world. He is currently doing some research on aspects of parliamentary law and assembly in Russia and Belarus. (Chapter 2.)

Edwin Bacon, Lecturer in Russian Politics at the Centre for Russian and East European Studies at the University of Birmingham. He was formerly a Senior Research Officer with the Foreign and Commonwealth Office. As well as a number of articles on Russian politics and security, he is also the author of *The Gulag at War: Stalin's Forced Labour System in the Light of the Archives* (Macmillan, 1994). (Chapter 10.)

John Berryman, Principal Lecturer in European and International Studies and a member of the Russian and East European Research Centre at the University of Wolverhampton. His primary research interests focus on Russian foreign and security policy in the European and North-East Asian regions. His recent publications include 'Russian Security Policy and Northern Europe' in William E Ferry and Roger E Kanet (eds), *Post-Communist States in* *the World Community* (Macmillan, 1998) and 'Russia, NATO Enlargement and the West: Fast Lane or Dead End?' in Paul Brett *et al.* (eds), *Europe: Real and Imagined* (PIC, 1998). (Chapter 18.)

Christoph Bluth, Professor of International Studies at Leeds University. His interests include: Soviet/Russian foreign and security policy, nuclear non-proliferation, German foreign and security policy, Anglo-German relations and cold war history. His many publications include *The Collapse of Soviet Military Power* (Dartmouth, 1994). (Chapter 12.)

Michael Cox, Professor in the Department of International Politics at the University of Aberystwyth. His teaching and research interests are American foreign policy and the history and theory of the cold war. His most recent publication is *US Foreign Policy After The Cold War: Superpower Without A Mission?* (RIIA/Pinter, 1995); he has also edited the volume *Rethinking the Soviet Collapse: Sovietology, the Death of Communism and the New Russia* (Pinter, 1998). (Chapter 14.)

Nadia Davidova, a Research Fellow at the Russian Independent Institute for Social and National Problems. She has been a member of a study of unemployment and employment policy in St Petersburg, Moscow and Voronezh (1995–98) and she will also be a member of another project on poverty, ethnicity and political unrest in Moscow, Voronezh and Chechnya. She is currently working on issues of youth and regional problems, and as part of that study she published 'Regional Specifics of Russian Mentality' in the Russian journal, *Social Sciences*, in 1998. (Chapter 8.)

Mark Galeotti, Director of the Organised Russian and Eurasian Crime Research Unit at Keele University and Senior Lecturer in International History. An expert in post-Soviet security issues, he has been seconded to the British Foreign and Commonwealth Office and advised NATO, Western governments and private companies. His most recent book is *Gorbachev and his Revolution* (Macmillan, 1997), and he is currently working on a book on the Russian mafia. (Chapter 7.)

James Hughes, Senior Lecturer in Russian Government at the London School of Economics and Political Science. He has published widely on regional politics and centre–regional relations in the Soviet Union and contemporary Russia. (Chapter 1.)

Roger E Kanet, Professor and Dean of the School of International Studies at the University of Miami. His recent publications include the following edited and co-edited volumes: *Post-Communist States in the World Community*, with William E Ferry (Macmillan and St Martin's, 1998); *Resolving Regional Conflicts* (University of Illinois Press, 1998); *The Foreign Policy of the Russian Federation*, with Alexander V Kozhemiakin (Macmillan and St Martin's, 1997); *Coping With Conflict after the Cold War*, with Edward A Kolodziej (John Hopkins University Press, 1996). (Chapter 15.)

Julie A Lund, a PhD candidate in the School of International Studies at the University of Miami and a defence economy analyst with the United States Department of Defense. She has contributed to several review essays which have appeared in the journal *Osteuropa*. (Chapter 15.)

Nick Manning, Professor of Sociology and Social Policy at Nottingham University. He is writing up a study on unemployment and employment policy in St Petersburg, Moscow and Voronezh (1995–98), and is about to start another study on poverty, ethnicity and unrest in Moscow, Voronezh and Chechnya. He has also co-edited a book, *Environmental and Housing Movements, Grassroots Experiences in Russia, Estonia and Hungary, 1991–4* (Avebury, 1997). (Chapter 8.)

Andrew Patmore, Senior Research Associate in the School of Economic and Social Studies at the University of East Anglia, Norwich. He has conducted research on the balance of power in the Asia-Pacific region. His current research is on Japanese foreign policy. (Chapter 17.)

Anthony Phillips, completing his PhD at the University of Melbourne on ideological discourse in the late Soviet period. (Chapter 6.)

Richard Sakwa, Professor of Russian and European Politics at the University of Kent at Canterbury. His books include *Gorbachev and His Reforms, 1985–1990* (Prentice-Hall, 1990) and *Russian Politics and Society* (Routledge, 1993; 2nd edition 1996). His current research interests focus on problems of democratic development, post-communism, and the global challenges facing the former communist countries. (Chapter 11.)

Peter Shearman, Senior Lecturer in Political Science at the University of Melbourne. He lectures on International Relations and Russian Politics. He recently edited the book *Russian Foreign Policy Since 1990* (Westview, 1995) and he is currently completing a book on *Globalisation and the Politics of Identity in Russia*. (Chapter 16.)

Mark Webber, Lecturer in Politics in the Department of European Studies at Loughborough University. He has written on Russian foreign policy and security issues. One of his more recent books is *The International Politics of Russia and the Successor States* (Manchester University Press, Manchester, 1996). (Chapter 13.)

Stephen Webber, Lecturer in the Centre for Russian and East European Studies at Birmingham University. He is the author of a number of publications on Russian education, including the book *School, Reform and Society in the New Russia*, to be published by Macmillan in 1999. (Chapter 9.)

Stephen White, Professor of Politics and a Senior Associate Member of the Institute of Central and East European Studies at the University of Glasgow. His recent publications (with others) include *How Russia Votes* (Chatham House, 1997) and *Values and Political Change in Postcommunist Europe* (1998). (Chapter 3.)

Matthew Wyman, Lecturer in Politics at Keele University where he has worked since 1994. He is the author of *Public Opinion in Postcommunist Russia* (Macmillan, 1997) as well as a number of articles in the fields of Russian public opinion, electoral behaviour and party development. He is currently co-authoring a book on regional electoral trends and a textbook on contemporary Russia. (Chapter 5.)

Preface

Mike Bowker and Cameron Ross

Russia is no longer a superpower, but it remains one of the most important states in the world. It is a huge country with a population almost double that of re-unified Germany. It is also rich in natural resources and has a well-educated work-force, all of which means that Russia should, by rights, emerge sometime in the next century as a great economic power once more. In addition, Moscow, for all its recent travails, retains a formidable military capability. It is a sobering thought that Russia still has more than enough nuclear missiles to destroy the entire planet in just a few hours.

In sum, Russia cannot be ignored. What happens in Russia matters to Europe, and beyond. However, Russia too can no longer hide behind a Berlin Wall and isolate itself from the outside world. Since the end of the cold war, Russia has become a more integrated part of an increasingly interdependent world. The events of August 1998 really brought this home as the economic crisis in East Asia spread rapidly westwards and threatened to undermine the whole reform process in Russia. Nationalists and communists might rage at Russia's dependency on international bankers and financiers, but any attempt to leap off the roller-coaster ride that is the modern international capitalist system promises little more than further pain. This is the true nature of dependency, as an increasing number of Russian politicians have come to recognise.

Russia's uneasy dependency on the outside world is the underlying theme of this book. Unique among volumes on the post-Soviet period, this work takes full account of Russia's much reduced status in the world and provides comprehensive coverage of both the internal and external factors of transition. In so doing, it offers a more complete picture of contemporary Russia than other books currently on the market. The book is divided up into three sections, the first two on domestic aspects of transition, the third on foreign policy, but all con-tributors have emphasised the interconnections between the domestic and the international.

Part 1 looks at the process of political transition in Russia. Although the progress made in Russia since 1985 can too easily be underestimated – Russia has now become used to regular, competitive elections and a free press – democracy in Russia is clearly far from fully developed. A return to more authoritarian leadership seems highly likely if there is no economic upturn in the near future and social problems continue to multiply. Economic and social issues are the central concern of Part 2 which outlines the bleak reality of an impoverished populace, widening differentials, and a state lacking the funds to provide basic education, health and welfare services for its citizens.

Considering the deprivations faced by the vast majority of ordinary Russians since the collapse of the Soviet Union, their stoicism has been remarkable. Nevertheless, there have to be doubts that this can continue for much longer. Russian history is full of examples of periods of calm and public docility followed by sudden eruptions of violence and revolt. This pattern could repeat itself unless the government can begin to generate some level of optimism among the people sometime soon. At present, Russians lack a focus and a sense of direction. The certainties of the Soviet period have gone. In the process, Russia not only lost its Marxist–Leninist ideology, it also lost a state and its place in the world. Confined within new, unfamiliar and sometimes unstable borders, Russia has faced confusion over its national and cultural identity, which in turn has led to furious debate over the fundamentals of foreign policy and Russia's future role in the world.

Part 3 takes up these issues explicitly. There can be no doubt that the effects of transition have greatly weakened Russia as an international actor. What this actually means in terms of foreign policy, however, remains hotly disputed. Most fundamentally, does Russian weakness mean that Moscow is a greater or lesser security threat to Europe and its neighbours? On the one hand, the current state of the Russian military suggests that Moscow is in no position to launch any kind of attack against the West. Moreover, there are also doubts that Russia can subdue its own increasingly rebellious regions at home, never mind take back the newly independent Soviet successor states as some nationalists would like. Since there are few signs of economic recovery, many argue that Russian military capability is unlikely to change in the foreseeable future. Others, however, argue that such an attitude is terribly short-sighted. To base Western security on continued Russian weakness will, according to such commentators, store up all sorts of problems for the future. Weakness is a source of instability at home which could create the conditions for an extreme nationalist resurgence in Russia. In those circumstances, a strong leader could rebuild the military at the expense of the civilian economy and, like Nazi Germany not so long ago, seek to avenge the perceived injustices of the recent past.

Thankfully, such worst-case scenarios have not as yet come to pass. Russia has not collapsed as a state, civil war has not broken out, the very real danger of nuclear accidents has thus far been contained. Moreover, Russia, for all its doubts, has continued to deal with the West and to seek accommodation with its former cold war enemies. However, these chapters show that there is no room for complacency. The crisis of the summer of 1998 starkly revealed the partial nature of transition in contemporary Russia. It would seem that the common supposition that the Russian transition, for all its difficulties, is still heading in the right direction might well be misplaced. For it is at least arguable that the first stage of transition is now over and a new, distinctively Russian system is already in place. If so, it looks a deeply unattractive beast, combining many of the worst features of capitalism and Sovietism. Many epithets have been used to describe the new reality in Russia, but perhaps 'bandit corporatism' is best.

For it is a system riven with crime and corruption and dominated by a handful of self-interested politicians and billionaires.

The tragedy for Russia is that the ultimate goals of transition – a mature democracy and a fully functioning market – seem as distant as ever. Of all the possible indictments that could be levelled against the Yeltsin administration and his advisers (both in Russia and the West), this is surely the most damning of all. Russia remains a highly unstable and unpredictable place, and the chapters in this book indicate that this is unlikely to change for some time yet.

A note from the editors

Acknowledgements

The editors of this volume would like to thank the Universities of East Anglia and Dundee for funding a conference at UEA, Norwich, in February 1998 where many of the contributors gave first drafts of the chapters included here. They would also like to thank the staff at Longman who have been so helpful throughout the process of writing, compiling, editing and publishing this book.

Transliteration

Transliteration from the cyrillic alphabet is a difficult and sometimes contro-versial topic. We have decided to use the standard Library of Congress system for end notes and referencing wherever possible, but the more common and simplified spellings for the general text. Thus, in the text we spell the current Russian President's surname as Yeltsin, not in the formal Library of Congress style as El'tsin.

Boxes and pen-portraits

Most of the boxed inserts and figures which appear in the chapters have been written by the respective author of the chapter. On occasion, however, they have been added by the editors, while all the brief pen-portraits have been written and inserted by the editors. Sources have been cited in the boxes and pen-portraits where relevant, but some sources which have been extensively utilised should be mentioned separately here. They are Martin McCauley, *Who's Who in Russia* (Routledge, London, 1997), *Kto est kto v Rossii i byvshem SSSR* (Terra, Moscow, 1994), Archie Brown (ed.), *Encyclopaedia of the Soviet Union and Russia* (Cambridge University Press, Cambridge) and *The International Who's Who. 1996–97* (60th edition, Europa Publications Ltd, London, 1996).

All the boxed inserts in the text are headed with the Russian translation, 'spravka' (СПРАВКА), and the pen-portraits with the word 'biografiya' (БИОГРАФИЯ). 'Spravka' literally means information, and 'biografiya' biography. The Russian (cyrillic) alphabet puts a lot of people off, but it is really not as difficult as some suppose. Many of the letters are the same in both the cyrillic and the Latin alphabets, while others exist in both but have a different sound in English. Thus, for 'spravka', the cyrillic 'C' is pronounced as 'S' in English, and 'B' as 'V'. Therefore, the only letter that is completely different in the word 'spravka' is the cyrillic for 'P' which looks rather like a Latin 'n' but with straight lines. Thus, 'S p r a v k a' is rendered in cyrillic script as СПРАВКА.

The cyrillic for 'biografiya' is rather more complicated, but at least 'O' and 'A' are the same in both alphabets, and the Latin 'R' sound is written as 'P' in cyrillic. The English 'B' in cyrillic is 'Б'; 'I' is rather like 'U' with straight lines: 'И'; 'G' is like a small English 'r' with straight lines 'Г'; 'F' is the rather lovely and extravagant 'Ф' – rather like a flower in bloom; the sound in English, 'ya' – as in the English word, 'yap' – is rendered by just one letter in Russian, the backward 'R', 'Я', like in Toys 'Я' Us, the famous international toy company. Thus, 'B i o g r a f i y a' is rendered in cyrillic script as БИОГРАФИЯ.

Acknowledgements

The publishers wish to thank the following for permission to reproduce material:

Addison Wesley Longman Ltd for Figure 4.1. Macmillan Press Ltd for Table 2.3. The Macmillan Press Ltd/The Royal Institute of International Affairs for the map in Chapter 17. Routledge, London, for the map in Chapter 13. Box 16.7 is © The International Herald Tribune (distributed by the New York Times Syndicate). Zavtra Newspaper, Russia for the prayer in Box 10.1.

Though every effort has been made to trace the owners of copyright material, in a few cases this has proved impossible and we take this opportunity to apologise to any copyright holders whose rights may have been unwittingly infringed.

APEC	Asian–Pacific Economic Cooperation
ASEAN	Association of South East Asian Nations
CAP	Common Agricultural Policy
CDPSP	Current Digest of the Post-Soviet Press
CEE	Central and East European States
CFE	Conventional Forces in Europe
CIS	Commonwealth of Independent States
CMEA	Council for Mutual and Economic Assistance (Comecon)
CPD	Congress of People's Deputies
CPRF	Communist Party of the Russian Federation
CPSU	Communist Party of the Soviet Union
CSCE	Conference on Security and Cooperation in Europe (changed name to OSCE in 1995)
EAPC	European–Atlantic Partnership Council
EBRD	European Bank of Reconstruction and Development
EC	European Community (changed name to EU in 1993)
EU	European Union (successor to EC)
FCO	Foreign and Commonwealth Office
FSU	Former Soviet Union
G7	Group of Seven Richest Countries
G8	G7 plus Russia
GATT	General Agreement on Tariffs and Trade
GDP	Gross Domestic Product
GNP	Gross National Product
ICBM	Intercontinental Ballistic Missile
IFOR	Implementation Force (in Bosnia)
IMF	International Monetary Fund
INF	Internediate Nuclear Forces
KGB	Committee of State Security
LDPR	Liberal Democratic Party of Russia
MEP	Member of the European Parliament
MFA	Ministry of Foreign Affairs
MVD	Ministry of Internal Affairs
NACC	North Atlantic Cooperation Council
NATO	North Atlantic Treaty Organisation
NMP	Net Material Product

OECD	Organisation of Economic Cooperation and Development
OMON	Special Purpose Police Unit (riot police)
OSCE	Organisation of Cooperation and Security in Europe (successor to CSCE)
PCA	Partnership and Cooperation Agreement
PfP	Partnership for Peace
PHARE	Poland and Hungary: Aid for the Reconstruction of Economies
PJC	Permanent Joint Council
PR	Proportional Representation
PSI	Private Security Industry
RSFSR	Russian Soviet Federated Socialist Republic
RF	Russian Federation
SALT	Strategic Arms Limitation Treaty
SDI	Strategic Defence Initiative
START	Strategic Arms Reduction Treaty
SWAT	Crime Police
TACIS	Technical Assistance for the Commonwealth of Independent States
UN	United Nations
USSR	Union of Soviet Socialist Republics
VtsIOM	All-Russian Centre for the Study of Public Opinion
WEU	Western European Union
WTO	Warsaw Treaty Organisation (Warsaw Pact)

Introduction

Mike Bowker

Introduction: the nature of the Soviet system

The political system inherited by Mikhail Gorbachev when he came to power in the Soviet Union in March 1985 had changed surprisingly little since Stalin's day. The state had abandoned the mass arbitrary terror of that era, but the political structures remained essentially neo-Stalinist. The Soviet Union was a highly centralised dictatorship which was dominated by the Communist Party of the Soviet Union (CPSU) through its control over the state, the economy and the means of repression. Society was atomised, unable to express its views openly and unable to organise into groups independent of the party and state. The party justified its dominant position with reference to both Marxist–Leninist ideology and the success of its policies. Over a period of time, the CPSU had some success in gaining legitimacy among the Soviet people. A large proportion of Soviet citizens came to support the long-term goals of the party – socialism, equality and the state ownership of property – while also acknowledging that life in the USSR had improved for the vast majority of people. Living standards had risen since 1945 (more people had luxury consumer goods, such as cars, televisions, freezers and so on); social welfare was basic but extensive (education and health care were free, housing and energy virtually free and the state promised a job to all of its citizens); the country had emerged from the rubble of World War II as an internationally recognised superpower.

СПРАВКА 1 Soviet leaders

Vladimir Lenin: 1917–24

Joseph Stalin: 1924–53

Nikita Khrushchev: 1953–64

Leonid Brezhnev: 1964–82

Yuri Andropov: 1982–84

Konstantin Chernenko: 1984–85

Mikhail Gorbachev: 1985–91

Nevertheless, towards the end of Leonid Brezhnev's time in office, pressures were building up on the Soviet political elite to reform the system. There were three main reasons why this was so: (1) internal political and social pressures; (2) economic pressures; (3) external pressures.

Internal political and social pressures

By the late 1970s, the Soviet political system appeared inflexible and out of touch. A small group of predominantly old men made decisions behind closed doors in Moscow. In good times, this might have been tolerable, but as problems mounted unease grew. The country had changed from the largely illiterate peasant society of Stalin's day to one which was far better educated and increasingly more white collar. In these changing conditions, the monist, one-party system was less able to satisfy the demands of an increasingly complex society. Expectations were also rising and Gorbachev recognised this. A year before he became Soviet leader, he confided to his friend and future Foreign Minister, Eduard Shevardnadze, that things had to change. Gorbachev wanted to reform the Soviet system to avoid the future possibility of revolution. Therefore, he tried to create a system which was more accountable and responsive to the needs of the people.

Economic pressure

Although the Soviet Union had experienced rapid growth rates into the 1950s, they began to slow thereafter. Limited reform under Khrushchev and Brezhnev failed to reverse the trend and by the late 1970s growth had virtually disappeared altogether. The centralised command economy was reasonably effective in increasing production in a few priority areas (mainly heavy industry and the military) through the imposition of simple output targets, but other non-priority areas (notably the consumer goods and service industries) remained backward and grossly underfunded. The Soviet economic system as a whole was generally unresponsive to consumer demands, slow to innovate and extremely wasteful. As a result, the Soviet economy was typified by inefficiency, shortages, queues and poor-quality goods.

External pressures

The Soviet Union had always been, in the words of Paul Dibb (1988), 'an incomplete superpower'. Moscow's status rested almost entirely on its military strength, and most particularly on its formidable nuclear arsenal. However, Moscow was experiencing difficulties in the early 1980s in maintaining its high levels of defence spending. Pressures were growing at a time when President Reagan was committed to a new military build-up in the US, especially in new-generation high-technology weaponry. Already Moscow was spending 15 per cent or more of its GDP on defence, while the US spent less than half that amount. As the Soviet economy fell into relative decline in the late 1970s, it was increasingly apparent that Moscow could ill afford a new arms race with the US.

Furthermore, the sacrifices the Soviet Union had made to become a military superpower had won it international respect but few friends. For a state with global pretensions, the Soviet Union was surprisingly isolated. All the major powers in the international system – the US, the EU, Japan and China – were lined up against Moscow, while even many of the second-rank powers in the Middle East, Asia and Latin America viewed the Soviet Union with considerable distrust and suspicion. Moscow's main allies were confined to Eastern Europe and a handful of impoverished states in the Third World. Many Third World allies were hanging on to power by their finger nails in the face of popular insurrection and civil war, in countries as far afield as Afghanistan, Angola, Ethiopia and Nicaragua. Even in Eastern Europe, Soviet influence was maintained more by force and the threat of force, rather than through a genuine alliance of mutual interest. In sum, the global position of the Soviet Union in 1985 was far less imposing in practice than the communist leadership pretended and the Western world feared at the time.

The Gorbachev era

Mikhail Gorbachev represented a real break in Soviet history. He was not a particularly young man when he assumed power – he was 54 years old, but he did come from a different generation to his immediate predecessors. Khrushchev, Brezhnev, Andropov and Chernenko all made their careers, to a greater or lesser extent, in the Stalinist years. None was entirely free of the stigma that that implied. Gorbachev, on the other hand, owed nothing to Stalin. He was still a student at Moscow State University when Stalin died in 1953, and he became open to the idea of reform after witnessing the hope and optimism generated by Khrushchev's thaw in the 1950s and early 1960s. Gorbachev was well educated – he was the first Soviet leader since Lenin to have graduated from university. He was also better informed about the West than any of his predecessors, having travelled to Italy as a private citizen and to Canada and Britain in a public capacity before his appointment as General Secretary. He was acutely aware that the West did not conform to the simplistic caricatures of Soviet propaganda and, as a result, he was far more willing than his predecessors to engage with the West in open and honest dialogue. From all accounts, Gorbachev enjoyed his vigorous debates with Mrs Thatcher; he respected her views even if he rejected most of her arguments.

Many reformers greeted Gorbachev's elevation to General Secretary with enthusiasm. Others, however, were more sceptical. Gorbachev was different from his predecessors in many respects, but he had still risen to the top in the conventional way – through the party as a full-time party official. Because of this, there were doubts that Gorbachev would wish, or be able, really to change the communist system to which he had devoted his life. To an extent, this was true. Gorbachev came to power to save communism, not to destroy it, and many of his reforms reflected this fact. However, Gorbachev did actively seek change. Using his own terminology, he wanted *perestroika* – restructuring. He met much opposition from the old guard, from the party and state elite (the *nomenklatura*), and

СПРАВКА 2 On the *Gulag Archipelago* and *Repentance*

Alexander Solzhenitsyn (born 1918) was a communist believer until he was imprisoned for writing a letter home critical of the way the war was being run. He was in prison or exile from 1945 to 1957. He was finally released as part of the so-called Khrushchev thaw. His first novel about the camps was *One Day in the Life of Ivan Denisovich* which was published with Khrushchev's approval in 1962. His other works were banned in Russia until the late 1980s. His three-volume opus, *Gulag Archipelago*, used documentary evidence to expose the terrifying nature and extent of the labour camp network in the Stalinist era. He was expelled from the USSR in 1974 shortly after the book was published in the West. When Solzhenitsyn returned to Russia after the fall of communism, he became a fierce critic of the Yeltsin government. A member of the Orthodox Church, Solzhenitsyn condemned the materialism and lack of spirituality in post-Soviet Russia. However, his views were largely ignored by the Russian public. To many, he seemed a figure from the Soviet past who had diminishing relevance to the current situation in Russia.

Tengiz Abuladze (born 1924) was a Georgian film maker whose film, *Repentance*, made him internationally famous. The film was made in 1984, but only released in 1986 during the early days of Gorbachev's *glasnost* campaign. The film was a sensation. It broke many of the taboos of the Brezhnev period by portraying the full horror and degradation of the Stalinist era. An estimated 17 million Soviet people saw the film in its first three weeks of release.

from the military and the secret services, but this was only to be expected. What was more surprising was the level of support at the top for some kind of radical reform, even among more conservative figures in the political establishment (see Ligachev, 1993, pp. 274–5). Opposition against Gorbachev only really became organised late in his term of office when the reform process began to threaten the very existence of communism as a system and the Soviet Union as a state.

Political reform

Gorbachev's first political initiative on taking power was *glasnost*. This was a call for more openness in public life and more personal freedom for Soviet citizens. Soon after coming to power, political prisoners began to drift home. By 1989, they had all been released. Censorship was eased with the party slowly giving up its control over the media, culture and the arts. By the late 1980s, independent newspapers were published, previously banned books, like Solzhenitsyn's *Gulag Archipelago*, were put on sale and films like Abuladze's *Repentance* were taken down from the shelves and put on general public release for the first time (Box 2).

Liberalisation was a slow and uneven process, but, by the time Gorbachev left office, the stagnant, conformist public facade of the Brezhnev years had disappeared forever. *Glasnost* was an important policy innovation which opened up the system to a fundamental re-assessment of its past and current role. Once Stalin had been branded as a mass murderer and his successors as corrupt and incompetent, it was difficult for the party to continue to claim its vanguard role and its constitutional right to rule (for a full analysis of this view, see Remnick, 1993). Gorbachev recognised that the party had made grievous mistakes in the past. To avoid similar ones in the future, he argued, the powers of the party had to be constrained, like in the West, by legal and constitutional means.

Thus, at the Nineteenth CPSU Conference in June 1988, Gorbachev began the process of democratisation and introduced the concept of the separation of powers (see Chapter 2). New powers were given to the Soviet legislature (the Congress of People's Deputies and the Supreme Soviet) and a Constitutional Commission was set up to monitor executive action and policy. The first competitive elections since the earliest days of the revolution took place in March 1989. Although democratisation at this stage was limited, the first session of the Congress of People's Deputies (CPD) was a lively affair. For the first time, the Soviet public could watch their elected deputies debate issues openly on live TV. As such, it became a defining moment in the Gorbachev era – the people were being invited to participate in the political process. They were being treated as mature, educated people who could determine their own interests for themselves. Henceforth, it would always be difficult to turn the clock back and, to be fair, Gorbachev made little attempt to do so. In fact, he made efforts to accelerate the reform process over the coming 12 months.

Thus, an embryonic multi-party system was introduced when in February 1990 Gorbachev formally abolished Article 6 of the Soviet Constitution which gave the CPSU a guaranteed, monopoly right to rule. In the following month, the role of the party was further reduced with the creation of a presidential system in the Soviet Union (see Chapter 2 for further details). Democratisation was not limited to central bodies either. Republic and regional elections were held through the year 1990 in all the 15 Union Republics. In the more democratic atmosphere that prevailed by the time of these local elections, nationalists performed well in many republics, putting further pressure on the Soviet Union as a unitary state.

Economic reform

These pressures were further exacerbated by growing economic problems. When Gorbachev came to power, he had hoped to reverse economic decline and to raise living standards for the majority of Soviet people. He hoped to do this through the introduction of some market indicators into the state system. Competition was encouraged through an increase in foreign trade and foreign investment in joint ventures. Gorbachev also introduced a highly ambitious reform programme, called 'The Law on State Enterprises', in January 1988 which sought to decentralise decision-making power from the central planners down to the individual enterprises and service outlets and to replace gross output targets with profitability as the main determinant of a firm's operational success. As such, Gorbachev was attempting to create a 'third way'. He sought

СПРАВКА 3   **Main arms control agreements since 1985**

1987: Intermediate Nuclear Forces Treaty (INF) eliminated all land-based nuclear weapons of a range between 300 and 3000 miles in Europe and Asia.

1990: Conventional Forces in Europe Treaty (CFE) placed limits on conventional weaponry in Europe and lowered force levels to rough parity between NATO and the Warsaw Pact. (This treaty was subsequently amended to take account of the abolition of both the Warsaw Pact and the USSR.)

1991: Strategic Arms Reduction Treaty (START I) reduced US and USSR arsenals of strategic nuclear weapons by about 30 per cent.

1993: START II cut strategic nuclear weapons held on each side to between 3000 and 3500 (still unratified by the Russian parliament).

the efficiencies of the market combined with the social conscience of socialism. However, the reforms proved to be a disaster. Production collapsed, inflation took off and the state finances reached crisis proportions by the end of 1990 (see Chapter 6). The reasons for collapse are many and complex, but a few general factors can be briefly mentioned here. First, the reforms were ill thought out, both in concept and in detail. No such hybrid system had been tried anywhere in the world before. It was ill advised to embark on reforms of this scale without at least limited trials beforehand. Second, the enterprise directors were untrained and unprepared to take on the new responsibilities being asked of them by the government. Directors were used to simply accepting orders. Now they were being asked to become risk-taking entrepreneurs and Western-style managers. Finally, bureaucratic opposition forced Gorbachev to water down the reforms to such an extent that they became unworkable.

The economic problems in the USSR worsened as state authority declined. Further reform became impossible, and from 1990 the economy entered a downward spiral from which it still has not recovered.

Foreign policy

In many respects, Gorbachev had more success in foreign policy. When he came to power, he was keen to improve relations with the West. To this end, he signed a series of important arms control treaties (see Box 3) in conventional and nuclear weaponry which reduced tension across the East–West divide. These agreements also allowed Gorbachev to fulfil his long-term aim of cutting back on Soviet defence spending from 1989.

Gorbachev also won much international support when he actively sought national reconciliation in a series of regional conflicts around the world. Most significantly, he extricated Soviet troops from the unwinnable war in Afghanistan in February 1989. This began a process of Soviet withdrawal from

СПРАВКА 4 The Brezhnev Doctrine

It is quite clear that an action such as military assistance to a fraternal country to end a threat to the socialist system is an extraordinary measure, dictated by necessity; it can be called forth only by the overt actions of enemies of socialism within the country and beyond its boundaries, actions that create a threat to the common interests of the socialist camp.

This was Leonid Brezhnev, in a speech on 12 November 1968, explaining the reason for the use of force to suppress the reform movement in Czechoslovakia. Later known as the Brezhnev Doctrine, it implied the limited level of sovereignty available to Soviet allies in Eastern Europe.

Military force was used by the Soviet Union to maintain its influence in Eastern Europe on three occasions:

- East Germany in 1953
- Hungary in 1956
- Czechoslovakia in 1968

Poland was a slightly different case. Moscow flexed its military muscles in 1980 and 1981 as the power of the Solidarity trade union movement threatened to overthrow the communist system, but martial law was actually imposed by the Polish authorities themselves in December 1981.

the rest of the Third World. Even more remarkably, the politburo formally decided to abandon the Brezhnev Doctrine (Box 4) in 1986 (Bowker, 1997, p. 89). This meant that the Soviet Union would no longer use military force in Eastern Europe in support of the Marxist–Leninist governments in the region. Thus, in 1989, when the peoples of Eastern Europe rose up against their communist leaders, Moscow did not intervene militarily. When the Berlin Wall came down in November 1989, it was clear at last that the cold war was over. The great ideological rivalry between Moscow and Washington had come to an end.

The peaceful end of the cold war must go down as one of Gorbachev's greatest achievements. However, it was an achievement borne at some cost to Moscow. Despite Gorbachev's protestations at the time, there was an inescapable feeling that the Soviet Union had lost the cold war. For it was the Soviet Union which had made all the major concessions. It was Moscow which had given up its ideology, its status as a superpower and even the USSR as a state. Russia emerged from the cold war as no more than a Eurasian power. Its global pretensions had gone. This had never been part of Gorbachev's plan. He hoped his new thinking in foreign policy would enhance the international status of the Soviet Union. Moscow would give up its revolutionary rhetoric in order to build trust and to forge closer relations with other major powers around the world. However, as stated earlier, the status of the USSR was founded almost entirely on military power. As Gorbachev de-emphasised the military as a foreign policy tool, he simultaneously downgraded the Soviet Union as an international power. Other than military aid, what had Moscow to offer its allies around the world?

The US, in contrast, emerged as the dominant power in the post-cold-war world and liberal democracy as the dominant social system. The West's victory was seen by nationalists and communists in post-Soviet Russia as something of a humiliation. Few in Moscow wanted a return to the cold war. Many, however, mourned the passing of the Soviet Union as a great power.

An overview of the Gorbachev years

To summarise, any analysis of Gorbachev's reforms must look at different areas of policy. In some he achieved more than in others. However, even in his own terms, he was never better than partially successful. His greatest achievement was recognising the need for change and, despite some setbacks and hesitations, maintaining that commitment throughout his time in office (see Brown, 1996, pp. 269–72). However, he was too often unclear about the direction and purpose of the reform process. Too often, his reform proposals were ill thought out, incoherent and inconsistent. On the one hand, Gorbachev appeared to underestimate the difficulties of reform. On the other, he seemed to think that the Soviet Union and the communist system were so robust that they could withstand almost any amount of reform and thrive. Instead, the Soviet Union's stability and strength was more apparent than real. The Soviet system rested on three pillars – ideology, the CPSU and a strong state. Gorbachev proceeded to undermine them all – either deliberately or as an indirect result of his reforms. Gorbachev promised a communist renaissance. What he actually produced was the destruction of the communist system and the collapse of the Soviet Union as a state. It was a far more negative legacy than anything he had envisaged for *perestroika* some six years earlier.

The rise of Boris Yeltsin

Boris Yeltsin was brought to Moscow by Gorbachev in the summer of 1985 and became party leader in Moscow a few months later. He brought dynamism to his job and a reputation as a fixer from his time as party secretary in Sverdlovsk. In Moscow, Yeltsin quickly turned his attention to attacking privilege, perks and corruption in the city. It was a policy which gained him much support among the people but deep suspicion among the old guard. Although his political skills were widely recognised, he became known as something of a maverick – a loose cannon. This reputation seemed to be confirmed when he made an unscheduled speech to the Central Committee of the CPSU in October 1987. He attacked the slow pace of reform and the personality cult which, he said, was forming around Gorbachev. He was summarily dismissed from his post as First Secretary of Moscow and later lost his seat on the politburo. Many believed that Yeltsin's career was over. Few ever made a political comeback in the Soviet Union. However, Yeltsin was never forgotten by the people. He was widely seen as a martyr who had risked his career by taking on the party establishment. After Yeltsin repeated many of his accusations in public at the Party Conference in June 1988, his profile began to rise once more.

Gorbachev unwittingly gave Yeltsin his political lifeline when he started the process of democratisation. Yeltsin seized his chance and stood for election in a Moscow constituency for the new Congress of People's Deputies in March 1989. He won an overwhelming victory over the official party candidate, Brakov, the director of the ZIL car factory, gaining almost 90 per cent of the vote. Moreover, this was achieved despite a vigorous campaign against him in the official media. The following year, Yeltsin was also elected a deputy to the Russian parliament and soon became its *de facto* leader when appointed its chairman. In April 1991, the people supported in a referendum the introduction of a presidential system and elected Yeltsin as Russian President in June. This gave Yeltsin a firm base to challenge Gorbachev's power as Soviet leader. Yeltsin could now claim greater legitimacy than his rival – he had been elected to power by the people in a competitive election. This was in stark contrast to Gorbachev who had always avoided any such challenge. Gorbachev had been elected as Soviet President not by the people but unopposed by the members of the Congress of People's Deputies. His unwillingness to face the people affected his popularity, and from May 1990 Yeltsin began to overtake Gorbachev for the first time in the opinion polls (Brown, 1996, p. 6).

The August coup of 1991

Politics became more polarised around this time as the economic and political crisis in the Soviet Union worsened considerably. From the winter of 1990, there had been repeated warnings in the Soviet media of an impending coup. So it was scarcely a surprise when the Soviet Union woke up on the morning of 19 August 1991 to hear that a State Emergency Committee had taken power. According to the official communique, Gorbachev was ill and a temporary state of emergency had been imposed on the country. The immediate cause of the action was the imminent signing of the new Union Treaty which hardliners believed would lead to the disintegration of the Soviet Union as a state. A year or two earlier, the coup might have been successful, but, by the summer of 1991, the Soviet Union had changed. It had ceased to be a simple, monist dictatorship. It was no longer enough for a section of the old guard to get together with a few army officers to take power and to reverse the reforms of the previous six years. In a real sense, the state had become more pluralist. Power was more dispersed and the coup only served to extend this process.

The political elite was split down the middle by the events of August. There were divisions both between institutions and within institutions. Crucially, neither the party nor the military was united in support of the coup. Even the Committee of State Emergency which had initiated the action seemed uncertain how to proceed. These uncertainties were exemplified by the incompetence of the leading members of the Committee, some of whom appeared to be drunk and absented themselves throughout the crisis. Yeltsin, on the other hand, rose to the challenge. On the first morning of the coup, he stood on a tank outside the White House (the Russian parliamentary building) and publicly declared his opposition to the conspirators. Yeltsin risked his life, but in that memorable moment he became the focus of the opposition movement throughout the Soviet Union. As a directly elected leader, he could always claim to speak on behalf of the Russian people to a far greater extent than the little known members of the self-appointed Committee of State Emergency.

The coup collapsed after just three days. Gorbachev returned to what he himself referred to as a 'different country' (Gorbachev, 1991, p. 38). The old guard had discredited itself – less in the fact that it mounted the coup (a large proportion of the public and many of the regions supported it), but rather in its shambolic implementation (see Shevtsova, 1992, p. 7). There was also a strong feeling among reformers in the Soviet Union that Gorbachev had taken the reforms as far as he could. His failed attempts after his return to Moscow to save first the party and then the Soviet Union only served to reinforce the view that he was out of touch. Gorbachev's time was past and Yeltsin seized the opportunity finally to cast his rival aside. Declaring that the Soviet Union could no longer be saved, a communique was issued in Minsk in December 1991 which announced the imminent abolition of the USSR and its replacement by the Commonwealth of Independent States (CIS). The 15 Union Republics of the Soviet Union became internationally recognised independent sovereign states on 1 January 1992, with Russia by far the largest and potentially the richest of them all.

No Soviet leader had ever left office voluntarily. Most were carried out in wooden boxes, Khrushchev alone was forced out by his colleagues. Gorbachev, however, was left after the Minsk communique in the curious position of being President of a state that was about to disappear. Gorbachev had no choice but to accept the inevitable and resign. This he did after a dignified valedictory speech on 25 December 1991.

Yeltsin in power

Yeltsin had achieved his aim. He no longer had a rival power base to contend with in Moscow. He used his new status to introduce radical reform which was designed to overthrow the last remnants of communism in his country. His first priority was the economy. On the advice of his close confidant, Gennadi Burbulis, he placed Yegor Gaidar, a young liberal economist with little experience of politics, in charge of economic policy. Following the lead of Poland, and with the support of many Western economic advisers, Gaidar resolved to make a dash for the market. He introduced a policy called 'shock therapy' (see Chapter 6). Gaidar argued that the command economy had failed. Gorbachev's attempts to forge a third way had only made matters worse. The Russian state by the end of 1991 was almost bankrupt; it no longer had the resources to support loss-making farms and enterprises. There was an urgent need, Gaidar said, to abandon the failed policies of the past and embrace capitalism and the market.

Shock therapy consisted of three inter-related policies, all of which had to be implemented as quickly as possible. They included cuts in state spending, the freeing of prices, and privatisation. All reformist economists were agreed over the need for such policies, but doubts were expressed over the timing and speed of reform. Concerns were also expressed right from the start about the possible social consequences of radical reform (see Aslund, 1995).

Initially, parliament backed shocked therapy, but its subsequent failure demanded an urgent re-assessment. Industrial and agricultural production collapsed, living standards fell and vital social services were slashed. Diseases, such as diphtheria and cholera, long conquered in the Soviet Union, returned to haunt the villages and towns of Russia. Life expectancy for Russian males fell to as low as 58 years – not only because of epidemics, but also as a result of stress and alcohol-related problems (see Chapter 8). At the same time, crime exploded onto the streets of Russia. Mafia operations took over large sectors of the economy and posed a threat to democracy itself. Moscow, once one of the safest cities in the world, overtook New York in the mid-1990s in the number of homicides per year (Smiley, 1995, p. 58). Reports of assassinations of politicians, business people and investigative journalists became common. Private security became one of the few boom industries in post-Soviet Russia (see Chapter 7).

In the circumstances, it was scarcely surprising that the Russian people became disillusioned with the reform process – or that parliament became more critical of the President. The problem was, however, that parliament failed to occupy the role of a constructive opposition. Instead, it became increasingly negative and obstructionist. Parliament acted to undermine the government while refusing to take responsibility for its own actions. To an extent, there was a genuine dispute over the nature of power in Yeltsin's Russia – the constitution suggested that ultimate power rested with parliament, while Yeltsin, for his part, claimed pre-eminence on the grounds that the Russian people had voted for an executive presidency in April 1991 and for him as President the following June. The result was a prolonged stand-off between the executive and the legislature through much of 1993.

The October 1993 events

After an unsuccessful attempt over the summer to get agreement on a new constitution, Yeltsin bit the bullet and decided to act. On 21 September 1993, he issued a decree which dissolved parliament, and he announced that a referendum on a new constitution and new parliamentary elections would take place simultaneously on 12 December. Yeltsin's opponents in parliament decided, in a conscious replay of August 1991, to occupy the White House. Opposition was led by Ruslan Khasbulatov, chairman of Congress, and Alexander Rutskoi, Yeltsin's former Vice-President. Citing the decision of the Constitutional Court which had earlier declared the state of emergency to be illegal, the rebels set up an alternative government with Rutskoi as leader. Yeltsin responded by sealing off the White House. People were still allowed to leave but they could no longer enter the parliamentary building.

The rebels failed to gain general support in the country. Few recognised Rutskoi's alternative government and the base of his support soon began to ebb away. On the first day of the crisis, 658 deputies out of a total of 1033 attended the parliamentary session called by the rebels; by the end, there were only about 100 still in the White House. The main support for Rutskoi and Khasbulatov came from extreme nationalists and communists, as well as many of the regional soviets in Russia.

The occupation reached a climax on Sunday 3 October 1993, when about 15 000 rebel supporters overwhelmed the interior troops to gain entry to the White House. The rebel success spurred Rutskoi and Khasbulatov to believe the military and security services had deserted Yeltsin. Thus, Rutskoi went on to the balcony of the White House and called on his supporters to take the mayor's office and then the main TV centre in Moscow, *Ostankino* (Kutsyllo, 1993, p. 112). The mayor's office was close by and easily overrun by the rebels. The TV centre proved to be more difficult and fighting broke out on the streets and continued throughout the night. Sixty-two people died in the subsequent street battles in Moscow. When radio and TV broadcasts were closed down in the early evening, Khasbulatov thought that *Ostankino* had been taken by his supporters and declared that the time was now at hand to 'seize the Kremlin' (*International Herald Tribune*, 9–10 October 1993). The crisis was only resolved in the small hours when Yeltsin finally got agreement from his Defence Minister, Pavel Grachev, to use military force against the rebels. Thus, for 10 hours the following morning, tanks shelled the White House building. The rebels finally gave themselves up in the evening when both Rutskoi and Khasbulatov were arrested.

Events after 1993

Yeltsin, it seemed, had won another great victory. His opponents were crushed. Many were in prison. His supporters, both inside and outside Russia, believed that he had finally conquered the opponents of reform. A new constitution was drafted aimed at creating a more efficient political system with the President as the dominant figure. Although Yeltsin reneged on a promise he had given during the crisis to hold an early presidential election, the referendum on the constitution and the elections to the new parliament went ahead on schedule. Yeltsin had great hopes that the people would once again show their support for his reform programme. It was not to be. A majority voted in favour of the new constitution (although there were rumours of irregularities), but the reformists performed badly in the parliamentary election and were unable to form a majority in the new State Duma. The communists, under the leadership of Gennadi Zyuganov, together with their close allies the Agrarian Party, effectively re-entered post-Soviet politics with a combined total of 81 seats, while the proto-fascists, the Liberal Democratic Party of Russia (LDPR), under the flamboyant leadership of Vladimir Zhirinovsky, got the highest proportion of votes among the parties, but, because of the complex electoral system, only 64 seats in all. (See Chapters 2 and 3 for more details.)

The result was a shock to reformers in Russia and to the world outside. It appeared that the Russian people had finally turned against reform. However, the vote had no direct effect on the government of the country. Yeltsin now had the constitutional power to dominate parliament and to continue his reformist policies, but he recognised the will of the people. There were changes in personnel with Gaidar shunted aside after his party, Democratic Choice, received only 15 per cent of the vote. Viktor Chernomyrdin, a man with a more conservative reputation, replaced him and shock therapy became a term of the past, although no attempt was made to reverse the general course of economic reform. In other areas of policy, however, Yeltsin proved more eager to steal some of the nationalist and communist clothing. Thus, he announced a crackdown on crime and introduced legislation in 1994 which severely curtailed civil liberties (see Chapter 7). He also declared a greater interest in the newly independent Soviet successor states (see Chapter 13) and adopted a more independent, nationalist rhetoric in foreign policy. Relations with the West soured on a whole series of issues, from the war in Bosnia, through arms sales to anti-Western states, to NATO enlargement. Relations reached an all-time low when Yeltsin made a speech in December 1994 in which he suggested that the cold war could be replaced by the 'cold peace' (*International Herald Tribune*, 6 December 1994).

The years 1994–95 were a bad time for Yeltsin personally. Well known for his drinking and bouts of depression, he entered a period when his behaviour became even more erratic. Being drunk in the Russian parliament was one thing; being drunk abroad on public duty was quite another – it was not merely a personal embarrassment for Yeltsin, it was perceived to be a public humiliation for the country he represented. Thus, his behaviour in Berlin in September 1994 received considerable media coverage back home in Russia. Yeltsin was in Berlin to attend a ceremony to commemorate the final withdrawal of Soviet troops from Eastern Europe. It was a serious occasion, but Yeltsin acted in a way that was wholly inappropriate. He suddenly seized the baton during the ceremony and proceeded to conduct the band in a manner that could best be described as enthusiastic rather than skilled. The following month, during a public visit to the US, he was reported drunk on a number of occasions, and on his way back failed to disembark from the plane when it landed in Dublin on a stop-over visit to Ireland. His later explanation for his non-appearance – that his advisers had failed to wake him – convinced no one. His popularity rating began to decline amidst further reports of ill-health and economic collapse. The heroic days of August 1991 seemed long past.

The war in Chechnya

In an ill-judged attempt to rebuild his reputation, he supported military action against the secessionist republic of Chechnya. The Chechens had refused to sign the Federal Treaty of March 1992 after their leader, Dzhokhar Dudaev, declared independence a year earlier (see Chapter 4). Russia refused to recognise Chechen independence and, as Dudaev's position inside Chechnya appeared to weaken, Moscow decided to compel the republic to return to the Russian Federation. The military action was launched on 11 December 1994. A quick victory was expected. The Russian Defence Minister, Pavel Grachev, famously declared that the Chechen capital, Grozny, could be taken in a couple of hours by a single regiment of paratroopers (*The Guardian*, 11 January 1995). There were just 15 000 armed Chechen rebels against the combined might of the Russian military, but the military intervention was incompetently planned and organised. In fact, it took the Russians to the middle of January before they captured the Presidential Palace in Grozny and another three months before the rebels were driven from their main strongholds in the republic. Despite the bloodshed and destruction, the Chechen rebels were still not defeated. They simply retired to the mountains and began a campaign of terrorism and guerrilla warfare against the Russian occupiers.

The war in Chechnya further battered Yeltsin's reputation as a leader. Few Russians had much time for the Chechens, who were widely believed to have close links to the mafia (see Chapter 7), but the military operation remained highly unpopular. It also split the political establishment, with long-time supporters of Yeltsin, including Yegor Gaidar, joining more conservative figures, such as Alexander Lebed, in their condemnation of the conflict. The conflict, which heated up again in the spring, was also a hindrance to Yeltsin's efforts to be re-elected President in 1996.

However, an agreement was finally reached in the summer and winter of that year. Moscow agreed that Russian troops would withdraw from Chechnya with elections following in 1997; the final decision over Chechnya's status as an independent state or republic within the Russian Federation was postponed until the year 2001. The agreement represented a defeat for Moscow. It endangered Yeltsin's long-term policy of maintaining the territorial integrity of the Russian Federation and threatened further unrest in other parts of the volatile Caucasus region. There are fears of a similar conflict in neighbouring Dagestan. However, the continuance of the war was never a realistic option. The war in Chechnya had cost at least 30 000 lives by the summer of 1996 and gravely endangered Yeltsin's international reputation as a democrat and reformer.

Elections of 1995 and 1996

Two debilitating heart attacks in 1995 were followed by disappointing election results to the Duma in December. The new establishment party, this time led by Premier Chernomyrdin and called Our Home Is Russia, won only 55 seats. Zhirinovsky's star appeared to be on the wane too although he maintained a presence in parliament. The main victors, however, were the leftists, and in particular the Communist Party of the Russian Federation (CPRF) (see Chapters 2 and 3). It seemed that a growing number of Russian people were despairing of economic reform. They increasingly looked back to the days of the Soviet Union as a period of stability and relative prosperity (see Chapter 5) and the communists appeared well placed to take power in the upcoming presidential election in June 1996.

Yeltsin entered the election year well behind the communist candidate, Zyuganov, in all the opinion polls. He was down as low as 6 per cent in a poll taken in June 1995 (*Moscow News*, 30 June–6 July 1995, p. 2). However, Yeltsin led a vigorous election campaign – at least in the first round while his health held out. He campaigned up and down the country. He made speeches, he danced to rock and roll. Like an early Father Christmas, he gave out money to unpaid workers and made extravagant promises for a better future once the election was won. Yeltsin's strategy of negative campaigning also had an effect. Arguing that a vote for Zyuganov would bring back the nightmare of Stalinism, he played on people's fears. This seemed to work. Slowly, Yeltsin reversed the decline in his popularity and began to move ahead of Zyuganov in the opinion polls by the spring of 1996. He finally defeated Zyuganov by 53 per cent to 40 per cent in the second-round run-off, despite being unable to campaign after the first vote owing to a re-occurrence of heart problems (see Chapter 2).

A summary of the Yeltsin era

Yeltsin's victory in the 1996 presidential election was greeted with relief by his supporters. Yeltsin, despite his flaws, was still generally seen as the best defender of democracy and reform in Russia. However, as all the chapters in this volume show, democracy in Russia is not firmly based. Although a return to Brezhnevism is highly unlikely – if not yet impossible – a shift towards a more authoritarian style of government cannot be ruled out. Indeed, Yeltsin himself has shown authoritarian instincts at times of crisis throughout his presidency. He used force against the White House in October 1993 and again, on a quite different scale, against the Chechen rebels a year later. He has also shown himself reluctant to work in the spirit of democracy and to seek a genuinely co-operative relationship with either the Congress of People's Deputies before 1993 or the State Duma afterwards (see Chapter 2). He has supported a crackdown on ethnic minorities in Moscow and backed a bill in 1997 which has explicitly restricted freedom for a number of religious minorities in Russia (see Chapter 10).

In a sense, Yeltsin can claim to be only following public opinion. Evidence provided by Matthew Wyman in Chapter 5 clearly shows that public support for the conventions of democracy remains limited. A democratic culture has not yet been firmly established in post-Soviet Russia. Indeed, as James Hughes warns in Chapter 1, the impact of the reform process on the economic and social fabric of society has been so deleterious that it has 'de-modernised' Russia and made the creation of such a culture even more difficult to achieve than when the process was started under Gorbachev in 1985. Yeltsin's victory in 1996 did not of itself secure democracy in Russia. Also, it did not resolve any of the outstanding policy issues which confront the country. Most central of all in this context is the economy (see Chapter 6). Despite Yeltsin's supporters almost continuously declaring the sighting of the green shoots of recovery, in practice the Russian economy has staggered from one crisis to another since Gaidar first inaugurated the policy of radical reform back in January 1992. The reason for the poor performance of the economy is still vigorously debated by economists the world over. Was it too much shock and not enough therapy or too much talk and not enough real reform? What is clear, however, is that the economy remains in deep trouble. The devaluation of the ruble in August 1998, in the wake of the financial crisis in the Far East, only confirmed the pessimists in their view that steady long-term growth remains a distant prospect for Russia. The 1998 crisis also starkly revealed the extent of Russian indebtedness to, and dependence on, the West – a matter of considerable resentment among nationalists and

---

СПРАВКА 5   **Yeltsin in 1999**

Yeltsin appears to have lost the support of the country and the confidence of parliament. In a TV poll in October 1998, he received only 1 per cent approval rating after hundreds of thousands of Russians throughout the country went out on to the streets to call for his resignation. Yeltsin still exercises great power on paper but in reality power has shifted to parliament and the government. Yeltsin is clearly very ill, and it is reported that he works only two or three days a week. He has sacked three Prime Ministers in two years and faced the possibility of impeachment in spring 1999. The impeachment vote in the State Duma failed to get the necessary two-thirds majority, but Yeltsin's future remains in doubt.

---

communists and of considerable embarrassment to Russian reformers. The position of Yeltsin in 1999 is summarised in Box 5.

Conclusion

The process of transition outlined above has an importance that extends far beyond the territory of Russia. Russia may no longer be a superpower, but it remains internationally important because of its size (it is still the biggest country in the world), its strategic position (it traverses the two continents of Europe and Asia), its economic potential (due to its very rich natural resources, including oil, gas, and precious metals) and its destructive capability (its military potential is much reduced but Russia still possesses the biggest land army in Europe and a nuclear arsenal second only to that of the US). The world looks on with interest and concern, therefore, to see how Russia copes with its transition and its much reduced status in the world. Will Russia act as a stabilising or destabilising force in the world? What is the evidence to date?

Theorists have increasingly viewed internal factors as a determinant of foreign policy. Some liberals, for example, have argued that mature democracies are less aggressive and less likely to go to war than dictatorships. Michael Doyle (1986), in an influential article both extended and modified this argument when he acknowledged that, of course, democracies do fight (the US in Vietnam, for example), but *they do not fight each other*. If this theory is true, then the process of democratisation in Russia is clearly of significance, not only to the Russian people themselves but also to the world outside. The enlargement of democracy in the former Soviet bloc would, according to this theory, broaden the so-called 'pacific union' and offer a far better guarantee of peace and security in Europe than all the tanks and nuclear missiles that NATO could muster.

In Russia, however, transition has been difficult. The economy has not stabilised, the central authorities have been unable to reach a workable arrangement with the regions, democracy is weak and the future of the Russian state itself is far from secure. In response, communists and nationalists have called for a more authoritarian system to bring back law and order to Russia: hence, the more nationalist line in foreign policy too. The more pessimistic observers of international affairs have not been surprised. Samuel Huntington (1996), for example, wrote about new clashes emerging in the post-cold-war world which would be based on cultural, rather than nationalist or ideological, differences. Interestingly, Huntington argued that one of the central cleavages in the world was that between the West and Orthodox Christianity, centred around Moscow. Hopes of liberals for peace and well-being after the collapse of communism and the Soviet Union were perceived by Huntington to be naive. Russia was different from the West. Its interests were different, its culture was different. Therefore, according to Huntington, a partnership between Moscow and Washington was likely to be short term and purely instrumental.

Although Huntington's ideas were highly controversial, the honeymoon between Russia and the West did not last long. Whether this was due to Huntington's clash of civilisations or a more traditional clash of national interests is a matter of continuing debate. What is clear is that relations between Russia and the West have cooled since 1993. In the Far East, where there was considerably less euphoria over the end of the cold war, relations remained more on an even keel (see Chapter 17). In regard to the West, however, Moscow is now far more ready to pursue its own interests even if this antagonises Washington or Europe. However, with one or two notable exceptions (Moscow viewed Chechnya as an internal matter), Moscow has generally not acted irresponsibly in foreign affairs. In fact, the rhetoric has often changed more than the practice over the preceding years. This may be because of its current weakness militarily (see Chapter 12), it may be because of its economic dependence on the West or it may be something more deeply rooted in the changes since 1991.

Whatever the reason, an opportunity exists for the West to co-operate with Russia, even if a long-term partnership remains unlikely. The West should encourage the democratising process in Russia and seek to underpin economic reform with aid and other programmes. Russia may be too big and too different ever to be fully integrated into the institutions of the West (see Chapters 15 and 16 for different views on this issue), but other less comprehensive but more complex arrangements could be reached to bind Russia into the political, economic and security systems of the West. Despite initial reluctance, Russia has generally proved willing to play ball in this regard. It is not a member of NATO, but since May 1997 the Russia–NATO Permanent Council was set up to give Moscow a voice on matters of European security. Russia has also played a useful peacekeeping role in Bosnia together with NATO's IFOR–SFOR troops despite not being formally under NATO command. It has also permitted international organisations, such as the OSCE, to mediate in conflicts and to monitor agreed cease-fires on the territory of the former Soviet Union (see Chapter 13).

It is right to be cautious about the prospects in post-Soviet Russia, but it is also important to remember the distance already travelled. Russia has abandoned Marxism–Leninism. The cold war is over. Russia has no troops stationed outside the CIS. Russian officers walk the corridors of NATO Headquarters in Brussels.

In the welter of depressing statistics and reports that come out of Russia, it is sometimes easy to forget the remarkable changes that have happened since Gorbachev came to power in March 1985. These chapters attempt to give the reader a clear but nuanced version of life in Russia today.

References

Aslund A 1995 *How Russia Became a Market Economy*, Brookings Institution, Washington, DC.

Bowker M 1997 *Russian Foreign Policy and the End of the Cold War*, Dartmouth, Aldershot.

Brown A H 1996 *The Gorbachev Factor*, Oxford University Press, Oxford.

Dibb P 1988 *The Soviet Union: The Incomplete Superpower*, 2nd edition, Macmillan/IISS, London.

Doyle M 1986 Liberalism and World Politics, *American Political Science Review*, Vol. 80, No. 4.

Gorbachev M S 1991 *The August Coup: The Truth and the Lessons*, HarperCollins, London.

Huntington S P 1996 The Clash of Civilizations and the Remaking of World Order, Simon and Schuster, New York.

Kutsyllo V 1993 *Zapiski iz belogo doma: 21 Sentiabria – 4 Oktiabria*, Komersant, Moscow.

Ligachev Y 1993 *Inside Gorbachev's Kremlin: The Memoirs of Yegor Ligachev*, Pantheon, New York.

Remnick D 1993 *Lenin's Tomb: The Last Days of the Soviet Empire*, Viking, London.

Shevtsova L 1992 The August Coup and its Collapse, *Survival*, Vol. 34, No. 1, Spring.

Smiley X 1995 Murder Most Common, *The World in 1996*, The Economist Publications, London.

Further reading

Bowker M 1997 *Russian Foreign Policy and the End of the Cold War*, Dartmouth, Aldershot.

Lloyd J 1998 *Rebirth of a Nation: An Anatomy of Russia*, Michael Joseph, London.

Gorbachev M S 1987 *Memoirs*, Bantam Books, London and New York.

Remnick D 1993 *Lenin's Tomb: The Last Days of the Soviet Empire*, Viking, London.

Yeltsin B N 1994 *View From the Kremlin*, HarperCollins, London.

Radio Free Europe/Radio Liberty provides up-to-date information on the situation in Russia, the former Soviet Union and Eastern Europe: http://www.rferl.org/

Two other good sources are http://www.russiatoday.com/ and http://www.russia.net

PART I

Politics

1 Transition models and democratisation in Russia

James Hughes

Introduction: What is transition?

The break-up of the Soviet Union on 25 December 1991 ended a four centuries old political regime of centralised authoritarianism based in Moscow. From being an expansionist imperialist state, Russia, the largest of the newly independent post-Soviet states, has become one of the great test cases of transition to democracy. Transition studies are a rather loose embodiment of political science approaches and ideas about the nature of political and economic development. A transition is defined broadly as the interlude between one type of regime and another. The common thread uniting the diverse transition approaches is a central assumption that the historical experience of transformation from authoritarianism to democracy and the emergence of capitalism in the states of Western Europe and North America in the eighteenth century provide generalisable lessons and an analytical framework for understanding and promoting similar processes of change and outcomes in other states. The basic premise is self-evidently normative and linear: that the values, structures and political procedures of advanced Western democracies are the most developed and should be transplanted. Critics of this developmental approach to the study of politics argue that it is ethnocentric and culturally bounded. What is indisputable is that the gradual ebb and flow of state development amidst the growth of the capitalist economy has resulted in the steady erosion of the political space for authoritarianism, culminating in the consolidation of democratic forms of government in most states in the course of the twentieth century.

Transition studies are a broad church within which we can identify two main schools: the 'functionalist' and the 'genetic'. The functionalist school is concerned with the study of the impact of long-term processes of socio-economic development, or modernisation, on the emergence of stable democracy. In contrast, the 'genetic' school focuses on the political contingency and the role of agents of change in the investigation of the genetic question of *causation*: how democracy comes into existence. These schools are not mutually exclusive, and, in fact, much of the more recent work on transitions takes an integrated approach, interpreting the two schools as mutually interacting and, in some respects, reinforcing.

Much of the transition literature and its hypotheses are derived from the application of these ideas to the comparative study of democratising change beginning in the early 1970s in authoritarian states of relatively homogenous cultures and diverse regime types and geographical locations, from military juntas to corporatist and patrimonial regimes in Latin America, South-East Asia and the Southern tier of Europe (O'Donnell and Schmitter, 1986; Huntington, 1993). The lessons of these 'Third Wave' democratisations were subsequently applied to post-communist democratisation in Eastern Europe from the late 1980s. For a time in the early 1990s it was widely debated whether the collapse of communism had led to the triumph of Western ideas of liberal democracy and capitalism as the *rerum natura*, the fundamental basis of a natural order of governance. Such triumphalism rapidly waned as the multidimensional character and simultaneity of post-communist transitions made them a very particularistic and problematic variant.

The functionalist model

Social requisites and democracy

Functionalism explains the existence of democracy by its *correlation* with modernisation. The latter is seen as a necessary underlying condition for stable democracy. Seymour Lipset and Barrington Moore were among the first social scientists to stress the link between democracy and broad trends of capitalist development, modernisation and the growth of affluence: the latter broadly meaning the enlargement of the middle class and development of social protection and security for the working class. Lipset (1981, p. 31) encapsulated the idea thus: 'The more well-to-do a nation, the greater the chances are that it will sustain democracy'. Moore (1967, p. 418) simplified the notion further: 'No bourgeoisie, no democracy'. These social requisites are functional for democracy because economic 'abundance is a condition for institutionalizing the give and take of democratic politics', while an expanded middle class brings the informed participation and moderation in politics needed to counter extremist demagoguery (Lipset, 1981, pp. 460, 467). The significance of capitalist development and the pivotal role of the middle class in democratisation are contentious. For some the key attribute of the middle class in democracy is its association with the values of 'moderation, tolerance, and democracy' (Diamond, 1996, p. 22). Others take a less benign view of the role of capitalism and the middle class in democratisation, arguing that 'it was the contradictions of capitalism and not capitalists that created democracy' (Rueschemeyer *et al.*, 1992, p. 300). By creating and concentrating the working class, capitalism immensely augments the capacity for working-class self-organisation, leading to demands for political change and social reform. The propensity of the middle class is not universally supportive of democratic change; indeed, historically there have been many cases when it preferred to reinforce authoritarian regimes when challenged by working-class demands for expanded political equality (Rueschemeyer *et al.*, 1992, pp. 270–1).

Nevertheless, the linkage between modernisation and democratisation is now an accepted wisdom not only for transition studies but also in democratic theory. Dahl's classic study of contemporary democracy, for example, accepted the assumption that 'a high level of socio-economic development not only favours the transformation of a hegemonic regime into a polyarchy but . . . may even be necessary to maintain a polyarchy' (Dahl, 1971, p. 63). Similarly, a recent sophisticated quantitative analysis of states confirms that high levels of economic development correlate with the plural distribution of power resources which leads to democratisation (Vanhanen, 1997).

Modernisation and post-communist transitions

The collapse of Soviet communism has been subsumed within the empirical body of evidence deployed to confirm the functionalist hypothesis (Lipset, 1994). A more circumspect hybrid variant of the functionalist argument advocates that while economics alone does not explain the late twentieth-century transitions, economic growth and middle-class creation and enlargement were important factors. The most active supporters of the 'Third Wave' of democratic trans-itions from 1974 on, it is argued, were the urban middle class. Moreover, in com-munist states it was poor economic performance that undermined the legitimacy of rulers and the system (Huntington, 1993, pp. 54, 67, 179). Certainly, by many of the multivariate measures of modernisation (GNP, per capita and disposable incomes, level and type of industrialisation, level of urbanisation, education and literacy rates, health care, ownership of consumer products, newspaper reader-ship, doctors per person etc.) Soviet society by the early 1980s was a modernised one (Lewin, 1988; Lane, 1992).

The context of Soviet-type modernisation, conducted in conditions of global competition with the rival ideology and system of Western capitalist democracy, created unsustainable pressures on the monist authoritarian political regime. The mismatch between a political structure built on one-party authoritarianism and the modernised, urbanised and well-educated society led to a fundamental opposition between the aspirations and expectations aroused by the communist party's ideological claim that 'developed socialism' was the 'most advanced' sys-tem and the increasingly obvious failure of the command economy to deliver the material abundance and diverse cultural goods required to satiate societal demands. The idiocy of the daily struggle in a shortage economy had import-ant structural explanations (for example, the military burden on the budget of the cold war arms race, the absence of a market and its discipline effect on producers, inherent production quality and bottleneck problems, plan dis-tortions arising from erroneous information flows, poor labour incentives and other 'human factors'). The point is that the revolution in communications technology and the radical narrowing of time and distance from the 1960s meant that Soviet citizens were increasingly aware of the growing political and economic gap with the West.

The contradictions and increasing ineffectiveness of Soviet modernisation, illuminated by key economic advisers such as Aganbegyan, were major factors informing the early stages of Gorbachev's liberalisation strategy of *perestroika* (Aganbegyan, 1988; Ellman and Kontorovich, 1992). The great turning point in the radicalisation of *perestroika* came when the disgruntled Soviet urban middle classes in many republics led the push for an all-out programme of democratisation by organising nationalist popular fronts and youth-oriented 'informal groups' to mobilise mass popular protests against monist authoritarianism (Hosking *et al.*, 1992; Sedaitis and Butterfield, 1991). In the sense that modernisation pressures were an important factor initiating the transition in Russia, the functionalist argument would seem to be plausible. It is less convincing as a predictive model, however, if one examines the transformative impact of transition on social conditions. The functional model is flawed in not recognising that a systemic transition can devour the modernised social structures from which it is born, and Russia is a vivid demonstration of this phenomenon.

Pauperisation and de-modernising transition

If abundance, an enlarged middle class and a protected working class are social requisites for democracy, then what conclusions can we draw from the pauperising impact of transition on Russian society since 1991? The impoverishment of Russian society began during *perestroika*, when Gorbachev's mismanagement of economic reforms undermined the basis of the Soviet social contract. What had been an incremental deterioration in social conditions under Gorbachev was transformed into a cataclysmic downturn by 'shock therapy', launched under Gaidar's tutelage in January 1992. The severe cuts in state orders for industry, price hikes and a government-designed course of hyper-inflation to wipe out savings plunged the mass of society into poverty and severely debilitated the modernised social structure inherited from the Soviet era. A comparison of graphics of income structure among social groups in Russia in the communist and post-communist periods would show a diamond-shaped structure before 1991, with a burgeoning middle class and narrow income differentials, transformed into a sharply elongated pyramidical spike after 'shock therapy' in early 1992, with a polarisation between the mass of poor and a small, immensely wealthy elite. The transition period in Russia, therefore, has been marked by two distinct socio-economic trends: a sharp fall in output, and hence in average real wages, and a surge in inequality (McAuley, 1995, pp. 186–7). The official economic indices are sobering: between 1991 and 1995 GDP plummeted by 39 per cent, industrial output was halved and agricultural output fell by a quarter, while real average wages fell by 30 per cent between 1985 and 1995. After six years of economic management by reformers Russia showed its first marginal GDP increase in the first quarter of 1997 of 0.25 per cent. According to official figures for 1997, 76 per cent of the population earn less than $200 per month yet most price indices are at world levels. Even allowing for the unrecorded off-book activities of the shadow economy (notoriously difficult to quantify), it is incontrovertible that income differentials have been sharply polarised by the transition process. This is the key indicator of de-modernisation.

While a new middle class of sorts has emerged in Moscow owing to the concentration of economic capital and foreign investment there, Russian society as a whole is characterised by poverty, rather than abundance. Thus, the social requisites for democracy that may have been present in the late 1980s are now absent. The chances of Russia attaining the economic growth rates necessary to recover its prior modernised social class income structure are bleak over the short term. Furthermore, the 'structural adjustment' pressures demanded by IMF loan

conditionalities are actually impelling the Russian government to pare back radically its social infrastructure expenditure. The fiscal crisis of early 1998 meant
that such IMF conditionalities were strengthened for Russia to secure a \$22.6
billion emergency loan in July 1998. This external pressure is a significant factor
in the consolidation of Russia's de-modernising transition to the free market.

A novel adaptation of functionalism suggests that a different correlate, a
specifically 'capitalist modernization', as opposed to modernisation *per se*, may
be the crucial factor for the development of democracy. The new correlation
here is with the property ownership and economic freedom of an emergent
capitalist class, a factor that was largely absent in communist modernisations,
particularly in Russia, and will take time to develop (Bova, 1991, p. 134). While
it is true that there are now 40 million shareholders in Russia as a result of
privatisation, the effects of this are largely negated by 'insider' privatisation and
crony capitalism. Small networks of administrative and managerial elites used
their positional power to capture economic assets via privatisation and to
subdue competition by regulation and corruption. These 'rent-seeking' practices
to protect elite interests and to subdue competition were endemic and are denoted
by the term '*nomenklatura* privatisation' (Clarke and Kabalina, 1995; Aslund, 1996;
Blasi *et al.*, 1997). Consequently, by the late 1990s just seven vast business conglomerates (so-called 'financial–industrial groups') dominated the economy in
a form of oligarchic capitalism, not unlike the 'robber baron' capitalism of
the late nineteenth century USA economy. The Russian economy is also highly
criminalised and permeated by corruption. Some 41 000 industrial companies,
50 per cent of banks and over 80 per cent of joint ventures are believed to have
criminal connections, and the shadow economy is estimated to account for up
to 40 per cent of the Russian economy (*Finansovye Izvestiya*, 18 February 1997). It
would be logically consistent, therefore, to argue from within the functionalist
model that the current de-modernising trends in Russia, its polarised rich–poor
social structure, the sharp political conflicts over the distribution of scarce resources and its criminalised economy are at odds with its transition to democracy.

There is much evidence from the study of the political economy of transition to demonstrate that democratic legitimacy may insulate a government to
some extent from a system crisis arising from a sustained economic downturn
of the kind that has occurred in Russia since 1991. The evidence also suggests,
however, that democracy is not sustainable in the face of a lasting economic
crisis, as key actors will then search for non-democratic alternatives (Linz and
Stepan, 1996, pp. 76–81). Some positively advocate the necessity for 'adequate
executive authority to overcome crippling institutional and political divisions'
during an economic transition (Haggard and Kaufman, 1995, p. 378). In
the case of Russia, the attractiveness of a 'strong hand' (*silnaya ruka*) ruler has
been advocated by some analysts from early in its transition (Klyamkin and
Migranyan, 1989) and such calls have increasingly focused on the potential of
former General Lebed. Functionalists trace the origins of fascism to changes
in social structures: the social displacement, 'stratification strains' and psychological distress of rapid industrial development. A specific fascism of the 'lower
class', Peronism (Peron, president of Argentina 1946–55), is described by
Lipset as 'a coalition between the nationalist officers of an underdeveloped

country and its lower classes oriented against foreign imperialists and local bourgeois "renegades"' (Lipset, 1983, p. 175). Another paradox of Russia's de-modernising transition may well be that it is generating forms of what Huntington (1993, p. 66) terms 'concentrated inequalities' and the kinds of social tensions that are a fertile breeding ground for fascism.

The genetic model

Political requisites and democracy

Political contingency and the agents of change are the focus of this model of transition, pioneered in a seminal study by Dankwart Rustow. In opposition to the functionalist emphasis on correlation, Rustow offers a more nuanced approach by investigating the genetic question of *causation*: 'how a democracy comes into being in the first place'. Transitions to democracy take many roads, and no minimal level of economic development is necessary, according to Rustow, but they uniformly begin only when elites make a conscious decision to negotiate a political settlement through a 'procedural consensus on the rules of the game' (Rustow, 1970, p. 337). In this sense a democratic transition is essentially a voluntaristic process the outcome of which depends greatly on how the process is 'crafted' (Di Palma, 1990).

Rustow mapped the trajectory of a transition into four key phases. The first 'background' phase has a zero condition: 'national unity'. He defines this as follows: 'the vast majority of citizens in a democracy-to-be must have no doubt as to which political community they belong to' (Rustow, 1970, p. 350). The absence of a problem of contested boundaries is an important prerequisite, for otherwise transition poses a danger to the cohesion of the state. The second 'preparatory' phase is when the dynamic of transition is set in motion by a 'prolonged and inconclusive political struggle' between old and new elites (Rustow, 1970, p. 352). National unity ensures that this conflict is akin to a 'hot family feud', which may well lead to political polarisation but not to the disintegration of the state (Rustow, 1970, p. 355). This is followed by a 'decision' phase, when competing elites deliberately choose to institutionalise some aspect of democratic procedure for, as Przeworski (1986, pp. 59–60) notes, the essence of democratisation is to 'institutionalize uncertainty'. This brokered process of elite compromise is often described as a 'negotiated' transition or '*reforma pactada*' after the post-Franco Spanish model. Leaders often play a disproportionate role at this crucial turning point in the decision to accept the risk of a democratic system, a point stressed in Huntington's (1993, p. 107) later formula: 'Democracies are created not by causes but by causers'. A 'grand compromise' in the form of an elite pact establishes a basis for completing the fourth, and final, 'habituation' phase of transition, which embeds 'the habit of dissension and conciliation over ever-changing issues and amidst ever-changing alignments'. These values and behavioural compliance with the rules of the game are best promoted by a competitive party system – the sole institutional requisite cited by Rustow (1970, p. 363).

Whereas Rustow is primarily concerned with explaining the 'how' of transition, the architecture of his framework has been developed by later transition studies which have focused more explicitly on the 'why'. From the perspective of contingency, as a rule, transitions begin with some 'dramatic event' or the 'culmination of a series of events' (Linz, 1990, p. 157). Such 'triggers' may be sudden leadership changes, such as the death of a reactionary leader and the ascent of a reforming leader, much as with Gorbachev's selection as General Secretary in March 1985 and Yeltsin's seizure of power after the failed August 1991 coup. We can also expect a dramatic test for Russia's consolidation of democracy by the death of Yeltsin. Transitions can be tripped by a traumatic event that radicalises public opinion, much as the Chernobyl disaster of April 1986 mobilised the first wave of 'eco-nationalism' in the Soviet republics and demands for greater media freedom. Legitimacy problems for authoritarian regimes may be triggered by defeat in war, much as the Afghanistan débâcle and the bungled putsch of August 1991 discredited the Soviet leadership. Long-term historical processes of liberalisation that open up the system to change, what the Latin Americanists term *abertura* and the Sovietologists referred to as a 'thaw', may also be classified as triggers. A distinction is drawn between 'state-led' or 'regime-led' transitions and those that are not (Linz and Stepan, 1996, p. 71). Accordingly, the liberalisation process in the Soviet Union could be traced to Khrushchev's de-Stalinisation in 1956, followed by a partial reversal under Brezhnev, and then a final democratising wave of reform under Gorbachev after 1985, and attempts at democratic consolidation under Yeltsin since 1991.

The literature on transitions is rich in categories, matrices and schemata (see Mainwaring, 1992). Explanations of the causes of transition may be broadly categorised into two groups of factors: the 'endogenous' internally generated factors, and the 'exogenous' external influences. This question immediately raises the relatively nebulous, although fundamental, issue of defining the boundaries of transition. What are the beginning and end-points of transition? It is on the contentious matter of how to define an end-point that transition models become a will-o'-the-wisp hazy combination of two concepts. The first concerns the obscure distinction between transition and liberalisation, and the second rests on a very limited proceduralist definition of democracy. One view is that transition is completed once 'agreement on democratic rules is reached' (Di Palma, 1990, p. 109). Liberalisation, then, is a process that may lead to a transition, but it is not part of the transition itself (Przeworski, 1991, p. 111). Another view is that the onset of transition begins with a liberalisation phase when 'authoritarian incumbents . . . begin to modify their rules in the direction of providing more secure guarantees for the rights of individual groups' (O'Donnell and Schmitter, 1986, p. 6). Both views are synthesised into a third approach which recognises that while democratisation may entail liberalisation 'it is a wider and more specifically political concept . . . there can be liberalisation without democratisation' (Linz and Stepan, 1996, p. 3). The distinction between liberalisation and transition is important in the case of Russia if we are to draw a line between the Soviet and post-Soviet periods. To adhere to any internal consistency in the genetic model, Gorbachev's *perestroika* reforms must be seen as a phase of liberalisation with the decisions of the Nineteenth Party Conference in June 1988 leading to a partial democratization in the 1989 USSR and 1990 republican and regional elections. The result of Gorbachev's liberalisation was a classic polarisation of the kind predicted by Rustow's 'preparatory' phase, leading to the August 1991 coup and the collapse of Soviet communism (Bova, 1991). The period since 1991 can then be viewed as a process of overcoming problems in democratic consolidation (Linz and Stepan, 1996).

Transition studies are predominantly informed by a procedural definition of democracy derived from Schumpeter and refined by Dahl (1971). By characterising democracy in terms of the extent of *contestation* and *participation* provided in a political system, the *method* of political legitimation, namely free competitive elections, becomes the principal distinguishing marker, hence Huntington's unequivocal assertions that elections 'are the essence of democracy', for they are 'a vehicle of democratisation as well as the goal' (Huntington, 1993, pp. 9, 174). This singular focus on elections entails two main types of structural change to politics in a transitional state. First, the organisational paraphernalia of modern 'vote-catching' machine politics must be constructed: political parties, professional politicians and managers, and centrally controlled nation-wide party organisations. Second, the process of electioneering tends to become 'Americanised' through the use of modern communications technology to improve image making, media manipulation, campaigning and advertising techniques. Evaluating the election criteria can be cumbersome, however, and a narrow focus on proceduralism may lead into the pitfall of the 'electoralist fallacy': when authoritarian regimes are superficially legitimated by relatively free and fair elections. To avoid this, leading advocates of the genetic model have come to distinguish along a wide spectrum between 'high' and 'low' grade democracies (Linz and Stepan, 1996, p. 6). The rather oblique notion that democracy is characterised by 'alternance' in power has also been accommodated into the proceduralist approach through Huntington's 'two-turnover test' – transition ends when an alternance in power occurs as a result of a democratic election (Huntington, 1993, p. 266).

If one follows the proceduralist definition the starting point in Russia's transition to democracy was, arguably, the first democratic presidential election of June 1991, won by Yeltsin. Post-Soviet Russia, moreover, has not been short of experience of competitive state- and local-level elections that have been widely accepted as 'free and fair' contests: there have been two national referenda (April and December, 1993), two national parliamentary elections (December 1993 and 1995) and one presidential election of two rounds (June–July 1996), and every region and republic has held local, regional and gubernatorial or presidential elections since 1993 (some more than once). Russia, nonetheless, fails the proceduralist test because it has not yet passed the 'turnover' test. There has yet to be a post-Yeltsin democratic alternance of presidential power, something which may occur in the next presidential elections due in June 2000.

In considering the question of embedding democracy we are again faced with the definitional problem of demarcating transition from consolidation. Rustow termed this the problem of *habituation*, while much of the transition literature refers to 'consolidation'. Linz and Stepan (1996, p. 6) have proposed that consolidation be tested along three dimensions: *behavioural* – when 'no significant

| БИОГРАФИЯ 1.1 | **Gorbachev (born 1931)** |

Gorbachev was very popular in the West. His book, *Perestroika: New Thinking For Our Country and the World* (1987), sold millions of copies when it first came out. The world became fascinated by the man and his radical reform proposals. When he visited West Germany in June 1989, Gorbymania was born. 'Gorby, make love not walls', they shouted to him in Town Hall Square in Bonn. 'Please, Gorbachev, stay the course!' (Gorbachev, 1997, p. 671). In the Soviet Union, the reaction to Gorbachev was always cooler. Increasingly, he was blamed by the people for the collapse of the Soviet Union, as well as the economic and political chaos in the country. Gorbachev tried to make a political come-back in the presidential elections of 1996, but he received a mere 0.5 per cent of the vote.

national, social, economic, political or institutional actor' challenges the legitimacy of the new structures; *attitudinal* – when a 'strong majority' accepts the legitimacy of the democratic structures and the support for anti-democratic alternatives is 'quite small'; *constitutional* – when all forces in the state are 'habituated' to the democratic process. The salience of values and behaviour in these three dimensions effectively creates a 'political culture' test for a consolidated democracy. This is one of the five main elements that are now recurringly formulated to explain the process of democratic consolidation: *actors, institutions, stateness, international dimension* and *political culture*.

The actor-based model: the role of elites and leaders

Why do elites choose to democratise and marketise? It is invariably easier to describe a pattern of political liberalisation in authoritarian regimes leading to a transition to democracy than it is to account for why communist elites chose to liberalise. The ethos and motivations of elites are not readily understandable from observation, as they can only be determined with some accuracy by systematic investigation. Transition specialists, on the whole, tend to speculate on the basis of observation.

The functionalist model follows the notion of the 'King's dilemma', first advocated by Huntington, in analysing the constraints on leaders and their approach to political change in transition periods. The main thesis is that the process of modernisation enhances certain key power resources of a state, principally military and economic power, and in order to compete with rival states authoritarian regimes are driven to keep pace with modernising trends. Modernisation then creates structural changes in society (urbanisation, functional specialisation, mass education, mass communications and so on) which lead to demands for political liberalisation. If the regime liberalises it undermines its own *raison d'être*; if it does not it may radicalise demands for reform, possibly prompt a revolution and certainly hinder its modernisation (Huntington,

1968). The 'King's dilemma' model concentrates our attention on the key political leaders who promote transformation, but impulses for change may originate from other individuals, elites and societal forces.

In the case of Russia, arguably, we have two phases where a 'King's dilemma' might apply. If not the 'most important', the Gorbachev 'factor' was clearly critical for the liberalisation phase that transformed the Soviet Union in 1985–91 (Brown, 1996, p. 318). In his book, *The Third Wave*, Huntington (1993, p. 136) surmised that Gorbachev's reforms were an attempt to increase the legitimacy of the Soviet regime without fundamental political change. Di Palma (1990, p. 199) vaguely asserted that Gorbachev deluded himself into thinking that reform would enable the Soviet Union 'to refurbish its international status'. Gorbachev's 'democratising' credentials are obviously suspect, given that he never put himself forward for election, was consistently wary of competitive multi-party elections and used force against breakaway republics. In his poem, *Half Measures*, Yevtushenko aptly wrote that Gorbachev was 'half mutineer and half suppressor'. Of no less dramatic importance for the democratisation of Russia is the 'Yeltsin factor'. To illustrate the difference made by leadership we can take two key turning-point events in each phase where compromise within the elite was critical to prevent a break-down into violence. In the case of Gorbachev he managed to harness the competing factions within his regime to a compromise at the Nineteenth Party Conference in June 1988, which resulted in the beginning of a shift of power from the CPSU to elected soviets. Yeltsin, on the other hand, appears less temperamentally attuned to the politics of compromise, and more to unilateral action (Colton, 1995). His struggle to assert presidential dominance over parliament in 1992–93 and his unease at constraints on his power ultimately led to the break-down into violence in the bloody events of October 1993, followed by the promulgation of a new democratic presidential constitution.

Rustow (1970, pp. 355–6) predicted that the crucial decision for a transition to democracy would come from the elites; he did not explain, however, why elites might be motivated to act in this way. Rational choice assumptions and game theoretical models have increasingly become a common method of analysing the calculations and conflicts of elite 'actors' in transitions. The leading exponent is Przeworski who schematises transitions into five stages: 'extrication' from the old regime, constitution making, economic reform, followed by the decline into a 'valley of tears' of economic recession and popular discontent and finally 'rule by decree' as the transitional government overrides public hostility to secure an economic upturn. This trajectory is affected by the 'initial starting conditions', that is the political, economic and social structure of a state, and the timing of certain strategic choices and policy options. The 'double' political and economic nature of post-communist transition inevitably makes for greater complexity. Przeworski views transition as a four-player game involving collective action problems and strategic alliances between four main groups of actors who are critical to the outcome: hard-liners, reformers, moderates and radicals. A pact in the form of a coalition between reformers and moderates, he argues, will neutralise hard-liners and radicals and offers the best route for an 'extrication' to democracy (Przeworski, 1991).

The notion that elite pacts arise from deep-seated beliefs in democracy is rejected by the game theory approach, which emphasises the role of powerful 'interests', their preferences and the incentives offered by the institutional crafting of a competitive political market (Di Palma, 1990, pp. 41, 46). Przeworski adds two main reasons why elites support transition: they secure themselves from the often arbitrary violence of the authoritarian regime and obtain 'real opportunities to improve their material welfare' (Przeworski, 1991, pp. 31–2). The first of these assumptions is not very satisfactory for Russia, however, as the post-Stalin era of communism saw the regime downscale terror so that it operated at a residual level and was virtually irrelevant to the everyday life of the ruling elites. Some elites, particularly in the cultural–professional intelligentsia, would have been most affected, but we should bear in mind that the scale of dissent in communist states varied widely, and in the case of Russia was marginal by the time of Gorbachev's liberalisation. The leitmotif of the Brezhnev era, after all, was 'stability in cadres', a policy which more than any other fostered complacency, ossification and corruption of communist ruling elites. Security from violence is not, therefore, a convincing explanation for why Russian elites have initiated and adhered to transition. The second rationale, an elite 'enrich yourself' logic, is not readily testable given the lack of transparency and, as noted earlier, 'insider' nature of post-communist privatisation and marketisation.

Under communism the senior levels of the *nomenklatura* had privileged lifestyles that, as a matter of policy, were covert. Arguably, democratisation and marketisation presented an opportunity to legitimise and normalise this privileged socio-economic status. Is the observed '*nomenklatura* privatisation' a cause of or a product of the initial shock therapy and subsequent economic policies pursued by Yeltsin's governments since 1992? Many of the main beneficiaries of the early stages of economic reform in Russia emerged from the younger levels of the ruling *nomenklatura* – from the Komsomol apparatus – and from the intelligentsia. They had the skill assets and foresight to anticipate the consequences of the economic reforms and to adapt quickly. The fact that the immediate result of shock therapy was a collapse of production which affected wide elements of the old elite, particularly in the regions, suggests that '*nomenklatura* privatisation' was more of a reaction to the free-market liberal policies of Gaidar, and then Chubais, than a premeditated asset stripping on the part of the old elite as a whole. The escalation of capital flight from Russia in 1992–97, estimated at some $60 billion total volume, largely deposited in banks in Switzerland and Cyprus, confirms an adverse elite *reaction* to the economic policies of the transition (*Finansovye Izvestiya*, 18 February 1997).

Clearly, it is of vital importance to differentiate between various elements and levels of elite power in determining how much and what kind of premeditation there was in the transition. Adaptive elite networks from the old communist *nomenklatura* are the driving force behind Russia's new 'crony capitalism'. Ironically, the fact that Russia's economy is dominated by seven competing 'financial–industrial groups' which are of a monopolistic orientation is a strong indication of the consolidation of a form of 'administrative' market that is closely intertwined with the upper echelons of the state (Kordonskii, 1995). This trend severely limits the space for the emergence of a competitive pluralistic capitalism, which has obvious implications for the development of a rich diversity of mediating institutions and organisations between state and market: the so-called 'economic society' that is made a condition of democratic consolidation by Linz and Stepan (1996, pp. 11–15). In any event, the success of democratic transition for Przeworski depends 'to a large extent on economic performance'. However, as we discussed above, Russia has experienced a de-modernising transition which produced a sustained economic crash, and this factor largely explains why consolidation in the political sphere has been so difficult. I will return to the question of the motivation of elites when I examine the 'stateness' and 'political culture' elements below.

Institutional design

Democratic institutions fulfil a core legitimising function, and the choice of institutional design will be a crucial determinant of successful consolidation (accepting that stability is a measure of success). There is now a substantial body of evidence from comparative studies to demonstrate that the way in which states are constitutionally equipped matters. Lijphart's work on the attribute of political leadership and the role of certain types of 'constitutional engineering' to promote compromise and reconciliation in the establishment of a stable democracy, such as parliamentarism instead of presidentialism, and proportional against majoritarian electoral systems, is underscored by subsequent studies of transition (Lijphart, 1977, pp. 2ff and 165). One of the problems faced by democratic transitions is that comparative experience in Latin America demonstrates that they can be reversed, particularly where the military formed the old regime and remains a reserve power in the new one. According to Huntington transition in one-party states, such as in Russia, will be more difficult but is likely to be more permanent precisely because of the nature of the institutional transformation. One of the difficulties that post-communist transitions encounter is the tendency for old ruling communist parties to remain as political actors. On the positive side, Huntington argues, they do not face the Latin American problem of a potentially reversible military 'withdrawal' from politics (Huntington, 1993, p. 120). What is overlooked here is the precedent established for military intervention in Russian politics by the August 1991 coup and October 1993 conflict. Moreover, former military leaders have played a prominent role as active politicians in Russia, for example Generals Rutskoi, Lebed and Rokhlin (with the former two currently serving as governors).

The institutional 'crafting' aspect of transition is elucidated by a combination of four factors: the nature of the institutions chosen, the mode of deciding on the choice, the 'craftsmen' involved and the timing imposed (Di Palma, 1990, pp. 8–9). Many of the general propositions concerning the 'crafting' techniques of a democratic transition are viable only where elites compromise and negotiate. In the case of Russia, it has been argued that the post-Soviet transition has been flawed because it was 'unpacted' virtually from the outset. Hence, Russia's transition has been 'revolutionary' and wholly incomparable

БИОГРАФИЯ 1.2 **Yeltsin (born 1931)**

Yeltsin became a populist when he first came to Moscow from his home town of Sverdlovsk. He very publicly rode to work on public transport instead of in his official limousine and made frequent unannounced visits to shops and factories to see how the people really lived. He was highly critical of the opulence of Gorbachev's life-style, which he recounts in his book, *Against the Grain* (Yeltsin, 1990, pp. 133–4). Everything changed, however, after the collapse of the Soviet Union, and he became the unchallenged leader in Russia. Increasingly, he has isolated himself from the common people and lives in a way little different from the communist leaders of the past. Yeltsin's family have thrived during his regime. His daughter, Tatyana Demychenko, is his political adviser, one of his sons-in-law is head of Aeroflot and his wife has recently become head of a major TV channel. There are rumours that Yeltsin has bought a house in the West for fear of facing criminal charges if he were to remain in Russia after losing office, which he and his supporters have always denied.

with the more 'evolutionary' transitions of Southern Europe and Latin America (McFaul, 1993). This interpretation views Russian politics as essentially polarised between communists and democrats from the late Gorbachev era, with the ending of polarised politics by the Yeltsin's victory and the triumph of reform in 1996 (McFaul, 1997). In practice, this seemingly straightforward distinction was not always clear, as elite grand compromises on reform occurred both under Gorbachev (for example at the Nineteenth Party Conference of June–July 1988) and in the early post-Soviet period (Yeltsin's alliances first with Rutskoi in 1990–91, and then with Khasbulatov in late 1991). There is no doubt that a crisis arose over institutional design in Russia, but it did so only in the course of 1992–93 and was entangled with a range of other policy and personal disputes between Yeltsin and parliament's leaders. The failure of the Constitutional Convention in the summer of 1993 confirmed that a consensus on the 'rules of the game' (a requisite for a stable transition) could not be reached. Russia's 'unpacted' transition of this period was marked by a tendency for unilateralism on the part of both president and parliament and a reluctance to engage in consensus-building multilateral negotiation. This was evident from uncompromising rhetoric and the refusal of both sides to accept the Constitutional Court as a mediator in the course of 1992–93 or the inconclusive results of the April 1993 referendum as a popular recommendation for consensus. The impasse arising from the 'dual democratic legitimacy' of president and parliament was an indication of a weakening of elite commitment to institutions and arbitration. Yeltsin's use of the military as an ultimate arbitrating 'deadlock-breaking device' to dissolve parliament forcibly in October 1993 has set a dangerous precedent.

The imposed constitution of December 1993 reflected Yeltsin's preference for a presidential over a parliamentary system. The institutional choice of presidentialism has been associated with unstable democracy, whereas a parliamentary constitution is seen as promoting a healthy, vibrant system of party competition and the stabilisation over time of party cleavages making for a stable democracy (Linz, 1994). Whether the choice of a proportional over a majoritarian electoral system for parliament promotes or hinders democratic consolidation is less clear, since both systems have been associated with consensus making or polarisation. The importance of these institutional dimensions lies in their likely impact on stunting the development of a party system – a factor that is almost universally regarded as the lynchpin of a stable democracy.

O'Donnell coined the term 'delegative democracy' to describe the preference for presidentialism and the reliance on decree powers and a strongly vertically organised power hierarchy to shore up the state during transition (O'Donnell, 1994, pp. 55–69). Such a system is viewed as a 'symptom of weakness', however, and does not augur well for overcoming the political and economic challenges of transition (Przeworski, 1995, p. 64). The term has achieved a wide currency among analysts to cover many post-communist presidents, most notably Yeltsin. In fact, the boundaries between presidentialism and parliamentarism are in practice marked by significant checks and balances under the Russian constitution of 1993, perhaps reflecting the urgency and immediacy with which it was promulgated. Russia may, in fact, be viewed as a hybrid system. The inconclusive struggle between president and Duma in 1997–98, for example, has centred on budgetary and other fiscal policies which constitutionally must be approved by the Duma, while Yeltsin's power of dissolution is tightly constrained to two areas: a vote of no confidence in the government (Article 117), and refusal to approve his nominee for prime minister (Article 111). For this reason Russia has been categorised as more of a 'presidential–parliamentary' system, which is potentially the most unstable combination of constitutional power sharing (Shugart and Carey, 1992). At the same time, we should note that 'presidential–parliamentary' type systems have worked well elsewhere, for example 'cohabitation' between ideologically opposed presidents and parliaments being the norm in the French Fifth Republic since the early 1980s.

The nature of this institutional conflict reveals how contradictory push–pull factors are shaping Russia's transition. On the one hand, the 1993 constitution is viewed as being overly presidential and obstructive of democratic practice. Consequently, it locks into a Russian tradition of absolutist polarised politics encapsulated in the Leninist authoritarian tradition of '*kto kogo*' – 'who will overcome whom' (Tolz, 1994). One of the more remarkable aspects, however, of Russian politics post-October 1993 is how, despite the absence of a negotiated pact, and the serious blow to the integrity of democratic practice delivered by the October 'events', the main political forces have more or less adhered to the rules of the game imposed by the constitutional settlement. I say 'more or less' guardedly because Yeltsin has refused to abide by constitutional norms over a few key decisions, with his unilateral pursuit of the war in Chechnya being the most flagrant case of non-compliance. Despite the intentions of the framers of the 1993 constitution to create a presidential republic, Russia's hybrid system is a case where constitutional engineering is incrementally enforcing behavioural compliance with the democratic practices of compromise, negotiation and agreement on its political elites. We should beware of being too optimistic about the possibilities for successful consolidation, however, since Yeltsin's widely emulated informal style (for which see below) in conjunction with a confusion of law-making powers under the 1993 constitution has led to authority leakage. It is these latter factors, more than any others, that have contributed immensely to the weakness of the rule of law in contemporary Russia and prolonged its existence as a weak state.

The 'stateness' question

As noted above, Rustow's zero condition for a successful democratic transition is 'national unity', by which he meant that the 'overwhelming majority' concur on national identity and that nationhood must be 'unthinking' (Rustow, 1970, p. 351). This understanding of democracy is, after all, the cardinal rule of democratic theory, for as Dahl observed 'The criteria of the democratic process presuppose the rightfulness of the unit itself' (Dahl, 1989, p. 207). Theory, then, has established a linkage between homogeneity and democracy that suggests that transition to democracy is next to impossible in a multinational state such as the USSR. The collapse of the USSR seems to be a proof of this, so what then are the prospects for a multinational state such as the Russian Federation? Many of the 'Third Wave' transitions, particularly in post-communist states, have been problematic precisely because they occurred in multi-national states where democratisation unleashed conflicts over the nature of the state itself. The collapse of the Soviet Union under the pressures of Gorbachev's liberalisation is generally understood to be a result of the failure of Soviet nationality policies to construct a Soviet 'nation' and, indeed, its reverse policy of 'institutionalized multinationality' through territorialising ethnic diversity in a formal federal state (Brubaker, 1996, pp. 26ff). Consequently, liberalisation led to an uncontainable mobilisation of nationalist separatism. Secessionist trends in some of Russia's ethnic republics after the Eastern European revolutions and the collapse of the USSR, notably Tatarstan and Chechnya, suggest that these events had significant demonstration effects on the Russian Federation.

Recent transition literature has engaged more with the 'stateness' question and its potential paralysing effects on transition. Linz and Stepan view 'stateness' as one of only two 'macrovariables' of transition (the other being prior regime type, for which see below). Adept 'political crafting', they argue, can rescue states where transition gives rise to acute 'polis/demos' questions and secession tendencies (Linz and Stepan, 1996, pp. 29–37). They suggest two principal institutional forms of crafting to stabilise this issue. The first is 'consociational democracy' as suggested by Lijphart (1977): grand coalitions, mutual veto rights, segmental autonomy or federalism, a PR electoral system. Second, they consider electoral 'sequencing' to be a crucial determinant in establishing the legitimacy of the state in these cases. The survivability of a multi-national state, they argue, is best ensured when the 'founding' democratic elections are conducted at the statewide level rather than at regional or other substate level. If the first competitive elections are held at substate levels they lead to a mobilisation around ethnic nationalism, a questioning of the legitimacy of the state and a fragmentation into 'ethnocracies'. To demonstrate this point they contrast the success of Spain in managing its national conflicts with the Basques, Catalans and Galicians following statewide legitimising national elections in 1977 with the collapse of the USSR and Yugoslavia where the first democratic elections were held at republican and regional levels in 1990 (Linz and Stepan, 1991).

The 'stateness' question as understood by Linz and Stepan is a legitimacy problem that contributed to the collapse of the USSR. The implication of their argument is that 'proper' electoral management might have saved the USSR, much as it saved Spain. This is a serious understatement of the fundamental illegitimacy of Soviet Russian imperialism and the understandable aspiration for national self-determination in most of the 15 Soviet republics. Their benign view of the prospects for democratisation under Gorbachev's leadership of the Soviet Union is counterposed against independence movements in the successor states which gave 'a plebiscitary "national liberation" quality to the transition path' and are seen as 'privileging' independent state building over democratisation. Similarly, democratic consolidation in Russia is hindered by the 'privileging' of the collective rights of 'titular nationalities' who took advantage of the political struggle between Gorbachev and Yeltsin to enlarge their autonomy from 1990. This is an argument that is widely disseminated by Moscow-based Russian analysts, and oft repeated in Western studies, who readily associate national liberation and autonomy movements in Russia as cynical moves by non-democratic elites to entrench their power (Linz and Stepan, 1996, pp. 386–400). Historically, state and empire have been conflated in the Russian identity. This is the undercurrent for the post-Soviet identity crisis for Russia, where, rather than come to terms with and adjust to the changed post-imperial balance of power, it tends towards re-imperialisation (Motyl, 1998). This is evoked by what Szporluk terms 'Russian discomfort with geography' (Szporluk, 1997, p. 85). One of the greatest challenges for the building of a plural democracy in the Russian Federation is that ethnic Russians perceive their identity as being congruent with the current territorial boundaries of the whole federation.

The asymmetric pseudo-federal hierarchy inherited from the USSR has now been given real political significance by the weakening of the centre and by elite-led ethnonational mobilisation in some of Russia's republics. The conflict between president and parliament in 1992–3 weakened the power of the centre and gave the republics an opportunity to extract important concessions on autonomy, particularly in the policy domains of culture and economy, that were enshrined in the federal treaty of March 1992. Inevitably, friction results when the ingrained Russian superiority complex inherited from the Russian and Soviet imperial experience is confronted by the transformation of Soviet Russian pseudo-federalism into a real federalism where ethnic republics have secured collective rights. Antagonism over perceived inequalities was stirred up by Russia's regional elites, and consequently the 1993 constitution imposed an equalised status of republics and regions of the federation. Faced with destabilising secessionist threats, however, from early 1994 Yeltsin began a process of signing bilateral treaties with the republics to grant them varying degrees of autonomy. Some economically key republics such as Tatarstan, Sakha and Bashkortostan achieved significant devolved powers. The process was later extended in a much diluted form to Russia's regions during the build-up to the presidential elections in 1996 (Hughes, 1996).

The question is whether this kind of asymmetric federalism is stabilising or destabilising with regard to the 'stateness' issue. On the one hand, it institutionalises an ethnic hierarchy of territorial status, and differences of rights and privileges which are a source of great discontent, particularly among ethnic Russian regions. At the same time, however, it defuses secessionist tendencies. In fact, a strong argument can be made that such a treaty of autonomy would have prevented the war in Chechnya, and indeed it seems likely that Chechnya will eventually secure a semi-independent status of confederation with Russia. Asymmetric federalism, morever, serves as an important institutional check on 'great Russian chauvinism'. Equalisation of status of the federal units inevitably means Russian domination of ethnic minorities, whereas the variegated autonomies of the treaties at least may offer some protection from assimilationist Russian trends. In any event, Russia's military defeat in Chechnya has for the moment checked its capacity to project force against recalcitrant republics. Nevertheless, Russia's asymmetric federalism is institutionally weak because the treaties are a product of Russia's post-imperial presidency: executive agreements between Yeltsin and republican leaders that are widely opposed in both chambers of parliament. To that extent the 'stateness' issue is not fully resolved and is closely interwoven with the wider question of a post-Yeltsin alternance (see Chapter 4).

The international dimension

The classic transition study of the 1980s concluded that 'domestic factors play a predominant role' (O'Donnell and Schmitter, 1986). This understanding has been substantially revised in the light of the post-communist transitions which have demonstrated the importance of the international dimension as a factor shaping the outcome. It would be clearly ludicrous to suggest anything other than that Gorbachev's reforms of the Soviet system were a trigger for the transitions in Eastern Europe and that there was a rebounding demonstration effect from national resurgence in Eastern Europe on the mobilisation of nationalism in the Soviet Union and in the Russian Federation. There is also a strong argument that the pressures from United States foreign policy, both Carter's emphasis on human rights and the military build-up under Reagan, propelled the liberalising trends in the Soviet regime. Furthermore, our analysis of the prospects for democratic consolidation in post-communist states would be severely limited without taking account of the convergence pressures and compliance conditionalities exercised by international organisations on these states. Consequently, as Whitehead, parodying a Stalinist slogan, observes: 'there is no such thing as democratization in one country' (Whitehead, 1996, p. 24).

Much as recent International Relations theory emphasises the interdependence of states in the international system, so transitions have come to be viewed as essentially 'interdependent' processes that are affected by the prevailing international environment (Przeworski, 1991). International factors of influence are generally grouped under four analytical headings: *contagion (demonstration effects), control (external imposition), consent (international recognition and support), and conditionality,* with the former pair tending to involve unilateral interaction between states and the latter pair multilateral interactions between states and subnational or supra-national actors (Schmitter, 1996, pp. 26–54; Whitehead, 1996, pp. 3–25). In the case of Russia, the control factor is not relevant given that a democratic transition was not imposed by an external agency. The other factors do illuminate key aspects of the Russian transition. Contagion, the influence of one country's transition on others, can be difficult to validate, although we can correlate a contagion effect in transitions with reference to time and geographical proximity. The so-called 'domino effect' in Eastern Europe and the Soviet Union in 1989–91 would clearly fit this category. The importance of political economy performance factors in transition outcomes suggests that geographical proximity of post-communist transitions to the EU may be significant, as those states geographically closest are more likely to benefit from any spillover effects in terms of membership enlargement and economic investment. In this model distant countries such as Russia are less likely to succeed in the consolidation of democracy and a market economy (Przeworski, 1991). The salience of the geographical proximity of the EU to clusters of democratic transitions could be a reflection of what Schmitter terms 'organizationally saturated interdependence', refering to the 'networks of public and private exchange' that develop and link these states to the EU (Schmitter, 1996, p. 33). Network linkages, after all, will be more effective if they are proximate. There are undoubtedly undertones of the 'Western Culture' thesis in such arguments (see below).

Whitehead sees 'transmission mechanisms' such as the media as crucial instruments for inculcating the 'attractiveness' of the political and economic success of capitalist democracy; hence, 'images of the good life' are a key contagion effect and they are as effective in distant Siberia as they are in the Baltic States (Whitehead, 1996, pp. 8, 21). Such information contagion effects are magnified by the visual immediacy of images via modern communications technology. The immense impact of this kind of contagion in the *glasnost* era under Gorbachev did carry over into the first years of the Russian Republic when there was a flirtation with Westernisation. This was most keenly felt in key policy areas in 1991–92, such as Kozyrev's 'Atlanticist' foreign policy and Gaidar's disastrous imitation of a Polish-style 'shock therapy' with the assistance of Western economic advisers. The impact of images is, however, subject to a diminishing effect over time, particularly if expectations are dashed. Consequently, as Russia's economic slump persisted, the early post-Soviet flirtation with Westernisation has been gradually displaced by a re-assertion of deep-seated Slavophilism and suspicion of the West.

The elements of consent and conditionality may be used to explain why the lure of the West has faded rapidly in Russia after its initial attraction. Transitions require the consent of the international system, which effectively means the dominant Western powers, in two principal areas: recognition of the territorial legitimacy of a transition state and adapting it to existing security arrangements (Whitehead, 1996, pp. 17–18). As regards the former, the territorial legitimacy and sovereignty of the Russian state was accepted without argument post-1991 and membership of major international organisations rapidly progressed: inheriting the USSR's permanent seat on the UN Security Council (1992) and joining the Council of Europe (1996). The war in Chechnya raised the issue of whether compliance with certain standards of behaviour was best promoted by inclusion or exclusion from international organisations, and indeed Russia's membership of the Council of Europe was delayed partly as a consequence of the war. The previously uncontested nature of Russia's sovereignty was also subverted by unilateral OSCE activities in Chechnya. Moreover, Russia is increasingly being de-aligned from security arrangements in Europe as NATO expands into the former Warsaw Pact states of Eastern Europe in breach of agreements reached during German unification. There seems little propect that EU enlargement will ever extend to Russia, membership of GATT remains elusive and while political membership of the G8 was finally conceded in May 1998 Russia is not regarded as a full member for economic strategy. The consent and conditionality elements for Russia's transition seem predicated, above all, on its former superpower status and continuing Western uncertainty over how to cope with its nuclear status and wide-ranging national interests.

Conditionality is one of the international factors of transition most relevant to contemporary Russia. In principle conditionality for aid is a reasonable proposition, particularly in order to avoid waste and corruption. Schmitter decribes it as a form of 'coercion': 'by attaching specific conditions to the distribution of benefits to recipient countries – on the part of multilateral institutions' (Schmitter, 1996, p. 30). The Russian transition has been affected by conditionality from two main sources. Firstly, its economic transition has depended heavily on financial assistance provided by the IMF. In the first years of transition the key condition for the G7 and IMF was a demonstration of political 'will' to implement some form of economic 'shock therapy'. Gorbachev's failure to show the requisite 'will' meant the so-called 'grand bargain' of massive aid to the USSR was rejected by the G7 at its July 1991 London summit. Some have suggested that it was the failure of the IMF to provide Russia with loans even after it had initiated 'shock therapy' in early 1992 that scuppered its whole reform trajectory (Sachs, 1995, pp. 60–1). Conditionality for IMF loans in the later transition period has focused more on the meeting of specific fiscal targets on low budget deficits and low inflation, deregulation and privatisation. The IMF's 1997–2000 $9.2 billion loan facility and the July 1998 $22.6 billion emergency loan to Russia to deal with the fiscal crisis that developed in the aftermath of the South-East Asia financial markets crash largely hinge on the implementation of a doctrinaire neo-liberal variant of monetarist fiscal rectitude and a free market philosophy on the eradication of state regulation. The argument is that the 'wider the scope of market forces, the less room there will be for rent-seeking by elites with privileged access to state power and resources' (Lipset, 1994, p. 3).

IMF loans are economically vital to bolster the Russian economy, but their conditionalities have been tremendously destabilising politically. Since late

1996 there have been incessant conflicts over budgetary issues between the president and government seeking to conform to IMF pressures, and the parliament seeking to avert the social costs of IMF conditionalities for the mass of impoverished Russian citizens. The conflict has intensified as a result of the 1998 fiscal crisis, and it has now widened to cover a range of issues such as deregulation of highly profitable natural monopolies (such as Gazprom), tax reform, reform of social provision and land privatisation. The IMF conditionalities for the 1998 loan are dependent on the Russian government implementing a range of fiscal and structural reforms and, if necessary, bypassing parliamentary opposition through the use of the president's decree power. This is a case where economic reform is being promoted at the expense of institutional development and the behavioural compliance with the 1993 constitution noted earlier. European organisations such as the EU and EBRD are even more overtly political than the IMF in their conditionality for loans and other assistance, insisting on certain democratic standards and convergence criteria.

Finally, we should note that external influences may be broadly felt at the multilateral level through the role of advisers, practitioners, NGOs and other specialists. The impact of this kind of influence is difficult to gauge, although the role of external advisers in assisting Russia with the crafting of new political and economic institutions has created much resentment at the way aid funds are siphoned off to Western consultants. In theory, democratic consolidation is promoted not only by the demonstration and emulation effects of interstate relations between governments but also by the developing of contacts between parliaments, parties and the work of specialist agencies such as the National Endowment for Democracy, Westminster Foundation for Democracy and the EU PHARE and TACIS programmes. The fact remains, however, that its great power status, coupled with its almost certain permanent exclusion from the principal international organsations in Europe, the EU and NATO, makes Russia less amenable to convergence pressures than other post-communist states.

Political culture: prior regime type and path dependency

The political culture factor in transition is fundamentally a history-based explanation. Obviously, there was a shared experience of communism, but each communist state had very different political traditions and starting conditions in terms of social, economic and political needs and orientations. Transition 'paths' and consolidation 'tasks', consequently, are seen as constrained in direct proportion to the strength and persistence of the legacy of the prior regime type (Linz and Stepan, 1996, pp. 55–65). The rejection of communism as a political system appears to be a smoother process in the states of East–Central Europe where it was often imposed from without and in fairly recent historical memory after 1945. In these states communism is essentially seen as conflictual with nation-state building and the re-assertion of national identity. In Russia, however, communism emerged from within, as a 'home-grown' phenomenon rooted in Russia's historical experience and established much earlier by the October 1917 revolution. Soviet communism was associated with modernisation and national resurgence and with the emergence of Russia as an industrialised society and a global superpower, for as Churchill remarked 'Stalin found Soviet Russia with the *sokha* (wooden plough) and left her with the atom bomb'. Communism had a much more durable impact in Russia than elsewhere, not only in terms of its institutional legacy but also in the way it shaped political tradition and the 'moral ethos' of the political actors who inhabit institutional spaces. After all, leadership style and character are deeply rooted in political culture.

'Western culture' and civil society

The notion that successful democratisation is inextricably linked to a Westernisation of political culture is most closely associated with Huntington, who argued that 26 of the 30 countries identified by him as 'Third Wave' democracies either were Western or have strong Western influences. This correlation led him to believe that democratic consolidation requires a Westernisation of culture. The lack of permeability to Western influences of countries with an Eastern Orthodox religious culture rooted in Byzantine traditions of theocracy led him to suggest that the boundary of Western Christendom in 1500 'may separate those areas where democracy will take root from those where it will not' (Huntington, 1993, p. 300). Huntington's cultural demarcation line also excludes countries with Islamic and Confucian cultures. Essentially, the argument is that such cultures are intrinsically incapable of developing fully democratic political institutions and practices because open adversarial politics and political competition are alien concepts.

The intellectual origins of such an argument may be found in certain Weberian strands of modernisation theory which emphasised the relationship between protestantism, capitalism and democracy. Similar arguments were made in the 1950s and 1960s to dismiss the prospects of democratisation in Catholic states such as Spain, Portugal and those of Latin America. These are precisely, indeed, those states which formed the bulk of the 'Third Wave'. The point is that we should not be too dogmatic or sectarian with regard to the cultural underpinnings of democracy. Indeed, Huntington himself is not logically consistent in his argument since he acknowledges that 'the most important cause of cultural change is economic development itself' (Huntington, 1993, p. 311). Consequently, we should expect that with the development of a modern market economy in Russia its political culture will adjust accordingly. As we observed earlier, however, Russia has experienced a demodernising transition with the collapse of its industrial society and impoverishment which has seen state provision of the services associated with a modern society substantially reduced.

Consolidation requires more than functioning democratic political institutions and a market economy. Dahl asserted that pluralist democracy was underpinned by a 'democratic credo' of toleration and compliance to the rules. It was not necessary for this credo to permeate mass society, indeed this could be destabilising, but it was absolutely essential that the elites adhere to it, because as he observed 'leaders lead – and often are lead' (Dahl, 1961, p. 325). It is a long-established axiom that successful democracy is underpinned by *civil society*, through the autonomous organisation of voluntary associations that have high participation levels and shared values (Diamond, 1996, pp. 228–30). Whether it hinges on a specific 'civic culture' (Almond and Verba, 1963) or depends on social capital and 'civic traditions' (Putnam, 1993), a vibrant civil society is widely seen as a fundamental check against the re-emergence of an authoritarian state power. This institutional dimension of civil society is bound together by values of toleration, engagement and trust, particularly among elites. These values are epitomised by what Gellner termed the 'modular' person of modern indus-trialised societies: complex voluntary associations of individuals in arrays of networks and organisations, and very unlike the forced activism and participa-tion of totalitarian societies, or the clan–kin blood ties of traditional societies (Gellner, 1994). We should be wary, however, of overstating the capacity of civil society to deter authoritarianism, as the example of Weimar Germany demon-strates. In the absence of strong state institutions, civil society offers little pro-tection against a democratic breakdown.

Totalitarian 'prehistories' and the 'flattened landscape' of a very weak or non-existent civil society are an obvious distinctive feature of Russian and other post-communist transitions (Linz and Stepan, 1996, pp. 235–54). Transitions from authoritarian rule are regarded as less problematical because their market econ-omies created a foundation for the self-regulating autonomous organisations that underpin civil society. Communist totalitarian systems, in contrast, for ease of control attempted to erase these traditions and transform society into 'atomised, isolated individuals' (Arendt, 1958, p. 323). Just how totalitarian the Soviet Union was is much debated. Soviet society was underlaid by a largely autonomous second economy, and there were pockets of overt private economic activity such as private plots and peasant markets. The great challenge of post-communist tran-sition is less a question of how to rebuild civil society, but how to develop and empower much of the unofficial organisational life of the Soviet system.

Democratic practice

The emphasis on the 'crafting' dimension of democratic consolidation inherent in the genetic model of transition tends to assume an institutional and values vacuum as regards a legacy of history. It is even suggested that a democracy like Russia's is being constructed 'from scratch' (Fish, 1994). This overlooks the significant role of formative influences such as tradition and experience on those doing the 'crafting'. As John Stuart Mill observed, institutions are 'the work of men'. The 'crafting' of new institutions does not therefore occur in a vacuum, nor in the absence of external imposition (as in post-war Germany and Japan) does it begin from a 'year zero' starting point. The building of democratic institutions develops amidst the reworking of the historical legacy of institutional structures and the values and practices of political culture. The history of trans-itions demonstrates that authoritarian pasts can be overcome by countervailing conditions, principally economic performance and the growth of prosperity.

The genetic transition model assumes that an elite pact is the most stable environment for overcoming the problems of institutional engineering required for a successful transition. A reproduction of some kind of communist era elites in politics, administration and business is intrinsic to this model. The assumption is that such elites must be behaviourally compliant with the institutional rules of the game and that over time such compliance will promote democratic values. Despite the crucial importance of elites in transition models, there have been remarkably few systematic studies of post-Soviet elite configurations and values. This weakness is partly derived from the legacy of a 'defensive' elite inherited from the communist era, as Russian elites generally operate in a much more non-transparent and inaccessible manner than their Western counterparts. Although elite attitudes are of immense importance to the progress of consolidation, much of the writing on this aspect of transition in Russia is focused on mass societal values. Moreover, studies of post-Soviet elites have focused on the state level, the traditional preoccupation of transition studies, while we know very little about substate elite configurations and attitudes – a level that is key for the consolidation of democracy. In principle, the absence of a 'lustration' (purging) process in Russia, unlike in some Eastern European states (East Germany, Czech Republic, Poland, Bulgaria), signifies that there was a political opportunity for old communist elites to adapt to the transition. There are, in fact, two conflicting hypotheses on post-Soviet elite trends: a *reproduction* thesis and a *circulation* thesis. Perhaps the most widely held view is that although communist era elites have been fragmented and become more differentiated, there has been a 'revenge of the *nomenklatura*' as old elites have reproduced themselves by converting their positional power under the communist regime into positional power in the democratic transition (Krystanovskaya and White, 1996). The trend for old communist elites to colonise new democratic bodies seems to be confirmed also at regional levels (Hughes, 1997).

Alternatively, other studies have suggested that the state-level political elite under Yeltsin is characterised by a trend of circulation from the Soviet era intelligentsia, with a Western and pro-market orientation (Lane and Ross, 1998). Our lack of knowledge about the moral ethos or values of the Russian elites is a serious weakness in evaluating the Russian transition given that the role of leading actors and groups is central to the transition models of analysis. The question is, to what extent have elite values been transformed in a way which will promote democratic consolidation and a marketised economy? Studies of state-level elites under Gorbachev and Yeltsin suggest that they are largely imbued by a communist era moral solidarity and lack of commitment to the values of democratic politics and a market economy (Lane, 1996, 1998).

The inherited elite 'moral ethos' imposes severe constraints on the development of democracy in Russia. It is the residues of this communist era 'moral ethos' that fostered the development of a highly patrimonial form of presidentialism, geared to unilateralism in politics and monopolising trends in business. It has also suppressed the growth of a democratic society in two other key areas: by undermining the independence of two crucial institutional checks on arbitrary power in developed democracies, the mass media and the judicial system and by marginalising social organisations and NGOs from influence on public policy. Political events in Russia since 1991 demonstrate a strong pull from past authoritarian practices. The autocratic political tradition of leadership unconstrained by institutional arrangements seems to appeal to Yeltsin's temperament, evident from his repeated references to himself as a 'Tsar'. This is a rhetorical affirmation of his preference for bypassing institutions, his personalization of power and the creation of a type of Byzantine 'court' politics around his presidency (see Chapter 2). Memoirs of former close officials reveal that Yeltsin's personal style favours informal norms of decision-making in the *dacha, banya, binge* and tennis court (Korzhakov, 1997; Kostikov, 1997). Such practices may well be fairly common among political leaders in many states, but few are as unconstrained by an institutionally weak state as Yeltsin.

Yeltsin extracts a plebiscitary legitimacy from his electoral victories and has given a new respectability to the traditional informal political practices of the communist era by obstructing the embedding of democratic institutions and practices. Much as the style of the CPSU General Secretary was replicated by leaders down the authority chain, so Yeltsin's presidential style has been emulated in the emergence of 'little presidents' in Russia's regions and republics, for example, such as presidents Shaimiev (Tatarstan) and Nikolaev (Sakha), governors Rossel (Sverdlovsk), Nazdratenko (Primorye) and Lebed (Krasnoyarsk) and mayor Luzhkov (Moscow). Finally, the Yeltsin style of politics has been influential in shaping not only the Russian transition but also those of other post-Soviet states. A presidential 'contagion' from Russia has influenced developments in states such as Belarus and Ukraine and in those of the Transcaucasus and Central Asia. Arguably, this preference for semi-authoritarian presidentialism would have been less popular had Yeltsin not blazed the trail since 1992.

Experience of democratic practice is self-evidently a crucial mechanism for transforming political culture. The sustained democratic practice of competitive elections in 1991–96 has established a one-dimensional democracy in Russia. Votes are merely symbolic, however, if they do not shape political outcomes. Russia's political leaders, its president in particular, have been remarkably unresponsive to voting preferences, a factor which contributes to voter apathy. This discounting of public opinion is partly a product of political will and partly due to the weakness of Russia's state capacity. Russia's fragile democracy is rendered even more brittle by the hollowness of its civil society. The prospects for democratic consolidation are also checked by a trend towards 'delegative democracy' and the far-reaching penetration of politics by the influence of corporate oligarchs. Hence, Russia is aptly described as an 'uncertain transition' (Linz and Stepan, 1996, p. 81). The best prognosis for Russia may well be that its democratisation will continue 'by fits and starts' (Lowenhardt, 1995, p. 152). On the positive side, there has been an incremental behavioural compliance among the political elites with the give and take of democratic politics. Russia's zigzagging transition may soon reach its critical point as, poised on the cusp of the post-Yeltsin era, the country is confronted by two alternative paths of political development: an authoritarian variant and a consolidated democratic variant.

The difficulties of the transition are summarised in Box 1.1.

СПРАВКА 1.1	**The difficulties of the transition in Russia**

1. *Simultaneity of change.* Russia had to change its economic and political system simultaneously with its efforts at state building.

2. *Totality of change.* Russia needed revolutionary change in every area of life. The command economy had to be transformed into a liberal market; a one-party dictatorship into a liberal democracy; an atomised, passive society into an active civil society.

3. *Post-imperial change.* Russia gave up its land-based empire, but still faces problems over borders, the Russian diaspora, its post-imperial political cuture and new economic relations with the Soviet successor states.

4. *Great power status.* Russia is the only nuclear power to have undergone the radical process of transition.

Concluding remarks: why is Russia's post-communist transition different?

The transition in Russia sparked a heated debate between area and comparative specialists over the relevance of transition models and their assumptions to the study of Russia (Schmitter and Karl, 1994; Bunce, 1995). A *modus vivendi* appears to have been reached whereby the analytical frameworks provided by comparative studies of transition are being applied, and in the process they are being modified to take account of Russian particularities. Models are blunt analytical instruments for they inevitably blur the more distinctive features of any transition. In the case of post-communist transition in Russia, there are certain features which, in combination, make for a radically different perspective compared with those elsewhere. The distinctiveness has four cardinal aspects: the simultaneity of change, the totality of change, the post-imperial nature of change and Russia's former superpower status. First, it is generally recognised that the simultaneity of post-communist transitions makes them more complicated and problem prone, whether it is the 'double' transition of concurrent political and economic transformation (Przeworski, 1991) or the 'triple transition' including the additional element of post-communist nation-state building (Offe, 1996).

Second, in contrast to transitions from authoritarianism, post-communist transitions involve a totality of change from monist political regimes with centrally planned economies and weak civil societies. Given that the communist system had its longest duration (70 years) and greatest penetration of state and society in Russia, the question of the totality of change becomes most salient in this case. As a starting point for transition it is as radically different as one could possibly imagine compared with those of Latin America, Southern Europe and South-East Asia. In these cases transition has involved change from authoritarianism, normally with a corporatist market economy, where there was a higher level of autonomous social and economic organisation (principally centred around religion and business) compared with communist regimes.

Third, problems arising from post-imperialism are, perhaps, the most distinctive trait of Russia's transition. Unlike many other empires, as the Russian state expanded from the late sixteenth century, there was never a clear distinction between the Russian *core* and its imperial *periphery*. This made for a conflation of core and periphery in the making of Russian identity – a legacy that continues to resonate in contemporary politics. Considering that the state is the fundamental unit of analysis for the transition approach, it is surprising how little attention has been drawn to this aspect of Russia's transition. Only recently have studies focused on this dimension (Dawisha and Parrot, 1997; Snyder, 1998). The issue of post-imperialism arises at four main levels: first, how Russia influences transitions in its former empire in the post-Soviet states of its 'near abroad'; second, how ethno-nationalism is to be contained within the Russian Federation itself; third, how elite mobilisation of regional separatism is to be managed; fourth, how the legacy of imperial economic dependencies and intra-state ties is to be refashioned.

Finally, although Russia's status is seen more as 'great power' than 'super-power' in the post-cold-war era, it remains the only nuclear superpower to have undergone a democratising transition from authoritarianism. As a former hegemonic power Russia exercised immense influence not only in the communist bloc of states but on the whole international system. The nuclear factor makes the potential dangers of a Russian transition more potent and, consequently, that its consolidation of democracy is a success is of crucial international importance. The transformation of its status from superpower to great power has meant that the transition in Russia has been affected more by international political factors than any other transition hitherto, with the corollary that this transition has been of supreme importance in shaping transitions throughout the former Soviet Union, in Eastern Europe and indeed in other parts of the world where democratisation was stalled by cold war politics.

Acknowledgements

The author would like to thank Chris Binns and Gwen Sasse for their comments.

References

Aganbegyan A 1988 *The Challenge: Economics of Perestroika*, Hutchinson, London.
Almond G and Verba S 1963 *The Civic Culture: Political Attitudes and Democracy in Five Nations*, Princeton University Press, Princeton, NJ.
Arendt H 1958 *The Origins of Totalitarianism*, 2nd enlarged edition, Meridian, New York.
Aslund A 1996 Reform vs. 'Rent-Seeking' in Russia's Economic Transformation, *Transition*, Vol. 2, No. 2 (26 January), pp. 12–17.
Blasi J R, Kroumova M and Kruse D 1997 *Kremlin Capitalism: The Privatization of the Russian Economy*, ILR Press/Cornell University Press, Ithaca, NY.

Bova R 1991 The Political Dynamics of the Post-Communist Transition: A Comparative Perspective, Bermeo N (ed.), *Liberalization and Democratization: Change in the Soviet Union and Eastern Europe*, Johns Hopkins University Press, Baltimore, MD, pp. 113–38.

Brown A 1996 *The Gorbachev Factor*, Oxford University Press, Oxford.

Brubaker R 1996 *Nationalism Reframed: Nationhood and the National Question in the New Europe*, Cambridge University Press, Cambridge.

Bunce V 1995 Should Transitologists Be Grounded?, *Slavic Review*, Vol. 54, No. 1 (Spring 1995), pp. 111–27.

Clarke S and Kabalina V 1995 Privatisation and the Struggle for Control of the Enterprise, Lane D (ed.), *Russia in Transition: Politics, Privatisation and Inequality*, Longman, London, pp. 142–58.

Colton T 1995 Boris Yeltsin, Russia's All-Thumbs Democrat, Colton T and Tucker R (eds), *Patterns in Post-Soviet Leadership*, Westview, Boulder, pp. 49–74.

Dahl R 1961 *Who Governs? Democracy and Power in an American City*, Yale University Press, New Haven, CT, and London.

Dahl R 1971 *Polyarchy: Participation and Opposition*, Yale University Press, New Haven, CT, and London.

Dahl R 1989 *Democracy and Its Critics*, Yale University Press, New Haven, CT, and London.

Dawisha K and Parrot B (eds) 1997 *The End of Empire? The Transformation of the USSR in Comparative Perspective*, M E Sharpe, London.

Diamond L 1996 Toward Democratic Consolidation, Diamond L and Plattner M F (eds), *The Global Resurgence of Democracy*, Johns Hopkins University Press, Baltimore, MD, and London, pp. 227–40.

Di Palma G 1990 *To Craft Democracies: An Essay on Democratic Transitions*, University of California Press, Berkeley, CA.

Ellman E and Kontorovich V (eds) 1992 *The Disintegration of the Soviet Economic System*, Routledge, London.

Gellner E 1994 *Conditions of Liberty: Civil Society and its Rivals*, Hamish Hamilton, London.

Gorbachev M 1997 *Memoirs*, Bantam Books, London.

Haggard S and Kaufman R R 1995 *The Political Economy of Democratic Transitions*, Princeton University Press, Princeton, NJ.

Higley J, Pakulski J and Wesolowski W (eds) 1998 *Postcommunist Elites and Democracy in Eastern Europe*, Macmillan, London.

Hosking G, Aves J and Duncan P 1992 *The Road to Post-Communism: Independent Political Movements in the Soviet Union 1985–1991*, Pinter, London.

Hughes J 1996 Moscow's Bilateral Treaties Add to Confusion, *Transition*, Vol. 19, No. 20 (September), pp. 39–43.

Hughes J 1997 Sub-National Élites and Post-Communist Transformation in Russia, *Europe–Asia Studies*, Vol. 49, No. 6, pp. 1017–36.

Huntington, S P 1968 *Political Order in Changing Societies*, Yale University Press, New Haven, CT.

Huntington S P 1993 *The Third Wave, Democratization in the Late Twentieth Century*, University of Oklahoma Press, Norman, OK, and London.

Krystanovskaya O and White S 1996 From Soviet Nomenklatura to Russian Élite, *Europe–Asia Studies*, Vol. 48, No. 5, pp. 711–34.

Klyamkin I and Migranyan A 1989 *Literaturnaya Gazeta*, 16 August.

Kordonskii S 1995 The Structure of Economic Space in Post-Perestroika Society and the Transformation of the Administrative Market, Segbers K and De Spiegeleire (eds), *Post-Soviet Puzzles: Mapping the Political Economy of the Former Soviet Union*, Vol. 1, Nomos, Baden-Baden, pp. 157–204.

Korzhakov A 1997 *Boris El'tsin: Ot rassveta do zakata*, Interbuk, Moscow.

Kostikov V 1997 *Roman s prezidentom: Zapiski press-sekretarya*, Vagrius, Moscow.

Lane D 1992 *Soviet Society Under Perestroika*, Routledge, London.

Lane D 1996 The Gorbachev Revolution: The Role of the Political élite in Regime Disintegration, *Political Studies*, Vol. 44, No. 1 (March), pp. 4–23.

Lane D 1998 Transition under Eltsin: the Nomenklatura and Political Elite Circulation, *Political Studies*, Vol. 45, No. 5 (December), pp. 855–74.

Lane D and Ross C 1998 The Russian Political Elites, 1991–5, Higley J, Pakulski J and Wesolowski W (eds), *Postcommunist Elites and Democracy in Eastern Europe*, Macmillan, London, pp. 34–66.

Lewin M 1988 *The Gorbachev Phenomenon*, Radius, London.

Lijphart A 1977 *Democracy in Plural Societies. A Comparative Exploration*, Yale University Press, New Haven, CT.

Linz J J 1990 Transitions to Democracy, *The Washington Quarterly*, Vol. 13, No. 3 (summer), pp. 143–63.

Linz J J 1994 Presidential or Parliamentary Democracy: Does it Make a Difference?, Linz J J and Valenzuela A (eds), *The Failure of Presidential Democracy: Comparative Perdspectives*, Vol. 1, Johns Hopkins University Press, Baltimore, MD.

Linz J J and Stepan A 1991 Political Identities and Electoral Sequences: Spain, the Soviet Union, and Yugoslavia, *Daedalus*, Vol. 121, No. 2, pp. 123–39.

Linz J J and Stepan A 1996 *Problems of Democratic Transition and Consolidation: Southern Europe, South America, and Post-Communist Europe*, John Hopkins University Press, Baltimore, MD.

Lipset S M 1960 *Political Man: The Social Bases of Politics*, Doubleday, New York.

Lipset S M 1981 *Political Man: The Social Bases of Politics*, revised edition, John Hopkins University Press, Baltimore, MD.

Lipset S M 1994 The Social Requisites of Democracy Revisited, *American Sociological Review*, Vol. 59 (February), pp. 1–22.

Lowenhardt J 1995 *The Reincarnation of Russia: Struggling with the Legacy of Communism, 1990–1994*, Longman, London.

Mainwaring S 1992 Transitions to Democracy and Democratic Consolidation: Theoretical and Comparative Issues, Mainwaring S, O'Donnell G and Valenzuela J S (eds), *Issues in Democratic Consolidation: The New South American Democracies in Comparative Perspective*, University of Notre Dame Press, Notre Dame, IN, pp. 294–341.

McAuley A 1995 Inequality and Poverty, Lane D (ed.), *Russia in Transition: Politics, Privatisation and Inequality*, Longman, London, pp. 177–89.

McFaul M 1993 Russian Centrism and Revolutionary Transitions, *Post-Soviet Affairs*, Vol. 9, No. 3, pp. 196–222.

McFaul M 1997 *Russia's 1996 Presidential Election: The End of Polarized Politics*, Hoover Institution Press, Stanford, CA.

Moore B 1967 *The Social Origins of Dictatorship and Democracy: Lord and Peasant in the Making of the Modern World*, Allen Lane, London.

Motyl A 1998 After Empire: Competing Discourses and Inter-state Conflict in Post-imperial Eastern Europe, Snyder J (ed.), *Post-Soviet Political Order: Conflict and State-Building*, Routledge, London.

O'Donnell G 1994 Delegative Democracy, *Journal of Democracy*, Vol. 5, No. 1, pp. 55–69

O'Donnell G and Schmitter P 1986 *Transitions from Authoritarian Rule: Tentative Conclusions about Uncertain Democracies*, John Hopkins University Press, Baltimore, MD.

Offe C 1996 *Varieties of Transition: The East European and East German Experience,* Polity Press, Cambridge.

Przeworski A 1986 Some Problems in the Study of the Transition to Democracy, O'Donnell D and Schmitter P, *Transitions from Authoritarian Rule: Tentative Conclusions about Uncertain Democracies,* John Hopkins University Press, Baltimore, MD, pp. 47–63.

Przeworski A 1991 *Democracy and the Market: Political and Economic Reforms in Eastern Europe and Latin America,* Cambridge University Press, Cambridge.

Przeworski A 1995 *Sustainable Democracy,* Cambridge University Press, Cambridge.

Putnam R 1993 *Making Democracy Work: Civic Traditions in Modern Italy,* Princeton University Press, Princeton, NJ.

Rueschemeyer D, Huber Stephens E and Stephens J D 1992 *Capitalist Development and Democracy,* Polity Press, Cambridge.

Rustow D 1970 Transitions to Democracy: Toward a Dynamic Model, *Comparative Politics,* Vol. 2, No. 3 (October), pp. 337–63.

Sachs G 1995 Consolidating Capitalism, *Foreign Policy,* Vol. 98 (Spring), pp. 50–64.

Schmitter P 1996 The Influence of the International Context upon the Choice of National Institutions and Policies in Neo-Democracies, Whitehead L (ed.), *The International Dimensions of Democratization: Europe and the Americas,* Oxford University Press, Oxford.

Schmitter P and Karl T 1994 The Conceptual Travels of Transitologists and Consolidologists: How Far to the East Should They Go?, *Slavic Review,* Vol. 53, No. 1 (Spring), pp. 173–85.

Sedaitis J B and Butterfield J (eds) 1991 *Perestroika From Below: Social Movements in the Soviet Union,* Westview, London.

Shugart M and Carey J 1992 *Presidents and Assemblies: Constitutional Design and Electoral Dynamics,* Cambridge University Press, Cambridge.

Snyder J (ed.), 1998 *Post-Soviet Political Order: Conflict and State-Building,* Routledge, London.

Szporluk R 1997 The Russian Question and Imperial Overextension, Dawisha K and Parrot B (eds), *The End of Empire? The Transformation of the USSR in Comparative Perspective,* M E Sharpe, London, pp. 65–93.

Tolz V 1994 Problems in Building Democratic Institutions in Russia, *RFE/RL Research Report,* Vol. 3, No. 9 (4 March), pp. 1–7.

Vanhanen T 1997 *Prospects of Democracy: A Study of 172 Countries,* Routledge, London.

Whitehead L 1996 Those International Dimensions of Democratization, Whitehead L (ed.), *The International Dimension of Democratization: Europe and the Americas,* Oxford University Press, Oxford, pp. 3–25.

Yeltsin B 1990 *Against the Grain: An Autobiography,* Jonathan Cape, London.

Further reading

Huntington S P 1993 *The Third Wave, Democratization in the Late Twentieth Century,* University of Oklahoma Press, Norman, OK, and London.

Linz J J and Stepan A 1996 *Problems of Democratic Transition and Consolidation: Southern Europe, South America, and Post-Communist Europe,* John Hopkins University Press, Baltimore, MD.

Przeworski A 1995 *Sustainable Democracy,* Cambridge University Press, Cambridge.

The president and parliament in contemporary Russia

Alexei Avtonomov

Introduction: the Soviet political system

The nature of the Soviet system has been much debated in the West. Was it totalitarian, authoritarian or a form of corporatism? How much did the system change over time? On one general issue, however, there was general agreement – the Soviet Union was a highly repressive, one-party dictatorship. The state was highly centralised with power concentrated in the hands of a few political leaders at the top. Their power, moreover, was unconstrained by legal or institutional means. There were no checks and balances in the system. Party writ was law. It was, in other words, a monist system dominated by the Communist Party of the Soviet Union (CPSU) which allowed no political input from the people or any independent outside groups.

Nevertheless, the Soviet Union contained many of the trappings of a pluralist state. There was no independent judiciary, but party and state bodies coexisted throughout the entire Soviet period. There were top party bodies, such as the politburo and secretariat, and top government bodies, such as the Council of Ministers. However, in practice, there was little separation between party and state. The CPSU had been the governing party for so long in the USSR that few could differentiate between the two. Every state body had a party cell within it to ensure that party policy was followed. Personnel and duties frequently overlapped. Differences that did occur within the Soviet system (usually kept firmly behind closed doors) were rarely between party and state as such, but between bureaucracies. Thus, the party and state bodies dealing with defence matters would usually work together to fight other sectors for a larger share of state funding. In effect, party and state had fused. There was little exaggeration in speaking of a party–state system in the context of the Soviet Union.

The system has also always had a legislature and elections at national, republic and local levels. Indeed, Lenin took power in October 1917 in the name of the legislature – the soviets (councils), not the Bolshevik Party. However, again, in practice, the executive dominated the legislature. Soviet elections to the legislature at local and national level were virtually meaningless (see Box 2.1). There was no choice of candidate, and although not all candidates were CPSU members (and therefore subject to party discipline), all candidates were approved by party and state authorities. Furthermore, the elections had no impact on the government of the country. The elected deputies did not make up the government, nor did the election have any impact on party policy. In fact, the

СПРАВКА 2.1   On Soviet elections

In Soviet times, there was only one name on the ballot paper. Theoretically voters had the right in a secret ballot to vote against the candidate by striking his name out with a pen or pencil. Cubicles were set aside where people could register their vote. However, most voters went to the polling station, picked up a ballot paper and put it straight into the ballot box without marking it. That counted as a positive vote in favour of the candidate. If someone took out a pencil or went into the cubicle, then the authorities had strong suspicions that the person was voting against the candidate. Thus, the ballot was secret in name only.

almost unanimous votes registered regularly in favour of the single official candidate were viewed by the authorities as a sign of public approval for the general line of the Communist Party. The national parliament, the Supreme Soviet, sat for only a short period of time during the year and had neither the time nor the power to propose its own legislation or to review effectively that of the government. The Supreme Soviet was there to applaud rather than to criticise or hold the government to account. The legislature offered no constraint on central power.

Articles 50 and 51 of the 1977 Soviet Constitution appeared to grant important individual rights to Soviet citizens, including the rights of free speech and association. However, the article also stated that these rights could only be exercised insofar as they were in the interests of the Soviet people and the development of socialism. This allowed the state to repress dissidence for the long-term, collective good of Soviet society.

The CPSU's dominant position in society was justified in reference to Marxist–Leninist ideology. The CPSU was not a normal party. It was not a body organised to develop policy and to seek power through the ballot box. The CPSU was a self-proclaimed vanguard party. The party, in theory at least, was made up of professional revolutionaries devoted to the communist cause. Supposedly well read in the classic Marxist–Leninist texts, they claimed to be uniquely well positioned to lead society towards the ultimate goal of communism. Since communism was in the long-term interests of all, any opposition to the vanguard party was, by definition, reactionary, precluding any need for parties other than the CPSU. Article 6 of the 1977 Soviet Constitution formalised this position by granting the party a guaranteed, monopoly right to rule. However, the justification for a limitation of democracy in the Soviet Union also became a justification for limiting it inside the party as well. For the party was dominated by the leadership. The rank and file were expected to carry out orders from above without question; discipline within the party was rather like in the army. Party rules spoke of democratic centralism, but it was all centralism and no democracy. There were no elections – personnel were selected from above and not elected from below; debate, in theory, was permitted before a decision was made (thereafter party members had to be committed to the implementation of agreed policy), but, in practice, the organisation of opposition to the party leadership was restricted after Lenin banned party factions in 1921 and all debate was effectively stifled soon after Stalin came to power in January 1924.

The monist system accorded the party leadership enormous power, but it was also a source of weakness. On the one hand, it allowed the party to make difficult decisions in the long-term interests of the country; on the other, it encouraged the abuse of power. Since the state denied the existence of conflicting interests in Soviet society, it devised no institutional means of mediating between them. The system was unresponsive to popular demands and the leadership was almost wholly unaccountable to the people. As a result, all change had to be initiated from above. The masses had no constitutional means of demanding change. This was not a recipe for gradual change but for long periods of passivity followed by sudden periods of violent upheaval. This was a pattern detected in Tsarist times. It was to be repeated in the USSR when, as the US diplomat and academic George Kennan had predicted back in 1947, there were splits in the political elite. 'If, consequently, anything were ever to occur to disrupt the unity and efficacy of the Party as a political instrument, Soviet Russia might be changed overnight from one of the strongest to one of the weakest and most pitiable of national societies' (Kennan, 1947, p. 580).

Gorbachev

Gorbachev was critical of the Brezhnev period, in part, like his successors, because he wished to establish his credentials as a new leader, but also because he recognised many of the weaknesses of the political system he inherited. He accepted much of the liberal critique of Marxism–Leninism. Gorbachev favoured a more accountable system which limited the overweening power of the executive. He hoped to create such a system through liberalising and democratising the political system. This, he argued, would not only reduce the risk of Stalinism re-emerging in the Soviet Union; it would also allow for more considered decision-making which would avert mistakes, such as the Soviet invasion of Afghanistan in 1979. Liberalisation was a necessary first step, and *glasnost* was introduced as a policy shortly after Gorbachev came to power in March 1985. Without the right of free speech and a more independent media, any future democratisation of the political system would be rendered virtually meaningless. Democratisation, however, involved changes to the political structures in the Soviet Union. The process was formally introduced as policy at the Nineteenth CPSU Conference in June 1988. There were three main innovations.

A reactivated legislative branch of government

Gorbachev introduced a two-tier parliament: the Congress of People's Deputies (CPD) which was formally the supreme organ of state power, and the Supreme Soviet. The CPD was a huge body with 2250 deputies who were elected in three

СПРАВКА 2.2 Why did people join the party in the USSR?

1. Ideological belief.
2. Interest in politics.
3. A desire to make policy and change society.
3. Career. Some jobs required party membership.
4. Perks and privileges. Generally only for full-time party officials.

different ways: a third were elected from single-member constituencies; a third were elected on a republic and regional basis; a third were elected by the CPSU and other public associations. This form of election was designed to limit democracy and ensure the presence in parliament of certain authority figures. It was notable that Gorbachev was one of the 100 CPSU members selected unopposed to fill the designated party places. The CPD then elected from among its number the 542 deputies for the Supreme Soviet. The indirect elections to the smaller and more influential Supreme Soviet had the intention of filtering out the more radical deputies to make the innovation more acceptable to the hardliners in the party. Nevertheless, the CPD proved to be a lively debating chamber, even if its record as a governing body was less impressive. Parliament proved too unwieldy and too ill disciplined to achieve very much in practical terms.

Competitive elections

The election on 26 March 1989 for the deputies to the CPD was the first competitive national election since the Leninist period. The elections were not at this stage multiparty (although they became so the following year for the republic and regional elections). Independents were allowed to stand, but all other parties, except for the CPSU, were still banned. This obviously gave a great advantage to the party establishment. However, party members could stand against each other in constituencies and compete for votes. This had the effect of revealing the extent of the differences in political views between CPSU members (see Box 2.2). It also greatly loosened party discipline. A factor that was further encouraged when Gorbachev repealed Lenin's ban on party factions in December 1989 and declared that the party no longer had to vote as a bloc in the CPD. The result was that the party split along ideological and national lines.

The Commission of Constitutional Review

Gorbachev also created a form of Constitutional Court to provide the third pillar of the checks and balances system of government – the executive (the state), the legislature (parliament) and the judiciary (the Commission of Constitutional Review). This commission had nothing like the powers of the US Supreme Court. Nevertheless, it was an important step forward. For the first time, the party implicitly acknowledged that no body or individual was above the law and the constitution of the country. No longer was the law to be whatever the party decreed.

The reduction in power of the CPSU

The national elections of 1989 were not the end of the democratisation process in the Soviet Union, they were only the beginning. In February 1990, Gorbachev formally abolished Article 6 of the Brezhnev Constitution which gave the CPSU a guaranteed monopoly right to rule. In effect, this was formalising the fledgling multi-party system that was already emerging in the Soviet Union at that time. Richard Sakwa estimated that there were already about 500 parties and 60 000 independent organisations in existence by the time Gorbachev made his announcement (Sakwa, 1990, p. 203), although the vast majority were small and of little political significance. The following month, he further reduced the power of the party by introducing a presidential system. Gorbachev was not elected President directly by the people as the rules seemed to demand (because of what Gorbachev described as exceptional circumstances), but unopposed by the deputies of the CPD. In many ways, the reform changed very little – the powers of the General Secretary were simply transferred to the presidential office. Nevertheless, it did have an impact on the party. It ceased formally to be a governing body and its top institutions met far less regularly. Gorbachev, for his part, argued that his position as executive President gave him far greater legitimacy to govern – only 10 per cent of the adult population of the USSR was in the party while the President, as head of state, could claim to represent the whole of Soviet society.

When all 15 Union Republics held elections in 1990, the state found itself under increased pressure. Nationalist blocs performed well in most republics and formed parliamentary majorities in the Baltic Republics and Georgia. Radicals, such as Yeltsin and his supporters in Russia, also performed strongly in many areas. Now there were not only checks on executive power at the top, there were also growing checks from below – from the republics and regions. Power was being dispersed and decentralised. The problem was that this was greatly undermining the authority of the centre, making the implementation of policy increasingly difficult. The process of democratisation might have been more successful over the long term except for a series of major problems which undermined the state. These included:

- economic decline from 1988;
- the collapse of Marxism–Leninism in Eastern Europe in 1989;
- growing national unrest in many republics.

Yeltsin

The period 1991–93

The first thing to emphasise about Yeltsin is that his power base lay in Russia, not in the Soviet Union. He was, it is true, a deputy in the Supreme Soviet of the USSR, but he rose to power and influence through the RSFSR. He was

Table 2.1 The first Russian presidential
election, 12 June 1991

Candidate	Vote (%)
Boris Yeltsin	57.3
Nikolai Ryzhkov	16.8
Vladimir Zhirinovsky	7.8
Aman Tuleev	6.8
Albert Makashov	3.7
Vadim Bakatin	3.4
Invalid votes	4.1
Turnout	74.7

Source: Richard Sakwa, *Russian Politics and
Society*, Routledge, London, 1993, p. 390

elected a deputy of the Russian parliament in the republic elections in spring
1990 before becoming its chairman in May. At the same time, Yeltsin left the
CPSU, claiming to want to represent all of the Russian people as chair of the
Russian parliament, and he has remained resolutely above party politics ever since.
Then, following Gorbachev's example, he sought to extend his power in Russia
through creating a parallel presidential system to that in the Soviet Union. Yeltsin's
proposal was accepted by the people in a referendum in April 1991 and he was
formally elected President of Russia from a field of six in June (see Table 2.1).
The political structures in Russia were, therefore, roughly the same as those at
the union level. Parliament was a two-tier system with a Congress of People's
Deputies and a smaller, more influential Supreme Soviet. The CPD was formally
the supreme organ of power in Russia and it could veto any decision by the
Supreme Soviet. It also had unilateral powers in a number of important areas,
such as the impeachment of the President. In practice, however, the Supreme
Soviet was the more important body because it sat in permanent session in contrast to the CPD's part-time status.

As already noted in the introduction, Yeltsin used his popular mandate to
defeat first the August 1991 plotters and then his great rival in the Kremlin,
Mikhail Gorbachev. Yeltsin finally forced Gorbachev to resign when he agreed
with other republic leaders to abolish the Soviet Union in December 1991 and
set up the CIS.

Yeltsin was then unchallenged in Moscow as Russian leader. However, unlike
almost all the other republic leaders he chose not to seek ratification for the
momentous events of 1991. He sought neither re-election nor a new constitution to take account of the new realities of post-Soviet Russia. The constitution
was based on the Russian one written back in 1978 when Brezhnev was still General
Secretary and the Soviet Union still a one-party state. It had been greatly
amended to allow for the changes that had taken place since 1990, but it was
scarcely a document which bore much authority. However, Yeltsin declared he
had no time for talk. He had to get on with the business of government, he
said, there had already been too much delay. Now was the time for action and
Yeltsin saw economic reform as his first priority. In some respects this attitude
was understandable, but his decision to ignore political structures in the new
Russia proved costly. Although Yeltsin was able to use his considerable prestige
after the August coup to get his policies adopted in the early stages of his

government, he found this increasingly difficult as time went on and there seemed no end to the mounting economic and social problems.

The CPD granted Yeltsin emergency powers for a 12 month period from December 1991. These powers included the right to issue decrees on economic policy and to appoint key government ministers and regional officials. Almost as soon as Congress gave Yeltsin these powers, it tried to claw many of them back. As the economy continued its downward spiral, parliament challenged the President in December 1992. In a highly charged atmosphere, there was a move towards impeachment, but it failed to get sufficient votes. Nevertheless, Congress rejected Yeltsin's appeal to extend his emergency powers because of the President's failure to effectively implement an acceptable reform programme. Thereafter, effective government in Russia became far more difficult.

In a system of checks and balances, the demarcation of power between the various institutions is vital. Some overlap and some competition are inevitable. Indeed, they are the very life-blood of democracy. However, there needs, at a very minimum, to be a general agreement on the rules of the game for the system to work at all. Too often this was lacking in the case of Russia. Although disputes between the President and parliament appeared to be based on policy disputes – on the economy, the budget, taxation, the war in Bosnia, and so on – in practice, the central issue was power. Who should rule Russia, the President or parliament? The President saw his election in June 1991 as a mandate from the people, while Congress claimed supremacy with reference to the Russian constitution. Neither side was willing to give way on this crucial issue. Yeltsin wanted a supine parliament; Congress wanted a President as a figurehead. Parliament in many ways acted irresponsibly, the President in an often high-handed and autocratic fashion.

It would always have been difficult for Yeltsin to get agreement with parliament over his reform policies. Many deputies were resolutely opposed to reform and were out to make things difficult for the Yeltsin administration. Yeltsin could never have won over the hard-liners. His real failure, however, lay in losing support of the more moderate members of Congress. According to Anatoli Chubais, a close Yeltsin ally at the time, the President had the support of 65 per cent of deputies in April 1992, but by October that figure had been all but halved (*Guardian*, 19 October 1992).

In a compromise move by Yeltsin, he dropped the liberal Yegor Gaidar in December 1992 as acting Prime Minister (although he was retained as an economic adviser and he returned to government in September 1993) and he was replaced by the more centrist Viktor Chernomyrdin. Yeltsin's closest political adviser, the man who had set Russia on the course of liberal reform, Gennadi Burbulis, was also sacked as a sop to Congress. Government policy began to shift under pressure from parliament away from its earlier economic liberalism and pro-Western foreign policy. However, parliament was not satisfied. In March 1993, it proposed further constitutional amendments to reduce still further Yeltsin's role as President. In April 1993, a referendum was called to try to end the political paralysis which had gripped the country. The result appeared to give backing to the President and his policies of economic reform, but the result was not overwhelming nor legally enforceable (see Table 2.2).

Table 2.2 Referendum 25 April 1993

	% of vote	
	Yes	*No*
1. Do you have confidence in Yeltsin?	58.7	39.2
2. Do you approve of the socio-economic policies of the government since 1992?	53.0	44.6
3. Do you want early presidential elections?	49.5	47.1
4. Do you want early parliamentary elections?	67.2	30.1

Source: adapted from Richard Sakwa, *Russian Politics and Society*, Routledge, London, 1993, p. 391

БИОГРАФИЯ 2.1 **Yegor Gaidar (born 1956)**

Yegor Gaidar was an intellectual and a trained economist, but he had little political experience when he was put in charge of economic reform in post-Soviet Russia. He was a supporter of Mrs Thatcher and Thatcherite economics, so it was of little surprise when he introduced 'shock therapy' – a dash to the market – in January 1992. However, when his reforms failed, he was replaced by Chernomyrdin in December 1992. Gaidar did make a brief comeback shortly before Yeltsin's suspension of parliament in September 1993, but, after his party's poor performance in the parliamentary elections later that year, he became a far less influential figure in Russian politics and even lost his own seat in the State Duma in the 1995 elections.

БИОГРАФИЯ 2.2 **Viktor Chernomyrdin (born 1938)**

Viktor Chernomyrdin was Prime Minister from 1992 to 1998. He was a centrist who was perceived by many at the time to have a 'safe pair of hands'. However, he was uncharismatic on TV. He looked to many Russians like a typical Soviet bureaucrat. Indeed, he had served on the CPSU Central Committee in the Gorbachev period while also acting as Minister for the Gas Industry. He moved from this latter position to become head of *Gazprom* in 1989 from which he made his fortune. As Prime Minister, his critics argued he continued to defend the interests of the energy lobby at the expense of manufacturing and other industries. Increasingly seen as self-serving, his hopes of becoming Yeltsin's successor were dashed when he failed to be reappointed Prime Minister in August 1998. However, he came to prominence again when he acted as Yeltsin's special envoy during the Kosovo crisis of 1999.

The stand-off between the executive and legislature was finally broken on 23 September 1993 when Yeltsin unilaterally closed down parliament. This action clearly exceeded the constitutional powers of the President and led to the events of October (see the introduction), but Yeltsin emerged clearly on top. The White House lay empty and blackened by gunfire while his most vitriolic opponents were in prison. A new constitution was drawn up by Yeltsin which was supported by the people in a referendum, but it was never debated or ratified by parliament. Elections were also held on 12 December 1993 for a new style of parliament.

The post-1993 political system

The power of the President

Clearly, Yeltsin's aim in drawing up the new constitution in 1993 was to create a political system in which the President was dominant. He was not wholly successful in his attempt, for Yeltsin was forced to accept a number of amendments to his draft before it was formally put before the Russian people in December. Nevertheless, the constitution did accord the President considerable powers and, most importantly from Yeltsin's point of view, clear supremacy over parliament. Thus, Article 80 declared that the President shall 'determine the guidelines for the domestic and foreign policies of the state' and 'represent the Russian Federation domestically and in international relations'. The Constitution went on to say that the President was head of state and Commander in Chief of the Russian armed forces. The President had considerable powers over key appointments, the right to preside over sessions of the government (Article 83), the power to submit bills to the Duma (Article 84) as well as the right to veto bills passed by parliament (Article 107). The President could issue decrees (Article 90), call a state of emergency (Article 88), call referenda (Article 84) and dissolve the State Duma in certain cases (Articles 111 and 117). Parliament was given, at best, a retrospective say over the declaration of a state of emergency, while there was no need to submit presidential decrees to either parliament or the people.

The power of the President was constrained by the will of the people. Most importantly, the President was required to seek election directly by the people every four years, and the same individual (as in the US) was not allowed to hold office for more than two consecutive terms (Article 81). However, it had become considerably more difficult to remove a sitting President than in the past. Impeachment was the only legal means of doing so and this became a more complex and lengthy business. Impeachment charges could only be brought if, in the judgement of the State Duma (supported by the Supreme Court and the Constitutional Court), there were grounds for thinking that the President had committed an act of 'high treason' or some other crime of similar gravity. A successful impeachment of the President required a two-thirds majority in both chambers of the Federal Assembly (Article 93).

The Federal Assembly

The most obvious change in the political system after 1993 involved the legislative branch of government. The old two-tier system was abandoned for a more traditional bicameral parliamentary structure. The new Federal Assembly consisted of two chambers, the State Duma and the Federation Council. The State Duma was elected, as in Germany, by two different methods of election. Half of the 450 deputies were elected in single-member constituencies by the first-past-the-post system; the remainder were elected from a party list, a system of proportional representation (PR) which required electors to vote for their preferred party on a national basis. Seats were distributed according to the percentage vote for each party, but with the one important proviso that a party had to get at least 5 per cent of the vote before gaining any seats on the party list. This 5 per cent threshold concept was borrowed from Germany and was an attempt to reduce the number of small parties in Russia, to marginalise extremists and to encourage greater coalition building between parties and political organisations. However, the 5 per cent threshold has not been so successful in the Russian case. Thus, communist and nationalist parties remain a considerable force in parliament, while the party system as a whole remains very weak (see Chapter 3).

In the Federation Council, two seats were reserved for each of the 89 regions in the Russian Federation. The method of selecting people for these two posts has changed over time. In 1993, the people voted for their two deputies directly, but, in 1995, deputies were selected on an *ex officio* basis from the heads of executive and legislative branches of regional government. However, these posts have been increasingly elected by the people rather than appointed by Yeltsin. As a result, the Federation Council has become less supportive of Yeltsin as oppositionists have won more elections in the provinces (see Chapter 4).

The State Duma is the more powerful body and sits in permanent session (except for a long summer vacation). It has the right to approve the President's choice of Prime Minister, the right to register a vote of no confidence in the government, the right to review government legislation, the right to initiate impeachment proceedings against the President and the right to initiate bills. Most bills passed by the Duma are passed up to the Federation Council for approval. If the Federation Council rejects the bill, a joint commission is set up to try to settle the differences. This has generally proved possible, although a two-thirds majority in the State Duma can override the Federation Council's veto. The President must sign all bills into law and s/he too has the right of veto. The presidential veto can also be overturned, again by a two-thirds majority, but on this occasion in **both** chambers.

The Federation Council is required to review legislation on the budget, taxation and other financial matters, as well as some foreign policy issues, such as the ratification of treaties and the declaration of war. The Federation Council, however, has played a particular role, as its name suggests, in protecting the interests of the regions and republics.

National elections 1993–95

The President expected the reformers to win a majority in the Duma after the 1993 elections, but he was disappointed. Instead, the nationalists and communists performed strongly and parliament remained essentially opposed to free market reform. Although these elections were judged by independent monitors to be generally free and fair, many criticisms were levelled against their organisation. First, the election took place soon after the October events and before a new constitution had been formally adopted. Parties frequently had difficulties in registering in time with the Central Electoral Commission (they needed 100 000 signatures in 1993 and 200 000 in 1995 in support of their registration) so that they could stand on the party list. Second, the campaign period was short, which was perceived to give the established reformist parties an advantage. Third, all registered parties were allowed to campaign on TV, but no debate was allowed on the constitution. In the end, only 13 parties were able to register for the election and only eight crossed the 5 per cent threshold. Other parties and blocs managed to gain seats, however, through winning in the single-member constituencies. Although a majority voted for the constitution, there have been persistent rumours of fraud, and some regions of Russia voted against, which created difficulties subsequently (see Chapter 4).

After the election, the reformists were on the defensive. Yegor Gaidar resigned as Prime Minister in January 1994 at the same time as the nationalists under Vladimir Zhironovsky and the communists under Gennadi Zyuganov could claim a legitimate voice in Russian politics. Yeltsin had created a political system that he could dominate, but it was difficult to avoid the judgement of the people. Although the rhetoric changed more than actual policy, there was a more nationalist and authoritarian feel to government policy. The Duma also kept the pressure on the President. One of its first decisions in February 1994 was to vote for an amnesty for all the conspirators in the August 1991 coup and the October events of 1993. Much to Yeltsin's displeasure, he found his arch enemies out of prison and in a position once again to conspire against him.

Yeltsin responded by isolating himself more from everyday politics and depending more and more on a close circle of advisers, many of whom supported a more hard-line policy, such as Mikhail Barsukov (Minister of the Interior) and Alexander Korzhakov (formally his bodyguard). Yeltsin also created a big presidential office to improve links with the government and to out-manoeuvre parliament – for example, he created the Presidential Council (the successor to the Presidential Consultative Council) in 1993. Such bodies had the advantage from Yeltsin's point of view of being immune from ordinary legislative oversight.

The first Duma was designed to be a transitional body which would sit for just two years. New elections were held, therefore, in 1995 for a parliament which would serve the full term of four years. In 1995, the nationalists performed less well, but the left, and particularly the Communist Party of the Russian Federation (CPRF), gained in seats to maintain the anti-liberal bloc in parliament (see Table 2.3). The elections were believed to be fairer and freer than those two years earlier. The atmosphere was calmer and the campaign period longer. As a result, as many as 43 parties were able to register for the party list

Table 2.3 Russian parliamentary and presidential elections 1993–96

	1993 State Duma election		1995 State Duma election		1996 presidential election		
	Parties	Party list vote (%)	Parties	Party list vote (%)	Candidates	First round votes (%)	Second round votes (%)
Pro-government	Russia's Choice	15.5	Our Home is Russia	10.1	Boris Yeltsin	35.3	53.8
	Others	6.7	Russia's Choice	3.9			
			Others	1.5			
Total		22.2		15.5		35.3	53.8
Democratic Opposition	Yabloko	7.9	Yabloko	6.9	Grigori Yavlinsky	7.3	
	Others	4.1	Others	5.5			
Total		14.0		12.4		7.3	
Centrists and others	Russia's Women	8.1	Russia's Women	4.6	Mikhail Gorbachev	0.5	
	Others	10.2	Party of Workers' Self-Government	4.0	Svyatoslav Fedorov	0.9	
			Others	7.2	Martin Shakkum	0.4	
Total		18.3		15.8		1.8	
Nationalists	Liberal Democrats	22.9	Liberal Democrats	11.2	Vladimir Zhirinovsky	5.7	
			KRO	4.3	Alexander Lebed	14.5	
			Others	4.2	Vladimir Bryntsalov	0.2	
					Yuri Vlasov	0.2	
Total		22.9		19.7		20.6	
Communists	CPRF	12.4	CPRF	22.3	Gennadi Zyuganov	32.0	40.3
	Agrarian Party	8.0	Agrarian Party	3.8			
			Communists – Working Russia – For the Soviet Union	4.5			
			Others	1.6			
Total		20.4		32.2		32.0	40.3
Against all		NA		1.8		1.5	4.8
Turnout (%)		54.8		64.4		69.8	68.9

Source: Matthew Wyman, 'Elections and Voting Behaviour' in S. White, A. Prauda and Z. Gitelman, Development in Russian Politics 4, Macmillan, Basingstoke, 1997

although only four crossed the 5 per cent threshold – the Communists (CPRF), the Liberals (LDPR), Our Home Is Russia and Yabloko (see Chapter 3).

The parliamentary elections of December 1995 were seen by many as a dress rehearsal for the far more important presidential elections in the summer of 1996. As stated in the introduction, the opinion polls seemed to suggest that Yeltsin had little chance of being re-elected. However, he was able to turn the position around in the spring as support flooded back to the Yeltsin camp. Reformers, such as Yegor Gaidar, who had deserted him after the attack on Chechnya, returned after realising there was no other viable reformist candidate. The majority of journalists backed Yeltsin as soon as it became obvious that the only other possible winner would be the CPRF leader, Gennadi Zyuganov, who they feared would re-introduce state control of the media. The bosses of big business in Russia also backed the Yeltsin campaign and gave him millions of rubles to prevent the return of communism. The West also supported Yeltsin. A group of American campaign advisers decamped to Moscow and helped to devise a more lively but also more negative campaign which portrayed Zyuganov as a Stalinist whose victory could lead to civil war.

It was important for Yeltsin that he came out on top in the first round of voting. This he managed to do, albeit with only 35 per cent of the vote (see Table 2.2). However, this victory was not sufficient to prevent a second round. According to the rules, a candidate needs an absolute majority of the vote to be elected, and if this is not achieved, then there has to be a run-off between the top two candidates. However, the relentless campaign effort almost killed Yeltsin and he was too ill to appear in public during the second round of electioneering. He won the vote, but it was noticeable that there was an eerie silence in the media on the subject of Yeltsin's illness. The image of a fit and dynamic man that Yeltsin had sought to portray in the first round had been revealed to be wholly disingenuous. At the moment of victory, Yeltsin was gravely ill and faced major heart surgery. He was unable to take up his duties for many months, and his recovery has been far from complete. It was depressing for many Russians to find themselves with another incapacitated leader. It brought back memories of the twilight years of the Soviet regime when the stagnation and paralysis seemed to be epitomised by the ill-health of Brezhnev, Andropov and Chernenko.

The Federal Assembly in action

The political system encouraged the formation of factions or party groups in the State Duma. Each faction or party group is accorded a seat on the influential Duma Council which oversees the workings of the lower body of the legislature. Chairs of the parliamentary committees (there were 21 in the first Duma and 28 in its successor) were also generally distributed according to the strength of the different parties and groups in the Duma. Parties which win seats from the party list are automatically attributed the status of a party faction, and these factions are usually joined by other party members who won election in single-member constituencies. Independents and others are able to join existing party factions, or they can form their own groups (if they contain 35

Table 2.4 Parties, factions and groups in the State Duma, 1996–98

Party	Total seats for Party February 1996	No. in faction or group April 1998
CPRF	157	134
Our Home	55	67
LDPR	51	49
Yabloko	45	44
Agrarian	20	
Others	45	
Independent	77	
Total	450	
Groups*		
Russian Regions		42
People's Power		45
Agrarian		35
No group or faction		24

* Groups were set up after the new Duma was convened from deputies elected in single member constituencies, many of whom had been nominated by parties which failed to win seats on the party list

or more members). Memberships of these factions and groups are quite fluid with deputies quite frequently shifting allegiance. Table 2.4 shows the state of the factions and groups in April 1998.

The Federation Council is organised differently. The deputies are more like part-time parliamentarians. They have full-time jobs in the regions or republics, so the Federation Council sits only once per month. Party factions are not permitted and very few deputies have any formal party allegiance at all. The majority of party members belong either to the CPRF or to the establishment party, Our Home Is Russia. There is no executive body leading the business of the Council, which means that the body is rather less disciplined than the State Duma. There are committees, however, as in the Duma (there were 11 in 1998), which review legislation and make recommendations to the government.

The Duma, on the other hand, has been able to act as a more coherent body than its predecessor, the Congress of People's Deputies, in part because of the strength of the party factions and groups. The factions, particularly in the present Duma, are better organised and more disciplined, and as a result far more likely to vote as a bloc (see Table 2.5).

There is also more co-operation across factions on a whole raft of policy issues (see Table 2.6). This allowed a consensus to be formed on many policy areas in the Duma. Thus, over two-thirds of all the deputies in the Duma voted in favour of draft bills on bankruptcy in October 1997 and on anti-corruption in November 1997.

This is not to suggest, of course, that there are not many problems in the workings of the new Federal Assembly. The main one is that the legislative process is slow and a backlog of bills has built up. The Federal Assembly remains decentralised and relatively ill-disciplined for all the improvements since 1995. Also, parliament still has the President to deal with. There is greater co-operation between the Federal Assembly and the President than before with commissions

Table 2.5   On faction voting in Duma

Percentage in factions voting the same way, 1996–97	
CPRF	81–87%
Our Home Is Russia	74–78%
LDPR	86–89%
Yabloko	78–82%
Russian Regions	67–71%
People's Power	66–71%
Agrarians	72–74%

Source: *Informatsionno-analiticheskii bulleten*, No. 9, 1997

Table 2.6   Co-operation between factions in the Duma

	Coincidence of attitudes in voting results: October–November 1997							
	CPRF	*LDPR*	*OHR*	*Yabloko*	*Agr. Gr.*	*PP*	*RR*	*Ind.*
CPRF		70.7%	48.3%	46.6%	82.8%	77.6%	39.7%	0
LDPR	70.7%		58.6%	46.6%	69.0%	67.2%	58.6%	20.7%
OHR	48.3%	58.6%		60.3%	60.3%	53.4%	72.4%	25.9%
Yabloko	46.6%	46.6%	60.3%		51.7%	43.1%	65.5%	36.2%
Agr. Gr.	82.8%	69.0%	60.3%	51.7%		77.6%	51.7%	12.1%
PP	77.6%	67.2%	53.4%	43.1%	77.6%		55.1%	15.5%
RR	39.7%	58.6%	72.4%	65.5%	51.7%	55.1%		51.7%
Ind.	0	20.7%	25.9%	36.2%	12.1%	15.5%	51.7%	

CPRF, Communist Party of Russian Federation; LDPR, Liberal Democratic Party of Russia; OHR, Our Home is Russia; Agr. Gr., Agrarian Party group; PP, People's Power; RR, Russian Regions; Ind., Independent, deputies in no registered faction or group.
Source: *Informatsionno-analiticheskii bulleten*, No. 9, 1997, p. 22

set up to deal with differences, but major conflicts have emerged – if not on the scale of the 1992–93 period. Below, we will consider three important cases.

No-confidence votes

Parliament has the right to initiate a no-confidence vote in the government if 20 per cent of deputies or a party faction wish it. However, the President is not obliged to dismiss the government if a no-confidence motion is passed. The appointment and dismissal of the government are entirely the President's privilege. Indeed, the vote of no-confidence can be a double-edged sword for the parliamentary deputies for, if such a vote is brought twice in three months, the President must dismiss either the government or the State Duma. This is obviously a difficult position for deputies. A vote of no-confidence can have a touch of Russian roulette about it since the deputies are often more likely to lose their relatively well-paid jobs than the government ministers they are criticising.

Nevertheless, a vote of no-confidence was brought against the government on 27 October 1994 following the collapse of the ruble on the international markets. On a single day, the ruble lost a quarter of its value. Although the ruble revived subsequently, the Duma blamed the government for the economic crisis. 194 deputies voted in favour of the no-confidence motion and only 54 supported the government. However, this was still not enough to pass the motion, for that would require an absolute majority of all deputies (not of votes cast), i.e. 226 votes in all.

A second no-confidence vote was held on 21 June 1995 in the wake of a terrorist attack on Russia by a number of Chechen rebels. On this occasion, an absolute majority (243) backed the motion attacking government policy on Chechnya. Yet Yeltsin ignored the vote and declared his full support for the government. When the Duma voted again in July (i.e. within the three month time-frame), Yeltsin made it clear he would dissolve parliament if an absolute majority supported the no-confidence motion. It was so close to the forthcoming parliamentary elections in December that many deputies were willing to take the risk. Others felt that Yeltsin would not dare dissolve parliament since the new establishment party, Our Home Is Russia, created by Prime Minister Viktor Chernomyrdin had only been registered in May. According to election rules, all parties had to be registered for a minimum of six months before they could participate in a parliamentary election. Early elections could have meant Our Home Is Russia could not run, thereby destroying Chernomyrdin's plans to dominate the Duma. Despite all the manoeuvring, the government still scraped through – only 193 voted in favour of the motion, 33 below the required absolute majority of 226.

The case of Sergei Kiriyenko

In March 1998, Yeltsin took the surprise decision to dismiss his entire government, including the Prime Minister, Viktor Chernomyrdin. The President proposed Sergei Kiriyenko as his replacement. The Duma had approved Chernomyrdin in 1996 as Prime Minister at the first time of asking, but deputies were far more dubious about the merits of Kiriyenko. He was only 35 years of age with little experience of government or business. He seemed a reasonably able man, but the deputies saw him simply as the President's puppet. Therefore, on 10 April, Kiriyenko was rejected as Prime Minister by the State Duma. 186 voted against and 143 in favour in a secret ballot. However, instead of Yeltsin seeking another candidate who might be more acceptable, as implied in the constitution, the President proposed Kiriyenko once more and declared there were no other suitable candidates for the post. He was rejected once again by parliament – this time by an even bigger majority in an open ballot (115 in favour; 271 against). The constitution states that if the Duma rejects the President's proposal for Prime Minister three times, the President 'shall appoint the Chairman of the Government of the Russian Federation [the Prime Minister], dissolve the State Duma and call new elections' (Article 111). In the face of this constitutional power, the State Duma reluctantly approved Kiriyenko as Prime Minister on 24 April. Two hundred and fifty-one deputies voted in favour of his appointment, 24 against and the rest abstained. Yeltsin's victory seemed to indicate the power of the presidency and the bloody-mindedness of Yeltsin. The President's imperious attitude towards the Duma was reflected by the fact that he refused to go and speak to parliament and explain his reasons for sticking by Kiriyenko. It soon turned out, however, that it was no more than a pyrrhic victory.

Table 2.7   Results of Duma vote on Primakov's candidacy for Prime Minister –
11 September 1998

Factions/groups	For	Against	Abstained	No vote
CPRF	122	1	2	6
OHR	33	1	5	27
LDPR	0	49	1	0
Yabloko	43	0	0	1
People's Power	36	3	2	4
Agrarians	36	0	0	0
Russian Regions	34	1	3	5
Independents	13	8	2	5
Total	317	63	15	48

Source: *Kommersant*, 12 September 1998, p. 1

Events of August 1998

In August 1998, only a few months after the appointment of Sergei Kiriyenko, Yeltsin faced economic meltdown. The economy was in free-fall as the ruble plummeted in value on the international markets. Moscow defaulted on debt repayment and the stock market was temporarily closed. Yeltsin lost the support of big business and parliament registered their discontent with government policy. The big business elite, the so-called 'corporate oligarchs' (see Chapter 6), were suspicious of Kiriyenko's reformist zeal and fearful of the consequences of the ruble devaluation. The oligarchs demanded the return to power of one of their own – Viktor Chernomyrdin as Prime Minister. Yeltsin fatefully undermined his reputation by again sacking his whole government and agreeing to back Chernomyrdin. The man he had dismissed just a few months earlier as out of touch and lacking new ideas was now presented by Yeltsin as the saviour of Russia.

This time, however, his dramatic action appeared to be a sign of weakness not strength. Yeltsin seemed out of his depth as the economic crisis threatened the small successes he had achieved in the previous seven years. A private deal was struck with the business elite which would allow Yeltsin to stay as President but with much reduced power. Chernomyrdin, as Prime Minister, would take over from Yeltsin as the prime mover and shaker in Russian politics. The deal appeared done and dusted, but the Duma would not play ball. The State Duma rejected Yeltsin's nomination for Prime Minister twice – on 30 August and 9 September. Not only the communists rejected his appointment, but the reformist Yabloko bloc as well. Its leader, Grigori Yavlinsky, explained his opposition by saying that it was Chernomyrdin who had brought Russia to its knees in the first place, and Yeltsin had been right to dismiss him (*The Guardian*, 2 September 1998, p. 11). This time, Yeltsin realised that the Duma was prepared to risk a political crisis by rejecting his nomination three times. In the circumstances, Yeltsin felt he had no option but to find a compromise candidate at the third time of asking. The Duma finally approved Yevgeni Primakov, the former Foreign Minister, as Prime Minister (see Table 2.7).

The crisis showed the weakness of Yeltsin's position in August 1998. He looked ill again and out of his depth. He had to compromise and offered Yevgeni Primakov as his nominee. Primakov had no expertise in economics, but he was

БИОГРАФИЯ 2.3　**Yevgeni Primakov (born 1929)**

Yevgeni Primakov is a trained Arabist who worked in the Middle East for the communist party newspaper, *Pravda*, from 1966. While working there, he struck up an acquaintance with Saddam Hussein. He used this acquaintance during the Gulf crisis (1990–91) to try to bring the stand-off between Iraq and the international community to a peaceful conclusion. Officials in the West, however, tended to view his diplomacy essentially as an attempt to save Saddam Hussein's skin. They were, therefore, very suspicious of him when he was named Foreign Minister in 1996, but he proved to be an adept operator. He calmed the nerves of the nationalists at home, while simultaneously striking up a reasonable working relationship with the West. Primakov performed a similar trick when he was appointed Prime Minister in September 1998, but his willingness to support opponents of Yeltsin led to his dismissal in May 1999.

his own man and power shifted perceptibly away from the president and towards parliament and the government. Such was Primakov's growing popularity and power that Yeltsin took action again in May 1999 and dismissed his Prime Minister for the third time in two years. With elections looming, the Duma ratified the presidential appointee, Sergei Stepashin, at the first time of asking.

Conclusion

There might well have been grounds for Yeltsin to view the Congress of People's Deputies as an obstructionist and irresponsible body. This was far less the case with the new State Duma. There were problems in the first session of the Duma (1993–95) as the deputies got used to the new constitutional arrangements, but since 1995 there have been great improvements in the working of parliament. Relations with the President also improved, although Yeltsin showed a continued eagerness to circumvent parliament wherever possible. There is a danger of the current system evolving into a more authoritarian kind of rule if a less reformist President comes to power after Yeltsin. There are sufficient gaps in the constitution which Yeltsin has already exploited and others could do to an even greater extent.

However, the events of August 1998 show that the President can be constrained. Yeltsin's power seemed greatly reduced in the face of the realities of the global economy and the unified opposition of corporate business and parliament. In the current crisis, the future of Russia is very uncertain. The CPRF is demanding changes to the constitution to abolish the presidential system and create a parliamentary one. Formally, changes to the constitution require a two-thirds majority in both chambers of parliament (except chapters 1, 2 and 9 which can only be changed by the adoption of a new constitution altogether) and this would still be difficult to achieve given the current distribution of parties in the Duma (see Chapter 3). Only the President can call a state of emergency and he can only be dismissed through impeachment. However, resignation is permissible, and Yeltsin already seems to have given up some of his powers as President. It is important for the democratisation process in Russia that future actions remain within the parameters of the 1993 Constitution. As Russia lurched from crisis to crisis, however, there were renewed fears that democracy would not survive in Russia.

БИОГРАФИЯ 2.4   Sergei Stepashin (born 1952)

On Wednesday 19 May 1999, Sergei Stepashin was ratified by the State Duma as Yeltsin's third Prime Minister in two years. The vote was 293 in favour; 55 against. The signs were that the deputies were not ready for another fight with Yeltsin so soon after the failed impeachment vote against the President four days earlier. Stepashin was promoted from his post as Interior Minister and is known as a loyal supporter of the President. The programme he has outlined to parliament does not suggest any great changes in policy. He has promised to crack down on the shadow economy; continue to pursue market reform; ensure back wages are paid; increase spending on defence; and he also supports the idea of a union between Russia, Ukraine and Belarus.

References

Kennan G 1947 The Sources of Soviet Conduct, *Foreign Affairs*, No. 25, p. 4.
Sakwa R 1990 *Gorbachev and His Reforms, 1985–1990*, Philip Allan, Hemel Hempstead.
Sakwa R 1993 *Russian Politics and Society*, Routledge, London.

Further reading

Sakwa R 1993 *Russian Politics and Society*, 2nd edition, Routledge, London, Part 2.
White S, Pravda A and Gitelman Z (eds) (1997) *Developments in Russian Politics 4*, Macmillan, London, Part 1.

For up-to-date information, see the web sites http://www.duma.gov.ru and http://www.russia.net/ which also has the 1993 Russian constitution on-line.

3 Political parties

Stephen White

Introduction: the emergence of a multi-party system

Under the Soviet system only a single party had enjoyed a legal existence ('two parties?'; local wits responded, 'isn't one bad enough?'). Mentioned in passing in earlier versions, the Soviet constitution that was adopted under the guidance of Leonid Brezhnev in 1977 had converted the effective dominance of the Communist Party into a formal political monopoly. The CPSU, according to an entirely new Article 6, was the 'leading and guiding force of Soviet society and the nucleus of its political system, of all state organisations and public organisations', and it imparted a 'planned, systematic and theoretically substantiated character to their struggle for the victory of communism'. In 1990, however, the party agreed to relinquish its monopoly, and Article 6 was amended to read: 'The Communist Party of the Soviet Union [and] other political parties, as well as trade union, youth, and other public organisations and mass movements, participate in shaping the policies of the Soviet state and in running state and public affairs through their representatives elected to the soviets of people's deputies and in other ways'. Article 7 was also revised to make it clear that 'all political parties, public organisations and mass movements' had to operate within the law, and Article 51 added the right of all citizens to 'unite in political parties and public organisations and to participate in mass movements contributing to their greater political activity and to the satisfaction of their diverse interests'. The party, Gorbachev told a meeting of the Central Committee in February, was not so much abandoning its political monopoly as acknowledging that the USSR had already become a multi-party society, although the parties and movements that had come into existence in the late 1980s had not yet acquired a legal basis; it would certainly make every effort to retain the leadership of a changing society, but it could do so only 'within the framework of the democratic process', without any kind of 'political or legal privileges'.

A legal framework for multi-party politics was established the following October when a new law on public associations was adopted, covering political parties as well as trade unions, women's and veterans' associations, and sport clubs. At least ten citizens were required to establish an association under the law; they were then required to hold a founding congress at which their statutes were adopted and executive bodies elected. The statutes of an association had then to be registered with the USSR Ministry of Justice or its counterparts at other levels of government, which could refuse registration if (for instance) the objectives of the association appeared to conflict with the law. Political parties, in particular, were supposed to have the basic goal of participation in elected institutions and in government; they were expected to have a programme, which had to be published for general information, and they had the right to nominate candidates for election, to campaign on their behalf and to form organised groups in the bodies to which their candidates were elected. The registration of new and existing parties, including the CPSU, began on this basis in 1991; 25 parties had been registered by the summer of 1992, although many claimed no more than a few hundred members and there were no more than 30 000 active members of all political parties put together (*Izvestiya*, 20 April 1992, p. 2). The new constitution nonetheless made clear that post-communist Russia was firmly committed to 'political diversity and a multi-party system', subject only to the requirement that parties and associations refrain from a forcible challenge to the state or from incitement to social, ethnic or religious strife; the same principles were affirmed in a new law on public organisations, approved by the Duma in April 1995, pending the adoption of a special law on parties themselves.

Parties at the Duma elections of December 1993

The first test of this emerging but still weakly formed party system was the election of December 1993, and in particular the election to the lower house, the State Duma, which was based in part upon a national competition among party lists and in part upon a series of contests in single-member constituencies. The suspension and bombardment of the parliament had created an inhospitable environment for the conduct of these first post-communist elections. Yeltsin's main rivals, parliamentary speaker Ruslan Khasbulatov and his Vice-President Alexander Rutskoi, had come out of the parliament building with their hands in the air and were in prison facing serious charges. There was a brief period of censorship; 15 newspapers were banned on the grounds that they had contributed to the 'mass disorder in Moscow', and three others were suspended. *Pravda* and *Sovetskaya Rossiya*, two of the papers that had been suspended, were also instructed to change their names and to replace their editors (in the end both retained their distinctive titles, but did not appear for an extended period); the parliament's own paper, *Rossiiskaya gazeta*, was taken over entirely by the Russian government. A state of emergency in Moscow, incorporating a ban on demonstrations and a curfew, lasted until 18 October. The Constitutional Court, which had ruled that there were grounds for Yeltsin's impeachment, was suspended and its chairman forced to resign; the prosecutor general was dismissed and replaced with a Yeltsin loyalist. Sixteen parties or organisations were suspended on the grounds that they had been involved in the 'events' of 3–4 October 1993; the Communist Party of the Russian Federation, whose leader had actually urged both sides to 'refrain from provocations', was eventually legalised, but most of the others, including the National Salvation Front and the hard-left Russian Communist Workers' Party, remained subject to a ban

БИОГРАФИЯ 3.1   **Vladimir Zhirinovsky (born 1946)**

Vladimir Zhirinovsky is generally seen as the wild man of Russian politics. He founded his party, the LDPR, in 1989 and burst on to the political scene after his party performed well in the 1993 parliamentary elections. His programmes are extreme nationalist and at times anti-Semitic, but there are persistent rumours in Russia that he is himself a Jew. His programmes are equally muddled, but he has engaged many in Russia with his good looks and unpredictable behaviour. He is best known for his maverick behaviour, for example, when he threw water in the face of an opponent publicly on TV. The public seems to be getting a bit bored with such antics, however, and his star appears to be on the wane.

that deprived them of any opportunity to take part in the proceedings. Western governments had supported Yeltsin's moves against parliament on the grounds that he had promised to submit himself personally for re-election in the summer of 1994 (an undertaking that was later withdrawn) and in the expectation that a new election would allow Russians to rid themselves of a 'communist parliament' that had represented an obstacle to reform. The result was a considerable shock, not just in Russia but also to the wider international community. Most successful of all were the independents, who won 141 of the 225 single-member constituencies; this gave them nearly a third of all the seats in the new parliament. The most successful of the parties was Russia's Choice, led by former acting prime minister Yegor Gaidar and fully committed to the policies of the Yeltsin government, with a total of 70 seats. However, there was a sensational result in the party list contest, which was won by the right-wing nationalist Liberal Democratic Party led by Vladimir Zhirinovsky with nearly a quarter of the vote, with the Communists in third place, and there was some disappointment that the level of turn-out was just 54.8 per cent, continuing a steady decline from the heady days of the first competitive elections in the last years of Soviet rule. The result was a fiasco for Russian pollsters, who had predicted a clear win for Russia's Choice; it was still more serious for politicians. Television coverage was suddenly suspended in the early morning because of 'technical difficulties', and US Vice-President Al Gore, who had been present to welcome the birth of Russia's new democracy, had to leave in some embarrassment. Gaidar's own reaction was that the reformers had suffered a 'bitter defeat'; the Moscow evening paper put it even more dramatically, warning that Russians had 'woken up in a new state' after the 'communo-fascists' success' (*Vechernyaya Moskva*, 13 December 1993, p. 1). The new Duma, however, was an extraordinary one, elected for a limited period of two years; its successor, to be elected in 1995, would define the shape of parliamentary politics for a normal four-year term and perhaps for rather longer.

СПРАВКА 3.1   **The general policy line of a selection of political parties in 1995**

1. Democratic or reformist

   Yabloko: leader, Grigori Yavlinsky

   Russia's Democratic Choice: leader, Yegor Gaidar

   Social Democratic Party: leader, Alexander Yakovlev

   Forward Russia: leader, Boris Fedorov

2. Pro-government centrists

   Our Home Is Russia: leader, Viktor Chernomyrdin

   Bloc of Ivan Rybkin: leader, Ivan Rybkin

3. National patriots

   Congress of Russian Communities: leader, Alexander Lebed

   Derzhava: leader, Alexander Rutskoi

   Liberal Democratic Party of Russia: leader, Vladimir Zhirinovsky

4. Communist–Agrarian left

   Communist Party of the Russian Federation: leader, Gennadi Zyuganov

   Agrarian Party: leader, Mikhail Lapshin

   Power to the People: leader, Nikolai Ryzhkov

   Communists – Working Russia – for the Soviet Union: leader, Viktor Anpilov

   All-Union Communist Party: leader, Nina Andreeva

Political parties in 1995

According to the Central Electoral Commission, 273 parties or other organisations had the right to nominate candidates to the Duma that was elected two
years later (see Box 3.1), and there were fears that Russia might set the 'world
record for the number of electoral associations per head of population'.
Candidates in single-member constituencies, under the law, had to secure the
support of at least 1 per cent of the local electorate; 2627 individual candidates
were successfully nominated on this basis, with between two and 23 candidates
registered for each of the seats available. Parties or 'electoral associations' that
wished to put forward candidates in the national competition for the other half
of the Duma had to collect the signatures of at least 200 000 electors, not more
than 7 per cent from any one republic or region; 43 parties and movements
were eventually registered, with a total of 5746 candidates on their lists (the Central
Electoral Commission claimed later it had validated 933 000 nomination papers
containing a total of 12 million signatures). The election law made it illegal to
offer financial inducements to potential supporters, and it was also illegal to

contribute to the nomination of more than a single list. Press reports, however, made clear that many of the parties ignored these requirements in obtaining their signatures; a week before nominations closed prospective signatories in the Belgorod region were being offered two kilograms of flour, and in Krasnodar a bottle of beer; the average price of a signature had reached 2000 rubles, and it increased still further as the deadline for nominations came closer. Very provisionally, the parties and alliances that were included on the ballot could be divided into four broad groups (For a more general discussion, see Lowenhardt (1998) and Wyman *et al.* (1998); details on the parties themselves are drawn from Korgunyuk and Zaslavsky (1996) and Oleshchuk and Pavlenko (1997), as well as press sources).

Democratic or reformist groupings

There were eleven 'democratic' or reformist groupings, of which the most substantial was 'Russia's Democratic Choice – United Democrats', led by Yegor Gaidar and committed to the fullest possible transition to a private ownership economy. The bloc was based around Gaidar's own Russia's Democratic Choice Party, founded in June 1994, together with the Peasant Party of Russia led by Yuri Chernichenko and the Social Democratic Party, formed in 1995 and led by the 'father of *perestroika*', Alexander Yakovlev. Gaidar's party had emerged from Russia's Choice, the broadly based coalition that had been founded to 'express the interests of all who in the referendum of 25 April [1993] had supported the reformist course of President Yeltsin'; it became the largest of the parliamentary fractions after the 1993 elections, but lost ground as some of its deputies gravitated towards the Chernomyrdin government, while others took up a more sharply critical position; so did Gaidar after the outbreak of the Chechen war, although this led to an open rift with President Yeltsin when Gaidar announced in February 1995 that the party would not support him for a second term. Russia's Democratic Choice adopted 'freedom, property, legality' as its slogan; it favoured a reduction in the role of the state, support for small business, the privatisation of agriculture and a cut in military expenditure. The party list in the elections was headed by Gaidar, together with the former parliamentary ombudsman who had become internationally known for his condemnation of the Chechen war, Sergei Kovalev, and actress Lidiya Fedoseeva-Shukshina. The party itself was represented in 78 of Russia's regions, with 5000–10 000 members throughout the country; the largest party organisation was in Moscow, with a thousand members, but branches more typically had between 100 and 150 members.

'Yabloko' was led by economist Grigori Yavlinsky. The party shared a commitment to economic reform but on a more gradual basis, and it was sharply critical of the policies the Yeltsin administration had been following with Gaidar's support since the start of 1992. Yabloko had officially been founded in January 1995, although its three founding members (whose surnames gave the party its distinctive title) had formed a bloc to contest the 1993 election and then a fraction in the new Duma. Yabloko's programme, adopted in September 1995, declared it a 'democratic movement committed to the creation of a

БИОГРАФИЯ 3.2   Grigori Yavlinsky (born 1952)

Yavlinksy dropped out of school and worked originally as a fitter and electrician at a glass factory in Ukraine. He later returned to education and became a respected economist. He helped to write the 500-day programme in 1990 which was a radical plan to introduce the market into the Soviet Union. The plan was never implemented. Despite his reformist credentials, he became a leading opponent of Gaidar's shock therapy programme. He was opposed to the break-up of the USSR, favoured the liberalisation of prices only after privatisation had taken place and feared the social impact of shock therapy on the people of Russia. In a surprising move he and his party, Yabloko, supported the nomination of centrist, Yevgeni Primakov, as Prime Minister after the economic crisis in the summer of 1998. His critics, however, would say his refusal to take up a post in the new Primakov government was typical of his role in Russian affairs. They see him as an egocentric outsider more willing to criticise than test his ideas in government.

rule-of-law state with a market, socially oriented economy and a strong army'; its list in the December elections was headed by Yavlinsky, former Russian ambassador in the US Vladimir Lukin and economist Tatyana Yarygina. Their aim, Yavlinsky told *Izvestiya*, was to demonstrate that there was a 'democratic alternative to the current regime'; they were critical of the bombing of the White House in October 1993 and the increasingly corrupt nature of the ruling elite and anxious to strengthen the place of parliament within the existing Russian constitution. Yabloko supported the free market, but not at the expense of those who were unable to defend their own interests, and they did not believe that science, education, health and culture could simply be handed over to market forces. Their electoral programme placed considerable emphasis in addition upon public morality, the environment and evolutionary rather than more rapid change. However, if Gaidar had become leader of Russia's Democratic Choice because he more than any others could articulate its political philosophy, Yabloko was much more clearly an organisational extension of its party leader, and in practice 'its leader G. Yavlinsky *was* its political line' (Korgunyuk and Zaslavsky, 1996, p. 75; emphasis added).

Pro-government centrists

The 'pro-government centre' was based around Our Home is Russia, founded in the spring of 1995 as a political movement that could sustain the Chernomyrdin government in the Duma elections and then provide the basis for a presidential campaign by Boris Yeltsin in the summer of 1996. In practice, Our Home is Russia was the 'party of power': a coalition of the post-communist political and economic *nomenklatura*, with differing views but a common interest in maintaining their position. It represented two constituencies above all:

the energy complex, with which Premier Chernomyrdin had a close association, and the metallurgical complex, with which the then first Vice-Premier Oleg Soskovets was connected. Chernomyrdin's reputed wealth as a result of the privatisation of the gas industry attracted unfavourable publicity, and some dubbed the group '*Nash dom, Gazprom*' (our home is Gazprom) after the name of the gas concern of which the premier had been chairman and which had made him, apparently, one of the richest men in the country. Our Home is Russia's list in the 1995 elections was headed by Chernomyrdin himself, together with film director Nikita Mikhalkov (whose *Burnt by the Sun* had won an Oscar in 1994) and General Lev Rokhlin, who had led the assault on Grozny in the Chechen war but refused to accept a state prize for his achievement. Our Home is Russia stood for a 'broad centre', including a stronger state and support for domestic producers and investors. Its pre-election programme, adopted in August 1995, emphasised three priorities: the 'spiritual renewal of Russia', including the rights and freedoms of the individual; the 'integrity of the country', including public order; the 'development of a market economy together with a greater degree of social protection'. Our Home is Russia's most obvious advantage was the support it received from big business, together with its access to the machinery of government and the mass media; it was able to spend liberally on campaign publicity and to attract celebrities (such as the German supermodel Claudia Schiffer) to its public events, although it was not clear that this would compensate for the middle-aged image of the prime minister – who had never before run for public office – and his ministerial colleagues. Their campaign slogan – 'On a firm foundation of responsibility and experience' – emphasised this bureaucratic image.

'Women of Russia' had a more ambiguous position; based on the Soviet-era Committee of Soviet Women and relatively successful with 8 per cent of the party list vote in the 1993 elections, it had come to reflect the centrist views of the President and of its leader Ekaterina Lakhova, a doctor who came from the same part of Russia as Boris Yeltsin and who had organised a commission on women, the family and demography within his administration. It was, in this sense, the female half of the 'party of power'; yet it had also supported a move by the Communists and Agrarians to halt the process of privatisation which led it to be called the 'women's department of the Russian Communist Party'. It was, *Izvestiya* (5 November 1995, p. 4) explained, 'one of the most pragmatic' of the Duma parties, in that it 'more often than others voted for diametrically opposite proposals'. Women of Russia had lost their unique claim to represent the female constituency with the inclusion of women in prominent positions in other blocs or indeed as the leaders of blocs, such as former social security minister Ella Pamfilova, who headed the Pamfilova–Gurov–Lysenko bloc, and businesswoman Irina Khakamada of the pro-market grouping Common Cause; at the same time they had the good fortune to obtain first place on the ballot paper, a source of some advantage in all electoral systems. The Women of Russia programme emphasised social issues, including protection for the family, a 'socially oriented market economy' and non-involvement in military conflicts, including Chechnya; as the programme pointed out, 'Without women there's no democracy!'.

National patriots

A further group of parties occupied a national-patriotic position, including a new and apparently promising grouping, the Congress of Russian Communities. Its leaders were certainly representative of key constituencies: former chairman of the Security Council Yuri Skokov, who had close ties with the military–industrial complex, economist Sergei Glazev, who had been minister of foreign trade up to October 1993 when he resigned in protest over Yeltsin's suspension of parliament, and the formidable figure of Alexander Lebed, the gravel-voiced general who had led the 14th army in the Dnestr region until a cease-fire was concluded and who was then dismissed when his outspoken views began to embarrass the Ministry of Defence. Some opinion polls in the autumn of 1995 suggested that Lebed was the most popular politician in the country; newspaper commentaries credited him with the 'brain of Albert Einstein and the physique of Arnold Schwarzenegger'. Lebed's autobiography, *Za derzhavu obidno*, was published in the late summer of 1995; it recalled his arduous military training, his service in Afghanistan and Moldova, and his commitment to the Orthodox Church, the army and the Russian people – but not necessarily democracy. The Congress had been founded in March 1993 to represent Russians living outside the federation, gradually evolving into a moderate national-patriotic grouping. Its programme was egalitarian but also eclectic. Its central elements were the gradual reconstitution of the USSR by peaceful means, defence of Russians abroad, a crackdown on crime, support for traditional Russian institutions such as the Church and family, the restoration of Russia's great power status and the formation of a 'highly effective and socially oriented market economy' in which there would be a 'sensible defence of domestic producers' as well as 'support for the high technology core of the Russian military–industrial complex'. The Congress made clear that it was an 'above-party movement' whose members could support a variety of views. It was very critical of the government's economic programme and blamed Yeltsin for the collapse of the USSR, the 'October events' of 1993 and the excesses of privatisation, but it had its own difficulties, partly because of the inconsistencies in its programme but also because of the unresolved ambitions of its leaders (Skokov, for instance, told journalists that Lebed 'lacked education' and was unready for the post of defence minister, let alone the presidency).

The other national-patriotic parties were Derzhava (Great Power), headed by former Vice-President Alexander Rutskoi, and Zhirinovsky's Liberal Democrats. The Liberal Democrats had been the sensational winner of the 1993 party list election, but their parliamentary fraction had been unstable and Zhirinovsky had in practice shown some willingness to co-operate with the Chernomyrdin government, in particular through his support of the 1994 and 1995 budgets. The party's earlier appeal had also been undermined by the emergence of other radical nationalist groupings, including the Congress of Russian Communities and the Russian All-National Union, which was led by Duma deputy Sergei Baburin. The Liberal Democrats, founded originally in 1989 with what appeared to be the tacit support of the KGB and Communist Party, were nationalist and anti-Western in their foreign policy, strongly in favour of the restoration of federal

БИОГРАФИЯ 3.3 **Alexander Lebed (born 1950)**

Alexander Lebed has had a remarkable career as war hero and now politician. He was briefly Yeltsin's ally after the latter's presidential victory in 1996. He has since distanced himself from the President and has made a new career as governor of Krasnoyarsk in Siberia. Governors are very powerful, and Lebed is making a clear bid to be Yeltsin's successor as President. He has managed to maintain a high profile in the Russian press. After the economic crisis of August 1998, Lebed took emergency measures in Krasnoyarsk and froze prices for gas, petrol, electricity and local transport, and committed himself to similar price freezes on locally produced goods and essential foodstuffs. This is unlikely to help the economic situation in the country as a whole, but faced with the prospect of three-figure inflation he hopes it will be a popular move in Krasnoyarsk.

control in Chechnya and pro-market but also protectionist in their domestic economic strategy. They were equally opposed to the dissolution of the USSR and called for it to be restored within its earlier boundaries or 'ideally' the boundaries the Russian Empire had enjoyed after the Crimean War, including Finland, the Baltic states and Alaska; they also favoured the restoration of at least indicative planning. The Liberal Democrats were well financed, had a national network of activists and enjoyed a high level of support within the armed forces, but they owed most of all to their leader, a charismatic campaigner who successfully identified the problems of ordinary Russians and suggested simple but plausible remedies – such as reviving arms exports or shooting the leaders of organised crime. The Liberal Democrats, indeed, were 'less a political party than an organisation serving the ambitions of a single person, its leader Vladimir Zhirinovsky', who had been elected chairman for ten years in 1994; the party congress added the words 'the party of Zhirinovsky' to its official title the same year (Korgunyuk and Zaslavsky, 1996, pp. 127–8, 129).

The communist–agrarian left

A more conventional range of parties occupied the communist–agrarian left, of which by far the most important was the Communist Party of the Russian Federation, founded in 1990 within the framework of the CPSU and led by Gennadi Zyuganov. It was a distinctive party in many ways: it was the only one with a mass membership, and it had the best network of local activists throughout the country; indeed for some it was the only one of these organisations that could properly be called a political party. In 1991, the party explained in its election platform, there had been a 'state coup' led by the 'old *nomenklatura*'. The Communists called for a 'national-patriotic majority' in the new Duma which would restore a 'people's power' based on the soviets with guaranteed socio-economic rights for working people, the renationalisation of 'strategic'

БИОГРАФИЯ 3.4   Gennadi Zyuganov (born 1944)

Zyuganov was a member of the old CPSU from 1964 to its dissolution in 1991. He was a full-time party worker from 1974 and worked in the Ideology Department of the CPSU Central Committee 1983–90, reaching the post of Deputy head of the Department. In June 1990, he was appointed Central Committee secretary and politburo member of the newly formed Communist Party of the RSFSR. He held both these posts until the dissolution of the RSFSR Communist Party in 1991. He was elected head of the Communist faction in the Russian State Duma in 1994 and is currently head of the revived Communist Party of the Russian Federation. Zyuganov ran Yeltsin close in the 1996 presidential elections, but in general he seems a rather colourless character. Eager to undermine Yeltsin, he nevertheless appears unwilling to take the responsibilty of power himself.

sectors of the economy and priority for domestic producers of all kinds. The party had been suspended and then banned after the attempted coup of 1991, but the Constitutional Court ruled in November 1992 that although its leading bodies had usurped the functions of government, its rank and file members had the right to form the political organisation of their choice; they did so in February 1993, adopting a commitment to 'socialist ideas and people's power' as well as a commitment to the 'formation of a planned market economy' based on an 'optimal combination of different forms of property'. The party's new programme, adopted in January 1995, called for a 'return to the path of socialist development' but without going back to the 'society that existed before the start of so-called *perestroika*'. Its main aims were the restoration of elected soviets, guaranteed employment, free education and health care, patriotism and internationalism. The party's list of candidates in the 1995 elections was headed by Zyuganov, who represented the dominant 'popular-patriotic' section of the leadership; it could claim 570 000 members and a presence in all of Russia's republics and regions, making it by far the most significant of all the post-communist groupings (see Urban and Solovei, 1997).

The Communists' ally in rural areas was the Agrarian Party, founded in 1993, and representing state and collective farm rather than commercial agriculture. Its leader was Mikhail Lapshin, director of the 'Behests of Lenin' farm in the Moscow region; its other leading figures included Alexander Zaveryukha, who was Vice-Premier in the Chernomyrdin government, and Alexander Nazarchuk, who was Minister of Agriculture, as well as Vasili Starodubtsev, who had been one of the conspirators in August 1991 and was the successful chairman of a collective farm in the Tula region. The Agrarians' election slogan was 'fatherland, people's power, justice, welfare', but they stood, effectively, for state support of the agricultural sector, and this had been the main objective of their parliamentary faction in the outgoing parliament. The Agrarians also opposed land privatisation, arguing that it would lead to a fall in production and that speculators, rather than farmers themselves, would be the most likely benefici- aries. There were two other left groupings, 'Power to the People' led by former Prime Minister Nikolai Ryzhkov and Sergei Baburin, which sought to defend the living standards of ordinary people but without returning to a 'super- centralised planning and distribution system'; and the harder-line 'Communists – Working Russia – For the Soviet Union' which was a coalition of the Russian Communist Workers' Party and the Russian Party of Communists which was committed to the restoration of soviet power and of the USSR and socialism more generally, and which was led by one of he most effective of the street orators, Viktor Anpilov.

Patterns of electoral behaviour

With 43 parties or alliances competing for places in the party list section of the Duma, it was clear from the outset that few of them would be able to surmount the 5 per cent threshold. In the event, only four did so: the Communist Party of the Russian Federation, with more than a fifth of the vote; Zhirinovsky's Liberal Democrats and Our Home is Russia, each of which secured just over a tenth; and Yabloko, with just under 7 per cent. The Liberal Democratic vote fell by more than half, but this was an improvement on poll forecasts; there was more surprise that the Congress of Russian Communities had failed to reach the threshold, a failure that was attributed to its amorphous programme and to its uncertainty about a possible coalition with other parties, in particular the Communists. Most of the parties that had won seats in 1993 were also unsuc- cessful, including the Agrarian Party, Women of Russia, Russia's Democratic Choice, and the Party of Russian Unity and Concord; the Democratic Party, which had won party list seats in the earlier election, did not put forward a list of its own. The hard-line grouping, 'Communist – Working Russia – For the Soviet Union', by contrast, came close to the threshold, reflecting a general leftward shift in the electorate, and it was one of the parties, together with the Agrarians, Women of Russia, Russia's Democratic Choice and the Party of Russian Unity and Concord, that won some representation in the single-member constituen- cies. However, with only four parties able to secure seats in the new Duma, nearly half the party list vote was wasted, and the successful parties obtained a share of the party list seats that was twice their share of the vote. There was no precedent anywhere in the world for this degree of disproportionality, and there was understandable concern that the 'rights of millions of voters had been violated' (*Izvestiya*, 23 December 1995, p. 1; for a full discussion see White *et al.*, 1997a, Chapters 10 and 11; White *et al.*, 1997b; Belin and Orttung, 1997; and for a detailed set of results, Beloborodov *et al.*, 1996).

Elections in the single-member constituencies did something to correct these imbalances and many of the parties that obtained no seats in their own right were able to win some representation, often through a strong campaign by a party leader with local links. The Communists, again, were the most successful, but the Agrarians also did well, and parties in general increased their control over the single-member constituencies as the share of the seats that were won by independent candidates fell by half (they still won more seats than any of the parties). Alexander Lebed won a seat in Tula, although the Congress of Russian Communities had fallen below the party list threshold; his brother won a seat as an independent in Khakasiya. Ekaterina Lakhova, one of the leaders of Women of Russia, won a seat in the Ulyanovsk region; the leader of the Party of Russian Unity and Concord, Sergei Shakhrai, won his party's only seat in the Rostov region. The film director Stanislav Govorukhin, appropriately, won the only seat that was taken by the bloc that bore his name; and Ivan Rybkin, speaker of the outgoing Duma, won one of his party's three single-member seats in a Voronezh constituency. Yabloko campaigned more effectively than before in the single-member constituencies, and won nearly half as many seats as in the party list competition (it won more than any of the other parties in reform-minded St Petersburg). The Liberal Democrats, by contrast, won just a single constituency seat, in spite of their network of activists. It was notable that the second most successful party in the single-member constituencies was the Agrarian Party, which had failed to secure representation in its own right; the Liberal Democrats, conversely, had finished second in the party list contest but once again did very poorly in the single-member districts even though they had nominated the largest number of party-sponsored candidates. Party labels, admittedly, were often misleading, as many candidates preferred to fight as independents in the belief that their chances would be improved: outgoing Foreign Minister Andrei Kozyrev, for instance, fought his Murmansk constituency as the nominee of his constituents, not a member of a party list.

There had, in fact, been relatively little movement in the overall distribution of party preferences. As before, there were several large blocs: the organised left, with about a third of the party-list vote, and then three roughly equal blocs each with a fifth or more of the vote, representing the national-patriotic, pro-government and reformist parties and movements. The Communists had certainly advanced their position, winning 62 of the 89 regions and republics. However, their successes were most often at the expense of the Liberal Democrats, not of the pro-government or pro-reform parties, while their 1993 allies, the Agrarians, lost more than half their share of the party list vote and failed to secure representation in their own right. The leading reform party in 1993, Russia's Democratic Choice, lost even more heavily, but Our Home is Russia, which had not been in existence at the time of the 1993 election, took more than a tenth; taken together, the main pro-government vote in the two elections had hardly changed. The biggest loser, at least in numbers of votes, was the Liberal Democratic Party, with a fall in its share of the vote in all but one of the republics and regions and an overall loss of 4.6 million votes, more than half a million in the Moscow region alone; it was particularly unsuccessful in the largest cities and in regions with a large non-Russian population. Our Home is Russia, by contrast, did well in the largest cities (especially in Moscow) and in the non-Russian republics, and Yabloko won more votes than in 1993, although its share of the party-list vote fell slightly; it won two of the regions, St Petersburg and Kamchatka, and had the most concentrated of the party electorates, with more than a fifth of its voters resident in St Petersburg and Moscow.

How had voters made their choices?

How had voters made their choices? The survey evidence had already made clear that Communist voters were likely to be older than those of other parties; Women of Russia, by contrast, had the youngest of the party voters, but those who had not voted at all were even younger. Women of Russia, predictably, had the highest proportion of female voters, the Liberal Democratic Party the lowest. The reform parties, Russia's Democratic Choice and Yabloko, had the most highly educated electorates; the Communists and Liberal Democrats, conversely, had the highest proportion with a basic education and the lowest with a university or college degree. The reform parties were also the most likely to draw their support from the biggest cities, with their more highly educated electorates, although Our Home is Russia, with its appeal to officialdom, had a similar profile. Similarly, there were marked differences between the parties in terms of the beliefs of their supporters. Those who had voted for reform parties were the most committed to the market economy; Communist voters, followed by Liberal Democrats, were the most hostile. Communists and Liberal Democrats were also the most likely to resist the claims of any of the Russian regions to leave the federation, although voters and non-voters alike were also opposed. There were sharp contrasts also in attitudes to parties and party systems; Communist voters, followed by Liberal Democrats, were the most likely to favour the restoration of a single-party system – for the Communists, although not the Liberal Democrats, this was the view of the largest number. Few supported the multi-party system that had come into existence by the mid-1990s; the reform parties, Russia's Democratic Choice and Yabloko, were the most supportive of a multi-party system of a more coherent kind, and this was the most strongly supported position across the electorate as a whole. Congress of Russian Communities voters were more favourable towards the market and a multi-party system than the average, but (in spite of their party programme) also more likely to support the right of regions to leave the federation; sociologically, they were close to a cross-section of the electorate.

Survey evidence made clear other characteristics of party choice. The Communist vote, for instance, was the most consistent: more than two-thirds of those who had voted Communist in 1995 reported that they had also done so in 1993. Liberal Democratic voters were the next most likely to have voted for the party in both elections (47 per cent), followed by Yabloko with 43 per cent; only a third (34 per cent) of those who voted for Russia's Women, by contrast, had voted for them in 1993, and of those who voted for Russia's Democratic Choice only 19 per cent had voted for Russia's Choice in the earlier election. The Communist vote was the 'hardest' in several other respects: its supporters were, for instance, more likely to have decided at an early stage on their choice of party, and they were more likely than any other group of party supporters to agree that the party reflected the 'interests of people like me'. Yabloko and the Congress of Russian Communities did best when voters were asked whether they trusted the party leaders (Communist voters, by contrast, were the least likely to say they had voted for their party because they trusted its leaders). Our Home is Russia voters, on the other hand, were the most likely (and with some justification) to believe their party was 'strong enough to change things' (Russia's Women voters were the least likely to think their party could make a difference of this kind), and voters for the Congress of Russian Communities were the most likely to have been impressed that its candidates had not 'been involved in financial scandal or corruption'. Communist voters were also the most likely to report that they 'fully and unconditionally' identified with the party's programme and slogans: 43 per cent did so without reservation, compared with just 17 per cent of those who had voted for Our Home is Russia.

The weakness of party politics

Russia by the late 1990s was certainly a multi-party state; and yet it was difficult to say that parties were central to the political process. There were certainly bodies that called themselves parties and nominated candidates for public office; at the same time they were often no more than vehicles for ambitious politicians, with a negligible membership and a poorly defined programme. 'Forward, Russia', for instance, had no individual membership at all, nor did the Party of Economic Freedom, headed by wealthy businessman Konstantin Borovoi, and nor did Our Home is Russia – one of the questions considered by its congress in 1997, indeed, was whether it should 'become a political party' (*Izvestiya*, 28 January 1997, p. 2). There were certainly parties that had a mass membership and a functioning organisation, like the Communists and (according to its own estimates) the Liberal Democrats; at the same time there were parties that had a membership of no more than a hundred or so, like the incongruously named People's Party, and there were organisations of quite a different character that also had the right to put forward candidates, like the Union of Utility Workers. All the parties, moreover, exaggerated their memberships. Zhirinovsky, for instance, had included all those who attended its inaugural congress as members of the Liberal Democratic Party; some reports suggested the party's entire membership was largely fictitious. Also, there were fringe, mostly short-lived parties, such as the Humour Party or the Idiots' Party of Russia with its persuasive slogan, 'give the people bread and sausages' (*Izvestiya*, 14 October 1991, p. 1). The smallest were sometimes called 'divan parties', in that their entire membership could in theory be accommodated on a single couch.

Given their loose organisation, it was not surprising that many of the new parties divided into smaller and sometimes hostile groupings. The CPSU had itself fragmented into as many as eight distinct tendencies during its last years of rule, including a 'silent majority' (*Politicheskoe obrazovanie*, No. 18, 1990, p. 6), and most of these became independent parties in the post-communist years. Other parties remained coherent but at the cost of a harsh internal discipline, such as the All-Union Communist Party (Bolsheviks), headed by Nina Andreeva, which claimed continuity with the Nineteenth Congress of the CPSU (the last over which Stalin had presided) and refused to register with the 'bourgeois' authorities. It was equally clear that ordinary Russians were reluctant to associate themselves with the parties that had begun to compete for their support. According to the survey evidence, just 22 per cent of Russians identified to some degree with a political party, compared with 87 per cent of the electorate in the United States and more than 92 per cent in the United Kingdom (White *et al.*, 1997a, p. 135). Parties, indeed, were the most distrusted of all the political institutions, and they were more distrusted in Russia than in the post-communist countries of Eastern Europe (Rose, 1998). There were much lower levels of membership or participation in the activities of political parties than in Eastern Europe, and there were 'extraordinary levels of electoral volatility, even by post-communist standards': the shifts that took place in voting support between elections in post-communist Russia were six times as large as in Western Europe in the 1980s, and twice as large as in Eastern Europe (Wyman, 1996, p. 278). The Russian electorate, in these and other ways, was 'very fluid', cleavage formation was 'indefinite' and there was 'little sense of patterned interaction or "systemness"' (Webb and Lewis, 1998, pp. 255–6).

The weakness of parties in post-communist Russia was partly a consequence of the fluidity of social structures, partly a consequence of the length of time that Russians had been denied an opportunity to form their own organisations and to choose among them at the ballot box. It was also a consequence of the political system itself. For a start, Russia had a strongly presidential system, with a head of state who claimed to govern in the interests of the nation as a whole and who enjoyed a mandate of his own; this undermined the position of political parties, whose purpose was typically to mobilise a section of the electorate in order to achieve a parliamentary majority. Moreover, even if they did so, a majority in the Russian Duma had no direct implications for the composition of the government or the direction of public policy. The prime minister owed his position to the confidence of the President, not the support of the electorate, and Chernomyrdin's immediate response to the defeat of Our Home is Russia in the 1995 election was indeed to declare that there would be no changes at all in the policies he was pursuing (conversely, the sacking of the entire cabinet that took place in March and August 1998, and again in May 1999, had nothing to do with the party balance in the Duma, still less a national election). Why, in these circumstances, should parties seek to gather the support they needed to win a majority of seats, and, why should ordinary Russians believe that their choice of party gave them any influence over the conduct of public affairs?

The choice of party at the ballot box was in any case rather loosely related to the distribution of party support within the Duma. This was partly because of the disproportionality that operated in a system that allowed a large number of parties to compete for seats, but insisted on a 5 per cent threshold. However, it was also because of the way in which seats were re-distributed after the election had taken place. In a Western democracy, deputies sit with other members of their party after an election, and if their party is in a majority, at least in a parliamentary system, they form the government. The position in Russia was rather different. Only the Liberal Democratic fraction in the new Duma coincided with the number of seats that the party had won in the election. Yabloko gained an independent, Our Home is Russia ten independents and the Communists six independents and another deputy who had originally been elected on a different party list. Most 'independents', indeed, joined one of the party groupings in the new Duma; the 'independent' group itself was for the most part composed of deputies who had been elected on a party ticket. Democracy is about more than elections: it is about the organised choice of alternatives. Russians had very different views about the future of their society, but political parties, in the late 1990s, were still an ineffective means of expressing those differences and relating them to the conduct of public policy.

References

Belin L and Orttung R 1997 *The Russian Parliamentary Elections of 1995*, Sharpe, Armonk, NY.

Beloborodov A G *et al.*, 1996 *Vybory deputatov Gosudarstvennoi Dumy 1995*, Ves'mir, Moscow.

Korgunyuk Yu G and Zaslavsky S E (eds) 1996 *Rossiiskaia mnogopartiinost'*, Indem, Moscow.

Lowenhardt J (ed.) 1998 *Party Politics in Post-Communist Russia*, Cass, London.

Oleshchuk V A and Pavlenko V B 1997 *Politicheskaia Rossiia: partii, bloki, lidery*, Ves'mir Moscow.

Rose R 1998 *Getting things done with Social Capital*, University of Strathclyde, Glasgow.

Urban J B and Solovei V D 1997 *Russia's Communists at the Crossroads*, Westview, Boulder, CO.

Webb P and Lewis P 1998 The Lessons of Comparative Politics: Russian Political Parties as Independent Variables?, Lowenhardt J (ed.), *Party Politics in Post-Communist Russia*, Cass, London, pp. 253–64.

White S, Rose R and McAllister I 1997a *How Russia Votes*, Chatham House, Chatham, NJ.

White S, Wyman M and Oates S 1997b Parties and Voters in the 1995 Russian Duma Election, *Europe–Asia Studies*, Vol. 49, No. 5 (July), pp. 767–98.

Wyman M 1996 Developments in Russian Voting Behaviour: 1993 and 1995 Compared, *Journal of Communist Studies and Transition Politics*, Vol. 12, No. 3 (September), pp. 277–92.

Wyman M, White S and Oates S (eds) 1998 *Elections and Voters in Post-Communist Russia*, Edward Elgar, Cheltenham and Northampton, MA.

Further Reading

Lowenhardt J (ed.) 1998 *Party Politics in Post-Communist Russia*, Cass, London.

White S, Rose R and McAllister I 1997 *How Russia Votes*, Chatham House, Chatham, NJ.

Wyman M, White S and Oates S (eds) 1998 *Elections and Voters in Post-Communist Russia*, Edward Elgar, Cheltenham and Northampton, MA.

4

Federalism and regional politics

Cameron Ross

Introduction

Local politics in Russia is a highly complex matter. For a start, there are now 89 subnational components of the federation, consisting of 32 ethnically defined and 57 territorially defined regions (Fig. 4.1). These areas are further subdivided into more categories, as you can see in Box 4.1. All these different local entities have varying powers within the federation and different relationships with the central authorities. There are conflicts within and between these regions, as well as an ongoing power struggle between the centre and the periphery which is the major focus of this chapter.

Since the regional elections in Russia in 1990, the localities have taken advantage of comparative weakness at the centre to wrest more power for themselves. Fears were expressed, especially in 1992–93, that Russia could go the same way as the Soviet Union and split into competing ethnic regions. This chapter will show that the Russian state is still not wholly secure. Pressures on the centre are indeed considerable. However, the central argument of the chapter is that the threat to the Russian state comes less from nationalist forces in Russia (although they do exist) than from regional elites (especially in the richer regions) seeking to increase their political autonomy and to defend their local economic interests from what they see as exploitation by the centre. The Yeltsin administration, for its part, tends to view the regions with suspicion. The exploitation by the centre often involves nothing more than seeking to collect taxes in order to redistribute some wealth to less well-off areas of the federation. As a result, Yeltsin has attempted to impose central authority over the regions but, as will be shown in this chapter, so far with little success. The stand-off has led to impotence at the centre with the government often unable to implement its decisions in the regions. Thus, the struggle between the centre and periphery continues with little prospect of it coming to an end in the near future.

The nature of the Russian Federation

The 89 subjects of the federation vary greatly in size, population, power and wealth. Political power is, to a certain extent, dependent on size and population (the biggest republic is Sakha which spans 3 million square kilometres, and the most populous is Moscow with almost 9 million inhabitants), but the greatest source of power in the Russian context is economic. Wealth is dependent on various

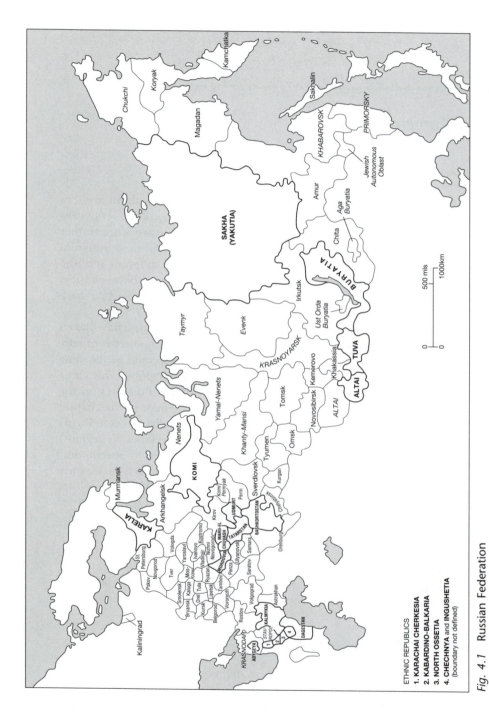

Fig. 4.1 Russian Federation

Source: G. Smith, The Ethno-politics of Federation without Federalism, in D. Lane (ed.), *Russia in Transition: Politics, Privatisation and Inequality*, Longman, London and New York, 1995, p. 22

ETHNIC REPUBLICS
1. **KARACHAI CHERKESIA**
2. **KABARDINO-BALKARIA**
3. **NORTH OSSETIA**
4. **CHECHNYA** and **INGUSHETIA**
(boundary not defined)

> ### СПРАВКА 4.1   Federal structure of Russian Federation
>
> 32 Ethnically defined subjects:
>
>   21 national republics
>
>   10 autonomous okrugs
>
>   1 autonomous oblast
>
> 57 Territorially defined subjects:
>
>   6 krais
>
>   49 oblasts
>
>   2 federal cities of Moscow and St Petersburg with the status of an oblast
>
> Total: 89 federal subjects

factors. The cities of Moscow and St Petersburg, for example, are comparatively well off owing in large part to their prestige which is attractive to foreign investors. In general, however, the availability of key natural resources, such as oil, gas, diamonds and gold, is the main determinant of wealth in the regions. Therefore, Sakha with its diamonds and Tatarstan with its oil are comparatively rich, while the resource-poor republics of Dagestan and Tuva remain mired in poverty with little prospect of escape (see Bird *et al.*, 1996, p. 326).

Disparities in wealth and power between localities are wide and have grown wider since the collapse of the Soviet Union in 1991. Moscow is performing strongly but it is not typical of Russia as a whole. Per capita income in Moscow in 1996 was over three times the national average, and more than 10 times that in impoverished Dagestan – where over half the population is living below the official subsistence level (Lavrov, 1997). Unemployment figures (including hidden unemployment, i.e. those on a short working week or sent home for 'extended holidays') vary greatly too, from a high of 44 per cent in Vladimir Oblast down to the much lower rates of 8 per cent in the capital and 4 per cent in the Sakha Republic (*Russian Federation Presidential Analytical Service*, 1997). The pressures placed on the federation as a result of these disparities are formidable.

The centre has attempted to deal with these pressures in different ways. These have included legal, political and economic methods to try and reassert central control over the regions. Yeltsin has found, however, that the regions are equally adept at utilising such levers to their own benefit.

Legal methods

Federal Treaty

There was general relief in Russia when the Federal Treaty was signed between the central authorities and the regions in March 1992. It was seen as necessary at a time when the future of Russia as an integrated state seemed in doubt (Nikolaev, 1995, p. 5)[1]. Most regions recognised the economic and political need to clarify relations between the centre and the periphery, but the treaty was a compromise document. It committed the signatories to remain within the federation while allowing the regions considerable autonomy within it. Some subjects of the federation, however, were granted more autonomy than others. For a distinctive feature of the treaty were the special privileges accorded to the 21 national republics which were recognised in the treaty as sovereign states with rights of national self-determination and, by implication, the right to secede from the federation. They were allowed to adopt their own constitutions and to elect their own executive heads. The other regions, on the other hand, were given no such rights. Instead of a constitution, the regions were permitted only local charters, while their top executives were not elected by the people, but appointed by Moscow. In this unequal treaty, as Stoner-Weiss (1997, p. 238) has pointed out, the 23 million people living in the republics had greater rights than the 123 million living in oblasts and krais. The special status contained not only political advantages but economic ones as well. The national republics were also allowed to keep a far greater proportion of the wealth generated locally from property and natural resources than other subjects of the federation.

Even this was not sufficient bait for some national republics. The wealthy republics of Sakha and Bashkortostan only signed the Federal Treaty after they were granted further concessions over foreign trade and mineral resources, while oil-rich Tatarstan held out until it was accorded special associate status within the federation. To all intents and purposes, this created a 'state within a state' and came as close as one possibly could to giving Tatarstan independent control over its economic and political affairs, including foreign trade and foreign policy. Yeltsin later admitted that the treaty was necessary to forestall 'the danger of a split in the Federation' (Yeltsin, 1997, p. 14). Only Chechnya refused to compromise at all – an independent stance which later led to war with Moscow. As a result of this unequal treaty, rich national republics became richer, while poorer localities found it ever more difficult to escape the trap of poverty.

This inequality of treatment led to a struggle between the republics and the other subjects of the federation. The republics fought to maintain their special status while the rest attempted to upgrade theirs. Thus, Astrakhan, Amur, Chelyabinsk, Chita, Kaliningrad, Perm, Orenburg, Kurgan, Sverdlovsk and Vologda oblasts, as well as the city of St Petersburg and Primorsky Krai, either declared their sovereignty or republic status, or announced their intention to do so in the future (Lapidus and Walker, 1995, p. 98). This was scarcely surprising, for, as Lapidus and Walker pointed out, the division between national republics and other subjects of the federation was often largely arbitrary:

> Why should the inhabitants of Karelia, where the Karelians make up only ten
> per cent of the population and Russians almost seventy five per cent, enjoy special

---

1 The Federal Treaty actually consists of three separate agreements signed with the republics, oblasts and krais, autonomous okrugs and the Jewish autonomous oblast.

economic privileges simply because they live in a region arbitrarily designated an autonomous area? Similarly, why should the people living in Sakha-Yakutia be given ownership of the enormous natural wealth of the republic while Russians living in resource-rich Tyumen are not granted that right? (Lapidus and Walker, 1995, p. 96)

Even the autonomous okrugs, which were at the bottom of the regional hierarchy, caught the sovereignty bug. They too began unilaterally to declare sovereignty, despite being trapped inside territorially based oblasts and krais (see map in Fig. 4.1). Recently we have witnessed okrugs demanding outright secession from their regions (for example, Khanty-Mansi and Yamal-Nenets from Tyumen Oblast) while others demand re-integration into their parent oblasts (for example, Komi-Permyak Okrug which wants to return to Perm Oblast, and Ust-Orda Buryatia which is seeking re-integration with Irkutsk Oblast). As Paretskaya rightly stresses, the motives for these apparently contradictory processes are identical – namely, economic advantage. Thus, Perm and Irkutsk oblasts are happy to be free of the financial responsibility of their impoverished okrugs, while Khanty-Mansi and Yamal-Nenents okrugs are fabulously rich oil and gas producers and want to retain as much of their wealth as possible (Paretskaya, 1997a). The majority of citizens in both okrugs boycotted the 1997 gubernatorial (governor) election in Tyumen Oblast and the heads of the okrugs (who were re-elected to their posts in the autumn of 1996) continue to refuse to recognise the authority of Tyumen Governor, Leonid Roketski (Sasaki, 1996, p. 6).

In sum, the Federal Treaty settled few of the issues it confronted in 1992. It even encouraged regions to seek greater autonomy through its unequal treatment of the subjects of the federation.

The Russian constitution

After his victory over the Russian parliament in October 1993, Yeltsin sought to regain control over the regions. He viewed the regions, often erroneously, as the centre of 'communist opposition' and was eager to reduce their powers. Thus, a presidential decree dissolved the local soviets and called for their replacement with much smaller, democratically elected legislative assemblies. A new constitution was drawn up in December whose intention was to reinforce further the supremacy of the centre over the periphery. After years of political paralysis in Moscow, Yeltsin was desperate to claw back some of the powers he had reluctantly been forced to give up during his debilitating struggle with parliament.

The new constitution set out the basic rights of the federal authorities and federal subjects in Articles 71–73. Article 71 lists those powers which were to be exclusive to the federal authorities and Article 72 outlined those to be shared between the federal authorities and its subjects. Article 73 stated that any powers not specifically covered in Articles 71 and 72 were to rest with the subjects of the federation. However, as Stoner-Weiss comments, the powers of the federal authorities appeared so extensive that they left very little for subnational levels. Also, since no article referred specifically to the powers exclusive to the regions, the struggle between the centre and periphery continued (Stoner-Weiss, 1997, p. 241).

Yeltsin further offended the regions by rejecting their demands to incorporate the text of the Federal Treaty into the new constitution. Article 5 was particularly controversial. It proclaimed that all the subjects of the federation were equal, which appeared to challenge the concept of special privileges for the national republics. However, Article 11 muddied the waters by implying, in highly convoluted language, that the Federal Treaty was still legally in force, including, presumably, its unequal treatment of the different subjects. Article 78, the so-called 'flexibility clause', seemed to extend this notion of inequality. It allowed federal authorities the right to transfer 'the implementation of some of their powers' to subjects of the federation, and vice versa. As Lapidus and Walker predicted, this only served to encourage bilateral agreements between Moscow and the subjects and the further development of an 'asymmetrical federation' (Lapidus and Walker, 1995, p. 102). This point will be taken up again later in the chapter.

The major institutional change was the introduction of the Federation Council as the second chamber in the new bicameral parliament set up after 1993. The Federation Council consisted of two representatives from each of the federation's 89 subjects. Yeltsin hoped that he could dominate the Federation Council through his appointment of its leading figures. The pressure on Yeltsin was such, however, that he was forced to allow elections in most of the regions by 1996. As a result, the Federation Council was able to play a more independent role in Russian politics. Increasingly, it became a major national forum for the articulation and promotion of regional interests.

The new Russian Constitution was supposed to provide the country with an effective presidential system. It was largely unsuccessful, however, in resolving the disputes between the centre and periphery. The Chair of Russia's Constitutional Court, Marat Baglai, has complained that his court is being overwhelmed by an avalanche of suits and counter-suits between the centre and the localities, especially over matters assigned in the constitution to joint jurisdiction (Shpak, 1998, p. 6).

Even the legality of the new constitution was contested in the regions. For although the constitution was supported officially by 58.4 per cent of the population nationwide, there was evidence to suggest that the actual vote had fallen below the 50 per cent required by the election rules. Indeed, some independent observers estimated that turn-out was more probably somewhere between 38 and 43 per cent (White *et al.*, 1997, p. 100). Even according to official statistics, turn-out was below the required 50 per cent in a total of 11 regions and six republics, and the vote was boycotted altogether in Chechnya (Smirnyagin, 1995). Furthermore, voters in 16 regions, and eight of the 21 republics, voted against the constitution (see Box 4.2). The result was, therefore, something less than the wholehearted endorsement for the new Russian Constitution that Yeltsin had been looking for. Nationalist leaders, especially in those 15 republics where the constitution was not ratified, were able to argue with some force that the federal constitution was not legally binding on their territory and that their own national constitutions should take precedence.

СПРАВКА 4.2 **Fifteen republics did not ratify the Russian Constitution in the December referendum**

A. Where less than 50 per cent supported the constitution

1. Kalmykia   48.5 per cent supported the constitution
2. Bashkortostan   40.7 per cent supported the constitution
3. Chuvash   39.9 per cent supported the constitution
4. Adygeya   38.2 per cent supported the constitution
5. Mordovia   36.1 per cent supported the constitution
6. Tuva   29.7 per cent supported the constitution
7. Karachai-Cherkessia   27.4 per cent supported the constitution
8. Dagestan   24.8 per cent supported the constitution

B. Turn-out below 50 per cent (and therefore vote invalid)

9. Komi   47.2 per cent
10. Marii-El   46.8 per cent
11. Ingushetia   46.0 per cent
12. Khakassia   45.6 per cent
13. Udmurt   44.2 per cent
14. Tatarstan   13.4 per cent

C. Boycotted referendum

15. Chechnya

Source: A. M. Lavrov (ed.), *Rossiiskie Regiony Posle Vyborov-96*, Iuridicheskaia Literatura, Moscow, 1997

Political methods

In 1990, Yeltsin had invited the republics and regions of Russia to take as much sovereignty as they could swallow. However, this was simply an attempt to out-manoeuvre Gorbachev, and by 1991 Yeltsin was seeking to re-impose central control over the regions. To this end, he created two new posts – the presidential representative and the regional governor. We will look at both in turn.

Presidential representatives

The system of presidential representatives was set up after the August 1991 coup. The representatives were often referred to as Yeltsin's eyes and ears in the regions. They were expected to monitor and report back to the President on the situation in the regions and, as far as possible, to ensure that federal policy was being implemented. To this end, the representatives could impose presidential decrees directly without reference to the local bureaucracies and even recommend the dismissal of recalcitrant local officials. The powers of representatives were more limited in the republics.

Yeltsin hoped that the representatives would serve as a direct, autonomous chain of command from the President down to the regions. However, it did not work out quite as planned. The legislation was too vague to be effective, while many of the presidential representatives, who were former regional executives, soon turned 'native', adopting the views of those they were supposed to be controlling. Thus, in 1997 the Kremlin was forced to replace 60 per cent of its presidential representatives because of fears that 'their loyalty had been co-opted by the regional power elites' (Helmer, 1997, p. 2). Others more loyal to the President found that they had neither the political authority nor the economic resources to stand up to the regional elites (see Hahn, 1997; Stoner-Weiss, 1997). Four presidential decrees have since been passed in an attempt to raise the profile of the representatives but each one has been a dismal failure. Effective power in the regions remains firmly in the hands of the regional governors.

The regional governors

The governor has the power to dominate the regions. Initially, appointed by and responsible to the President, Yeltsin allowed a number of gubernatorial elections to take place at irregular and rather infrequent intervals after 1993. However, by 1997 most of the top governorships had been popularly elected. This gave the local governors more legitimacy in their regions, and a more independent voice at national level too as *ex officio* members of the Federation Council. The elections also tended to give more power to the communists. In a careful study of 73 elections by Michael McFaul and Nikolai Petrov over the period from August 1996 to June 1997, they concluded the following: 'If before this electoral cycle, only three governors could have been considered ideological communists, we now count 19 governors with a firm communist orientation. Ideological liberals suffered; 10 ruled before these elections but only 5 won re-election.' Nevertheless, they went on to state that the common picture of local government being controlled by the communists (or nationalists, for that matter) was greatly exaggerated. For, 'the vast majority of governors – over two thirds,' they wrote '. . . have no ideological affiliation whatsoever' (McFaul and Petrov, 1997, p. 533).

More important than the ideological affiliation of the governors, however, is the fact that power seems to be shifting inexorably to the localities. With elections to regional and municipal legislatures also nearing completion, thousands of new local deputies have come to power since 1996 with Yeltsin no longer able to simply appoint loyal supporters to top positions. As one presidential adviser on regional affairs has warned:

> . . . a drastic strengthening of regional power is taking place against a backdrop of the destruction of federal power at the local level. Governors are no longer subordinate to the President, the vertical chain of federal authority is being destroyed . . . little by little real chaos has seized the entire system of relations between the Federation and the regions.   (Smirnyagin, 1996, pp. 3–4)

The governors, once seen as a means of control for the President, are now viewed as having the power and the political will to undermine the authority of the federal institutions.

Exerting pressure from below

Yeltsin has tried to counter this growth in regional power by supporting sub-regional administrative areas. This was a tactic earlier employed by Gorbachev, with little success, as he attempted to avert the collapse of the Soviet Union. Thus, Yeltsin backed the Mayor of Vladivostok Viktor Cherepkov in his battle against the Governor of Primorsky Krai Yevgeni Nazdratenko and was at least partially successful in undermining Nazdratenko's authority in the region (Paretskaya, 1997c, p. 3). The Yeltsin administration also pushed through legislation in August 1995 which significantly enhanced the powers of mayors and municipal governments at the expense of the larger republic, krai or oblast of which they were a part (see *Rossiiskaya Federatsiya*, No. 6, 1995, pp. 17–32). However, in April 1996, the republic of Udmurt responded by defiantly passing a decree which abolished all municipal bodies on its territory, thereby taking direct control of local budgets and municipal property (Paretskaya, 1997d, pp. 3–4). Despite rulings by the Constitutional Court and the President which declared the actions unlawful, Udmurt was able to hold out for almost two years. In January 1997, the Yeltsin administration introduced further legislation aimed at strengthening the financial independence of municipal authorities. According to this law on the 'Financial Foundations of Local-Self Government' (which was originally vetoed by the Federal Council), municipal authorities were entitled to their own guaranteed minimum federal and regional tax receipts paid directly from the centre, bypassing the higher regional or republican bodies (Kamyshev, 1997, p. 14).

There is little sign that this tactic has strengthened Yeltsin's hand overall. Indeed, as Gorbachev found earlier, its immediate effect has been to devolve power to ever smaller entities undermining the larger republics, krais and oblasts, but with the prospect of ultimately undermining central authority too in the longer term.

An 'asymmetrical federation'

One of the more curious developments in Russian federalism, already alluded to in the discussion on the new Russian Constitution, has been the proliferation of bilateral treaties signed between the federal government and federal subjects. Such treaties are rapidly replacing the federal constitution as the primary basis of federal relations. These bilateral accords often give the local signatories substantial extra rights over the disposition of natural resources on their territory, special tax concessions and other economic and political privileges. In many cases such treaties have been signed on the eve of parliamentary and presidential elections which could be seen as part of a package to encourage the regions to support the President.

In energy-rich Tatarstan and Bashkortostan, bilateral agreements have led to such profitable industries as petroleum extraction, petroleum refining and power generation being removed from the centre's jurisdiction and handed over to local control and ownership. In June 1995, Sakha signed a treaty with Moscow which gave the republic ownership of 26 per cent of its diamond output, 30 per cent of its gold output and a slightly smaller percentage of its oil and gas reserves (Emelyanenko, 1995, p. 14) According to Lavrov, outright tax losses to the federal authorities caused by just four special budgetary deals with the republics of Karelia, Tatarstan, Bashkortostan and Sakha, came to at least 2 trillion rubles, or 2.3 per cent of the federal budget's revenues for 1994 (Lavrov, 1995, p. 2). The treaty with Tatarstan signed on 15 February 1994 represented the first significant move towards this 'asymmetrical federation'. Other bilateral agreements followed and by June 1998 a total of 46 had been signed. Other types of mini-agreement were also signed between regions and individual federal ministries. As just one example of many, the Ministry of Fuel and Energy had signed 26 such deals by 1996.

While the constitution does allow for some flexibility in relations between the centre and periphery (see Article 78), there is a danger that such treaties can seriously undermine its authority. As Anatoli Sychev (Chair of the Federation Council Committee on Federation Affairs) wrote:

> All of these agreements ... have elements contradicting the Russian Federation Constitution and federal laws. This means that the so-called treaty law exists alongside constitutional law in our country, and the former effectively supersedes the latter for the signatories of treaties. (Sychev, 1996, p. 1)

The treaties also make a mockery of Article 5 of the federal constitution which states that relations between the centre and all the federal subjects are equal. Moreover, it is clear that the bilateral treaties have, in all but name, elevated a select number of oblasts to the status of *de facto* republics. Yeltsin has clearly adopted such a policy towards the regions as part of a divide-and-rule strategy, but there are questions as to how long this policy can be sustained. According to Yuri Stroev (Chair of the Federation Council):

> every time a new treaty is signed, misunderstandings and tensions arise in relations among regional leaders. Each suspects the other of having signed some sort of secret document, in which he wangled some kind of preferential treatment for himself. ... (Kozyreva, 1998, p. 7)

Sergei Mitrokhin, a deputy to the Russian parliament, agrees. He has warned that, 'a treaty-based Federation is a weak Federation that will ultimately destroy itself' (Mitrokhin, 1996, p. 5).

Economic methods

The distribution of state funding to the regions has proved to be a key weapon in the armoury of the central authorities. Some areas, such as Dagestan, are almost wholly dependent on state subsidies, while others, such as Tatarstan and Sakha, are wealthy enough to manage without them. However, the distribution of funding has not always been according to economic need. Indeed, favours have often been granted simply as a means of buying off regional oppositionist leaders. This can mean funds going to already wealthy areas at the expense of those such as Dagestan which are in desperate poverty. However, such tactics are clearly short sighted. It simply acts as an encouragement to obstructionism in the regions while adding to the economic inequalities across the country.

СПРАВКА 4.3 **In 1997 there were eight donor regions**

1. Moscow Oblast
2. Lipetsk Oblast
3. Samara Oblast
4. Sverdlovsk Oblast
5. Krasnoyarsk Krai;
6. Bashkortostan Republic
7. Khanty-Mansi Autonomous Okrug
8. Yamal-Nenets Autonomous Okrug

Table 4.1 Federal transfers as a percentage of total budget income

	1994	*1995*	*1996*
Group A			
Aga-Buryatia AO*	83.3	69.4	68.6
Altai Republic	85.0	74.7	61.9
Dagestan Republic	91.9	64.4	55.5
Koryak AO*	81.6	81.6	68.1
Tuva Republic	86.0	78.7	68.5
Group B			
Bashkortostan Republic	2.6	0.2	2.8
Yamal-Nenets AO*	3.7	1.2	2.0
Khanty-Mansi AO*	3.1	0.4	3.6
St Petersburg	6.9	0.4	2.7
Tatarstan Republic	7.7	0.9	2.2

* AO, autonomous okrug
Source: A. M. Lavrov (ed.), *Rossiiskie Regiony Posle Vyborov-96*, Iuridicheskaia Literatura, Moscow, 1997

Indeed, the system of economic bribery can work both ways. The centre can distribute funds but it is also dependent on the regions to collect taxes. The regions, however, have proved notably reluctant to pass on taxes to the centre ever since the latter days of the Gorbachev administration. The withholding of taxes has inevitably hit state finances and played a role in undermining the whole reform project. In 1993, the centre collected only 40 per cent of the taxes owed, and over two dozen subjects of the federation refused to pay Moscow anything at all (Sakwa, 1996, p. 188). Rich and financially independent republics, the so-called 'donor regions' (those regions which pay more into the federal coffers than they receive back), find themselves in a strong bargaining position with the centre (see Box 4.3 and Table 4.1). They have been able to get more political rights to defend their own narrow economic interests at the expense of the poorer regions of Russia. As a result, the rich become richer and more powerful, and the poor become increasingly marginalised.

As Leonid Smirnyagin observes,

> It cannot be considered acceptable when some regions differ from others several times over in terms of such important indicators of social development as per capita income, production downturn, unemployment, infant mortality, or per capita support from public funds . . . citizens' rights are inevitably violated here. After all, the right to enjoy identical benefits regardless of place of residence is one of the citizen's fundamental rights.
> (Smirnyagin, 1998, p. 2)

Ethnic separatism

The attempts by the centre to contain the centrifugal forces in Russia have been largely unsuccessful. Some strategies, such as increasing state funding to oppositionist regions and signing bilateral treaties with individual subjects of the federation, may have made sense in the short term but are almost certainly storing up problems for the future. In the light of this, what is the likelihood of the Russian Federation following the Soviet Union's example and splitting up altogether?

In fact, the chances of the Russian Federation splitting up along ethnic lines are remote. Ethnic pressures on the scale witnessed in the former Soviet Union simply do not exist in Russia. While Russians made up barely half of the Soviet Union in its later years, the overwhelming majority of citizens in the Russian Federation are Russian (about 83 per cent). Russia remains a huge, multi-ethnic state, with 172 different ethnic groups living on its territory, but the non-Russian minority groups are small. The Tatars are the largest minority ethnic group in Russia, but they only constitute 3.8 per cent of the total population (Pain and Susarov, 1997, p. 10). Furthermore, the titular population constitute a majority in only 10 of the 32 ethnically based regions in Russia (Aga-Buryatia, Chechnya, Chuvash, Dagestan, Ingushetia, Kabardino-Balkaria, Kalmykia, Komi-Permyak, North Ossetia and Tuva)[2] and a plurality in just Tatarstan (48.5 per cent Tatars). Russians, on the other hand, have an absolute majority in 18 and a plurality in three and make up a substantial minority in most of the others (for example, 43.3 per cent of the population in Tatarstan is Russian). In other words, ethnic Russians dominate the new state and the pressures from minority groups for secession can be expected to be correspondingly weaker.

This does not mean, of course, that nationalism is not a problem in Russia. The demands for secession have been strongest in those republics situated on the outer rim of the Russian Federation bordering foreign states and where the majority ethnic group is non-Russian. With the exception of Tuva (which borders Mongolia), all such republics are to be found in the North Caucasus (Chechnya, Dagestan, Ingushetia, Kalmykia and North Ossetia). These are certainly very volatile areas, but they are also among the poorest in Russia. They are, therefore, heavily dependent on federal subsidies and this may act as a constraint on secessionist demands. Richer states, on the other hand, which also have strong nationalist claims, such as Tatarstan, are landlocked within Russia, making full independence less practical even if it is never impossible.

2 In Dagestan, there are a number of small indigenous national groups which together make up the majority of the population.

Chechnya has been the one republic prepared to fight for independence. Chechens are predominantly Muslim. They constitute the majority ethnic group in the republic, although Russians make up a sizeable minority (about 25 per cent). Chechens have a long history of rebellion against Russian occupation which long pre-dates the Bolshevik Revolution. However, Chechnya, like many other regions in the Soviet Union, took the opportunity of Gorbachev's reforms, to declare full independence in autumn 1991. Chechnya was an important region to Russia. It had oil and gas deposits and important oil pipelines and rail links crossed the republic. Moscow was reluctant, therefore, to let political control pass into the hands of the rebel Chechen leadership. An agreement, similar to the one struck in Tatarstan in February 1994, always looked the most likely outcome of the stand-off between the two parties. However, it was not to be. The Chechen leader, Dzhokhar Dudaev, refused to compromise and Yeltsin's patience wore out in the winter of 1994.

At that time, Dudaev's position in Chechnya looked relatively weak. His support in the republic was fading as the country faced economic disaster and the prospect of civil war. Against this background, the Yeltsin administration decided to back the Chechen opposition leader, Umar Avturkhanov, in his attempt to overthrow Dudaev. However, Avturkhanov's coup attempt failed and a number of Russian soldiers were captured in the process. Russia was in a bind. Should Yeltsin go forward or retreat? Yeltsin decided to press on after consultation with his Defence Minister, Pavel Grachev, and other members of his close entourage. Grachev convinced Yeltsin that victory against the Chechen rebels would be quick and relatively painless. How wrong he was. The Russians intervened in the Republic of Chechnya with massive force in December 1994, but Moscow was unable to defeat the rebels. The war ebbed and flowed, but a cease-fire was only signed in the summer of 1996. A peace agreement was signed later in the year which committed Russia to withdraw all its troops by the end of the year and the Chechen leadership to hold republic-wide elections the following year. The Chechen nationalist, Aslan Maskhadov, emerged the victor and is devoted to the cause of Chechen independence. He is convinced that this will be formally achieved early in the next millennium. If this does happen, it will certainly represent a major defeat for Moscow. Further moves towards independence might well follow, although neighbouring states in the North Caucasus are well aware of the costs of independence. Chechnya remains in a state close to anarchy. Its economy is devastated, lawlessness reigns and a return to war cannot be discounted.

Autonomy short of secession

In fact, most regions in Russia do not want independence, but they do want considerable autonomy within a loose federation. Already some regions have opted for what has become known as economic and legal separatism – a process whereby a number of areas 'seek to withdraw from close ties with the rest of the federation and establish autarkic political and economic systems on their territories' (Paretskaya, 1996, p. 1).

Legal separatism

According to former Justice Minister Valentin Kovalev, the constitutions of 19 of Russia's 21 republics (all except Kalmykia and Karelia) violate the federal constitution, 'either by declaring the given republic to be a subject of international law, outlining parameters of republican monetary systems, or delimiting the republic's borders with other federal subjects and even foreign countries' (Parish, 1996, p. 3). Prosecutor General, Yuri Skuratov, declared that over the period 1996–98 prosecutors at all levels had contested some 2000 resolutions and laws passed by regional legislatures because they violated the Russian Constitution in some way (*ITAR-TASS* 17:32 GMT, 19 January 1998). Nikolai Medvedev (Chair of the Russian Parliament's Commission on National Affairs) noted that federal laws were no longer enforceable in many republics. Presidential decrees, he said, were ignored in Tatarstan and federal laws in Dagestan could be overturned by referendum. There is, Medvedev concluded, 'no mechanism codifying the right of precedence for federal laws . . . We have yet to admit that we have a confederation made up of 21 members of the Federation' (Malash, 1993, p. 10).

A number of republics (Buryatia, Bashkortostan, Ingushetia, Karelia, Kalmykia, Sakha and Tuva) have declared the primacy of their own republican laws over those of the federation (see Lowenhardt, 1995, p. 125; Kirkow, 1998, p. 51). According to Kovalev, about one-third of regional laws and regulations registered with the Justice Ministry contravene federal legislation (Parish, 1996, p. 3). Indeed, some regions, he says, '. . . claim the right of regional authorities to ratify international treaties, determine the responsibility of judicial and law enforcement agencies, and revise federal borders', duties which clearly belong to the federal government (Paretskaya, 1997b, p. 2). Peter Kirkow has also noted that regional and republican parliaments have indirectly contravened the Federal Constitution by adopting legislation which violates human rights. Violations have included the denial of citizenship, the use of a non-Russian official state language in regions where the majority of the population is Russian and state bodies staffed only by certain nationalities (Kirkow, 1998, p. 51).

In sum, what we appear to be witnessing is a new 'war of laws' between the federal authorities and the regions reminiscent of the struggle between the Union Republics and the federal authorities during the Gorbachev period. This current dispute has been fuelled by the failure of the Russian parliament to enact key legislative measures which would tighten up centre–periphery relations.[3] Representatives of the regional elites, many of whom are in the Federation Council, have been able to block such legislation as they wish to retain as much flexibility as possible in their relations with the centre.

Economic separatism

Increasingly, regions have also sought economic separatism from the centre. As Graham Smith writes, 'seven decades of centrally directed economic coordination

---

3 For example, we still await the Parliament's adoption of the following key laws, 'On Ensuring the Integrity of the State and Compliance with the Russian Federation Constitution and Federal Laws' and 'On Principles and Procedures Governing the Demarcation of Objects of Jurisdiction and Powers Between Bodies of State Power of the Russian Federation and Bodies of State Power of the Members of the Russian Federation'.

between the regions has given way to the anarchy of regional autarky' (Smith, 1995, p. 29). Fierce battles have raged between the centre and the regions over the spoils of the privatisation programme, while regional taxation has remained a major issue of contention. Regions have imposed their own import duties and sales taxes on certain goods, prohibited the export of various products from their regions and set their own prices on certain goods – all in clear violation of federal legislation. Thus, Omsk Oblast put a 50 per cent duty on imported alcoholic beverages and 10 per cent on foods, measures designed to bring in an additional revenue of 830 billion rubles for 1997 (Grushina, 1997, pp. 7–8). This, on top of the non-payment of taxes due to the centre, represents a significant loss to the federal authorities since regional budgets make up more than half of the consolidated state budget.

The process of economic separatism has gone further in a number of cases with some republics and regions engaging directly in economic and diplomatic activity with foreign states. Many of the republics now have their own foreign consulates (Tatarstan has 'representative offices' in 15 foreign states) and many are independent members of international trade organisations. Over the period 1991–96, the regions and republics signed more than 300 trade agreements with foreign states and in many cases such deals were struck without the participation, or sometimes even the knowledge, of the relevant ministries in Moscow.

The future of the Russian Federation

From the above discussion it is clear that Russian federalism is in deep crisis. There would appear to be almost as many kinds of federal relations as there are subjects of the federation. Constitutional federalism has been superseded by a new kind of treaty-based federalism which at present is codified in some 46 bilateral agreements. Power politics has replaced constitutional law as the basis of centre–periphery relations. Economically powerful republics, such as Bashkortostan and Sakha, have demanded, and won, additional economic and legal concessions from the centre, while Tatarstan continues to insist that it is only an 'associated member' of the federation. Thus, the greatest threat to the federation does not come in the main from ethnic separatists, but from the richer regions which seek ever more economic and legal autonomy.

This process has been reinforced by the elections in the localities since 1993 which have significantly increased the powers of regional governors. The elections have also changed the composition of the Federal Council, the upper chamber of parliament, where regional governors are *ex officio* members. Before these elections Yeltsin could be confident of controlling the upper chamber through his powers of appointment; thereafter, the Federal Council was more independent of the President and better able to exercise its veto powers over the lower chamber to promote its own sectional interests (see Chapter 2). As a result, the 'war of laws' between the federal government and federal subjects continues unabated. Republics and regions appear able to violate federal legislation and the Russian Constitution almost at will. According to Sergei Mitrokhin, it is the absence of federal sanctions to discipline unruly federal subjects that is at the heart of Russia's constitutional dilemma. The President, he argues, should be given executive powers to suspend laws which violate federal legislation and to fire regional executives who disobey court rulings (Paretskaya, 1997e, p. 7). In fact, the President does have such powers in law but he has been loathe to exercise them in practice for fear of unleashing nationalist unrest or losing the support of economically powerful regional elites.

Reform of the federal system in Russia has long been on the agenda in political circles in Moscow. Two models have been put forward as possible alternatives to the current system. Both argue the need to reduce the number of regions and to simplify relations between the centre and the periphery. Thus, the first model envisages Russia divided into 50 territorial regions roughly equal in size. According to this model, no account would be taken of the ethnic composition of the regions and many of the present ethnic republics would be amalgamated with neighbouring regions. The second, more radical alternative, supported by the highly influential mayor of Moscow Yuri Luzhkov, would reduce the number of federal components still further, from 89 to just eight. The eight regions would correspond to the eight inter-regional associations already in existence. The inter-regional associations have played an important role in aggregating and articulating the demands of regions and republics which are situated in close geographical proximity. The most powerful is the Siberian Accord Association, headed by Vitali Mukha, the Governor of Novosibirsk, which unites the powerful and wealthy oil- and gas-producing regions of Siberia. Both these models would be intended to facilitate communications between the centre and the periphery, to reduce the risk of ethnic conflict and to encourage economic co-operation across the country.

The fact that these two alternatives were seriously aired at all reveals the concerns in Moscow over the current state of federalism in Russia. However, it is highly unlikely that either of them will be adopted in the near future. Although the aims of both models are highly desirable, the practical problems look insurmountable. Any such radical reform would require changes to the constitution which the regions, and in particular the ethnically defined regions, would fiercely contest. Without support in the localities, the reforms would be dead in the water. Thus, the present, highly complex, two-tier federal system, involving a combination of ethnically defined and territorially defined regions, will probably stumble on until the end of the next round of parliamentary and presidential elections (due in the year 2000). However, reform of the current system seems vital if political stability is to be restored in Russia. To declare the need for reform, however, is far easier than to specify the exact course the reform should take. A pessimistic but authoritative report written by members of the Federation Council in 1998 could see no way out of the dilemma currently facing the country. It stated: 'If the treaty process continues on special terms for a number of Federation components . . . it will ultimately lead to the collapse of Russia . . . But ending the treaty process will not change the situation for the better either. If the regions' autonomy [is threatened] . . . they will respond with inter-ethnic clashes, and it will all end in the establishment of an authoritarian regime' (Kuzina, 1998, p. 2). Authoritarianism or collapse? This is scarcely an appetising choice. Russians may end up with no choice – the scenario of authoritarianism *and* collapse seems a possibility. Stumbling on from crisis to crisis remains, however, the most likely outcome.

References

Bird R M, Ebel R D and Wallich C I 1996 *Decentralization of the Socialist State: Intergovernmental Finance in Transition Economies*, World Bank, Avebury.

Emelyanenko V 1995 Russia: Waiting for IOUs, *Moskovskie Novosti*, No. 44 (June 25–July 2), *CDPSP*, Vol. XLVII, No. 26, pp. 14–15.

Grushina N 1997 Local Authorities Resort to Unlawful Means to Raise Money, *OMRI Russian Regional Report*, Vol. 2, No. 10 (13 March).

Hahn J 1997 Democratization and Political Participation in Russia's regions, in Dawisha K and Parrot B (eds), *Democratic Changes and Authoritarian Reactions in Russia, Ukraine, Belarus, and Moldova*, Cambridge University Press, Cambridge.

Helmer J 1997 Russia: Regions Pressure Kremlin Into Policy Shift – An Analysis, *RFE/RFL Daily Report*, 4 November.

Kamyshev D 1997 Mayoral Revolution, *Kommersant Daily*, October 1, *CDPSP*, Vol. XLIX, No. 39, pp. 13–14.

Kirkow P 1998 *Russia's Provinces*, Macmillan, Basingstoke.

Kozyreva A 1998 What Kind of State Do We Live In, *Rossiskaya Gazeta*, 23 January, *CDPSP*, Vol. 50, No. 3, p. 7.

Kuzina N 1998 The Federation Is Bursting At the Seams, *Rabochaya Tribuna*, 17 January translated in *FBIS* (SOV-98-019), 17 January, p. 2.

Lapidus G W and Walker E W 1995 Nationalism, Regionalism, and Federalism: Centre–Periphery Relations in Post-Communist Russia, in Lapidus G W (ed.), *The New Russia: Troubled Transformation*, Westview Press, Boulder, CO, pp. 79–113.

Lavrov A M 1995 Russian Budget Federalism: First Steps, First Results, *Segodnya*, 7 June, *CDPSP*, Vol. XLVII, No. 23 (5 July), pp. 1–4.

Lavrov A M (ed.) 1997 *Rossiiskie Regiony Posle Vyborov – 96*, Iuridicheskaia Literatura, Moscow.

Lowenhardt J 1995 *The Reincarnation of Russia: Struggling With the Legacy of Communism*, Longman, Harlow.

Malash L 1993 Debates, *Megapolis-Express*, 3 March, *CDPSP*, Vol. XLV, No. 9, pp. 10–11.

McFaul M and Petrov N 1997 Russian Electoral Politics After Transition: Regional and National Assessments, *Post-Soviet Geography and Economics*, Vol. XXXIII, No. 9 (November), pp. 507–49.

Mitrokhin S 1996 It's a Rare Governor Who Doesn't Dream of Becoming a Khan, *Obshchaia Gazeta*, Vol. 44 (November), *CDPSP*, Vol. XLVIII, No. 43, pp. 5–6.

Nikolaev M 1995 The Federal Treaty and Russia's Statehood, *Respublika Sakha*, 31 March, *FBIS*, 28 October, pp. 1–9.

Pain E and Susarov A 1997 Line Five in the Mirror of Demography, *Rossiiskie Vesti*, October 30, *CDPSP*, Vol. XLIX, No. 44, pp. 10–12.

Paretskaya A 1996 Russian Central Authorities Seek New Formula for Relations With the Regions, *OMRI Russian Regional Report*, Vol. 1, No. 12 (13 November), p. 1.

Paretskaya A 1997a Lysenko: Autonomous Okrugs Problems Should Be Solved Individually, *OMRI Russian Regional Report*, Vol. 2, No. 2 (15 January), pp. 4–5.

Paretskaya A 1997b Justice Ministry Warns Regions That They Are Not Complying With Federal Legislation, *OMRI Russian Regional Report*, Vol. 2, No. 9 (6 March), p. 2.

Paretskaya A 1997c Centre Wants to Use Mayors to Counterbalance Governors, *OMRI Russian Regional Report*, Vol. 2, No. 10 (13 March), p. 2.

Paretskaya A 1997d Udmurt Conflict Had Economic Basis, *OMRI Russian Regional Report*, Vol. 2, No. 11 (20 March).

Paretskaya A 1997e Central Authorities Urgently Need Compulsory Tools for Regions, *OMRI Russian Regional Report*, Vol. 2, No. 2 (15 January), p. 7.

Parish S 1996 Center Continues to Rail Against 'Legal Separatism', *OMRI Russian Regional Report*, Vol. 1, No. 11 (6 November), p. 3.

Russian Federation Presidential Analytical Service 1997 Internet source http://www.region.rags.ru/table7.htm.

Sakwa R 1996 *Russian Politics and Society*, Routledge, London.

Sasaki R 1996 Oil Factor in Tyumen Elections, *OMRI Russian Regional Report*, (November), p. 6.

Shpak V 1998 Federalism Does Not Yet Exist in Russia, *Kommersant-Daily*, 20 January, *CDPSP*, Vol. 50, No. 3, p. 6.

Smirnyagin L 1995 Iuridicheskaya Literatura, *Rossiiskie Regiony Nakanune Vyborov*, Moscow, pp. 7–43.

Smirnyagin L 1996 At a Fork in the Road of Federalization, *Rossiiskie Vesti*, 24 October, *CDPSP*, Vol. XLVIII, No. 43, pp. 3–4.

Smirnyagin L 1998 Power Without a Strict Chain of Command Could Be Weakened Unless Action To Strengthen and Develop Federalism Is Taken, *Rossiiskie Vesti*, 16 January, *FBIS* (SOV-98-028), 28 January, p. 2.

1997 *Vybory Glav Ispolnitel'noi Vlasti Sub'ektov Rossiiskoi Federatsii 1995–1997* Ves' Mir, Moscow.

Smith G 1995 The Ethno-Politics of Federation without Federalism, in Lane D (ed.), *Russia in Transition*, Longman, Harlow.

Stoner-Weiss K 1997 Federalism and Regionalism, in White S, Pravda A and Gitelman Z (eds), *Developments in Russian Politics – 4*, Macmillan, Basingstoke.

Sychev A 1996 Russian Federalism: Problems and Prospects, *Delovoi Mir*, 31 May, *FBIS* (FBIS-SOV-96-132-S), 31 May, p. 1.

White S, Rose R and McAllister I 1997 *How Russia Votes*, Chatham House Publishers, New Jersey.

Yeltsin B 1997 The Might of the State Grows Through the Independence of the Regions, *Rossiiskie Vesti*, November 1, *CDPSP*, Vol. XLIX, No. 44, pp. 13–14.

Further reading

Stoner-Weiss K 1997 Federalism and Regionalism, in White S, Pravda A and Gitelman Z (eds), *Developments in Russian Politics – 4*, Macmillan, Basingstoke.

Kirkow P 1998 *Russia's Provinces*, Macmillan, Basingstoke.

McAuley M 1997 *Russia's Politics of Uncertainty*, Cambridge University Press, Cambridge.

For the Russian Constitution, see the internet source: http://www.russia.net.

5

Political culture and public opinion

Matthew Wyman

Introduction

What are the prospects for democratic consolidation in Russia after the end of the cold war? The extent of democratisation will be affected by a range of factors, many of which are considered in other chapters of this volume. These include whether the government can deliver to its people an acceptable standard of living, whether tensions between Russians and ethnic minorities within the country can be contained, whether the international context of Russian democratisation is supportive or destructive, institutional choice, the behaviour of Russian political elites, adaptation to the new order on the part of the armed forces. This chapter considers another central factor, the wishes of the Russian people themselves, as reflected in their political culture (see Box 5.1).

Before the start of political reform in the mid-1980s, most commentators (see, for example, Pipes, 1974) regarded Russians as having a distinctive set of political cultural attitudes which were supportive of a strong state which restricted individual freedom. An historical vulnerability to invasion and the periodic outbreak of civil unrest led over time to the emergence in Russia of an autocratic system of government where the absolutist ruler was able to dispose of all people and property according to his or her whim, without reference to the interests of society. For a complex set of reasons, social groups such as the nobility or the middle classes failed to gain the strength needed effectively to challenge the autocracy. Historically, therefore, Russian politics was characterised by decision-making concentrated in the hands of a limited number of individuals, with little societal input and virtually no mass participation, and by a state which interfered in individuals' lives to an extent which would not have been acceptable in many other parts of the world. The concept of individual rights was largely absent, and law was not seen as something which was universally applied, but as something which was only arbitrarily applied, and often only applied to crimes against the state, with individuals having only limited means of redress against each other.

The consensus of opinion in the Soviet period was that this political culture had largely persisted, with the only important difference, once the contours of the Soviet system had been established in the 1920s and 1930s, being that the rulers were the communist party elites rather than the Tsar and his entourage (Brzezinski, 1976). What little empirical evidence became available, from surveys of émigrés from the Soviet Union conducted in the 1950s and 1970s, tended

СПРАВКА 5.1   Political culture and democracy

Political culture indicates the orientations of individuals towards the political system in which they live. This has a number of levels:

1. *Beliefs about the current authorities:* how trustworthy; how effective; whether a better alternative exists. Lack of faith in the existing incumbents may have little significance for regime stability in democracies because it is always possible to replace governments by peaceful means in a democracy. It can be much more serious for non-democratic regimes.

2. *Support for the political system:* whether political decisions are made in an acceptable way; whether the right institutions have power; whether elections are desirable and effective; whether individual citizens have enough say; whether it is appropriate to take part in politics. Lack of popular confidence in the way in which political systems function may be a much more serious problem, implying major institutional reform, or even regime collapse if there exists a serious support for an alternative.

3. *Attachment to the political community:* do individuals see themselves as a part of the community, e.g. as Russians? Who are their national heroes and with which historical events do they most identify? Are there any sections of the political community which they mistrust and seek to exclude? Fundamental divisions within the political community about these issues tend to be very serious indeed, often leading to separatism, oppression and even civil war.

Source: adapted from Easton (1975)

to confirm these views, in that it found that former Soviet citizens tended to favour relatively high levels of government interference in politics and in the economy (Inkeles and Bauer, 1959; Millar, 1976). For example, this was reflected in large numbers approving restrictions on strikes and the banning of certain political parties in their adopted country, as well as having a preference for a high level of state intervention in the economy and for public rather than private ownership of the means of production and distribution.

Of course not all commentators agreed with the conclusion of cultural continuity. Others preferred to stress elements of change in Soviet society, and in particular the influences of urbanisation, rising levels of education in society, the growth of a dissident movement and the impact of improvements in communications technology which meant that information from elsewhere in the world was more easily available. All of these changes meant that Soviet society had become more complex, and therefore a more sophisticated and responsive political system was a self-evident requirement (Lewin, 1988). Several historians were also keen to point out that, despite the appearance of an excessively strong state, in both Tsarist and Soviet times governments always faced the problem of

СПРАВКА 5.2 Major sources for Russian public opinion

Russian pollsters: the first polling organisation, the All-Russian Centre for Public Opinion, VTsIOM, was founded in 1987 after Mikhail Gorbachev decided that it would be helpful for democratisation to attempt to find out what the public thought about what was going on in the Soviet Union. It publishes a bi-monthly summary of the state of Russian attitudes, called *Economic and Social Changes: monitoring of public opinion*. Many more commercial polling and market research organisations now exist in Russia.

The New Russia Barometer: organised by the Paul Lazarsfeld Society in Vienna in conjunction with the Centre for the Study of Public Policy, Strathclyde University. Has carried out extensive studies annually in Russia since 1991.

Central and Eastern Eurobarometer: commissioned by the European commission and carried out annually in Russia since 1991. Each survey asks about attitudes to democracy and to marketisation, with other issues investigated less regularly.

World Values Survey: from 1991, Russia was included as one of the 40-plus countries in this ongoing study of social and cultural change across the world.

New Soviet/Russian Citizen surveys: conducted in Russia by researchers from the University of Iowa regularly since 1990.

Public Opinion and Democratic Consolidation Project: conducted by a team from Glasgow University at mass and elite level in Russia and other post-communist countries in 1993 and 1996.

ungovernability. Thanks to its sheer size and communications difficulties, it was in fact remarkably difficult for the state to see its wishes put into practice, however forceful its methods of attempting so to do. This, indeed, is the theme of much classic Russian and Soviet literature, such as the satirical masterpieces of Nikolai Gogol. Several analysts also stressed the elements of Russian history which contradicted the traditional interpretation, such as examples of constraints on authority in pre-revolutionary Russia provided by tradition and custom, and by social institutions such as religious groupings who, although formally subordinate to the state, never in reality accepted this subordination (Petro, 1995; McDaniel, 1996).

Since the emergence of a programme of radical reform and democratisation in the Soviet Union in the mid-1980s discussion about mass values in Russia has mostly followed the latter approach, stressing change rather than continuity in Russian mass values. For the first time, scholars have been able to carry out surveys of mass attitudes, and move from inferring what ordinary Russians think about political matters to actually asking them (see Box 5.2). Having done this, most recent analysts who have studied Russian's views about democracy have concluded that they are in general supportive of democratic values, in that for example they reply to pollsters that they approve of regular elections, of a range of civil and political rights, of a multi-party system and so forth. For example, one prominent team of analysts has concluded in a recent study that their data 'challenge those who rule out successful democratic consolidation because the Russian . . . people lack a political culture that is ready for it' (Reisinger *et al.*, 1994, p. 220). Another team has been just as assertive: 'in terms of democratic consolidation in the [former Soviet Union] . . . Political values in the early 1990s were part of the solution, not part of the problem' (Miller *et al.*, 1998, p. 28). The cause of the change is often held to be the economic and social modernisation of the post-war period (Miller *et al.*, 1993).

Political culture and political change

Political cultures are one aspect of the set of norms, values, beliefs, identifications and expectations which societies possess. Some of these may be ones which virtually everyone agrees are appropriate beliefs: for example, that it is wrong to commit murder. Others may be more ambiguous in their effect, such as the view that all politicians cannot be trusted to keep their word. Whatever the case, they are beliefs which, like most beliefs in life, are not particularly susceptible to change. This is because of their origins, which most believe to lie in processes of political socialisation during childhood. Cultural beliefs tend to serve as 'standing decisions', which lead us to respond in certain habitual ways to certain situations, with our expressed beliefs reflecting our identities and emotional loyalties rather than our reactions necessarily being rational and considered ones.

A political culture, therefore, contains a great deal of inertia, which is why it is possible to use the term at all. However, the thing about tribal thought patterns is that they tend not to be appropriate eternally or in all situations. There may come a time when reality makes it impossible to continue thinking the same way. Indeed, Russians have found their political assumptions seriously challenged on a relatively frequent basis in the course of the twentieth century. The first time was in the years leading up to the 1917 revolutions, when old assumptions about the divine right to rule of Tsar Nicholas II were challenged in people's minds by the perceived incompetence of the ruling authorities as well as by the increasing influence of Western liberal and Marxist ideas. Much the same happened in the period leading up to the collapse of the Soviet Union at the end of 1991, by which time it was increasingly impossible to believe Communist Party rhetoric about equality and progress in the face of staggering official corruption and self-evident economic stagnation.

However, the crucial, and often missed, point to understand about the process of political cultural change is that it is not something which happens overnight. It is a big thing for people to change their basic orientations, since they have the character of standing decisions reflecting basic identities and loyalties (Fleron, 1996; Wyman, 1997). The views of a nation, then, in a period of change, will enter a period of what can only be described as chaos, where old ways of viewing things gradually fade away since they no longer reflect reality, but there is little clarity or consensus about what might take their place. There is a parallel in political life to the process of change in individuals, where it is frequently necessary to break down old ways before breaking through to new ones.

If the above is true, how could it possibly be the case that Russians have adapted to the ideas of democracy and the market economy as easily as some commentators have argued is the case? Indeed, it is tempting to argue that the idea that Russia is in a period of transition to democracy and a market economy is a flawed one, and an unfortunate consequence of the cold war triumphalism surrounding the collapse of communism. Just because a system which had existed for more than 70 years collapsed in acrimony and chaos does not mean that Russia is inevitably on the path to a 'Western-style' democratic system. The projection of an imaginary future into Russia's present may indeed blind analysts to many central features of contemporary Russia, such as the continuing prevalence of official corruption, nepotism and lack of accountability, the penetration of the economy by organised crime, the extent to which Russia is still not a unified market and the tendency for cynicism and lack of hope among her people.

At present, therefore, Russia's political culture should not be taken as a given, having a fixed set of characteristics. On the contrary, it should be seen as something which is in a process of transformation, where we have some idea of the starting point, but cannot know the final destination. What it is possible to do, however, is to identify some of the elements out of which it is made, elements which might in some possible futures grow and become dominant.

How can we best identify these elements? One source is clearly surveys of public opinion. Of course respondents' snap responses to interviewers are not necessarily an accurate reflection of more deeply held beliefs, but nonetheless the great advantage of the survey method is that of representativeness. Professional sampling procedures ensure that the selection of interviewees is a selection which is typical of the country as a whole. This representativeness is a characteristic which more qualitative approaches, which seek to establish why respondents hold particular beliefs, cannot emulate.

What an opinion poll can tell the analyst is what the most *typical* responses in a society or a section of a society are. However, if we are seeking to identify elements which could be the basis for a new political consensus, these may be beliefs which are at present by no means typical, or may even be largely unexpected. Therefore it is also necessary to balance quantitative survey evidence with more impressionistic sources: qualitative interviews, speeches, literature, media, discussions among intellectuals and so forth.

Beliefs about the current authorities

Any observer of the contemporary Russian political scene is bound to note the high degree of mistrust in politics and politicians to be found in present-day Russia. This contrasts greatly with the mood in 1988–89 when public opinion polls were first conducted in Russia. At that time, respondents had a great deal of trust in virtually all the major institutions of state, including even the

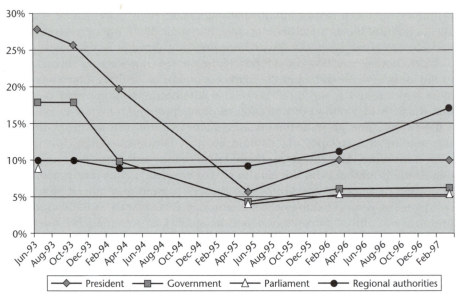

Figure 5.1   Trust in political institutions, 1993–97
Source: VTsIOM

Communist Party. The fatal moment for Mikhail Gorbachev came in the first half of 1991, during which time many Russians visibly transferred their trust from the Soviet President to his main rival Boris Yeltsin, who had been elected President of Russia that summer. By contrast, Yeltsin was able to survive his conflicts with the Russian parliament at the end of 1993 and to 'bust' successfully a constitution he disapproved of in part because public opinion, evidenced in the referendum of April 1993, remained broadly supportive of the President and suspicious of his opponents (Wyman, 1997, Chapters 3 and 4).

Figure 5.1 illustrates trends in Russians' views about the major institutions of their political system from 1993 to 1997. It gives responses to the question 'In your opinion, to what extent do(es) [name of individual or institution] deserve trust?' with possible responses fully, partly or not at all, and it shows the percentage who have complete confidence in the institutions in question. Three main trends emerge: a fall in the number of Russians who trust President Yeltsin and his government; the continued high level of mistrust of the Russian parliament; increasing popularity for institutions of regional and local government.

The post-1993 period was certainly a difficult one for the Yeltsin administration. Having disposed of its most obvious political opponents in the aftermath of the events of October 1993, there was no longer any credible internal opponent to blame for the continuing economic crisis, rising levels of crime, corruption and the fiasco of the war in Chechnya. In addition, new problems, in particular the issue of the non-payment of wages by the state to its employees, as well as increasing clarity about the extent to which several senior political figures have been enriched by several recent policies, emerged to add to the general level of dissatisfaction with the government. All of these undermined the previously widespread hope that Yeltsin would at last be a political leader who governed in the interests of the ordinary people rather than the ruling classes. In this context, falling levels of trust in President and government are scarcely surprising. The trend reinforces just how remarkable a victory Yeltsin was able to engineer in the 1996 presidential elections.

Readers may, however, be surprised at the continued level of distrust of the Russian parliament (Federal Assembly) evidenced in these data. It was never hard to see why the Russian Congress of People's Deputies, the parliament prior to 1993, had failed to gain legitimacy in the public mind. It was not fairly elected, it was dominated by deputies who looked and sounded like representatives of the old regime and were evidently unrepresentative of Russian society and it failed to distinguish itself in its behaviour or even adequately to address many of the central political issues of its time. However, optimists had hoped that the introduction of a new, professional, full-time and fairly elected parliament with properly specified powers would help to raise its esteem in the public mind. The data suggest that this has manifestly failed to happen. Indeed, out of the institutions pollsters have asked about, only political parties are more unpopular than the current State Duma. Supporters of a parliamentary system argue that this is because the constitutional arrangements of Russian presidentialism make it impossible for a parliament to perform adequately, since it simply does not have the power. The Duma's critics argue that many parliamentarians have failed to move towards more responsible behaviour patterns as rapidly as might have been wished. Most on both sides of the fence also accept that the idea of representation has weak roots in Russian culture. Ordinary people continue to have a great deal of difficulty in accepting that their deputies might be motivated by a desire for public service as well as personal aggrandisement.

One significant trend which emerges from these data is about trust in regional and local authorities. Since 1995 there has been an effort to ensure that all local executive and legislative bodies in Russia have been chosen through popular election rather than the previous system of appointment from above. Clearly this has served greatly to boost the levels of trust in these institutions in many parts of Russia. The ongoing disputes between centre and regions about the distribution of power and responsibility, and indeed assets, have certainly been one of the most important from the point of view of understanding the likely future distribution of power in post-communist Russia, and the fact that if anything public confidence lies more with the republics and regions than with the central government may have a significant bearing on this continuing process (see Chapter 4).

How does trust in political institutions in Russia compare with that which is found elsewhere in the world? Box 5.3 compares Russian responses as of 1997 with those of the United States, Great Britain and France in 1991. It should be noted that the responses are not completely comparable, since, while the questions are virtually identical, Russians had three possible answers to choose from, while there were four options in the other countries. However, this should if anything lead to greater levels of trust being expressed in Russia than in those countries where 'not very much' was also a possible response. What the data perhaps reinforce more than anything is that Russians are far from being unique in the nature of their feelings about the current operation of their

СПРАВКА 5.3 Comparative levels of trust in social and political institutions (in percentages)

	Russia	United States	United Kingdom	France
President	49			
Legislature	46	42	44	43
Army	59	48	80	54
Police*	42	75	77	65
Churches	57	67	45	48
Trade unions	37	32	27	30
Press**	67	56	15	37

Table entries are the percentages with 'a great deal' or 'a fair amount' of trust in the institution in the UK, USA and France, and 'a great deal' or 'some' in Russia
* In Russia, 'police, courts and procuracy'
** In Russia, 'press, radio and television'

Sources: adapted from *1991 World Values Survey*; *VTsIOM Bulletin*, Vol. 3, 1997, p. 59

political institutions. Across the world publics are sceptical about the shape of their governing institutions, although the precise focus of the scepticism tends to differ with local circumstances (Dalton, 1996). In established democracies, however, the interpretation of such a mood is somewhat different, and usually taken as an indication of a desire for the promises of democracy to be fulfilled. However, in a country such as Russia where constitutional choice is far from being settled, the mood may signify continuing indecision in institutional choice, and contribute to the lack of 'institutionality' and the general sense of instability of the political system.

Support for the political system

Unhappiness about the current operation of a country's political institutions does not necessarily imply that there will be pressure for basic decision-making procedures to be altered. Problems which lead to substantial political change are more likely to arise where there is basic unhappiness about the way in which leaders are chosen and political systems operate. So to what extent have Russians approved of the way in which the political system has functioned in the recent period?

Detailed consideration of this question presents a picture which can only be described as ambiguous. Russians appear to want to maintain the principle that their leaders are chosen in democratic elections. Thus, for example, a study by the University of Glasgow immediately after the December 1995 State Duma elections found that over half of respondents wanted a multi-party system (although one with fewer parties than at present) while just under 30 per cent wanted a return to a one-party system. Overwhelming majorities feel that elections are 'free and fair'. However, Russians remain sceptical about the effectiveness of elections: the 37 per cent who at that time thought that regular elections had a great deal or some effect in making politicians do what the people want were outweighed by the 52 per cent who thought that they had little or no effect (Miller *et al.*, 1998, Chapter 9).

Russian public opinion, however, demonstrates a basic unhappiness with many other aspects of the present political system (White, 1997, pp. 200–5). Recent New Russia Barometer surveys, as well as studies by the All Russian Centre for Public Opinion Research (VTsIOM), have found that many respondents believe that the communist system was more effective than the current one. While respondents believe that the situation has improved regarding freedom of speech, movement and religion, they are more likely to believe that their wishes were taken into account under communism than in the present day. Thus, for example, VTsIOM in 1994 found 54 per cent agreeing, compared with just 29 per cent disagreeing, that things would have been better if the country had remained as it had been before 1985, when Mikhail Gorbachev became General Secretary. Asked what attracted them about the period before 1985, the most common answer was that people were able to have confidence in the future, in other words that stability in people's lives at least gives the possibility of some forward planning. By January 1997, around one-third of Russians said that they were 'on the whole in favour of that kind of socialism we had in our country before 1985', just 30 per cent were opposed and the remainder were neither for nor against it.

Russians were equally divided when faced with questions about the possibility of a more authoritarian political system. In 1994, 25 per cent agreed and 43 per cent disagreed that 'the only way out of the predicament in which the country finds itself is the establishment of dictatorship'. By early 1997, around eight times as many said that order was more important than democracy as the number who believed democracy to be a greater priority. There was also a belief that mass disorder might occur. As of June 1997, fully 35 per cent of Russians thought that 'demonstrations with political demands for the resignation of the President, Government and Russian Parliament' were 'completely possible' in their area, and over one in four said that they would be certain or quite likely to take part in such demonstrations.

Evidently then the current situation is far from being a stable one. Regime change may normally occur when a clear alternative exists, but many revolutions simply reflect the collapse of an existing order, with the contours of the future state only being determined subsequently. While it is an exaggeration to say that protests against the current state of affairs are likely to lead to the violent overthrow of the system, they would certainly indicate the likelihood of another abrupt change of political direction.

Attachment to the political community

Successful political systems usually operate on the basis of consensus about the boundaries of the political community, the basic values of the political system, the objects of national pride and national attachment. Political conflicts about such issues tend to be the most intense and destructive kinds of conflict. Despite the evident flaws, Russia under late communism was largely united under a value system in the Brezhnev era described so eloquently by many commentators (e.g. Zaslavsky, 1982; Smith, 1976). The country was united, powerful, and with a military strong enough to prevent a repeat of the experiences of World War II. Of course, standards of living were not high, citizens were compelled to lead a dual existence in which behaviour in public was greatly different from that in private life and to turn a blind eye to official corruption and nepotism on a grand scale. However, prices were low, life was stable enough and the consequences of speaking out were unpleasant enough that the system managed to maintain itself successfully until 1985. Issues such as the place of ethnic or social minorities in the political system were simply not on the agenda. To be sure, there were a few dissenting voices, but their message scarcely penetrated into the wider society.

The Gorbachev era most importantly represented the progressive unravelling and then collapse of this consensus, as the mode of behaviour of the ruling authorities became intolerable to large sections of the population. Gorbachev's attempt to establish a new consensus around ideas of honesty and public-spirited behaviour made, to say the least, little headway.

The rhetoric of the Yeltsin administration after 1992 was that Russia should abandon attempts to be unique and adopt 'common Western values' of democracy and a market economy. In practice this meant standing for changes such as the acceptance of private property and the privatisation process, an end to price fixing and price stability, the opening up of the economy to the outside world and the attempt, at least, to respect human rights, including, freedoms of speech, assembly and movement.

However, observers of contemporary Russia may be struck with how little all of this reflects the value systems one encounters in contemporary Russia. Far more commonly one sees a mood of fatalism and resignation, reflected in statements along the lines that 70 years of communism destroyed any value systems which Russians might have had, and that therefore any kind of destructive or immoral behaviour is to be expected, or even justifiable. Treatment of minorities, especially ethnic and religious ones, is frequently poor. The utter destruction of political opponents remains the goal of significant sections of Russia's political elite. All kinds of corruption and dishonesty are accepted business and everyday practice. This can scarcely be seen as the adoption of the values of democracy and an effectively regulated market.

Public opinion studies reinforce the sense that 'western' values are not only not dominant, but are not even the strongest impulses that exist in present-day Russian public opinion. Figure 5.2 displays the most popular answers to the question 'In your opinion, which ideas could most unite Russian society today?' There is no majority preoccupation with the values of democracy and the market economy, and nor is there any evident desire for national strength and superpower status, or the values of the socialist system. If anything emerges from these data it is the desire for stability, honesty and order. This reinforces the view that the kinds of changes which are occurring in contemporary Russia

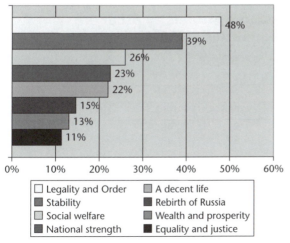

48%
39%
26%
23%
22%
15%
13%
11%

0%   10%   20%   30%   40%   50%   60%

☐ Legality and Order   ◼ A decent life
◼ Stability   ◼ Rebirth of Russia
☐ Social welfare   ☐ Wealth and prosperity
◼ National strength   ◼ Equality and justice

Figure 5.2   Unifying values, May 1997
Source: VTsIOM

are elite driven rather than emerging from popular demand. A few analysts have argued that the impulse for privatisation and marketisation in Russia came largely from a narrow social group with strong connections with the communist party elite, and also that politically there has been surprisingly little turnover of personnel in the Yeltsin period (Kryshtanovskaia and White, 1996). In this the current period is scarcely different to most of Russian history where the concerns of elites and masses have always tended to diverge to a very significant degree.

What then of issues surrounding the boundaries of the political community? It is evident from many political systems across the world that integrating minorities of various kinds is one of the most difficult and divisive tasks a system can face. It took virtually two centuries for the ideals of political equality embodied in the American Declaration of Independence to be given even statutory form. What is clear is that, without an open airing of grievances and concessions from all parties where such tensions exist, there is little possibility of alleviation.

Russian pollsters have approached the study of ethnic-related issues by looking at how respondents stereotype various ethnic groups within Russian society. Thus, VTsIOM asked 'What is your usual attitude to people of other nationalities, for example towards _____?'. Box 5.4 shows the responses.

Researchers would normally expect there to be a certain amount of self-censorship in responses to questions of this nature, although less so in parts of the world where political correctness is not so great a barrier to honesty. Given this, the level of negative feelings about gypsies and about people from the Caucasus region remains a matter of some concern (see also Wyman, 1997, Chapter 5). It is evident that the policies of the Yeltsin administration concerning the attempted secession by Chechnya would have been less acceptable in a more tolerant climate of public opinion.

СПРАВКА 5.4 Russian attitudes to other nationalities, 1993–95 (in percentages)

	Positive			Negative		
	1993	*1995*	*1996*	*1993*	*1995*	*1996*
Chechens	35	30	53	48	51	47
Gypsies	39	36	59	48	48	41
Azeris	43	42	72	43	39	28
Armenians	41	46		45	35	
Uzbeks	61	59		20	18	
Estonians	64	58	88	16	19	12
Jews	68	64	90	17	17	10
Tartars	71	74		13	12	
Ukrainians	81	83		7	7	
Russians	91	92		2	2	

Positive responses were 'with complete trust', 'with sympathy/with interest', 'calmly, without concern, just like anyone else'; negative responses were 'with fear/mistrust', 'with irritation, hostility or enmity'

Sources: adapted from Gudkov (1995b, 1996)

Another approach to the study of ethnic stereotypes is, rather than asking direct questions which might produce guarded responses, to ask respondents what they believe to be the most typical characteristics for representatives of particular ethnic groups, which is also an exercise which VTsIOM have carried out. Box 5.5 shows what the most typical qualities of various ethnic groups were believed to be in 1994. As can be seen, this method indeed brings out racist attitudes among a significant minority, towards Jews in particular, a fact which was not identified by a more direct approach. Other similarly disturbing attitudes are also manifest in public opinion: thus, for example, as of 1996, 40 per cent (the same proportion as in 1990), according to VTsIOM, agreed with the statement that 'people of non-Russian nationality now exercise too great an influence in Russia' (Gudkov, 1996, p. 23). Clearly, then, a significant level of intolerance and mutual misunderstanding complicates efforts to understand Russia as a unified political community.

Do mass attitudes to Russia's history allow us to shed any further light on values which might unite Russian society? Again, conclusions here are somewhat pessimistic. VTsIOM has on a number of occasions asked its respondents what they think the most important events of the twentieth century have been for Russia. On each occasion, victory in World War II was cited by a substantial majority. As of 1994, the next most commonly cited events were the October Revolution, the break-up of the USSR, the Chernobyl explosion and Yuri Gagarin's space flight. Similarly, a 1996 study, asking 'What in our history evokes the most pride for you?', found that victory in the war was again the most often mentioned (by 44 per cent of Russians), followed by 'the endurance of

СПРАВКА 5.5   **Ethnic stereotypes, 1994**

English
  Cultured, educated (53)
  Have a sense of personal dignity (4)
  Rational (36)
  Energetic (30)
  Freedom loving, independent (24)

Russians
  Open, honest (65)
  Hospitable (60)
  Long-suffering (56)
  Prepared to help out (55)
  Peace loving (47)
  Dependable, trustworthy (40)
  Love their work (38)
  Impractical (35)
  Irresponsible (26)
  Freedom loving, independent (25)
  Idle (23)

Uzbeks
  Respect the elderly (44)
  Religious (31)
  Hospitable (30)
  Downtrodden, humiliated (25)
  Idle (18)

Jews
  Hypocritical, sly (42)
  Stingy (31)
  Rational (25)
  Energetic (23)
  Secretive (23)
  Religious (20)

Lithuanians
  Arrogant (29)
  Freedom loving, dependent (22)
  Secretive (22)
  Have a sense of personal dignity (22)

Source: adapted from Gudkov (1995a)

the people' (39 per cent), 'great literature' (19 per cent), 'olden times and antiquity' (16 per cent) and, last of all, 'the Soviet state' (12 per cent) (Dubin, 1996). A study in 1997 found that several important falsehoods about the war remained central to popular beliefs: overwhelming majorities thought that victory in the war was due entirely to the efforts of the Russian people, not the Soviet people as a whole, and not a combined effort of the countries allied against Nazi Germany. Seventy-one per cent (up from 62 per cent in 1991) agreed that the Soviet Union had achieved victory in the war without the help of its allies (Gudkov, 1997).

What then of attitudes to Stalinism? VTsIOM in early 1998 investigated this by asking respondents to choose from a list of several statements about Stalin the ones with which they most strongly agreed. The most popular view, held by almost one in three, was that Stalin should be remembered for leading the Soviet Union to victory in the war, rather than for the injustices of his rule. A slightly smaller proportion thought that he had been 'a cruel inhuman tyrant guilty of the extermination of millions of innocent people'. One in six believed that Stalin had been a wise leader who turned the Soviet Union into a superpower, and one in seven thought that only a strong leader such as Stalin could preserve order in such an unruly country as Russia (*Russia Today*, 5 March 1998, p. 7).

These interpretations of war and Stalinism have significant consequences for Russian political development, since they form the basis of the appeals of communist and nationalist opponents of development on the basis of peaceful co-operation and free discussion. They reinforce beliefs that Russia cannot trust other countries and justify for their holders a state of affairs where there is a continued subordination of private life to the interests of the state. Overall, the penetration of a new set of social values and goals is only likely to be possible in the context of a national re-evaluation of its own history, which might seem a remote possibility in a period of mass culture and consumerism.

Conclusions

How then should we characterise Russian political culture after more than six years of the Yeltsin Presidency? The evidence cited above certainly suggests that a new value system which might replace the coherent if problematic set of values of the late Soviet period has not yet emerged. Elements of the old co-exist with new attitudes, in ways which are often contradictory, and in a state of flux. One can draw an analogy with work done in the natural sciences to help understand this process.

The analogy is with work done in physical chemistry by the Russian–Belgian scientist Ilya Prigogine, who was awarded the Nobel Prize in 1977 for his work on the thermodynamics of non-equilibrium systems. A non-equilibrium system is any one which is not closed and is involved in continual interchanges of various kinds with the environment in which it is located. A country is such an 'open system' because it is not closed off from the rest of the world, and the same is true of a social culture. Prigogine's theory was that, while any system which is open to outside influences always shows some fluctuation, as long as this does not go beyond a certain point – Prigogine's term is 'singular moment' or 'bifurcation point' – things remain stable. However, there reaches a point at which fluctuations and disturbances become so great that the system is moved into a state of 'creative chaos' where the old order of things can no longer continue and a crisis occurs. According to Prigogine, out of this chaos and breakdown of the old system, a new, more complex and differentiated way of ordering things eventually emerges – his term is a 'dissipative structure', and, importantly, there is a certain degree of chance about what the nature of this new order of things will be (Prigogine, 1980; Prigogine and Stengers, 1984).

The parallel with the processes of change in Russia is clear. For well-known reasons to do with external influences, economic failure, moral degradation and ecologicide, the set of values and behavioural and organisational norms associated with communism ceased to be functional. A crisis occurred and the old order collapsed. This being a human society, this collapse was initially associated with much denial, anger and subsequently depression. However, one can also identify a sense of acceptance that things cannot return to the past. Clearly, also, imported ideas such as 'greed is good' and society should tolerate a high level of inequality can scarcely be said to have sunk deep roots in the Russian value system.

Optimists had hoped that the Yeltsin Presidency would offer the opportunity for a process of articulating a new value system to take place. However, the 1991–98 period has seen preoccupation with issues surrounding state construction, including attempts to ensure that the state is solvent and can perform the most basic functions of protection of citizens and national defence. Complex and often fraught processes of renegotiating the relationships between Russia and its former subject republics, the distribution of power between central government, local government and the people, and between institutions at the centre, have dominated the period. There has been little sense that politicians have been concerned with articulating a new national purpose or set of ideas which can motivate and inspire. Stability has rightly been their priority.

We perhaps remain unclear as to the extent to which the new relationships are stable ones. Certainly it can be argued with some conviction that, for example, the balance of power between President and parliament embodied in the new constitution is not likely to be sustainable in the long term (see Chapter 2). Furthermore, the relationship between centre and periphery is so complex that accountability either upwards or downwards seems impossible, and one wonders whether this state of affairs is workable over a period of time (see Chapter 4). It follows therefore that Russian politics in the immediate future is likely to continue to be dominated by this process of settling new ways of doing things, and it may be some time before Russia is governed by leaders who articulate a new set of values which can motivate and inspire her citizens.

References

Brzezinski Z 1976 Soviet Politics: From the Future to the Past, in Cocks P, Daniels R V and Heer N W (eds), *The Dynamics of Soviet Politics*, Harvard University Press, Cambridge, MA, and London, Chapter 17.

Dalton R J 1996 *Citizen Politics: Public Opinion and Political Parties in Advanced Western Democracies*, Chatham House, New Jersey, Chapter 12.

Dubin B 1996 Proshloe v segodnyashnikh otsenkakh rossiyan, *Ekonomicheskie i sotsial'nye peremeny: monitoring obshchestvennovo mneniia*, Vol. 5, pp. 28–34.

Easton D 1975 A Reassessment of the Concept of Political Support, *British Journal of Political Science*, Vol. 5, pp. 435–57.

Fleron F J 1996 Post-Soviet Political Culture in Russia: an Assessment of Recent Empirical Investigations, *Europe Asia Studies*, Vol. 48, No. 2, pp. 225–60.

Gudkov L 1995a Dinamika ethnicheskikh stereotipov (sravnenie zamerov 1989 i 1994 gg.), *Ekonomicheskie i sotsial'nye peremeny: monitoring obshchestvennogo mneniia*, Vol. 2, pp. 14–16.

Gudkov L 1995b Ethnicheskie stereotipy naseleniia: sravnenie dvukh zamerov, *Ekonomicheskie i sotsial'nye peremeny: monitoring obshchestvennogo mneniia*, Vol. 3, pp. 22–6.

Gudkov L 1996 Ethnicheskie fobii v strukture natsional'noi identifikatsii, *Ekonomicheskie i sotsial'nye peremeny: monitoring obshchestvennogo mneniia*, Vol. 5, pp. 22–8.

Gudkov L 1997 Pobeda v voine: k sotsiologii odnovo natsional'novo simbola, *Ekonomicheskie i sotsial'nye peremeny: monitoring obshchestvennogo mneniia*, Vol. 5, pp. 12–19.

Inkeles A and Bauer R T 1959 *The Soviet Citizen: Daily Life in a Totalitarian Society*, Harvard University Press, Cambridge, MA.

Kryshtanovskaya O and White S 1996 From Soviet Nomenklatura to Russian Elite, *Europe Asia Studies*, Vol. 48, No. 5, pp. 711–33.

Lewin M 1988 *The Gorbachev Phenomenon*, Hutchinson Radius, London.

McDaniel T 1996 *The Agony of the Russian Idea*, Princeton University Press, Princeton, NJ.

Millar J R 1976 *Politics, Work and Daily Life in the USSR*, Cambridge University Press, Cambridge.

Miller A H, Reisinger W M and Hesli V L (eds) 1993 *Public Opinion and Regime Change: the New Politics of Post-Soviet Societies*, Westview, Boulder, CO.

Miller W L, White S and Heywood P 1998 *Values and Political Change in Postcommunist Europe*, Macmillan, Basingstoke.

Petro N N 1995 *The Rebirth of Russian Democracy*, Harvard University Press, Cambridge, MA.

Pipes R 1974 *Russia Under the Old Regime*, Penguin, London.

Prigogine I 1980 *From Being to Becoming: Time and Complexity in the Physical Sciences*, Freeman, New York.

Prigogine I and Stengers I 1984 *Order Out of Chaos: Man's New Dialogue with Nature*, Flamingo, London.

Reisinger W M, Miller A H, Hesli V L and Maher K H 1994 Political Values in Russia, Ukraine and Lithuania: sources and implications for democracy, *Europe–Asia Studies*, Vol. 24, No. 2, pp. 183–224.

Smith H 1976 *The Russians*, Sphere, London.

White S 1997 Russia, in Eatwell R (ed.), *European Political Cultures: Conflict or Consensus*, Routledge, London, Chapter 12.

Wyman M 1997 *Public Opinion in Postcommunist Russia*, Macmillan, Basingstoke.

Zaslavsky V 1982 *The Neo-Stalinist State*, M E Sharpe, Armonk, NY.

Further reading

McDaniel T 1996 *The Agony of the Russian Idea*, Princeton University Press, Princeton, NJ.

Miller W L, White S and Heywood P 1998 *Values and Political Change in Postcommunist Europe*, Macmillan, Basingstoke.

Petro N N 1995 *The Rebirth of Russian Democracy*, Harvard University Press, Cambridge, MA.

Wyman M 1997 *Public Opinion in Postcommunist Russia*, Macmillan, Basingstoke.

PART **II** Economics, culture and social policy

6 The political economy of Russia: transition or condition?

Anthony Phillips

Introduction

Since 1992, Russia has embarked on the complex process of economic transition. Russia was not the first country to initiate systemic change, but there was little theoretical work done on the problem of transforming a communist command economy into a functioning capitalist one. What theories existed related mainly to the reform of rural subsistence economies rather than developed industrial ones. Russia had to experiment. Transition was largely a leap in the dark. It was clear what had to be done. The economy had to be privatised and the disciplines of the market had to be introduced, but how? The Yeltsin government received plenty of advice, but Yeltsin and his colleagues argued they had no time to indulge in academic debate, and they had to act quickly and decisively to save Russia from ruin.

This may have been true, but the radical reforms which were introduced in January 1992 under the name of 'shock therapy' were not a success. Instead of a flourishing market economy, a curious mix of capitalism and Sovietism emerged. Although many economists expected the hangovers from the Soviet period to disappear as the disciplines of the market took hold, in fact the old ways have proved stubbornly resistant to change. Indeed, it is at least arguable that the transition is already over, and a distinctively post-Soviet economic system is in the process of forming in Russia. For market economies do not burst fully formed from nowhere in line with clear academic concepts and principles. On the contrary, economies, like individuals, are at least partly formed by culture, the past and the process of change itself.

Shock therapy transformed the economy in Poland into a market system. In Russia, however, it seemed less suited to local conditions. Russian political culture was different and more resistant to the idea of capitalism and the market. It was not enough for Yeltsin simply to lift the restrictions on private enterprise to produce an efficient, functioning market system. The communist ideology was more deeply ingrained in society than elsewhere in Eastern Europe. Transition in Russia was always going to be particularly difficult.

The Soviet economic system

The chief distinguishing characteristic of the Soviet economy was its explicitly political nature. Unlike in the market, there was no invisible hand in the Soviet

Union; no neutral arbiter which determined the behaviour of consumers and the economic units within the system (the firms, farms and service outlets). Market indicators – such as supply and demand, and profit and loss – were largely irrelevant to the authorities in Moscow. The realities of finite resources and consumer demands could not be ignored altogether, but state decisions and state commands were the primary dynamic in the Soviet system. The state owned and managed almost the entire economy. The state, therefore, made key decisions on investment, production, price and distribution. The state sent down commands in the form of output targets to individual economic units and they simply had to fulfil those targets to continue in operation. The quality and saleability of the product or service were definitely of secondary importance. As a result, many enterprises were producing poor-quality goods that nobody wanted at prices that were internationally uncompetitive. Such enterprises were able to survive in the Soviet Union, however, because of state subsidies and protectionist trade policies. The Soviet people wanted Japanese televisions and cars like everybody else, they simply could not get hold of them.

Unquestionably, the Soviet economy was highly inefficient and unproductive but it was a producers' rather than a consumers' market. The workforce remained largely supportive of the system because it offered regular pay, full employment and extensive, if rather basic, welfare facilities. It was also true to say that the situation was not equally bad in all sectors of the economy. The state set clear economic priorities, and from the days of the first five-year plan in 1928, the priorities for the Soviet state were heavy industry and the military. These sectors received the lion's share of state investment and many of the best workers, attracted by comparatively high wages and other privileges and perks of the job. As a result, these sectors performed relatively well. Soviet production of steel outstripped that of the West in the 1980s, while the USSR soon became an acknowledged military superpower after the war. However, in the modern era, iron and steel became comparatively less important as determinants of economic power and development. The most successful economies of the late twentieth century were those which concentrated more on high-technology products, consumer goods and services. It was precisely these sectors which the Soviet authorities had so grievously neglected throughout the Soviet period. Ideology and vested interests had prevented any significant shift in priorities until the mid-1980s.

When Gorbachev came to power in 1985, he inherited a declining economy. Growth in the period 1980–85 was probably zero (or very close to it), and, as the Soviet economy slowed, it was overtaken as the second biggest economy by Japan (Rutland, 1996, p. 156). Gorbachev favoured reform. He wanted to de-politicise management of the Soviet economy and, over time, to introduce certain market disciplines into the system. Thus, in January 1987, Gorbachev tried to encourage more foreign investment by allowing joint ventures on Russian soil; in July the state monopoly over ownership was broken when private retailing and service outlets (generally in the form of cooperatives) were legalised; the following year state monopoly control of foreign trade was ended. However, even these limited reforms met with much opposition from hard-liners. Declaring their opposition to speculation and the excesses of the market, hard-liners were able to impose caps on profits and higher taxes on the new cooperatives.

Gorbachev's most ambitious reform, however, was the Law on State Enterprises which came into operation in January 1988. It was a complex piece of legislation, but essentially it sought to devolve decision-making power down to the individual enterprise which, under Gorbachev's new scheme, was obliged to make a profit. The reform, officially known as 'cost-accounting', required a revolutionary shift in the way the Soviet economy operated. It was the centre-piece of Gorbachev's attempts to forge a 'third way' – somewhere between the centrally planned system and the free market. It was not a success. There were many reasons for its failure, but perhaps most important of all was the fact that prices continued to be set centrally. Without prices that reflected true value, profitability made no sense. As a result, state subsidies continued to flow to 'unprofitable' enterprises and the reforms did not fundamentally change the way enterprises operated. It simply disrupted the plan and made it operate at an even less optimal level.

As it became increasingly obvious that Gorbachev's economic reforms were not working, some economists began to contemplate more radical options. Thus, in 1990, Shatalin and Yavlinsky proposed the 500-day programme which called for the rapid conversion of the Soviet economy into a fully functioning market economy in about 16 months. Initially, Gorbachev seemed to approve the plan, but he was unable to deliver on it. His authority had been gravely weakened by earlier economic failures and he found he was unable to overcome growing opposition from more hardline colleagues, most particularly in the agricultural and defence-industry lobbies (see *Pravda*, 6 September 1990). When the 500-day plan lay still-born on the drawing board, and with no viable altern-ative on offer, the economy in 1990 began its precipitate decline, from which it has yet to recover.

As the economy declined, a political vacuum opened up at the centre. Regional officials and even enterprise directors took more power for themselves. This devolution of power was often interpreted by outsiders as a conscious move towards democracy and the market. This, however, was a rather simplistic view. Some regional elites took power in the name of reform, but the majority acted either to defend their locality from economic collapse or to shore up their own personal position. The effect of this extreme localism, which on occasion meant tariffs on trade between cities and regions, was sadly predictable – more short-ages and higher prices for the country as a whole while differentials between localities widened considerably (see Chapter 4).

The central authorities also moved close to bankruptcy as regions, enterprises and individuals refused to pay taxes. By 1991, the state's budget deficit had reached critical proportions at almost 30 per cent of GDP. In sum, the Soviet economy was in terminal crisis. As Peter Rutland noted, Gorbachev did not reform the Soviet economy; it simply collapsed (Rutland, 1996, p. 152).

The dash for the market 1992–93

Yeltsin believed that the only realistic way to rebuild Russia's shattered economy was through market reform, but he still faced considerable opposition inside Russia. Even those who supported the transition to the market – and this

СПРАВКА 6.1   Russian Prime Ministers

Yegor Gaidar, 1991–December 1992

Viktor Chernomyrdin, December 1992–March 1998

Sergei Kiriyenko, April 1998–September 1998

Yevgeni Primakov, September 1998–May 1999

Sergei Stepashin, May 1999–

included Yeltsin himself – had very little idea of what this actually involved in practical terms. Nevertheless, after his victory in the August coup of 1991, Yeltsin finally had the authority to press ahead with systemic economic reform and appointed Yegor Gaidar, a liberal economist, as acting Prime Minister (Russian Prime Ministers since 1991 are listed in Box 6.1). Gaidar realised, however, that the window of opportunity for reform would be open for only a brief moment. The communists and other hard-liners could be expected to gain ground if the economic decline continued. Therefore, Gaidar argued for shock therapy – the dash to the market – on political as well as economic grounds. It was necessary to dismantle the remains of communism as quickly as possible and to establish a new social base which would act as a vital support for the market system in the future. Although Yeltsin understood little of economics, he encouraged Gaidar to be ambitious and told his acting Prime Minister to make the reforms 'quick and beautiful' (Gaidar, 1996).

Shock therapy was launched in January 1992. In this first phase it contained two main strategies – first, the liberalisation of prices and foreign trade, and, second, financial stabilisation through tight monetary and fiscal policies. However, privatisation and other equally important issues, such as reforms of the commercial and bankruptcy laws, were put off to a later date. The influential reformist, Gennadi Yavlinsky (1992), was particularly critical of the delay in privatising state assets. He argued that the liberalisation of prices in monopoly conditions would fuel inflation without necessarily increasing production or improving productivity. Gaidar acknowledged the importance of privatisation as a means of breaking up monopolies and encouraging competition, but privatisation remained perhaps the most sensitive issue of all in post-Soviet Russia. Yeltsin, even at the height of his powers, expressed doubt that he could push through such policies in January 1992. In any case, privatisation was a huge and complex project which would take many years to complete. It was not something that could be done over night. Reform could not wait that long.

Nevertheless, shock therapy went ahead and 80 per cent of domestic prices were freed on 2 January, and trade was also greatly liberalised by the end of the month. These reforms had an immediate impact. Goods found their way back on to the shelves but, as Yavlinsky had predicted, at a cost. Inflation soared as managers put up prices to maximise their profits (see Fig. 6.1). Investment collapsed, while industrial and agricultural production fell to less than half their pre-reform levels over the period 1992–96 (*Russian Economic Trends*, 1995,

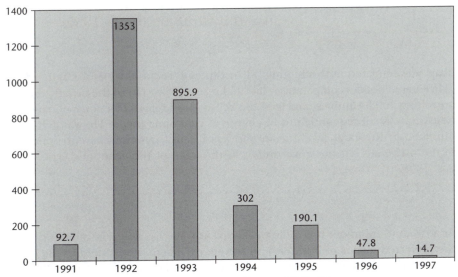

Figure 6.1   Russian inflation, percentage yearly rate, 1991–95
Source: World Economic Outlook May 1998, IMF, Washington, DC

pp. 113 and 116). Shock therapy had a truly devastating impact on the vast majority of Russian people: annual per capita income dropped from $4 110 in 1990 to $2 650 in 1994 (World Bank, 1996, p. 21), and the consumption of goods and services fell by a third from 1991 to 1995 (*Russian Economic Trends*, 1995, p. 117). Inflation wiped out savings overnight as over a third of Russian people were designated officially to be living below the poverty line in 1994 – triple the number at the time of shock therapy's launch two years earlier (*Russian Review*, 21 February 1994). A new class of poor had been created. Those on fixed incomes, such as pensioners and public sector workers, suffered the most. Although adjustments have to be made for the relative costs of living, some teachers and health service workers often found themselves on wages the equivalent of US$10 a month. In the circumstances, it was scarcely surprising that many public sector workers sought alternative employment or took second jobs to supplement their meagre incomes.

The initial surge in inflation after the introduction of shock therapy had been expected, but reformers were disturbed that prices did not respond more quickly to the disciplines of the market. Indeed, inflation became a major obstacle to economic recovery, varying between 10 and 30 per cent per month for the first three years of market reform (see Fig. 6.1). Inflation persisted within the system for some of the following reasons:

● the weakening of tight monetary policy
● high wage rises
● continued state subsidies to unprofitable enterprises
● the slow progress in breaking up monopoly businesses
● political opposition to the market, especially from the central bank and parliament.

БИОГРАФИЯ 6.1   Anatoli Chubais (born 1955)

Chubais was educated at the Leningrad Institute of Technology and Engineering. He entered politics comparatively late and rose rapidly to head the privatisation reforms from 1992. Chubais managed the Yeltsin presidential election campaign in 1996 and was subsequently put in charge of economic policy. He was generally disliked in Russia as a politician and has faced accusations of corruption from the press. He left the government in the wake of the economic crisis of August 1998.

As a result of inflation, the ruble weakened and the US dollar became for many the preferred means of business and private exchange. Investment in the economy remained weak as investors feared the volatility of the new Russian market. A Russian analyst, Tabata (1997, p. 565), estimated that capital flight from Russia in the period 1992–95 reached $30 billion per annum as potential investors sought less risky investment opportunities in the West. As a result, manufacturing slumped, while speculators, financiers and criminals made some big profits.

The difficult issue of privatisation was finally taken up by the liberal reformer, Anatoli Chubais, when a voucher scheme was set up in the summer of 1992. Vouchers were given out free to the Russian people in October and they were redeemable (up to the middle of 1994) for shares in companies which came up for privatisation over the period. The most popular privatisation scheme allowed management and workers to gain control of their businesses through the purchase of up to 51 per cent of a company's equity. Nevertheless, to bring some capital into the business, at least half of the investment had to be paid in currency not vouchers. Under this scheme, managers with access to some capital were in an ideal position to ensure effective control of their enterprises. The workforce also tended to support such buy-outs, since the managers usually offered job security and continued welfare benefits which remained of vital importance for most workers (see Chapter 8). Outsiders, on the other hand, were an unknown quantity who could be expected to want to maximise profits. This was wholly commendable in so far as it led to more productive work practices, but many workers feared for their jobs and believed such privatisation, in practice, would involve little more than asset stripping. As a result, management buy-outs became the most common form of privatisation in Russia. In 1993, 78 per cent of private firms were the result of insider buy-outs, and the figure had only dropped to 58 per cent by the end of 1996 (Fortescue, 1998, pp. 2–3).

The main aim of voucher privatisation was to create a large class of Russian shareholders committed to the idea of market reform. The scheme may have fulfilled this essentially political aim – many former communist bosses made millions from privatisation – but in economic terms it was far less successful. For the scheme brought little new capital into the enterprise, and in the case

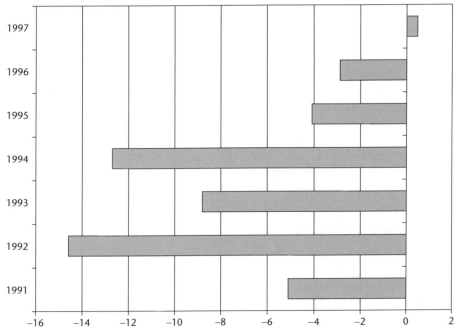

Figure 6.2   Russian GDP yearly growth 1991–97

Source: *World Economic Outlook May 1998*, IMF, Washington, DC

of management and worker buy-outs little in the way of new management skills or techniques. In fact, most managers of newly privatised firms kept their promise to the workforce and initiated little in the way of rationalisation or the restructuring of their businesses. Although this was welcomed by the workers, it meant that many unprofitable firms continued to operate. This was possible because managers, the reforms notwithstanding, still expected the state to cover their debts and to ward off any threat of bankruptcy through subsidies. The state, fearful of the social consequences of mass unemployment, generally obliged, at least until the end of 1993.

In most respects, the economic reforms of 1992–93 can be viewed as an abysmal failure. Inflation became locked into the system, investment was weak, real wages fell and the economy continued to decline until at least 1997 (see Fig. 6.2). The state also faced a major fiscal crisis, largely because of its failure to collect taxes. However, shock therapy was, as stated earlier, also a political project. In this respect, it could be interpreted more positively. In this early phase of reform, the people tended to be more supportive of the changes than some of the political institutions in Russia. Thus, while the Russian parliament was attempting to stymy Gaidar's reform programme, the people voted in favour of their continuation in a referendum in April 1993 (see Chapter 2). Furthermore, a small, but influential, group of the 'new rich' was beginning to form in Russia which made any return to the state-run command economy far less likely.

The new rich favoured the market, but they were not necessarily committed to all its values. Many, for example, were reluctant to allow greater competition into the system – either in the form of anti-monopoly legislation or through a relaxation of the regulations on imports. The new rich in 1992–93 had largely gained their position through their monopoly dominance of the market and there was little incentive for them to allow this to change. Economic reform, therefore, legalised private enterprise; it allowed a few people to become rich (and a greater number to become very poor), but it did not, however, create much of a competitive market, nor did it create a clearly regulated market. Commercial law, where it existed at all, went largely unobserved. As debts were often unpaid, it was scarcely surprising that crime and corruption became endemic to the system. Indeed, mafia gangs began to fulfil a function of sorts, becoming for many the best (and sometimes the only) means of extracting money from debtors (see Chapter 7).

Russian reform 1994–97

The new structure

The economic situation continued to deteriorate through 1994. In a major financial crisis in October, the ruble lost 27 per cent of its value in a single day. As a result, three government ministers resigned along with the head of the Central Bank, Viktor Gerashchenko, who had been a leading proponent of loose money. Anatoli Chubais, the last remaining member of Gaidar's reform team still in government, was placed in charge of macro-economic policy. Despite ongoing battles with the Duma over financial policy and continuing difficulties in collecting tax, Viktor Chernomyrdin, who had been elected as Prime Minister in December 1992, was able to bring inflation more under control. In March 1995, inflation fell below 10 per cent per month, and by August it was below 5 per cent (*Goskomstat*, 1995, p. 44). Many hoped that this signified an end to the struggle over the stabilisation of the economy.

However, the stabilisation was in most senses illusory. Since tax avoidance was still a major problem, the only way for the state to cut the budget deficit, which remained high, was through cuts in state spending. Health, education and defence were hard hit by such measures and subsidies to private enterprises were also cut. However, private industry tended to redirect their debts on to workers and creditors by refusing to pay debts and wages. By early 1998, it was estimated that only 25 per cent of the Russian workforce was being paid in full and on time (Hutchison, 1998). Thus, in the emerging market in Russia, bankrupt enterprises continued to operate and unpaid workers continued to turn up for work – to qualify for certain welfare benefits linked to the workplace (see Chapter 8). Market signals continued to be ignored. Faced with the prospect of the non-payment of bills, many firms either demanded cash up front or reverted to some kind of barter as a means of exchange. In agriculture, things were particularly bad. Agriculture had been little affected by privatisation. Farm labourers were poor and generally unable to afford buy-outs – or even to buy the necessary fuel or machinery to make their farms operational and more productive. As agricultural production slumped, the resultant food shortages forced town dwellers to rely on their own produce grown on their private plots and allotments.

Cash payment, barter and subsistence farming were all types of economic activity which were beyond the control and supervision of the state. For although money had regained much of its economic meaning since the economic reforms – it had become a more accurate measure of value – a large part of the Russian economy was, in effect, operating outside the official money economy. What had, in fact, emerged by 1997 was an economy split into three different tiers. At the first tier was an economy which was acting rationally according to the market signals received, but was generally operating outside the official money economy. As a result, it had links with the criminal underworld and was able to avoid taxes and state regulation. This economy was mainly concerned with trade and services. The second tier was big business which was unable to act outside the official economy owing to its sheer size and visibility in the market. This tier was largely engaged in legal market activity although it sought to manipulate the market to its own advantage and to use its economic power to influence the government's economic policy. Finally, there was the Soviet-style economy – composed mainly of old industries, such as coal and steel, which had been privatised but were often unprofitable. The style of management at this tier had changed little since communist days. The main aim of such managers was simply to survive in the new post-Soviet conditions. This had been largely achieved through state subsidies and the non-payment of wages, taxes and bills.

This three-tiered economy has led to enormous problems in the economy as a whole. These different tiers have acted as a drag on each other and slowed down overall economic recovery. The reformers wish to encourage the legal official economy, but divisions within the political and business elites have prevented the introduction and implementation of effective legislation.

Thus, much of the Russian economy operates in an essentially covert way. Businesses either are determined to avoid the attention of the state (to avoid taxes and because of their links with the criminal underworld) or do so more inadvertently as a consequence of barter, cash payments and subsistence farming. The existence of this massive shadow economy – some estimates suggest it makes up either a half or a quarter of the total economy (see Neshchadin, 1997; Kraynii, 1997) – makes it almost impossible to collate reliable statistics (Koen, 1996; Voronkov, 1998). However, some commentators believe that the size of the shadow economy suggests that the actual performance of the Russian economy is somewhat better than the official figures suggest. In particular, the official figures underestimate the rise in the service industry (see Fig. 6.3) – an important part of the shadow economy – and agriculture, since perhaps 43 per cent of food is now grown privately on small allotments for personal consumption (Kuddo, 1997, p. 21).

All of which does not mean that official statistics serve no purpose at all. They do reveal trends within the economy, but they must always be treated with extreme caution. The Russian economy is undoubtedly in crisis, but the official figure indicating a 41 per cent drop in GNP between 1990 and 1997 may be something of an exaggeration. Per capita estimates also need to be adjusted to take account of factors such as relatively low housing costs, access to private allotments, welfare benefits from work and second jobs which are often undisclosed to the state.

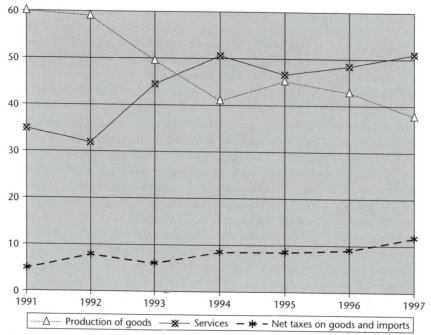

Figure 6.3　Russian GDP by sector 1991–97

Source: Statisticheskoe obozrenne Goskomstat Moscow, selected edition 1993–97, FIU Intelligence Reports – Russia

The new actors

No significant Western-style middle class has emerged in Russia yet. This is a serious omission, for a middle class which is law abiding and relatively secure economically is seen as vital by most commentators as a support for the market system. In fact, the only significant pro-market group to emerge since 1992 is the super-rich who were able to consolidate their vast wealth during the second wave of privatisation from late 1994. During this period (1994–97), new assets came up for sale, such as metal, energy and communication businesses, which, unlike many enterprises in the first wave, had real value both on the domestic and international market. Voucher privatisation ended in June 1994, so these assets had to be bought with real money. However, the market price for such businesses was still relatively low owing to a lack of capital in the country. The government could have sought to maximise its revenues through seeking foreign investment or it could have gone for a slower form of privatisation – for example, by breaking up some of the bigger conglomerates into smaller, more affordable units. Both these options, however, were deemed politically unacceptable. On the one hand, the government was vulnerable to the accusation from Russian nationalists of selling off national assets, while, on the other, the government was desperate for a quick sale to help to fund its burgeoning budget deficit.

The only Russians with money were millionaires such as Boris Berezovsky, Vladimir Potanin and Vladimir Gusinsky. They had made windfall gains in the early days of privatisation which allowed them to establish bases in banking and the mass media. During the second wave of privatisation from 1994, they began to move into positions of control and influence over hugely profitable firms with major export earnings. Moreover, they were able to acquire these valuable assets at relatively low prices. The shares for loans scheme, for example, which began in October 1995, was a particularly cheap source of wealth transfer for these tycoons. Desperate for revenue, the government handed over assets not for cash but as security for loans. When the loans were not re-paid, the firms were privatised at bargain basement prices. Thus, Berezovsky secured the ninth largest oil concern in Russia, *Sibneft*, for just $100 million, a fraction of its worth; Vladimir Potanin, founder of the country's largest private bank, *Uneximbank*, bought *Norlisk Nikel*, which produces 20 per cent of the world's nickel and more than 40 per cent of its platinum group metals, for a mere $130 million. He also paid only $130 million for a 51 per cent share of *Sidanco*, Russia's fourth largest oil company (*Transition*, 1997, pp. 11–12). These men made vast sums of money out of these privatisations. Unlike some of the earlier beneficiaries of privatisation, they were not dependent on political connections for their position. On the contrary, their vast wealth gave them considerable influence over the political elite in Russia. They bought into media operations to set the political agenda in Russia and also bankrolled favoured candidates in elections. Berezovsky, for example, became a key backer for Yeltsin in his presidential campaign in 1996 (see Box 6.2).

There are now three main groups constituting the new elite in Russia, corresponding roughly to the three-tiered economy referred to earlier. The first group was the old *nomenklatura*, whose power remained rooted in the state, and their influence was largely political and a result of their position within the state. The second group, which could be called 'early *nomenklatura* capitalists', possessed wealth through the ownership of private businesses, but still relied for their economic survival on their contacts with the political elite. They were the opportunists who made money from the first wave of privatisation, but were generally unable to transform their often unproductive assets into profitable enterprises and, therefore, depended to a greater or lesser extent on state subsidies. The 'early *nomenklatura* capitalists' are now the group which looks most vulnerable in the new conditions in Russia. Finally, there are the 'new capitalists'. This new group has accumulated vast wealth owing to its monopoly position in the Russian economy. This wealth has translated into political power, and the 'new capitalists' have shown themselves able to influence government policy to their own advantage on a number of policy areas, including taxation, privatisation, foreign trade and commercial law.

However, the old and new *nomenklatura* have made efforts recently to try to contain the growing power of the new capitalists. Therefore, some efforts have been made to regain some political control over the whole privatisation process. For example, the government in 1996 decided to limit private shares in 'strategic industries' to 49 per cent. However, this has not prevented their effective control by single individuals. Berezovsky, for example, has effective control over a number of companies, such as Russian Public Television (ORT), without being a majority shareholder, largely because he has the wealth to offer managing

СПРАВКА 6.2   **The rule of the seven bankers (*Semibankirshchina*)**

After President Yeltsin's re-election in 1996, Boris Berezovsky, worth an estimated US$2 billion, gave an interview to London's Financial Times in late October of that year. In it, he referred to seven prominent new Russians who ran seven of the major banks and credited them with co-operating to bankroll and master-mind Yeltsin's presidential campaign. Moreover, he made an even more exaggerated claim that between them they controlled more than 50 per cent of the Russian GDP.

The political power of the seven bankers seemed to grow in the autumn of 1996 as Berezovsky was appointed to the Security Council and Vladimir Potanin, head of *Uneximbank*, and probably the richest of all, ascended to a deputy Prime Ministership. However, by mid-1997, battles for influence had broken out among the bankers, principally around the contest for new privatisation prizes in telecommunications and oil. They began trading insults and accusations through their different media outlets against each other and against their various proteges and allies within the political system.

Thus, by November 1997, when Berezovsky was removed from the Security Council, the unity of the seven bankers had obviously been sacrificed in the battle for the spoils of further privatisation. While the term 'oligarchs' continued as a shorthand description for the powerful businessmen clustered in alliances with various political figures such as Yuri Luzhkov, Ivan Rybkin and Viktor Chernomyrdin, the notion of collective rule that *Semibankirshchina* conjured up no longer existed. It was replaced in many Russian minds with a metaphor of absolutist court politics – where various economic robber barons (the 'oligarchs') clustered around an enfeebled monarch (President Yeltsin) and intrigued against each other for the spoils of the kingdom.

directors irresistibly high loyalty bonuses. Even the state as part-owner is unable to match such sweeteners. Another example took place on 29 September 1997 when the Moscow Arbitration Court ruled that the 41 per cent share acquired in the chemical plant, *Cherepovets Azot*, by *Uneximbank* had to be returned to the government since the investment money had been illegally channelled into an offshore bank (*RFE/RL Daily Report*, 3 October 1997).

However, moves such as these did little to halt the general direction of privatisation in Russia. By 1996, 70 per cent of all firms were in private hands and the new super-rich had already acquired immense, independent power. The government was unable (and, in practice, often unwilling) to do anything about it.

Conclusion

As 1997 drew to a close, the economic situation in Russia looked a little brighter. Inflation had decreased to under 15 per cent for the year and positive growth (albeit slow) was registered for the first time since 1989. However, even then, it was clear that problems still existed. The budget revenue was 48 per cent behind target and 30 per cent of enterprises owed money to the state. In addition, there were debts to ordinary workers in February 1998 equivalent to US$8.9 billion (Economist Intelligence Unit, 1998b, p. 33). The underlying weaknesses of Russia's three-tiered economy were starkly revealed by the crisis of August 1998. For a couple of years, the government had been able to hide many of the country's economic problems through the profits from the energy industry and other natural resources – 40 per cent of all export revenue in Russia came from mineral fuels in 1997 (Economist Intelligence Unit, 1998a, p. 25), but this all changed when the Asian crisis led to cuts in energy prices and the subsequent collapse in confidence in the Russian economy. After raised hopes in 1996–97, the Russian economy by the end of summer 1998 had fallen 8.2 per cent on the previous year. Interest rates remained high (60 per cent) as the ruble continued to fall against the US dollar.

The new Prime Minister, Yevgeni Primakov, was left to pick up the pieces. It proved difficult to construct a government to deal with the economic crisis. Disaffection was growing in the country. Primakov promised to print money to pay off the backlog in wages, but the debt mountain had grown so high that any attempt to carry out the policy was bound to fuel inflation. The West was opposed to any such change in direction, but in fact Primakov was able to stabilise the economy and restore at least some level of confidence. However, this was all threatened once again when Yeltsin sacked his Prime Minister in May 1999 for what appeared to be political rather than economic reasons.

In sum, a market of sorts has been created in Russia, but it is not as yet self-sustaining. There are social supports for reform, but many political and even business elites remain suspicious of the market. There is certainly little support for the classical liberal market envisaged by Yegor Gaidar when he launched shock therapy back in January 1992. The public has also lost its early enthusiasm for change. The grinding poverty of the vast majority of Russians shows no sign of ending. The hopes for growth have been dashed by the August 1998 crisis. Yeltsin is clearly coming to the end of his time in office. He is ill and has no new ideas for the future. The hybrid, three-tiered economy lurches from crisis to crisis. It is far from clear that Russia will be able to cast off its Soviet past and create a fully functioning market economy anytime soon.

References

Economist Intelligence Unit 1998a *Country Profile: Russia 1998–99*, Economist, London.

Economist Intelligence Unit 1998b *Country Report: Russia Second Quarter 1998*, Economist, London.

Fortescue S 1998 Privatisation, Corporate Governance and Enterprise Performance in Russia, *Russian and Euro-Asian Bulletin*, Vol. 7, No. 5, pp. 1–10.

Gaidar Y 1996 *Public Lecture at the University of Melbourne*, 3 April.

Goskomstat 1995 *Statisticheskoe Obozrenie (Current Statistical Survey)*, p. 10.

Hutchison J 1998 Russia: What's Up, What's Down, What's Left?, *The San Francisco Flier*, 12 February.

Koen V 1996 Russian Macroeconomic Data: Existence, Access, Interpretation, *Communist Economies and Economic Transformation*, Vol. 8, No. 3, pp. 321–33.

Krayniy V 1997 Transformations: The Shadow Economy Comes into the Light, *Argumenty i fakty*, June 2–8.

Kuddo A 1997 Peculiarities of Russia's Employment Statistics, *Transition*, Vol. 8, No. 4, p. 21.

Neshchadin A 1997 The Shadow Economy: Today and Tomorrow, *Executive and Legislative Newsletter*, May.

Rutland P 1996 The Rocky Road From Plan To Market, in White S, Pravda A and Gitelman Z (eds), *Developments in Russian and Post-Soviet Politics*, Macmillan, Houndsmill.

Tabata S 1997 The Investment Crisis in Russia: A Research Report, *Post-Soviet Geography and Economics*, Vol. 38, No. 9, pp. 558–66.

Voronkov V 1998 The Corruption of Statistics, *Transitions*, Vol. 5, No. 3, pp. 40–5.

Yavlinsky G 1992 Spring 1992 Reforms in Russia, *Moscow News*, pp. 21–2.

Further reading

Aslund A 1995 *How Russia Became a Market Economy*, Brookings Institution, Washington, DC

Rutland P 1996 The Rocky Road From Plan To Market, in White S, Pravda A and Gitelman Z, *Developments in Russian and Post-Soviet Politics*, Macmillan, Houndsmill.

A web page for business and economic reports is
http://www.mosinfo.ru:8080/news/ber/index.html

7 Crime, corruption and the law

Mark Galeotti

Introduction

Russia is a country of long and rich traditions: of literature, of faith, of absolutism and also of crime. Successive Tsars and then General Secretaries battled against corruption within the state bureaucracy, just as the life of the peasant and, later, worker often revolved around the black economy and lynch law. Since the collapse of the USSR, however, crime in Russia and, especially, the Russian '*mafiya*' (mafia) have become a hot political issue, both at home and across the globe. In part, this is because it is a sexy topic for journalists to cover. In part, it reflects continuing amazement that such a powerful criminal community can emerge so quickly from such a controlled society (in fact, it was there all along, but largely hidden behind the Party). Russian criminals have quickly replaced Soviet tanks as a convenient enemy figure, to justify security budgets and even to fuel the plots of James Bond movies (Williams, 1996).

None of this can detract from the seriousness of the present criminal crisis gripping Russia. The raw statistics are terrifying: the crime rate may be stabilising, but it is still up by fully a third from 10 years ago, 75 per cent of all police officers think the battle against criminality is 'already lost' and the *mafiya* extorts protection money from up to 80 per cent of all businesses (Serio, 1992, p. 55; ITAR-TASS, 13 October 1997; Williams, 1997, p. 56). The general importance of the actual and potential 'criminalisation' of Russia comes down to five main issues:

1. *It weakens the moral authority and legitimacy of the state.* If the government appears to be unable to protect the rights, property and even lives of its citizens, it looks powerless. This is one reason why so many people are prepared to pay off the *mafiya*.

2. *It undermines democracy.* Democracy is still very new to Russia and, in the light of the above, it is perhaps hardly surprising that already too many people now link democracy with lawlessness and insecurity. This helps to explain the appeal of figures such as the maverick general-turned-politician Alexander Lebed or even the ultra-nationalist Vladimir Zhirinovsky, who promise to restore law and order to the streets. This is hardly helped by the fact that even many within the government see democracy and law enforcement as an 'either/or' choice. One worrying example was Presidential Decree 1226, 'On Urgent Measures to Protect the Population

Against Banditry and Other Manifestations of Organised Crime', pushed through in 1994. The then security chief, Sergei Stepashin, frankly admitted that it was a return to practices of the Soviet era. He added that he was 'all for the violation of human rights, if the person is a bandit or criminal' (ITAR-TASS News Agency, 9 November 1994).

3. *It weakens the state's actual resources.* Not only is policing an unruly country expensive, it also has a more direct effect on the treasury. Tax evasion, capital flight (sending money abroad without paying duties on it), embezzlement of state funds and similar crimes are rife. They have contributed to the crisis of the Russian budget, where even the establishment of an armed paramilitary Tax Police has not helped much. A state cannot function without money.

4. *It distorts the shift to a market economy.* Organised crime has taken advantage of the opportunities offered by the move from state control of the economy – especially privatisation – but it then twists them to its own ends. It creates and protects artificial monopolies in defiance of the market using violence and political clout to eliminate competitors. It forces business to spend excessive amounts (30–40 per cent of profits, according to some) on security. Furthermore, just as criminality undermines the very idea of democracy, so too does this perpetuate the dangerous idea that capitalism is just about making money, whatever it takes. In one opinion poll, only 5 per cent of Russians thought that honesty, ability and hard work were the way to prosperity: 44 per cent cited illegal speculation and 20 per cent money-laundering (Interfax News Agency, 12 July 1995).

5. *It threatens Russia's political and economic integration with the rest of the world.* There is a danger that the old cold war of communism versus capitalism is being replaced with a new one, in which the Russians are treated as if they are all frauds and criminals. Given the extent to which the Russian *mafiya* has penetrated the country's economic and even political system, this is perhaps understandable. However, it does mean that Russians are beginning to feel discriminated against and resentful. It is also an obstacle to foreign investment which would help to rebuild the country.

Illegality and disorder: a tradition

Russia has long been prone to unruliness, unrest, disorder and criminality (Chalidze, 1977, pp. 4–19). In the Tsarist era, the state largely left the peasants to police themselves through the village lynch law known as *samosud*, 'self-judging' (Frierson, 1987). This rough-and-ready form of social control was essentially based on the interests of the community. Theft from outsiders or from crown lands, for example, was accepted, but crimes which threatened the survival or social order of the village were dealt with harshly. Lesser offences resulted in public humiliation and the payment of fines (usually in the form of vodka for the village elders!), the most serious – such as horse-theft – in particularly painful and inventive deaths, typically involving sharpened, carved wooden spikes. The state did not like the idea of peasants policing themselves (especially given their tolerance for crimes against the state, such as tax dodging), but lacked the legitimacy and the officers to enforce its own writ more effectively.

Traditional forms of social control had little authority or relevance in the late nineteenth century's growing cities and their working-class slums such as St Petersburg's infamous Haymarket or the Moscow *Khitrovka* (Lincoln, 1993, pp. 123–8). There, the state's police had little authority, and, when they did venture into these rookeries, they went mob handed and fully armed (Thurston, 1980; Weissman, 1985). Furthermore, the cities were also the playgrounds of Russia's distinctive professional criminals, the members of the so-called *Vorovskoi mir* or 'Thieves' World' (Chalidze, 1977, pp. 33–64). This was not a criminal organisation so much as a criminal culture, whose members accepted a harsh code which set them apart from the rest of society. Most criminals were not members of this *Vorovskoi mir*, but it was to prove an institution able to evolve as Russia changed and became a powerful criminal force in the twentieth century.

Vorovskoi mir

The culture of the 'Thieves' World' was built around a rejection of the outside world and its own hierarchy and values (Glazov, 1976, pp. 144–50). Its strength is perhaps best illustrated by the fact that it had its own secret language, *fenya*, which incorporated words from beggars' slang, Yiddish, Romany, German and a number of other sources. It even had a visual language in the form of tattoos, whereby criminals would boast of their times in prison (a tattoo of a traditional Russian church on the back, for example, would gain one onion-domed tower for every term served in jail), their crimes, even their views. At a time when the Russian language itself was still fragmented into countless local dialects, criminals from across the country, who could hardly speak to each other, would still be able to understand the 'code' of each others' tattoos (see below).

They had a strict code to live by (Serio and Razinkin, 1995). This changed in detail but its main elements were:

- Never work within 'normal' society or have a family.
- Never serve or co-operate with the state.
- Accept the discipline and culture of the *Vorovskoi mir*.

- Look after the rest of the gang, giving money to the collective kitty (*obshchak*), teaching novice thieves the tricks of the trade and the like.

The code was enforced by the 'godfathers' of the 'Thieves' World', the *Vory v zakone* ('Thieves-within-the-Code' – the literal but misleading translation is 'Thieves-within-the-Law'). These *Vory* (thieves or criminals) were respected leaders of the criminal community, chosen by other *Vory* for their adherence to the code, their exploits and their authority. Nevertheless, as is discussed below, their culture also changed over time.

Imperial and Soviet corruption

In its own way, illegality was just as rife among the elite. There, corruption was the norm. Indeed, the low salaries paid to civil servants meant that it was in effect *expected* that they would supplement their income by *kormlenie*, 'feeding' off their jobs, whether accepting bribes, running private businesses as a sideline or appropriating to themselves state assets (Pipes, 1974, pp. 282–4; Clark, 1993, pp. 31–35).

Soviet Russia thus inherited a powerful criminal legacy and, when Bolshevik idealism met this culture of illegality, it was the latter which won. The Communist Party became, over time, just as corrupt and self-serving as the Tsarist bureaucracy. If anything, the scope for corruption increased given the greater control the Party exerted over every aspect of the economy and day-to-day life. Furthermore, the party found itself actively promoting certain forms of crime and criminal groupings for its own reasons. In order to bypass the bottlenecks and shortages created by the attempt to plan the economy centrally, for instance, a factory manager would turn to a *tolkach*, a 'fixer', who would be able to find the necessary spare parts, raw materials or whatever else was needed to meet the demands of the centre (Berliner, 1954). The Kremlin realised this, but accepted it in the name of efficiency: as Stalin himself put it, 'the victors of production are not judged'. The only real crime was not to meet the output targets set by Moscow.

Crime, Soviet style

Perhaps more strikingly, the massive expansion of the Gulag prison camp system during Stalin's reign of terror in the 1930s and 1940s led to increasing collaboration between the state and the *Vorovskoi mir*. While Stalin was sending millions of Soviet citizens into the Gulags, criminals were offered perks and positions of authority so long as they kept the political prisoners in line. Many were tempted to do this, thus breaking the code against collaboration. In criminal slang, they became *suki*, 'bitches' or 'scabs.' Then, during the Second World War, many others were conscripted or voluntarily joined the army to defend their motherland. To the purists, this was also collaboration, and when they were returned to the camps after the war, they also found themselves labelled *suki*. The result was the so-called 'Scabs' War', which raged through the Gulag system in the late 1940s and early 1950s (Glazov, 1976, pp. 152–5). An unknown number of criminals died, but eventually, not least thanks to the support of the authorities, the 'scabs' won. When, after Stalin's death in 1953, the Gulag system began to be run down, they were released into the wider *Vorovskoi mir* of the USSR. Their 'revised' code prevailed. With the taboo against collaboration lifted, a new breed of criminal emerged, willing to work with an increasingly corrupt party bureaucracy for mutual advantage (Vaksberg, 1991; Gurov, 1995).

In order to survive despite both the pressures of daily life and the inefficiencies of the economy, Soviet citizens themselves turned to crime, even if only the ubiquitous black market. In Robert Sharlet's vivid words, 'beneath a planned environment of acute and persistent scarcity, nearly everyone steals goods from the state, sells one's services on the side or, if neither is possible, at least "steals time" on the job' (Sharlet, 1984, p. 135). The *militsiya* (police) were no exception to this. A traffic police officer would, for example, routinely ignore a speeding offence if the driver had conveniently left a five ruble note folded in his or her driving licence. More generally, in a manner reminiscent of the Tsarist government's 'hands-off' approach to rural policing, the *militsiya* maintained overall order, but often by closing a blind eye to much low-level criminal activity, from black marketeering to absenteeism from work. After all, until 1981 the state itself also adopted a similar approach for ideological reasons. Crime simply should not exist in a mature socialist state, and so the Kremlin simply pretended it was falling.

The reason for this rather lengthy historical detour is that it is important to understand just how far Russia has for centuries operated under two sets of rules, the 'official' laws and the actual way the country operated (Lovell *et al.*, 1999). Russia's elites have become used to (mis)using their positions for personal gain, and the Russian people are as accustomed to being ruled by a corrupt clique and themselves breaking the law on their own behalf, and for their friends and families. Concepts such as respect for authority, a belief in the impartiality of the courts and the law and even faith in the police have been and still are largely absent.

The crisis of the law

The last years of the Soviet Union and the birth of the new Russia saw a dramatic collapse of law and order. As communism lost its final shreds of legitimacy and the economy ground to a halt, the black market came into its own. With the party no longer able to control it, the *mafiya* also emerged into the open to take advantage of the new opportunities available. The police were increasingly underfunded and demoralised, often sucked into an unwelcome role fighting nationalist unrest (Galeotti, 1993). Furthermore, public awareness and fear of crime rose even more rapidly, fuelled by lurid tales in a newly liberated press enjoying to the full its ability to break the old taboos.

Policing the new Russia

Through revolutions and coups, Russia's Ministry of Internal Affairs (MVD) has almost uniquely kept the same name since Tsarist times. Unfortunately, it has also often proved slow and reluctant to evolve to keep up with changing times and challenges. Today's MVD is thus strikingly similar to its Soviet-era counterpart. In most Western societies, there is a distinction between the politicians and civil servants in the equivalent ministry (the Home Office in Britain, the Justice Department in the USA) who establish the overall political line and the police officers who carry it out. The minister of the MVD and all his deputies are police generals and it is closer to a disciplined, military style operation. The chain of command runs down from the central ministry in Moscow through regional ministries (in the constituent republics of the Russian Federation) and local police commands (Galeotti, 1997b).

The police can be broadly broken down into four main types. There are the Local Inspectors, who carry out a form of community-based policing. The Patrol-Guard Service operates car and foot patrols. There are the usual plain-clothes detectives. There is also an increasing paramilitary component. As crime becomes more powerful and violent, not only are all Russian police turning to firepower instead of finesse (even traffic police often carry submachine guns) but heavily armed SWAT-type units have grown. The most notable of these are the 'black berets' of the Special Designation Police Units (OMON), who have acquired notoriety for their often brutal tactics. There is also a fifth type, halfway between the police officer and the private security guard: some regions and cities (most notably Moscow) have begun establishing their own 'Municipal Police' forces. They operate alongside their regular counterparts but separately from them, and tend to be better paid and better equipped, even if not much more respected or effective.

The *militsioner* (police officer) is typically male, of below-average education, with a respectable if not glittering police record, who signed up in his early twenties. Female officers make up around 15 per cent of the total, and are still far from being treated as equals, being assigned disproportionately to traffic and investigations work and dealing with minors. The majority of *militsionery* are married, and all have seen their standard of living decline steadily since the collapse of the Soviet Union. A normal police officer receives a salary broadly comparable with that of a municipal bus driver, even while facing very real danger: 201 officers were killed on duty in 1994, 248 in 1995, 263 in 1996 and 297 in 1997 (ITAR-TASS, 6 January 1998). In this context, it is hardly surprising that corruption is so widespread (see Box 7.1).

Given this poisonous legacy described in the last section, it was inevitable that post-Soviet Russia would suffer a continued crisis of policing. The list of problems facing the Ministry of Internal Affairs (MVD) is intimidating:

● *A lack of resources.* The continuing crisis of the Russian budget has hit the MVD hard. Policing has always had a lower priority than defence and political policing (Galeotti, 1993) and, although the post-Soviet government has tried to even the balance, this has not been easy. By 1998, the budget was still below what the MVD described as its 'operational minimum' and three-quarters of all funds received were being swallowed up by salaries and minimal upkeep. There simply is too little money for modernisation,

СПРАВКА 7.1 **A modern odyssey**

General Anatoli Kulikov, Russia's hard-line Interior Minister between 1995 and 1998, was especially concerned about corruption within the force – at various times he estimated that between 75 per cent and 90 per cent of officers took bribes. Shortly after his appointment, he secretly sent a truckload of vodka 700 kilometres across southern Russia as a test. It was stopped by police 24 times – and on 22 of them, the driver was asked for a bribe. Along the whole journey, the driver paid out a total of 2.16 million rubles (just over $500). As a result, Kulikov launched his 'Operation Clean Hands' anti-corruption campaign. Although this campaign was originally intended as a 'short, sharp shock', it has developed into a permanent institution with a special department, the Internal Security Directorate, established to run it, suggesting that corruption is deeply rooted in the MVD.

retraining or often even basic operations. In some cities, patrols have had to be limited because of a lack of petrol! As a result, the main 'front-line' police units are generally 30 per cent under-staffed, while in some regions this is as high as 70 per cent (MVD, 1997, p. 18).

- *A lack of new ideas.* Part of the problem is precisely that all Russia's top police officers are products of the Soviet era and have trouble coming to terms with both new approaches and the new demands of both government and society. Despite suggestions that it adopt a more 'community-based' approach, for example, the MVD continues to use confrontational paramilitary tactics which as often alienate the public the police are meant to protect.

- *A lack of public faith.* Public approval for and faith in the police is dangerously low: polls showed it at 40 per cent in 1996 (MVD, 1997, p. 1) and down to 34 per cent in 1997 (Galeotti, 1997b, p. 4). This is, of course, a vicious circle: without public support, policing is all the harder, and less likely to achieve the results which could increase public support.

The legal and moral vacuum

Ultimately, however, no police force can be more effective than the legal system it is there to uphold. The legal system is still half way through a messy transition as it amends and replaces Soviet-era laws and tries to introduce new ones more in keeping with the new Russia's aspirations to become a stable, democratic mixed economy. This is particularly true in the field of property law and rights (Varese, 1996b, pp. 16–33). The courts are backlogged and tangled in often contradictory and half-formed laws, and thus, for example, the *mafiya* may be the only means of recovering a debt or enforcing a contract.

СПРАВКА 7.2   **Private security = public insecurity?**

A real growth sector in Russia has been the private security industry (PSI). This has expanded dramatically, and by the end of 1997 comprised around 10 000 firms (MVD, 1997, p. 8) employing over a million people, compared with the 400 000 working within the *militsiya* (Galeotti, 1997a, p. 339). To a large extent, this reflects the prevailing lack of faith in the police and courts. In some ways, this is a modern-day answer to *samosud*, as individuals, communities and organisations seek instead to protect their interests themselves. Thus, companies have established their own security forces (the major gas firm *Gazprom*, for example, has 20 000 security personnel, many of them heavily armed), while many others buy in protection from the PSI or pay off the *mafiya*. However, there is another vicious circle at work here. This is not only a symptom of insecurity and a lack of faith in the police, it also worsens it:

- They bleed away respect and the best officers from the *militsiya*. When salaries in the PSI are as much as ten times as high as in the police, many of the most talented police officers are 'head hunted' away (Morvant, 1996, p. 26). Increasingly, people come to feel that security is only for those who can afford to pay for it.

- Many of these PSI firms act outside the law. The 1995 Law on Private Security gives them considerable powers of surveillance, search and even arrest and the right to use light pistols, for example, but many private guards openly flaunt large-calibre imported pistols, rifles and even machine guns.

- Many PSI firms are fronts for *mafiya* protection rackets.

Increasingly, organised crime offers one of the few reliable means of bringing order to a dangerously anarchic economic and legal system. The *mafiya* can collect on your debts (for a fee) and arrange short- or long-term finance as well as protect you from other gangs and ordinary street crime (see Box 7.2). It is, therefore, now an established practice to 'buy a roof', or pay protection money: some 70–80 per cent of firms pay 20–30 per cent of their profits for this 'roof' (*krysha*) (Williams, 1997, pp. 54, 56). For most entrepreneurs, the question is not whether to pay off the *mafiya* so much, as whether they are paying the right gang: the one with the power, the best contacts and, perverse though it may sound, the strongest reputation. After all, the more sophisticated criminals have come to realise the value of having a name for fair dealing!

Yet this is also a question of moral and even spiritual uncertainty and decay. A population for so long told that capitalism is evil is now being exhorted to enrich itself. More to the point, while a few Russians are becoming extraordinarily rich – and, unlike their corrupt party predecessors, flaunting their wealth at every opportunity – for most, life is extremely hard. By 1997, perhaps some 20 per cent of the population was living below the (already artificially low) poverty

Table 7.1 Official Crime rates 1991–97

Year	Crimes Reported	Change
1991	2 167 964	–
1992	2 760 700	+27.3%
1993	2 799 600	+1.4%
1994	2 632 700	–6%
1995	2 755 700	+4.7%
1996	2 625 100	–4.7%
1997	2 387 000	–9.1%

Sources: Morvant (1996, p. 25); MVD (1997, p. 26); *ITAR-TASS News Agency*, 30 January 1998

СПРАВКА 7.3 How to rig crime statistics

While Russian crime statistics are a little more credible than those of the Soviet era, they are still prone to heavy manipulation for political purposes. There are three main ways to massage the statistics:

- *Lie.* The least subtle approach. However, unlike the Soviet MVD, today's authorities must deal with inquisitive journalists and parliamentarians, so this crass method has fallen out of favour.

- *Re-classify.* If you need to be seen to be dealing with serious crimes, then simply record many as less serious offences. For example, many assaults in 1996 were classified as mere 'hooliganism' (a less serious crime, and one which jumped 13 per cent that year when the overall trend was downwards).

- *Base them on lies.* It is not always governments which distort the truth. Interior Minister Kulikov introduced tough new performance targets for the police. Instead of forcing them to work harder, however, in many cases these simply encouraged local commanders and their officers to under-report crimes – that way they seem to be solving a greater proportion of the total.

line: the figure was around 40 per cent if the UN's definition is applied (BBC *Summary of World Broadcasts: Russia*, 16 June 1997). For many, petty crime becomes simply a way of surviving.

'Disorganised crime'

The official crime rates show a slow turning of the tide of crime (Table 7.1). This is both a result of statistical anomalies (Box 7.3) and cooking of the books. Under pressure to produce good news, the MVD has ignored the growing tendency towards under-reporting, where the victims of crime simply do not bother telling the authorities as they expect no positive result – only a half-day filling in forms at the local police station. This is typical in cases of minor theft and similar offenses which have a relatively low clear-up rate (MVD, 1997, p. 31).

Nevertheless, the figures are not completely false. While 1996 did not see the 4.7 per cent fall that the MVD claimed, it probably did see stabilisation: at last the crime rate stopped rising, and 1997 is likely to have seen a real fall. This is both encouraging and, given the problems besetting the police, a genuine achievement. On the other hand, there are still many grounds for concern. Drug abuse and drug-related crime are growing rapidly, with the latter up 95 per cent in 1996 alone (Reuters, 6 January 1998). There is also still a huge amount of economic crime. As much as 40 per cent of Russia's economy may be 'hidden', for example, to avoid paying tax (Suetin, 1997). The future trend is likely to show a slow decline in the crime rates, but public perceptions tend to lag behind the facts. For some time to come, most Russians will probably feel insecure and unprotected, with the ensuing dangers outlined at the beginning of this chapter.

Organised crime

'The *mafiya*', one recent Russian joke goes, 'is like a government – except that it works'. There is much truth behind the humour. Organised crime in Russia has a long and brutal tradition, but it has been able to grow and evolve precisely because of the failings and failures of the state. From the roots of the nineteenth-century *Vorovskoi mir*, organised crime emerged to meet the unfulfilled needs of the Soviet people through the black market and to work with and within the Party itself. It was thus in an excellent position to benefit from the collapse of the USSR and the rise of the new Russia. The rush to privatise state assets allowed it to snap up large portions of the Russian economy at bargain prices. At the same time, it has managed to penetrate the political system, acquiring allies and clients in local and national government. The emergence of a new financial sector allowed it to set up banks and finance houses to launder its money, to develop its resources and to spread further into the legal economy. On the streets, the near collapse of state authority meant that organised crime could assert its ability to offer protection.

It is important to stress that this is by no means a single, monolithic criminal organisation. There is no single *mafiya*, no central controlling agency. Instead, the *mafiya* is, as much as anything else, a phenomenon, a collection of varied criminal groupings, ranging from swaggering Chechen gangsters (see Box 7.4), through shadowy ethnic Russian '*biznismeny*' (businessmen) building business empires on the back of money laundering and rigged privatisation auctions, to rings of demoralised army officers selling guns to make ends meet. Sometimes, when it is to their advantage, they work together; at other times, they will compete – often very violently. Along with overtly criminal activities such as protection racketeering, drug smuggling and prostitution, the *mafiya* is also involved in much legal business. As is mentioned above, it also provides services of a sort to the rest of the economy, where a solid 'roof' is often a vital business asset (Varese, 1996).

Russian police figures suggest that, in 1998, there were some 9000 *mafiya* groupings (Reuters, 6 January 1998), but their definition is far too loose, and includes groups which are really bandit gangs or small-time outfits. It is more likely that there are about 300 substantive and stable *mafiya* organisations, including about

СПРАВКА 7.4   Chechnya: Russia's Sicily?

Russia's turbulent southern region of Chechnya is often equated with Sicily. They share strong traditions of banditry and clannishness. They were both incorporated into their respective states by force in the nineteenth century. Both have become centres of international organised crime, but why? There are some striking similarities. Both regions felt alienated from their respective states, which they saw largely as imperial masters. While attitudes are slowly changing in Sicily, *glasnost* and the collapse of the USSR only heightened the nationalism of the Chechens, a people who had suffered a brutal mass deportation to Siberia and Central Asia in 1944 and had only been allowed to return home in 1956. Both cultures are also clannish, defined by a close-knit sense of loyalty to the family and community, not the state. However, from these traditional roots, modern, flexible and entrepreneurial criminal empires have grown, with the Chechen *mafiya* having established a presence across Europe.

12–20 major criminal cartels. The total membership may be anywhere between 20 000 and 100 000, but this misses the point. After all, it represents only the hard core of full-time criminals, not the millions who choose or are forced to co-operate with them, whether in paying protection money or returning 'favours', or who are unknowingly dealing with one of the myriad front organisations, from finance houses to haulage firms.

Criminal evolution

Today's *Vorovskoi mir* is still evolving, though. First of all, a new breed of 'godfather' has arisen: the *Avtoritet* ('Authority'). If the *Vory v zakone* are traditionalist leaders, elected by their peers because they have widespread influence and prestige within the criminal world, the *Avtoritety* are typically younger, more entrepreneurial criminals. They are usually gang leaders, less concerned with the thieves' code and more likely to be juggling both criminal and legal business empires (Williams, 1997, p. 199). Some, such as Federico Varese, believe these *Avtoritety* are taking over, as the old *Vor* elite declines (Varese, 1996, pp. 277–9). On the other hand, Joseph Serio and Vyacheslav Razinkin argue that the *Vory* are simply doing what they have always done: adapting. They have moved into international crime, expanded into new regions of Russia and begun inviting promising younger criminals into their ranks (Serio and Razinkin, 1995, pp. 84–6). It certainly seems too soon to write off Russia's 300–400 *Vory v zakone*.

If nothing else, Russian organised crime has proven astonishingly quick to globalise. There are four main reasons for this:

- *Access.* With the end of the cold war, making contacts and travelling abroad became far easier.

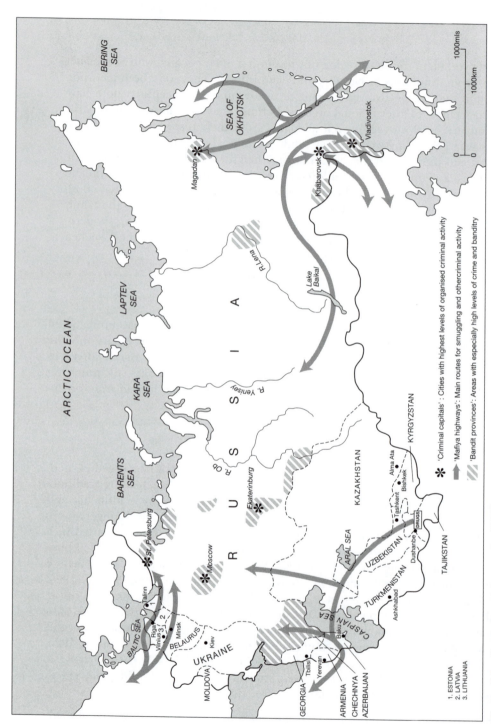

Figure 7.1 Successor states to the USSR

СПРАВКА 7.5   The *Organizatsiya*: Russian crime hits the USA

Since the 1970s, the Russian–Jewish émigré community of New York's Brighton Beach had been the focus of the *Organizatsiya* ('Organisation'), a small outfit specialising in white-collar fraud and local protection racketeering (Rosner, 1986). As the end of the USSR loomed and the *mafiya* looked to its global expansion, the *Organizatsiya* was targeted at its bridgehead in North America. In December 1991, senior *Vory* met at Vedentsevo, outside Moscow, to plan for the future. They appointed Vyacheslav Ivankov – known as '*Yaponchik*' ('the little Japanese man') – to bring the *Organizatsiya* to heel. He arrived in 1992 and by 1994 had removed or intimidated the *Organizatsiya*'s leadership. Under him, it expanded into a loose coalition including five major cartels comprising 220 gangs run by ex-Soviet citizens in 17 North American cities, including New York, Chicago, Los Angeles, San Francisco and Miami. Their activities include everything from sophisticated frauds to the sale of stolen weapons and provision of KGB-trained hitmen. Ivankov was arrested by the FBI in June 1995 and imprisoned for masterminding a scheme to extort $3.5 million from two Russian business-men, but the empire he has founded continues to grow.

- *Contacts.* The criminals had existing contacts with counterparts within other post-Soviet states and the former Warsaw Pact nations of Eastern Europe.
- *Outlook.* Criminals used to operating across the multi-ethnic USSR were already used to cutting cross-border deals and, indeed, realised how valuable they could be, especially in evading the police.
- *Incentive.* The uncertainty felt about Russia's future applied just as much to the criminals as everyone else. There was a clear desire to hide away funds and set up operations abroad just in case Russia exploded or suddenly began to fight crime seriously.

As a result, Russia's distinctively disorganised form of organised crime is, as Fig. 7.1 shows truly globalised. Many *Vory* have moved abroad (especially to Austria, Germany, Israel and North America – see Box 7.5). Many more gangs have begun expanding into new territories, investing abroad and forging international alliances. Already, for example, certain major gangs – especially *Solntsevo*, the biggest group in Moscow – have been working with the Sicilian Mafia, buying drugs through the Italians to sell in Russia and northern Europe. Again, however, this should not be over-dramatised. This is not, as Claire Sterling has argued, a *Pax Mafiosa*, a global criminal alliance (Sterling, 1994). Instead, this is just a piece-meal and essentially entrepreneurial process, as criminals and their gangs take advantage of what opportunities they can in what is, after all, an increasingly integrated and – thanks to the aircraft, email and mobile telephone – shrinking world.

Towards a mafiocracy?

It is difficult to sound too upbeat about the prospects for the emergence of a stable, safe and law-governed state in Russia. Lawlessness and a suspicion of authority are deeply ingrained and the police's successes against crime in general have not been matched by much progress against the *mafiya*, nor does the flagrant corruption of the new ruling elite help. Even relatively 'clean' politicians appear openly prepared to benefit from their office. In late 1997, for instance, it emerged that seven officials who had been central to the campaign to privatise state assets received a large advance of $45 000 for a book that is not likely to appear, paid for by a company which has flourished since the privatisation campaign. This triggered a political row in which allegations of favouritism were made. Many were sacked – but the most senior, the then First Deputy Prime Minister, Anatoli Chubais, was simply deprived of his additional post (Finance Minister) and otherwise survived unscathed.

In part, such scandals could be explained away as being driven by the smear tactics of a still rough and unsophisticated press and political system. There is some truth in this, but it is clear that there is far more to it than that. The new elite is largely the old elite, ex-party bosses and managers re-inventing themselves as politicians and *biznismeny*, but retaining many of their old ways. Boris Yeltsin himself, for all his regular pronouncements on the evils of corruption, appears content to turn a blind eye when it is politically convenient (Lovell *et al.*, 1999).

Hope

However, it is best to conclude by looking for signs of hope, and here, ironically, the very corruption of the system may help deal with the *mafiya*. After a series of violent turf wars in 1990–94, a status quo began to emerge. Increasingly, the main gangs are competing not against each other but against the *bespredelchiki* ('disorderly'), hungry newcomers trying to fight their way into the criminal big league. Many of the senior criminals are now looking for security, public respect and legitimacy, not least as they see the advantages in being able to operate within legal business. It may well be that they can be brought into the legal order, turning their money laundries into legal banks, their hired guns into private security guards. The experience of countries such as the USA is that organised crime can almost never be simply policed out of existence, it also needs to be allowed to legitimise itself (Galeotti, 1998).

Perhaps most importantly, there are signs that Russians are aware of the limitations and dangers of their current criminalised state of 'half-reform' and want and hope to move beyond it. Market traders may pay the *mafiya* protection because they feel there is no alternative, but they resent it. A new generation of police officers realise that at the moment they cannot avoid adopting paramilitary tactics, but they see the advantages in a community-based approach, working with the population, not against or in spite of it. The crime situation is stabilising. Some *mafiya* bosses are behind bars; others look willing to rejoin legal society. The high profile given crime in the media reflects the efforts of courageous investigative journalists prepared to probe the murky underside of the new Russia, even, in some cases, at the cost of their own lives. Russians may be heirs to a long criminal tradition, but that does not necessarily mean that they must remain its passive slaves.

References

Berliner J 1954 Blat is higher than Stalin, *Problems of Communism*, Vol. 3, No. 1, pp. 22–31.

Chalidze V 1977 *Criminal Russia*, Random House, New York.

Clark W 1993 *Crime and Punishment in Soviet Officialdom*, M E Sharpe, Armonk, NY, and London.

Frierson C 1987 Crime and punishment in the Russian village, *Slavic Review*, Vol. 46, No. 1, pp. 55–69.

Galeotti M 1993 Perestroika, perestrelka, pereborka: policing Russia in a time of change, *Europe–Asia Studies*, Vol. 45, No. 5, pp. 769–86.

Galeotti M 1997a Boom time for the Russian 'protectors', *Jane's Intelligence Review*, Vol. 9, No. 8, pp. 339–41.

Galeotti M 1997b Policing Russia, *Jane's Intelligence Review Special Report*, 15.

Galeotti M 1998 The mafiya and the new Russia, *Australian Journal of Politics and History*, Vol. 44, No. 3.

Glazov Y 1976 'Thieves' in the USSR – a social phenomenon, *Survey*, Vol. 22, No. 4, pp. 141–55.

Gurov A 1995 *Krasnaia mafiia*, Miko Kommercheskii Vestnik, Moscow.

Lincoln W B 1993 *In War's Dark Shadow*, Oxford University Press, Oxford.

Lovell S, Ledeneva A and Rogachevskii A (eds) 1999 *Bribery and Corruption in Russia*, Macmillan, Basingstoke.

Morvant P 1996 Corruption hampers war on crime in Russia, *Transition*, Vol. 8 (March 1996), pp. 23–7.

MVD 1997 *Itogi operativnogo-sluzhebnoi deyatelnosti organov vnutrennikh del I sluzhebno-boevoi vnutrennikh voisk MVD RF v 1996 godu*, MVD, Moscow.

Pipes R 1974 *Russia Under the Old Regime*, Penguin, Harmondsworth.

Rosner L 1986 *The Soviet Way of Crime*, Bergin & Garvey, Boston, MA.

Serio J 1992 *USSR Crime Statistics and Summaries: 1989 and 1990*, Office of International Criminal Justice, Chicago, IL.

Serio J and Razinkin A 1995 Thieves professing the code: the traditional role of vory v zakone in Russia's criminal world, *Low Intensity Conflict & Law Enforcement*, Vol. 4, No. 1, pp. 72–88.

Sharlet R 1984 Dissent and the 'contra-system' in the Soviet Union, *Proceedings of the Academy of Political Science*, Vol. 35, No. 3, pp. 135–46.

Sterling C 1994 *Crime Without Frontiers*, Little, Brown, London.

Suetin D 1997 Ekonomika Rossii: iz sveta v ten' pereletaya, *Ekonomika i zhizn'*, Vol. 13, p. 14.

Thurston R 1980 Police and people in Moscow, 1906–1914, *Russian Review*, Vol. 39, No. 3, pp. 320–38.

Vaksberg A 1991 *The Soviet Mafia*, Weidenfeld & Nicolson, New York.

Varese F 1996a What is the Russian Mafia?, *Low Intensity Conflict & Law Enforcement*, Vol. 5, No. 2, pp. 129–38.

Varese F 1996b *The Emergence of the Russian Mafia*, DPhil Thesis, Oxford.

Voslensky M 1984 *Nomenklatura*, Bodley Head, London.

Weissman N 1985 Regular police in Tsarist Russia, 1900–1914, *Russian Review*, Vol. 44, No. 1, pp. 45–68.

Williams P 1996 Hysteria, Complacency and Russian Organized Crime, *PSBF Briefing*, 8.

Williams P (ed.) 1997 *Russian Organized Crime: the New Threat?*, Frank Cass, London.

Further reading

Chalidze V 1977 *Criminal Russia*, Random House, New York.

Handelman S 1994 *Comrade Criminal*, Michael Joseph, London.

Williams P (ed.) 1997 *Russian Organized Crime: the New Threat?*, Frank Cass, London.

The issues of crime and policing in Russia are well served by the internet, which allows students to access a wide range of Russian and outside sources. The following sites are especially useful:

Office of International Criminal Justice (includes the on-line version of its excellent journal *Criminal Organizations*) at http://www.acsp.uic.edu/index.shtml

Committee for a Safe Society's Organized Crime home page at http://www.alternatives.com/crime/index.html

Organised Russian and Eurasian Research Unit (ORECRU) at http://www.keele.ac.uk/depts/hi/orecru.html

St Petersburg Times at http://www.spb.ru/times/current/

8 Social policy after the cold war: paying the social costs

Nick Manning and Nadia Davidova

Introduction: the Soviet legacy

Under the old system, social policy achievements were measured, as in so many areas, in terms of gross inputs rather than the quality or effects of final outputs. The numbers of doctors, nurses, flats and teachers or the early retirement age were proudly displayed as signs of the inexorable upward growth of 'developed socialism'. However, in practice these were subject to the restraint of the 'residual principle' whereby capital investment was firstly directed towards industrial goals, while housing, the raising of living standards and other improvements in people's lives only received what remained. Thus, 'final' welfare indicators, such as the meeting of social needs, or the quality of the goods and services provided, or the kind of social relationships that were produced or reproduced, were not so impressive.

The strong link between work history and social security resulted in neglect of a number of 'pure need' groups, such as poor children, disabled and unemployed people. Resources devoted to health care, by comparison with international trends, were extremely meagre – about 4 per cent of NMP (equivalent to about 2.5 per cent of GNP), compared with 6 per cent of GNP in the UK and 10 per cent in the USA (Davis, 1990). Housing provision was a continuous source of dissatisfaction from the October revolution onwards. Young couples could rarely find their own flat to begin married life in and normally had to share with one set of parents. In addition, a significant proportion of tenants remained in communal flats, sharing cooking and bathing facilities. This stressful situation led to divorce and inhibited reproduction (Shlapentokh, 1989).

Overall, Soviet welfare was largely reminiscent of 'occupational welfare'. Social policies were not so much a compensation for social risks as an adjunct to the labour market. While coverage in some areas was impressive, benefit and service levels were low. Many benefits were distributed through the workplace, either directly as enterprise services (e.g. housing, health care, and food) or managed through official trade unions (benefit claims and holidays). Strictly speaking, this was entirely compatible with the socialist principle of 'to each according to their work', with social need being the guiding principle for distribution only under future communism. To make it more oriented to need would have been to break the links with the labour market.

Federal priorities

Clearly the environment within which social policy exists has changed dramatically since the collapse of the Soviet Union. Public administrative structures and
budgetary arrangements are in turmoil. Income support, including pensions, has
not kept pace with inflation, health and education are increasingly varied
regionally and locally. Unemployment continues to be relatively low but living
standards are growing steadily more unequal.

Reaction to the old system favoured reduced planning control in favour of
markets and reduced central control in favour of decentralised and democratic
administration. In theory, this should correct the key technical failure of the
old system which suffered from an overload of, and hence loss of, information
as a result of central decision-making. It had been hoped that this would release
self-interest and political empowerment, which would invigorate a demoralised
and passive population. These gains have been very unevenly developed, if at
all, while the changeover has brought with it some very severe social costs. Widening
incomes have left more women, children and old people in poverty, and undermined the security of public sector workers, such as doctors and teachers.
Classic social problems such as infectious disease, alcoholism, prostitution and
crime have grown, and consequently birth rates have dropped while death rates
have climbed. Pressures on social services have escalated at the same time as
inflation, tax evasion and corruption have reduced the resources available and
administrative and legal capacities have shrunk.

The policy options here are stark. In the short run, a total absence of social
support might enable the quickest restructuring of the economy, but it could
only be possible through the draconian suppression of social unrest (hardly possible now in Russia). The alternative is to seek more gradual economic reform
and to target help as precisely as possible in the short term, with the longer-
term goal of a Western mix of social insurance and private provision (Barr, 1994,
pp. 26–27). Although benefits are still closely tied to enterprises and poorly targeted, Russia appears to have opted for the latter course. However, despite repeated
declarations of social policy reforms, for example, in 1993 prior to the new constitution and in 1997 arising out of the 1996 presidential election campaign ('The
Social Reform Programme for 1996–2000'), little is being effectively implemented, particularly if a regional view is taken.

In legal and administrative terms, the most significant development has been
the new Russian Constitution adopted in December 1993. Social policy issues
are covered in a variety of proposals, but there are also omissions. The constitution has to be read against a background of more detailed social policy
proposals issued by Yeltsin in November, a month before the referendum of
that year. The constitution, as many observers have noted, is heavily weighted
towards the powers of the President. While ministers take responsibility for managing various parts of the domestic policy programme, for example, in Ministries for Labour, Social Protection or Health, presidential decrees continue to
take the lead in policy initiatives.

On 3 November 1993, Yeltsin published his review of policy goals a month
after the October confrontation with parliament. While it can be read partly as

an election manifesto, the review appeared to form the basis of intended social policy plans. They included:

- a system of minimum social guarantees
- allowances for the needy
- better targeting of social welfare benefits
- a minimum living standard
- a minimum wage
- a minimum pension

In January 1998, the Russian Government published a further key document on social policy, called 'The Twelve Main Tasks in the Area of Social and Economic Policy'. The programme appeared less ambitious than the earlier 1993 proposals. Among the main social goals were:

- the payment of pensions and wages on time;
- targeted social support for the poorest strata of the population;
- reducing non-payments of social welfare;
- construction of housing for servicemen and officers.

There have been major problems in attaining even these less ambitious goals. The main ones have been a shortage of funds, high expectations among the Russian people for the continuation of universal state benefits as in the Soviet period, economic difficulties which were exacerbating already-existing social problems and growing regional differences in wealth which were making a central policy on social welfare more difficult to implement.

Shortage of funds

The shortage of funds was perhaps the most crucial problem. Ellman and Layard (1993, p. 58) argued that only 3 per cent of GNP was spent on education and 2 per cent on health – only half the average rate in OECD countries. Even though higher spending was accepted by the Duma in later years, only a fraction of the money earmarked in the budget was finding its way into the social services. Up to 1996, a large percentage of the budget debt occurred in the social sector (*Russia – 1997*, 1997, p. 9), resulting in wage arrears for public sector workers and shortages of medicines, textbooks and so on. Indeed, the Institute for the Economy in Transition argued that there had been a substantial reduction in state funding in 1996 with spending on health care, education and other social services down to just 65 per cent of 1991 levels (*Russian Economy in 1996*, 1997, pp. 116–19). This level of funding, however, is dwarfed by the costs of income support, which are now technically outside the state budget in four separate funds: employment, social insurance, pensions and medical insurance. Generated since 1991 by a 39 per cent payroll tax, in 1994 they amounted to 17 per cent of GDP. The 'Social Reform Programme for 1996–2000' states that, in the medium term, a significant rise in the share of social spending cannot be expected.

As in many Western countries, spending on social services is particularly sens-itive to two factors – the rate of unemployment and the level of pensions. Labour force surveys indicate that, in 1997, the unemployment rate was about 9 per cent with a further 6 per cent on involuntary leave and 5 per cent on short time (Chetvernina, 1997, pp. 227–9; Standing, 1994). Although these rates are much higher than official figures indicate, unemployment in Russia remains relatively low. Unemployment pay is also low – only about 10 per cent of average wages. Pensioners, however, have done rather better. The minimum pension has been indexed to roughly one-fifth of average wages, while the average pension is about one-third (see below for further details). As a result, pensions rather than dole money have become the main burden on the social welfare budget.

An end to universal benefits

Better targeting of social benefit has become a necessity in the new economic conditions in post-Soviet Russia. This has been recognised by the new Social Affairs Minister, Sysyuev, who was appointed in April 1997, and by President Yeltsin in a speech to the Federal Assembly in 1998. The state can no longer afford the kind of universal benefits that existed in Soviet times. Although the benefits look generous, in fact they only serve to reinforce existing inequalities in Russian soci-ety. Thus, the highest income groups (upper deciles, 8–10) receive 42 per cent of the social welfare budget, while the lowest income groups (deciles 1–3) only receive 27 per cent (Dmytriev, 1997).

Public views on social policy

Public opinion polls show that most people in Russia are opposed to Yeltsin's initiatives on social welfare (see *Information Monitoring Bulletin*, January 1998, p. 19). Most people still want the extensive social protection they had got used to in Soviet times (Institute of Sociological Analysis, 1997). Surveys in 1991 and 1993 showed that a growing number favoured free schools (41 per cent to 58 per cent), free health care (22 per cent to 46 per cent), free housing (24 per cent to 32 per cent), full employment (90 per cent) and a guaranteed minimum income (90 per cent) (*Information Monitoring Bulletin*, January 1994, pp. 24–6). In view of these findings, it is clear that further radical changes in social policy would meet with considerable public opposition.

Regional differences

Regionalism is also a growing problem in Russia (see Chapter 4). Inequalities across the federation have made central policy formulation on social issues far more difficult. Social problems are greatest in the North Caucasus and the adja-cent regions in the south. There, industrial production has slumped, per capita income is low and unemployment is high (University of Birmingham–Russian Expert Institute, 1996, pp. 45–6). However, in some other regions with rich nat-ural resources and more modern industry, the situation can be very different.

СПРАВКА 8.1   **Moscow**

Life in Moscow has changed greatly since the collapse of the Soviet Union. It is now a truly cosmopolitan city. Yuri Luzhkov, Moscow's mayor, has given the capital city a face-lift. He has rebuilt the Cathedral of Christ the Saviour after it was destroyed by Stalin and built a new shopping and cultural complex in Manezh Square in front of the Kremlin. Moscow is now full of shops, bars, cafes and restaurants and can boast a booming nightlife. However, prices have also shot up. So it is only a handful of very rich Muscovites, along with wealthy Western tourists and business people, who can afford to sample many of the delights of the new Moscow.

Table 8.1   Annual per capita Incomes in major Russian economic regions (December 1996) (in thousands of rubles)

Moscow	4031
St Petersburg	1171
North (six regions)	1017
Northwest (three regions)	703
Central Russia (12 regions)	625
Volgo-Vyatka (five regions)	563
Black Soil Area (five regions)	663
Volga Region (eight regions)	649
Northern Caucasus (10 regions)	499
Ural (eight regions)	737
Western Siberia (nine regions)	980
Eastern Siberia (10 regions)	761
Far East (10 regions)	1347
Kaliningrad Oblast	639
Average in Russia	1002

Source: Russia – 1997

In Moscow (see Box 8.1), for example – the city most foreigners visit and know – the situation is comparatively good. It is not necessary to travel far from Moscow, however, to find poverty. Ivanovo, for example, a couple of hundred miles away, has a per capita income of less than half that of Moscow. Even when some necessary adjustments are made regarding the cost of living in the capital, Moscow is still far wealthier than even other comparatively wealthy areas, such as Western Siberia, the North and Far East, let alone the poorer South, Volga-Vyatka and the old industrial Centre of Russia (see Table 8.1).

It is clear from such statistics that the Russian North, Far East and Siberia cannot survive without federal support. However, it should just be mentioned briefly here that per capita income is not the only means of determining individual living standards. Other factors include local prices (sometimes regulated by local authorities), the availability of goods (many Russians grow their own food) and traditional life-styles (Davidova, 1998, pp. 36–48). Thus, the cost of living can vary greatly from region to region too. For example, the cost of living in the agrarian south is some four or five times lower than in the Far East (*Delovoi Mir*, 24 January 1997).

If the central authorities are really serious about addressing social problems in Russia, it is vital that policies take account of these very great differences between regions. 'The Programme of State Stimuli for Economic Activity and Development' adopted in 1995 attempted to do this by, among other things, prioritising support for depressed regions, and especially the North and Far Eastern territories. However, the success of these initiatives depends, to a large extent, on the future performance of the Russian economy.

Employment and enterprise welfare

Turning now to specific areas of social policy, we will start with the most significant – employment. In Soviet times, this was not merely the source of income for most households (as in all industrial societies), but also the major supplier of social services, especially housing, that are normally delivered in other countries through governments or markets. Many people continue to receive substantial benefits through their enterprise, and approve of this arrangement, but the process of Russian privatisation did not include adequate planning for the reorganisation of social provisions, which had always been unprofitable. The vast majority of Russian enterprises are now technically in private hands and they have been encouraged to transfer their housing to municipal control and to sell off their social facilities, mostly in sport, leisure and pre-school facilities. However, employees are then unable to afford to use these facilities as they become expensive private services. The main consequences of this process have been a reduction of social support for employees, a gradual change in the pattern of social protection and a failure of local authorities, which are struggling with meagre budgets to make up for the social services lost to private business.

In this shifting climate, the enterprise operates as a multiplier of advantage; those enterprises doing well provide significantly higher levels of help and social benefits than do others. Rose found in 1992 that more than 50 per cent of the urban population have at some time received help from their place of work with medical care, child care, and holidays, and a third help with housing, food and other goods (Rose, 1992a, p. 10). In 1997, a Ministry of Labour and Social Development Survey showed that 70 per cent of enterprises still provide free health care, with 48 per cent of employees stating that they have received it personally during the last three years; corresponding figures for 'material support' are 55 and 33 per cent, for pre-school and leisure facilities 33 and 10 per cent and for transport and food 50 and 25 per cent (Kovaleva, 1997, pp. 26–32).

Employment is thus about more than money incomes, and hence labour market changes are crucial determinants of people's welfare. The response of the Russian labour market to the transformation shock has differed in many respects from that of other East European countries. Notwithstanding an enormous decline in production, unemployment is at a comparatively low level and has not yet reached 10 per cent. Unemployment seems to be mitigated by the flexibility of the Russian labour market, reflected in high rates of job turnover. In 1995, both *Goskomstat* and the Russian Economic Barometer reported a hiring rate of 19–21 per cent of average annual employment, and a separation rate of 27–28 per cent (Kapeliushnikov, 1997).

A study in 1992 of redundant workers by Gimpelson and Magun (1994, pp. 57–75) shows that more than 50 per cent were re-employed within three months, with over a quarter entering the non-state sector. This process accelerated in 1993, with about one third of medium-sized industrial firms expanding their employment throughout the year (*Russian European Centre for Economic Policy*, 1994, p. 90). In some areas, notably Moscow, this appears to have created a labour shortage in some sectors, particularly for skilled workers (Solovyev, 1994, p. 167). In 1996 the number of unemployed grew at a lower rate than in the preceding three years (*Russian Economy in 1996*, 1997, p. 62). On the whole this pattern can be read as a favourable one regarding economic reform – suggesting a flexible labour market with relatively modest unemployment.

The meaning of this pattern is disputed, however, and highly regionally varied – as discussed earlier. There are three contrasting views of this issue. First are those who do not expect there to be a massive shake-out, since the labour market is already making a successful adjustment to flexible restructuring (OECD, 1996; Layard and Richter, 1994). However, a high labour turnover conceals a large segment of the labour market which is very stable, amounting to the 'hoarding' of labour by worker-controlled managements according to other commentators, with a smaller segment turning over employment at a furious rate – the so-called 'churning' of jobs (Commander *et al.*, 1995). A third view suggests that excess employment exists as a result of the wages tax (Roxborough and Schapiro, 1996) or simply the costs of change – 'enterprises retain labour because they need it and it costs them little to keep it' (Clarke, 1996, p. 52). A major reason for this is the continued, and even developed, role of the old trade unions as purveyors of enterprise welfare goods and services. 'Occupational welfare' has changed far less than state social policy (Ashwin, 1997). This has been a major factor in the willingness of Russian workers to put up with being technically on leave – i.e. employed, but with no work or wages – since a substantial part of their income continues to be supplied in the form of non-money goods and services.

Household survival beyond employment: income, social security benefits and poverty

There has been a very sharp growth in income inequality in Russia. The ratio between incomes of the wealthiest and the poorest 10 per cent was 15:1 in 1994 (Goskomstat, 1997b), and the inter-regional income gap is also large. In terms of income polarisation, Russia is now ahead of Brazil. However, across the whole country since 1995 there has been a halt to the growing redistribution of incomes in favour of the higher income groups; the income ratio of the wealthiest and the poorest 10 per cent had narrowed somewhat to 13:1 in 1996.

Beyond primary employment in the labour market, many people have a mixture of secondary work, friends, family and unwaged work to maintain their incomes. Shlapentokh (1989) has shown the importance of these connections under the old regime. Since 1991 they have become, if anything, more important – at least during the years of acute adjustment in the labour market and consumer prices. Rose (1993a, p. 25) distinguishes three types of economic activity: official (employment, or pensions); uncivil (secondary work for money, or exploiting connections); social (non-monetary work, or exchange). He argues that those relying on the first type only are *vulnerable*, on the first and second are *enterprising*, and on the first and third are *defensive*; the rest are *marginal*. In his 1992 survey, he found a distinctive pattern for Russia compared with other East European countries in that a higher proportion were *vulnerable* (a third) and a lower proportion were *marginal* (10 per cent) (Rose, 1992b, p. 21). Even so, more than a quarter of the Russian sample of working age people declared that their main job was not the most important for their standard of living. About the same proportion declared that growing food was important; indeed, overall more than half of the sample grew food, and more than a third reported that they grew most or some of their food during the previous year. Other important activities included exchanging help for house repairs, and giving or receiving connections for essential services, particularly medical care and medicines (over half the sample). Our own data for 1996 and 1997 confirm this general pattern (Manning *et al.*, 1997).

The third main source of income is of course the state. Here the most important activities have been related to pensions, family allowances and unemployment. The reform of pensions came in 1991 (Barr, 1992, Chapter 2) when the pension fund was created, financed by a payroll tax of 28 per cent from employers and 1 per cent from employees, relieving the state budget from responsibility, and since 1991 this fund has been generating a large surplus (4 per cent GDP in 1994). The fund is subject to the control of the Ministry of Social Protection which co-ordinates policy and calculates benefits and entitlements. Pensioners are entitled to a minimum, enhanced by the number of years' work, and previous earnings, although there is as yet no retirement test to qualify. In principle the benefit rate should be calculated automatically, but rapid inflation has politicised the rate, for example, when the President reduced the State Duma's recommended rise in the summer of 1994 from 50 per cent to 15 per cent, as a result of which the Minister of Social Protection resigned. Current proposals by the new Ministry for Labour and Social Development are for a Western-style 'funded' system (such as occupational pensions) based on genuine insurance principles, with a clear relation between lifetime payment and benefit. However, this is not easy to achieve. For example, the British and American government schemes still work on a pay-as-you-go basis, with each generation in effect taxed to pay for the previous generation. A fully funded scheme for Russia would involve the transfer of a massive amount of resources into pension funds, which would have to be built up over many years, in addition to paying for current unfunded pensioners.

Family allowances have almost by default become a significant element in federal policy towards poorer people, since children have become increasingly represented among the poor. A new system has been in operation since January 1994 (Russian European Centre for Economic Policy, 1994, p. 48). All children under 18 months are entitled to an allowance of 150 per cent of the minimum wage (up from 60 per cent, and now totalling about 15 per cent of the average wage); up to 6 years of age the rate is 105 per cent (up from 45 per cent), and thereafter 90 per cent of the minimum wage. This is quite high by international standards. It is enhanced for families in the north. The pension fund disburses the money, but the funding comes from the state budget. Clearly, this benefit is dependent on the political fortunes of the minimum wage level, which has not been stable – between May 1992 and May 1993 this benefit in real terms declined to one-third of its previous value, but the 1994 change re-instated it.

The cornerstone of social security under the old system was the right to work (Article 40 of the old constitution), upon which other policies for income maintenance were based. Therefore, the main problem looming on the horizon is the possibility of mass unemployment (even if as yet it has not materialised). Fear of this problem generated the Employment Law drafted in the autumn of 1990, and formally adopted on 15 January 1991. This officially signalled the end of the right and duty to work by imposing a 1 per cent payroll levy to generate funds to finance unemployment benefit, retraining, public community work and career guidance (Standing, 1991). However, unemployment benefit has not been as big a cost to the government as was expected. This is because few claimed it, either because they were moving between jobs or because the rate of benefit was so low. For the first three months it was 100 per cent continuation of wages, then 75 per cent from the employment service for the next quarter, 60 per cent for the following quarter, and finally 45 per cent for the quarter after that. The minimum is equal to the minimum wage (i.e. 10 per cent of average wages). Since this is calculated on the basis of the previous year's wages, and is not indexed, with the high inflation rates of 1992 and 1993 most recipients were in effect on the minimum. Conditions of receipt include work-seeking and the acceptance of at least the second appropriate job offer. Benefits are paid from the 1991 Employment Fund. Proposals for a flat rate benefit (to simplify administration) and means-tested unemployment assistance (for those whose benefits are exhausted) continue to be discussed.

Underlying this discussion on incomes is the question of poverty. Goskomstat data in 1996 suggested that average per capita monthly incomes of 22.6 per cent of households were below the Ministry of Labour subsistence minimum. In 1997, this figure was down slightly to 20.9 per cent (*Socio-Economic State of Russia*, 1997, p. 69). Since the minimum pension is currently around 20 per cent of the average wage or half the Ministry of Labour minimum subsistence poverty level, and the average pension is around 31 per cent of the average wage or 80 per cent of the subsistence level, the pension rate might be expected to determine the poverty rate. However, the average pension has closely matched the average wage since the mid-1980s, suggesting that the image of impoverished Russian pensioners should be replaced by one of impoverished children, particularly since it is quite common for pensioners also to take on paid work.

Surveys in 1992 and 1993 by the Russian Longitudinal Monitoring Survey and Goskomstat respectively, reported by *Russian Economic Trends* (Russian European

СПРАВКА 8.2   On the cost of living

Prices and wages do vary greatly over time. Wages, of course, vary according to a person's age, experience and seniority. The figures below, therefore, can act as no more than a very rough guide to prices and wages in Moscow in October 1998. The ruble stood at 16 to one US dollar.

Average pay of a doctor: 500 rubles

Average pay of a nurse: 400 rubles

Average pay of a teacher: 500 rubles

Price of a loaf of bread: 3 rubles

Price of a bottle of milk: 6–11 rubles

Price of a packet of pasta: 46 rubles

Price of a washing machine: 8000–9000 rubles

Approximately 25 per cent of a person's wage is spent on rent, electricity, gas and water.

Centre for Economic Policy, 1994, p. 47), show that the composition of the poor was significantly tilted towards children – for both 1992 and 1993 the proportion of children in poverty (about 40 per cent) was roughly twice that of men over 60. We have found in our own project that in 1997 the primary cause of poverty, and especially profound poverty, was the respondents' family circumstances – one-parent families with children under 18 and families with many children; families of the disabled. Among families with one parent or many children, the number of those who found themselves in very poor material circumstances exceeded the average by a ratio of three (Manning *et al.*, 1997). Since the rate of pregnancy among young unmarried women is growing rapidly (in contrast to the overall birth rate which has fallen sharply in the 1990s), family and child poverty is likely to become worse (UNICEF, 1996).

Examples of the cost of living are shown in Box 8.2.

Health, illness and health care

In the health service, lack of funding, poor administration and unregulated health insurance remain the biggest problems. Total investment did rise in 1994 to 2.8 per cent of GNP, up from 2 per cent in 1992. Much of the money, however, was not spent directly on health services. Wages in the health sector are only 75 per cent of those in industry, and morale is low (*CDPSP*, 1994, Vol. 46, No. 33, p. 22). New sources of money in future will have to be private. Budget caps on hospitals which have now been imposed, combined with an explosion in the price of pharmaceuticals, have forced health carers to charge for services. In his 1992–93 surveys, Rose reported that half of the population had to use connections to get goods and services which were difficult to find – usually medicines and doctors (Rose, 1992a, p. 16). An estimated 10–15 per cent of the population still receive health care from their place of work (Preker and Feachem, 1994, p. 309) but, as mentioned earlier, these services are gradually winding down. This is a problem, because it leaves the already stretched health service with a substantial additional burden.

This crisis in the health service has been highlighted by the decline in general health among the Russian public. There have been a series of epidemics in Russia, including diphtheria, cholera, measles and general intestinal problems. Poor public hygiene and the cost of health care have meant that fewer people have sought immunisation and other important health services. Thus, in 1993, 2992 people died from drinking dirty water. The authorities simply urged Russians to boil drinking water, saying they lacked the money to clean up supplies (Yermakova, 1994, pp. 17–18). Air pollution is also a big problem with records for 1993 showing that respiratory diseases have become the most common health complaint in Russia, with a 20 per cent increase among children from 1992 to 1993 (*CDPSP*, 1994, p. 20). Russian children generally are less healthy than they used to be, partly because they cannot afford school meals and medical services. Life expectancy for the average male has dropped to just 58 years.

Housing

Despite very cheap rents in the Soviet period, housing remained a traditional source of public dissatisfaction. Accommodation was generally poor, unattractive and the waiting lists were long. The 27th CPSU Congress in 1986 committed itself to tackling this massive problem with a promise to provide all families with their own flat by the end of the century. Since an estimated 20 per cent of the Russian population lived in communal flats, this implied a major increase in housing investment (Trehub, 1987, p. 13). To raise the necessary revenue, there was a need to institute a more realistic pricing system. Traditionally, rent and energy costs rarely absorbed more than 3 per cent of the household budget, but this move was still very controversial.

The Yeltsin Government was keen to privatise accommodation, but the process has been slow. Few householders could afford to buy and maintain their own homes. Although about half of all flats were in private ownership by 1997 (Russian European Centre for Economic Policy, 1994, p. 84; Dmytriev, 1997), about 20 per cent of enterprises continued to provide their employees with free accommodation (*Information Monitoring Bulletin*, 1997, pp. 30–1). Two presidential decrees (in December 1993 and June 1994) have tried to tackle the thorny problem of finance by authorising mortgage lending, housing savings accounts and local government construction funds for low-income housing. However, the policy had too many loopholes and failed to encourage lending. For example, it gave too few guarantees to lenders in the case of default. State building of housing has virtually stopped, exacerbating the already existing shortage of accommodation in Russia. This has led to a massive increase in homelessness in Russia.

The exact number of homeless is difficult to estimate, but various reports suggest there might be as many as 50 000 in St Petersburg (Orebro Workshop, 1994, p. 34) and perhaps double that figure in Moscow (Andrusz, 1994, p. 15). The personal cost of homelessness in a country with a cruel winter climate could be gauged by the gruesome statistics assembled by Sokolov who reported that 525 corpses of homeless people were found on the streets of St Petersburg in 1992, a figure that more than doubled just a year later (Sokolov, 1994, pp. 161–3).

Housing remains a hot issue in post-Soviet Russia, not only because of the continuing dissatisfaction over availability, quality and cost, but also because it is potentially such a rich source of income both for the new Russian entrepreneurs and the criminal classes.

Conclusion: which way for the Russian welfare state?

Barr (1994, pp. 26–7) has drawn attention to the distinction between short-term, sometimes emergency, social policy measures forced by events that have developed in the early transition phase and the medium-term reconstruction of social policy. There have been two clear points at which President Yeltsin has attempted to give overall shape to the development of the Russian welfare state. The first, in the run-up to the 1993 referendum, focused on basic rights and expectations that Russian citizens could have about social policies. For example, it was proclaimed that a system of minimum social guarantees, including living standards, wages and pensions, would provide for those without sufficient means, and that social protection would be targeted on the needy. These promises have not been fulfilled. There is widespread and very deep poverty for many Russians, whatever method is used to measure this. The targeting of social support is also regressive, in that those on higher incomes get more than those on lower incomes. This is in part a result of the continued support coming through enterprises, but particularly through more successful enterprises, and to the better-paid staff in them. As we have seen, a growing number of Russian citizens are calling for the state to secure basic social support while some members of the government recognise that the market may not be the solution to social policy.

More recently, in January 1998, there was a further pronouncement on the 'Twelve Main Tasks in the Area of Social and Economic Policy'. They exhibit a mixture of political expediency and realism. For example, the aim to ensure that wages and pensions are paid on time reflects the widespread public discontent over arrears in the last year or two, and the emergence of strike action once again among miners, which might spread. Similarly, the offer to finance housing for the military direct from the Ministry of Finance addresses the pressing issue of returning servicemen from abroad, but more significantly it is designed to appease a still significantly powerful group in Russian society that Yeltsin may well yet need. Other items are more organisational. The recognition that with limited resources the government will inevitably have to target them on the poorest if they are to be of any use is a notable break from the 1993 declarations. This will entail challenging monopolies in the system, political or economic, and the development of a clear understanding of the way the finance and organisation of social policy have developed in the 1990s. It is significant in this respect that there is planned to be an inventory drawn up of budget-financed organisations, starting with education and health. The chaos and *de facto* decentralisation of finance and organisation that have developed since 1991 appear to have left the government ignorant of even the most basic knowledge of how social policy is currently working.

Are these tasks any more realistic or workable than those of 1993? They are certainly more realistic in the sense that they have been formulated against a far more accurate assessment of the difficult circumstances for social policy, and an admission that the organisation and implementation of social policies have been perverse – the pretence that universal social guarantees could be maintained has in effect resulted in guarantees for the better off and dire poverty for others. However, realism does not mean that the implied massive shift in priorities towards the poor can actually be achieved. The barriers to this shift are the ones that have distorted social policy in the first place. The continued delivery of social policies through the enterprise as 'occupational welfare' means that enterprises are a major multiplier of disadvantage, since they channel social support to those who are relatively better off. Just as the retention of surplus labour in these very large organisations has kept unemployment under control and, importantly, suppressed the potential for political disaffection, it has also contributed to the sharp rise in inequality in Russia in recent years.

The continuities of enterprise welfare activities can be contrasted with the rapid changes evident in a second barrier to changing social policy priorities on the ground, the *de facto* regionalisation that has developed surprisingly quickly in the 1990s. Regional inequality has arisen out of the differential effects of rapid inflation, and the adjustment in economic restructuring that has been possible in some areas but not others. This has been compounded for some regions by local political elites which have tried hard to resist the economic changes, for example, by blocking the development of new small and medium-sized enterprises in the private sector. Regional differences are now so large that there would have to be an enormous re-centralisation of government services to even them out – hardly possible now. It is difficult to see how the federal government will be able to slow down, let alone halt or reverse, these regional inequalities which have had such a marked impact on social policy (see Chapter 4). Key events of social policy are summarised in Box 8.3.

While the 1993 Russian Constitution retains national level policy-making in principle for health, education and social security, privatisation and regionalisation in these areas have pulled planning and provision away from central control and increased regional inequalities. However, the tension between presidential decree and State Duma policy-making, and between policies and their implementation, still make prediction about the future of social policy fairly hazardous.

The use of high payroll taxes as the key funding mechanism is reminiscent of the French system (Pfaller *et al.*, 1991). While there remains a strong enterprise commitment to employee welfare, this is acceptable to managers, but strong international competition has forced the French to cut these relatively

СПРАВКА 8.3   **Key events of social policy**

Social context for social policy

- rapid growth of regional inequality
- continued uncertainty over health and education policy
- guaranteed income minima are very low
- deep poverty for certain families, especially with children
- worsening health and demographic patterns
- slow growth of unemployment, but with labour market flexibility
- continuity of enterprise welfare functions

General areas of social policy

- move from state budget to payroll finance funding
- more informed debate and realism in social policy
- privatisation of housing and parts of health care and education
- more targeting of social welfare

high additions to labour costs. It may be that, in the longer term, Russian managers will come to feel the same. On the other hand a good example of such enterprise welfare is offered by the USA, where employers provide greater social support than is common in Europe and where government programmes are much more meagre and subject to great regional variation. For example, the Clinton health security plan was to give employers a key role in health insurance. However, Russian longer-term plans seem to be for a state-regulated national insurance system along German lines, rather than the more minimalist American tradition.

In terms of a model that currently dominates comparative social policy analysis (see Esping-Andersen, 1990), the Russian welfare state is moving strongly towards social welfare as a *commodity*, towards a sharply graded system of *stratification*, and in favour of a greater role for *markets* rather than state control. In terms of this model, it is moving away from any social democratic tradition towards a mixture of corporatist policy-making combined with a residual minimum for those unattached to the labour market.

References

Andrusz G 1994 The Causes and Consequences of Homelessness in Moscow and Sofia, paper for the ESRC East–West Workshop on the Social Consequences of Marketisation, London, 9–10 December.

Ashwin S 1997 Shop Floor Trade Unionism in Russia, *Work, Employment and Society*, Vol. 11, No. 1, pp. 115–32.

Barr N 1992 *Income Transfers and the Social Safety Net in Russia*, World Bank.

Barr N (ed.) 1994 *Labor Markets and Social Policy in Central and Eastern Europe, the Transition and Beyond*, Oxford University Press, Oxford.

Chernina N 1994 Poverty as a Social Phenomenon in Russian Society, *Sociological Research (SOTSIS)*, Vol. 3, pp. 61–8.

Chetvernina T 1997 Forms and Main Features of Hidden Unemployment in Russia, in Zaslavskaya T (ed.), *Kuda Idet Rossia*, Intertsentr, Moscow.

Clarke S 1996 Structural Adjustment Without Mass Unemployment? Lessons from Russia', in *The Restructuring of Employment and the Formation of a Labour Market in Russia*, Centre for Comparative Labour Studies, University of Warwick.

Clarke S 1997 Poverty in Russia, working paper, Centre for Comparative Labour Studies, University of Warwick.

Commander S and McHale J 1995 Russia, in Commander S and Coricelli F, *Unemployment, Restructuring, and the Labour Market in Eastern Europe and Russia*, World Bank, pp. 147–91.

Davidova N 1998 Regional Specifics of Russian Mentality, *Social Sciences*, Quarterly Review of Russian Academy of Science, No. 1, pp. 36–48.

Davis C 1990 National Health Services, Resource Constraints and Shortages: A Comparison of Soviet and British Experiences, in Manning N and Ungerson C J (eds), *Social Policy Review 1989–90*, Longman, Harlow.

Dmytriev A 1997 Unpublished Report for Annual International Symposium, Russia, Moscow Inter-Disciplinary Academic Centre for Social Sciences, 17–19 January.

Ellman M and Layard R 1993 Prices, Incomes and Hardship, in Åslund A and Layard R, *Changing the Economic System in Russia*, Pinter Publishers.

Esping-Andersen G 1990 *The Three Worlds of Welfare Capitalism*, Polity Press, London.

Gimpelson V E and Magun V 1994 Nouvel emploi et mobilité sociale des travailleurs licenciés, *Cahiers Internationaux de Sociologie*, Vol. XCVI, pp. 57–75.

Goskomstat 1997a *Socio-Economic State of Russia*, Moscow.

Goskomstat 1997b *Russia in Figures*, Moscow.

Institute of Sociological Analysis 1997 Public Opinion Foundation Nation-Wide Survey, 1996, *Current Digest of Post-Soviet Press*, Vol. 49, No. 1, p. 4.

Kapeliushnikov R 1997 Job and Labour Turnover in the Russian Industry, *The Russian Economic Barometer*, Vol. VI, No. 1.

Kovaleva N 1997 Conflicts, Trade-Unions, Social Support: Opinions of Employees and Employers, *Information Monitoring Bulletin*, Vol. 31, No. 5, pp. 26–32.

Layard R and Richter A 1994 Labour Market Adjustment in Russia, *Russian Economic Trends*, Vol. 3, No. 2, pp. 85–104.

Manning N, Shkaratan O and Tikhonova N 1997 Social Policy and Unemployment Survey, 1995–98, Unpublished Working Paper, INTAS-94-3725.

Nefedova O and Treivish A 1996 Post-Soviet Space of Russia, *Mir Possii*, Vol. 2, pp. 3–12.

OECD 1996 *Labour Restructuring in Russian Enterprises: a Case Study*, OECD.

Orebro Workshop 1994 Unpublished Report, Moscow.

Ovcharova L 1997 The Definition and Measurement of Poverty in Russia, Working Paper, Institute of Population of Russian Academy of Science, Moscow, and Centre for Comparative Labour Studies, University of Warwick.

Pfaller A, Gough I and Therborn T 1991 *Can the Welfare State Compete?*, Macmillan, Basingstoke.

Preker A S and Feachem R G A 1994 Health and Health Care, in Barr N (ed.), *Labor Markets and Social Policy in Central and Eastern Europe, the Transition and Beyond*, Oxford University Press, Oxford, pp. 288–321.

Rose R 1992a *Russians Between State and Market*, Studies in Public Policy No. 205, Centre for the Study of Public Policy, University of Strathclyde.

Rose R 1992b *Divisions and Contradictions in Economies in Transition*, Studies in Public Policy No. 206, Centre for the Study of Public Policy, University of Strathclyde.

Rose R 1993a *Is Money the Measure of Welfare in Russia?*, Studies in Public Policy No. 215, Centre for the Study of Public Policy, University of Strathclyde.

Rose R 1993b *How Russians are Coping with Transition*, Studies in Public Policy No. 216, Centre for the Study of Public Policy, University of Strathclyde.

Roxborough I and Schapiro J 1996 Russian Unemployment and the Excess Wages Tax, *Communist Economies & Economic Transformation*, Vol. 8, No. 1, pp. 5–29.

Russia – 1997 1997 Statistical Bulletin of the Governmental Centre of the Economic Situation, Moscow.

Russian Economy in 1996 1997 Issue 16, Institute for Economy in Transition, Moscow.

Russian European Centre for Economic Policy 1994 *Russian Economic Trends*, Whurr Publishers, Lawrence, KS, and London.

Shlapentokh V 1989 *Public and Private Life of the Soviet People*, Oxford University Press, Oxford.

Socio-Economic State of Russia 1997 State Statistical Committee of the Russian Federation, Moscow, January–August.

Sokolov V 1994 Homelessness in St Petersburg, in *St Petersburg in the Early 1990s: Crazy, Cold and Cruel*, Charitable Foundation 'Nochlezhka', St Petersburg, pp. 161–3.

Solovyev A 1994 The Situation in St Petersburg Labour Market, in *St Petersburg in the Early 1990s: Crazy, Cold and Cruel*, Charitable Foundation 'Nochlezhka', St Petersburg, pp. 166–70.

Standing G (ed.) 1991 *In Search of Flexibility: the New Soviet Labour Market*, International Labour Organisation, Geneva.

Standing G 1994 Why Measured Unemployment in Russia is So Low: the Net With Many Holes, *Journal of European Social Policy*, Vol. 4, No. 1, pp. 35–50.

Trehub A 1987 Social and Economic Rights in the Soviet Union, *Survey*, Vol. 29, No. 4, pp. 6–42.

UNICEF 1996 *Transmonee Data Base*, ICDC, Florence.

University of Birmingham–Russian Expert Institute 1996 How People Adapt to the New Reality, *Vlast*, Vol. 9, pp. 45–6.

Vishnevsky A 1998 Report for the International Inter-Disciplinary Academic Symposium of Social Sciences, School of Social and Economic Sciences, Moscow, 16–19 January.

Yermakova M 1994 In Terms of Health We Are in 68th Place, *Rossiiskiye vesti*, 29 April, p. 3, in *Current Digest of the Post-Soviet Press*, Vol. 46, No. 17, pp. 17–18.

Further reading

Manning N 1995 Social Policy and the Welfare State, in Lane D, Russia in Transition: Politics, Privatisation and Inequality, Longman, London and New York.

A good web site is Professor Simon Clark's at Warwick: http://www.csv.warwick.ac.uk/fac/soc/complabstuds/russia/russint.htm

There are also a lot of very useful data in the UNICEF Social Policy Regional Monitoring Reports for Central and Eastern Europe which includes a lot on Russia. They also have some good free data available – the latest is a Windows package called *Trans MONEE 3.0.*

9 The meanings of reform in the Russian school system

Stephen Webber

Introduction

What are the meanings of education in contemporary Russia?[1] If Russia is to make progress towards the consolidation of democratic values and practices discussed elsewhere in this volume, and if it is to achieve any success in its attempts to revitalise its economy, the education system must have a vital role to play. A comprehensive and ambitious set of reform policies were, indeed, introduced in Russia just after the dissolution of the Soviet Union, in the Law on Education of 1992, with the declared aims of rendering the school capable of promoting these goals. As will be shown, change is taking place in the school system, although at a slower pace than some observers claim, and along policy lines which, I argue, are based on a 'false consensus' with regard to the premises and aims of reform. Further, despite signs of a certain settling down of change within the system, the vulnerability of the school in the harsh social climate of contemporary Russia has become increasingly evident, most notably in the form of a severe decline in what was already, under the Soviet system, a weak funding base, and in such negative phenomena as the mass exclusion of children of school age. In this way, in addition to acting as a mirror of social problems, the school (or educational policy) has contributed to these crises itself.

Given the complexities of such issues, the aim of this chapter is not to provide a comprehensive analysis of school reform in post-Soviet Russia, but to focus on a select number of developments seen in the school system since 1991, both *internally* (i.e. within the system) and *externally* (i.e. the school's relations with society at large), through the following course of analysis:

- a critique of the agenda for reform
- an appraisal of the progress made to date in implementation, and a review of the problems encountered in this process
- a brief examination of the nature of the social meanings of the school

1 The reader may guess from the use of the plural form 'meanings' that I do not intend to give a positivistic account of developments in the Russian school system. As with all social processes, one person's interpretation of the nature of education will be different, perhaps greatly, from another's – what may appear to be 'choice' in selecting a school for one, may be exclusion and the denial of opportunities for another.

СПРАВКА 9.1　**The meanings of Soviet education**

The history of the Soviet education system mirrored that of the USSR as a whole: after an initial period of turmoil, there was an attempt to introduce radical change and put into practice the principles of Marxism–Leninism, which then gave way to a more traditional, conservative and authoritarian model of organisation, which allowed the country to achieve some impressive results in certain areas, but which ultimately proved too inflexible to adapt to changing social, political and economic conditions.

This should serve as a starting point for the reader's further investigation of these issues, and to highlight the importance of education as a key factor shaping the present and the future of Russia.

The development of the reform agenda

Assessing the need for change: looking forward, looking back

The reform programme currently under way in Russia's schools was officially announced in the July 1992 Law on Education of the Russian Federation, but, in fact, the momentum for change had begun some years earlier, in the mid-1980s, at the grass roots level. The work of the so-called 'teacher innovators', who promoted approaches to teaching and learning which gave more emphasis to the needs of the individual, and which stood in contrast to the unitary (and strictly controlled) curriculum endorsed by the communist authorities, attracted attention from within the teaching profession and from the public at large, and fed into an apparently widely felt impression that the Soviet school was in urgent need of reform (see Box 9.1). In this way, the education debate both mirrored the wider societal debates of that time, opened up by Gorbachev's policy of *glasnost*, and fed into them. When Boris Yeltsin named Eduard Dneprov as Minister of Education in the RSFSR in 1990, it seemed that the reformers now had their people in power, ready to put into practice in the Russian republic, and then, after December 1991, the independent Russian Federation, the ideas which the grass roots had generated and which seemed to have widespread support. The main directions of change enshrined in the Law on Education, then, can be summarised thus:

- humanisation (of the content of the curriculum and the process of teaching–learning)
- democratisation (establishing greater public accountability, encouraging more 'democratic' forms of interaction between various levels–actors in the system)

- de-ideologisation (breaking the monopoly of the communist ideology in curriculum content and other areas of school life, fostering plurality and tolerance in approaches to education)
- diversification (of the type of education provided and the types of establishment providing it)
- humanitarisation (giving more emphasis to the humanities element of the curriculum)
- decentralisation (devolution of power to the regional and municipal authorities and the schools themselves)

On the surface, these appear to be aims which are very similar to those being pursued by systems in 'liberal democracies' around the world – indeed, when the agenda was announced it received a positive reaction from a good number of Russian and foreign observers (see, for example, Coons, 1993, p. 87). We need to scratch beneath the surface, however, to investigate what a linguist might term the 'deep structure' of the agenda, i.e. the premises on which these policies are based. If we isolate and examine the case of one policy area – humanisation – for instance, a certain duality can be observed, in which the reforms represent both a forward-looking, 'progressive' approach, but also a rather remedial, even destructive, stance with regard to the perceived Soviet legacy.[2]

Humanisation is an inherently vague concept, which has been open to a wide range of interpretation since it was introduced into Soviet educational debates, although a common thread – albeit a very broad one – underlying calls for humanisation centres on the need to devote more attention to the individual pupil, and her or his personality (*lichnost*). In the Soviet system, so reformers claimed, a process of what a social psychologist might call de-individuation was encouraged by the nature of the curriculum, which was, ostensibly, common for all pupils, regardless of abilities or interests (see, for example, Kohli, 1991). Further, it was claimed by some that the authoritarian, even totalitarian nature of the school had meant that children were educated in a 'prison-like' atmosphere (Dneprov, 1994, p. 4). Accordingly, the need for humanisation was given considerable emphasis in the Law on Education, with Article 2 ('Principles of State Policy With Regard to Education') declaring a commitment to:

> The humanist character of education, the priority of universal humanitarian values, the life and health of citizens, the free development of personality . . .
>
> (The Law on Education of the Russian Federation, 1993, p. 118)

All laudable sentiments, of course – but was it right to view the ethos of the Soviet school as the antithesis of such values? Perhaps to an Anglo-Saxon observer, accustomed to the pupil-centred approach to teacher–pupil relations which has developed in recent years in the USA and UK, the atmosphere in the Soviet school (and its Russian successor) does seem to be excessively authoritarian – but an observer from a system with similar roots to the Soviet–Russian model (e.g. from France or Germany) may well be less likely to come to such

---

2 In broader terms, this duality can be seen to reflect features of post-Soviet Russian society, in which the relationship between the past, present and future – or people's perception of them – involve a complex web of tensions and contradictions.

a conclusion, viewing the maintenance of a more 'authoritarian' set of relations as more acceptable. This is not to say that there was not a need (in my opinion, at least) to foster a more 'democratic' approach to teacher–pupil relations – indeed, this feeling was shared by many respondents to a range of studies conducted in the USSR and Russia in the late 1980s and 1990s. However, the extent of the criticism levelled at the Soviet school in this and other issues belies a tendency inherent in the reform agenda towards exaggerating such ills, with the consequent risk that the pendulum might swing too far in the opposite direction.

This tendency to over-react was understandable, given the contexts in which discussion of change was taking place in the late 1980s and early 1990s. The Soviet Union was in a state of flux, with an oppressive uncertainty hanging over the future of the Soviet system and Soviet society, a condition which was only slightly ameliorated (and, in other ways, intensified) by the emergence of an independent Russia. The comfort of hindsight from our vantage point of today can cause us to talk with a confidence about developments in post-Soviet Russia which was simply not apparent to those living through the upheaval of transition: to the radical reformers in the Ministry of Education, under the dynamic and bullish leadership of the minister, Dneprov, it appears that the course of school reform was seen as a struggle against the old order, with educational change viewed as a key which could help to bring down and remove the Soviet legacy, not just in the schools but in society at large.[3] Hence the motivation behind the calls for rapid decentralisation and devolution of power in the system, for instance, and the need for diversity in curriculum, methods and the type of establishment available – again, all policies which, although they might not receive universal support, are commonly employed in many systems across the world – seem to have stemmed at least partly from a backward-looking stance on change. These reforms, moreover, were to be implemented as quickly as possible, in order to secure the dismantling of the old system.

While shock-therapy tactics may have been considered appropriate by some for dealing with the Russian economy in 1992, however (and there are many who would feel that such policies were, in fact, not justified), in the school system the adoption of what Johnson (1996, p. 41) has termed a 'big bang' approach to school reform carried even more risk: school systems are inherently conservative institutions which react slowly to change, but which are also vulnerable to radical and rapid policy shifts (it is worth reflecting on what has happened to the school system in England and Wales over the past 30 years to appreciate this point). I would suggest that if the Russian school system had tried to take on board, and to implement, the agenda for change in the style and at the pace being demanded by Dneprov, serious internal tensions would have emerged, as teachers, pupils and parents tried to come to terms with a complex set of policies, some of which they may not have supported and may have opposed

---

3 Perhaps I may be accused by some of overstating this point, although, in conversation, many Russian educationalists have agreed with me in this interpretation, indeed, a good number actually suggested this line of analysis themselves, from their perspectives as insiders. To gain your own impression, read the pieces by Dneprov and other Russian authors in Eklof B and Dneprov E, *Democracy in the Russian School*.

СПРАВКА 9.2 Russian educational establishments catering for the 6–17 age band

This table summarises the types of establishments found in the education system of the Russian Federation, showing those which existed at the end of the Soviet period (and which still exist today), and the 'new' establishments which have emerged since the late 1980s. It should be noted, however, that (a) the 'new' titles are often taken from traditional, pre-revolutionary titles (e.g. gymnasium) and (b) a change of title does not necessarily mean that much has changed within the establishment (cf. Independent Russia and the Soviet Union).

Age (grade)	Soviet model	'New' establishments
6–17 (I–XI)	Secondary school (*Obshcheobrazovatelnaia shkola*) Specialised school (in-depth study of particular discipline) (*Spetsializirovannaia shkola*)	Gymnasium (*gimnaziia*) Lycée (*litsei*)
15–17 (IX–XI)	Evening school (*Vecherniaia crediaia shkola*)	
15–17 (IX–XI)	Professional-technical College (*Professionalno-tekhnicheskoe uchilishche* – PTU)	College (*kolledzh*)
15–19	Technical college (*Tekhnikum*) Pedagogical college (*Pedagogicheskoe uchilishche*)	

strongly. In fact, as I will argue below, the realities of reform have allowed a relatively more stable (although still difficult) transition from the Soviet to Russian school (see Box 9.2).

Before we examine the course of implementation, however, I wish to reflect a little more on the background to the reforms and set the attempts to introduce them into a broader context by posing the following questions:

- was the Soviet school really in a state of crisis?
- can a consensus really be achieved on national educational needs (and at what cost)?

Was the Soviet school really in a state of crisis?

By the end of the Soviet period, there appeared to be a widespread assumption that the school system was experiencing considerable difficulties. In a 1991 survey, for instance, 69.3 per cent of teachers and 62.7 per cent of parents stated that they felt schooling was in 'a deep crisis and requires fundamental reform' (Sobkin and Pisarskii, 1992, p. 77). This message was echoed by senior politicians, including Boris Yeltsin (Yeltsin, 1989) and Mikhail Gorbachev himself (Gorbachev, 1989).[4] To some extent, of course, the perception that a crisis exists can be as significant as providing tangible proof of its presence: a lack of confidence in the schools was likely to lead to further decline, not improvement. However, such claims of crisis need to be examined more closely.

To do so, we must try to separate aims from outcomes in any analysis of the Soviet system. The exaggerated perceptions of the problems of the Soviet school, contained in the reform agenda, can be traced at least partly, I suggest, to a failure on the part of the reformers to *decontextualise* the Soviet school, i.e. to take the school out of its societal contexts and examine it as an educational institution which was or is, in its characteristics, very similar to those found in many other countries. It has often been the case, for instance, that an over-concentration on the significance of the ideological content of Soviet education has rather clouded analyses. This is not to say that such issues should be ignored or downplayed too far – indeed, a follow-up process of *recontextualising* the school back into its societal setting (thus opening up opportunities, in turn, for a deeper understanding of that society) is essential, in order to identify the part that such factors played in shaping the meaning of Soviet education. However, a more balanced assessment, which attached less weight to the perceived importance of the communist 'wrappings' of the school, could have enabled the reformers to recognise that the sense of crisis in education, of dissatisfaction with existing practices and the search for approaches better suited to the demands of contemporary societies, are issues which are familiar to school systems the world over.

In the USA, for instance, the publication in 1983 of an influential report entitled *A Nation At Risk* indicated the amount of unease among certain sections of US society with regard to their education system; in the UK, the 1988 Education Reform Act was also a reaction by the Conservative Party to a negative appraisal of the state of education. While the scale of the funding problem in the Soviet system and the general crisis in the Russian economy renders direct comparisons with Western countries somewhat problematic, it is clear that Russian schools are facing problems and demands which are very similar to those of their counterparts in, say, Holland or Canada. Even the perceived need for de-ideologisation (which appeared to be based on an exaggerated impression of the extent to which the aims of teaching communist values coincided with the actual outcomes in terms of the level of commitment by the population to these ideas) shares certain features with debates over the role of compulsory religious instruction in the UK, for instance. I am not suggesting that such matters were not more pressing in the Russian than in the English case, but merely wish to point out that the rather intense, and inward-looking, nature of the transition from the Soviet Union to Russia caused many to ignore the lessons of international experience by focusing principally on the Russian case, thus limiting the scope for useful comparison. Once more, this can be understood to a point, as the Soviet educational community had, at least until the late 1980s, been cut

4 For an excellent review of the 'crisis' in Soviet education in this period, see Jones A 1991, Problems in the Schools, in Jones A, Connor W and Powell D (eds), *Soviet Social Problems*, Westview Press, Boulder, CO, pp. 213–26.

off from the mainstream international debate on the development of schooling. Research into the sociology of education, for example, had been heavily restricted by the Soviet authorities, rendering it a much tamer field than its controversy-ridden counterpart in the West.

Trying to define national educational needs

The tension between the progressive and remedial characteristics of the policies for school reform mentioned above reflect a wider set of dynamics present throughout the countries engaged in a post-communist transformation. As the following comment seems to suggest, the backward-looking nature of change was, perhaps, inevitable, given the risks associated with challenging the established order:

> Some have argued that the political changes in Central and Eastern Europe were a revolution against communism, but not necessarily *for* any single thing . . .
>
> (Löwenhardt, 1995, p. 146)

This situation clearly makes it difficult to talk of the definition of long-term plans for the development of education in such countries, when it is hard enough just to predict what will happen in the near future. Further, given the fundamental reshaping that is, evidently, taking place in the social fabric of Russia, it is clear that there is the potential for considerable, even violent, disagreement with regard to the nature of education which is (or, as the case may be, is not) to be provided to the population. Even in relatively stable countries with a strong democratic tradition, however, the pursuit of some kind of consensus on 'national' educational goals can be an illusory goal.[5] While politicians (and the mass media) prefer to reduce the debate on education to clear-cut 'rights' and 'wrongs', the nature of schooling is, alas, far more complex than that, and does not readily submit itself to obvious solutions which will prove agreeable to a majority (or even a sizeable minority) of the population.

In post-Soviet Russia, however, something of a consensus *has* actually been achieved on the development of education, albeit somewhat by default, in the form of what I term a 'false' consensus. This stems from the fact that the public debate over education policy has remained rather shallow, progressing relatively little from the restricted debate seen in the pre-1985 Soviet period, when the communist authorities commanded a dominant position in any public discussion of such issues. Although political pluralism, freedom of speech and comparatively free mass media now exist in Russia, the country is so consumed with what seem to be the rather more urgent problems of soaring crime rates, unemployment and political instability, that education is often neglected as an issue for public discussion. Even among those who do take an active part in talking about education, there often seemed, in the early 1990s at least, to be a reluctance to challenge what have proved in the West to be highly contested notions, such as the ambiguous concept of 'choice' in educational provision,

5 See, for example, a description of such matters as they relate to the school system in England: Jonathan R 1996 Education and 'The Needs of Society', in Hartness A and Nash M (eds), *Education and Society Today*, Falmer Press, London, pp. 134–45.

and a willingness to support calls for, say, 'humanisation' and 'democratisation' without fully being aware of the meanings of the terms.

Through this false consensus a rather eclectic set of education policies, which in the UK would be labelled as examples of both right- and left-wing stances on education, have managed to cohabit in the reform agenda, a situation that holds both positive and negative implications. Positive, in that the potential for conflict which the introduction of the reform agenda entailed has been somewhat softened by the lack of substantial debate on these issues (and, indeed, perhaps the Russian experience shows that constructive coexistence of seemingly opposing ideas is possible, a potential lesson for many systems), and negative, in that this somewhat artificial level of agreement (or, more accurately, consensus through disinterest and lack of awareness) is not helping the development of a stronger and more active social conscience with regard to education, which will be necessary if Russian society is to address effectively the internal contradictions and tensions inherent in the agenda.

Towards implementation

In the previous section I have shown that an understanding of the social contexts which have shaped the reform agenda is essential, if we are to appreciate the nature of change in the Russian school system. However, it is also important to bear in mind that the outcomes of school reform may diverge considerably from the aims set out by the policy-makers, and that certain concerns over the premises of reform outlined above may well prove less significant as policies move into the implementation phase, and are adapted and distorted, face practical obstacles and are even opposed, as they pass through what I call the 'prism of change'. In this section an appraisal will be made of the course of change in Russia's schools during the 1990s, and some tentative conclusions drawn on the internal state of the system in the first decade after the Soviet Union.

Some observers, Russian and foreign, have overestimated the pace and scale of real change in the Russian school system, arguing that strong evidence of successful implementation is already visible. In 1995, for instance, it was claimed that a complex innovation in teaching and learning called 'developmental education' (Box 9.3), designed by Russian researchers working on the foundations of the great Russian psychologist Vygotsky, had been effectively introduced into 42 per cent of all primary-level classes in the country (Ob itogakh . . . , 1995, p. 63). In fact, we should be more cautious: the experience of educational change across the world, even in cases of relatively small reforms in stable, prosperous countries, indicates that the change process is a long, drawn-out affair, which has more often than not ended in failure, or at least only the partial achievement of aims. In the case of the developmental education initiative, it is extremely unlikely that such a large number of schools had, in fact, managed to implement it successfully, less than two years afters its introduction, especially given the resources problem faced by the schools (see below). Overall, the pursuit of the highly ambitious and comprehensive package of reforms launched in the Russian school system, against a backdrop of severe political, economic

СПРАВКА 9.3 **On Vygotsky and developmental education**

Developmental education, is the term used to describe an approach to learning devised by teams of psychologists working in the traditions of the famous Russian psychologist, Lev Vygotsky, whose work continues to exert a major influence on educational psychology in Russia. Vygotsky's work, which includes such concepts the 'Zone of Proximal Development', has been adapted by Zankov, Davydov and others to promote the creation of a learning environment which is more child centred than the traditional Soviet approach allowed.

and social crises which cannot but adversely affect the schools, suggests that we should not expect too much success too soon.

Change, then, is an elusive concept which is difficult to evaluate and almost impossible to quantify. Rather than attempt a definitive account of change in Russian schools, therefore, I will refer to the patterns change experience which I observed in Russian schools in my own research.[6]

While I will suggest a likely distribution of such experience in the system as a whole, the reader should be aware that it is still, even at the time of writing in 1998, too early to speak with confidence of the results of the reform programme launched in 1992.

Innovation and over-experimentation

There is no doubt that some of the innovative work being practised in certain Russian schools is of very high quality, and is in the avant garde of such work anywhere in the world. The implementation of Bibler's 'dialogue of cultures' approach to learning, for example, and the experience in democratic school organisation of such educationalists as Tubelsky in Moscow and Frumin in Novosibirsk deserve (and have attracted) the attention of Western educationalists (see Box 9.4). Apart from such prominent examples, one can also observe considerable change in a wide range of schools, with the adoption of innovative approaches encouraged vigorously by the federal-level ministry, especially under the first Russian Minister of Education Dneprov, and a certain momentum has also been generated by such initiatives as the founding of the Russian Association of Innovative Schools (see Frumin, 1997).

In my field-work, I interviewed staff in a secondary school in St Petersburg in which a highly detailed programme for change had been drawn up, with the

---

6 This research was conducted between 1990 and 1997, and included field-work in the cities and regions of Yaroslavl, Moscow and St Petersburg, during which I visited a wide range of educational establishments and conducted interviews with a large number of educationalists, pupils, administrators, journalists and researchers. The findings will be presented in my forthcoming book, *School, Society and Reform in the New Russia*, to be published by Macmillan Press in 1999.

СПРАВКА 9.4 **Innovation in Russian schools**

Bibler's dialogue of cultures

The dialogue of cultures approach to learning established by the educationalist Bibler aims, as the name suggests, to develop cross-cultural understanding, through organising the curriculum around inter-disciplinary projects in which the pupils follow the development of European society from Ancient Greece onwards.

Democratic school organisation

Alexander Tubelsky and Isak Frumin are headteachers (from Moscow and Novosibirsk respectively) who have gained a national and international reputation for their work on democracy in education. Tubelsky, for instance, has created a 'School of Self-Determination' in a secondary school, in which pupils play a major part in organising the life of their establishment.

involvement of all members of staff, and with clearly defined goals and evaluation procedures. Although it was difficult to assess the extent to which these plans were proving successful, this approach stands in marked contrast to the lack of freedom for initiative which existed under the Soviet system, in which teachers could face severe reprimands for straying too far (i.e. just a little) from the officially approved and prescribed line. Indeed, even in systems which have not endured such restrictions, the practice of the school described above might be seen as untypically advanced, promoting the development of 'change agents' among the staff (i.e. encouraging teachers to take responsibility for change), and setting strategic goals for innovation, thus achieving the kind of 'vision' of change which theorists on reform consider essential.[7]

The pursuit of innovation can be taken too far, however. As the rigid controls of the Soviet system were relaxed further and further, even before December 1991, some educationalists, schools and even municipal and regional authorities began to take advantage of the opportunity this presented to 'do their own thing', while paying insufficient attention to the need to ensure that their innovations were justified and scientifically well grounded, and to the need to maintain a degree, at least, of commonality within the school system. With regard to the management of the system, for instance, although it would be going too far to suggest that system-wide cohesion has been compromised since 1991, concerns were expressed by some over the implications of the rush to devolve

7 For a key text on school reform, see Fullan M 1991 *The New Meaning of Educational Change*, Cassell, London.

responsibility before adequate measures had been taken to ensure a smooth transition to a decentralised model (see, for example, Bolotov, 1994), with some regions, for instance, adopting policies for change which contradicted those promoted by the centre. It is true that this is something which is not uncommon in other decentralised systems, as seen in the conflict between left-wing Local Education Authorities and the right-wing Conservative Government in the UK in the 1980s. However, the disruption which such conflicts cause to the school system is likely to be exacerbated in the Russian case, with a more violent swing seen in some areas away from a hyper-centralised model to one in which an increasing amount of dislocation is possible, if such trends are left to develop, between the educational policies followed in the country's 89 regions.

At the school level, I can refer to an example which, again, shows how the policies advocated by the centre have contributed to problems of fragmentation. As part of the democratisation strand of the reform agenda, schools were urged to build upon the momentum of the late 1980s, in which one element of the drive to introduce greater 'pluralism' into school life had been the attention given to the role of school councils, which, it was hoped, would give a voice to the parents, pupils and local community representatives in the running of the schools. The amount of influence afforded to the pupils in such democratic councils could be taken too far, however: in one case, reported by the First Deputy Minister of Education, the pupils had voted to have mathematics and other 'difficult' subjects removed from the curriculum, replaced by increased emphasis on 'easier' disciplines. Since the decision of the vote was final, according to the constitution of the council, the removal had to be upheld – setting an example which, perhaps, many school-children across the world would find alluring, but which is surely not a sound basis for establishing curriculum guidelines! (Bolotov, 1994, p. 4).

Cases such as these highlight the flaws in the reform agenda mentioned earlier: a more forward-looking, evolutionary approach to managing school reform may have helped the reformers to predict, and thus to try to avoid, some of the problems of fragmentation seen in recent years, which prompted a good number of the educationalists I interviewed to complain of pedagogical anarchy in the schools. Such an assessment is, fortunately, overly pessimistic, as a false impression of the frequency of such problems is provided by the amount of coverage which they have received in the educational community. They do represent a significant problem to the authorities, however, which must try to tap into and exploit the potential for change which innovative teachers and schools possess, but at the same time ensure that such energy is channelled into productive innovation, rather than over-experimentation.

Much of this innovation and over-experimentation is to be found in so-called 'alternative' schools, a loosely applied term which covers establishments ranging from the private sector, which includes what would in the UK be considered traditional academically oriented schools as well as schools with Montessori and Steiner approaches to education (Box 9.5), to the state and semi-state-controlled gymnasia and lycées. Increasingly, such schools have come to charge fees for attendance, often attract relatively highly qualified staff through offering higher salaries, and they have a pupil cohort which will often be of the above-average

СПРАВКА 9.5   **Montessori and Steiner approaches to education**

Maria Montessori (1870–1952) based her ideas on her experiences with mentally handicapped children. She developed a method of teaching based on an informal approach, incorporating instructive play and allowing children to develop at their own pace. Rudolph Steiner (1861–1925) was an Austrian philosopher who developed his own mystical and spiritual teaching. His method of teaching emphasised the arts as a means to develop the whole human being. His first school was set up in Stuttgart, Germany, in 1891, but many others have followed the Steiner method. The educational approaches of Montessori and Steiner, which are well known and established in the West, but have not generally been integrated into the educational mainstream, have been adopted with varying degrees of success by a good number of schools and kindergartens in Russia.

ability range (although the parents' ability to pay can also be a deciding factor, of course). As a result, these schools can (that is not to say they necessarily do) have an advantage over state-run secondary schools, in terms of resources (material and human), and thus may enjoy a potentially better capacity for change; moreover, a good number were set up on the initiative of a head teacher and colleagues who had worked in the state sector before, and who had some motivation (and subsequent stake) in engaging in innovation. Despite such advantages, however, the alternative schools have not always proved capable of meeting the expectations of, among others, the reform team under Dneprov, that they might become 'beacons of change' for the system as a whole; furthermore, while their numbers have grown (by 1997 some 50 500 pupils were enrolled in non-state schools, in comparison with 32 600 in 1993) (Osnovnye napravleniia . . . , 1998, p. 11), this represents a mere 0.24 per cent of the total of 21 million children of school age (6–17 years) in Russia (Bolotov, 1997, p. 9). In general, some 1.5 million pupils (7 per cent of school-age population in Russia) were studying in 'profile' schools in 1997 (i.e. schools in which certain subjects, such as mathematics or foreign languages, are studied intensively), and over one million pupils were enrolled in gymnasia and lycées (768 000 and 406 000 respectively), again representing just some 5.6 per cent of the school age population (Osnovnye napravleniia . . . , 1998, p. 11). It is therefore the under-funded state 'comprehensive' which must shoulder the responsibility for the development of the system.

Shallow coping

From the evidence of my own research, and drawing on the insights into educational change provided by a sizeable body of research in Western systems, however, it is likely that the true extent of real change, up to the late 1990s at least, was actually quite limited in the Russian school system. Although many teachers claimed that they had introduced change (and this, in itself, can be a positive sign of inclination to innovation), many would, in fact, have been paying lip-service to change, repeating buzz-words such as humanisation and differentiation, without having actually introduced anything substantially new into their teaching. This is only to be expected, as similar patterns are found in any school system; in the Russian case, it had, quite understandably, proven difficult to break free of the culture of the Soviet system, in which attempts at unsanctioned change were strongly discouraged. In order to become 'change agents', Russian teachers needed to receive an adequate level of support and retraining; unfortunately, the question of teacher education, which should be the number one priority in any educational reform effort, was neglected for much of the 1990s (see, for example, Webber and Webber, 1994; Webber, 1996). As a result, I would suggest (although, to reiterate, I have no way of proving so conclusively with hard figures) that the majority of schools and teachers found that they were engaged, consciously or not, in what Louis and Miles refer to, when writing about American schools, as 'shallow coping' – in other words there was a semblance of change, but it was rather superficial, existing more in statements and reports than in actual practice (Louis and Miles, 1990).

Towards a settling down of reform?

As the initial dust of the turbulent post-Soviet transition cleared a little in the late 1990s, however, it was possible to discern, I would suggest, a certain amount of 'settling down', or institutionalisation of the reform effort. The mechanisms of cohesion which the central authorities had been slow to introduce in the early 1990s had now been developed and introduced (see Webber, 1997), albeit with delays and encountering certain obstacles, and comprised:

- a Federal Programme for the Development of Education (a framework for devolution, establishing a strategic agenda for change at the federal, regional, municipal and school levels)
- a set of educational standards (to provide a more flexible pattern of benchmarks than the discarded, rigid Soviet curriculum)
- a system of teacher appraisal
- a new system of school inspection and accreditation.

Progress had been made in adapting the teacher-education network to suit the demands of the post-Soviet school, and a more reasoned, evolutionary approach to change appeared to have emerged at all levels. Central and regional authorities seemed to be engaged in greater co-operation, for instance, and educationalists seemed to have a more informed attitude to the nature of change, having had the opportunity to stand back and evaluate the successes and failures of the early years of reform. In short, it seemed that the rather aggressive and remedial nature of the reforms as they were promoted in the immediate aftermath of the dissolution of the USSR had given way to a more promising, constructive and forward-looking approach to change – or is this a naive, premature assessment?

Practical obstacles to change

Perhaps so, for while one might argue with my contention that there are signs of settling down in the reform process itself, there can be no dispute over the severity of the funding crisis in education, and the consequences it has held for the state of the schools and their ability to implement change. The proportion of GDP spent on education has, apart from short-lived revivals, declined continuously from the end of the Soviet into the post-Soviet period, with a figure of 3.5 per cent recorded in 1995 (*Finansy v Rossii Statisticheskii sbornik*, 1996, p. 18). As a comparison, the United States allocates some 5.5 per cent, the United Kingdom 5.3 per cent and France 5.4 per cent (*Russia: Education in the Transition*, 1995, p. 15); more tellingly, one needs to bear in mind also the tremendous economic decline since 1991 which has further exacerbated the problem (see Williams, 1996, p. 13). The federal education authorities frequently complain that even the money that has been earmarked for education in the budget is often delayed, diverted or frozen: in 1994, for instance, only 61.3 per cent of the minimum funding requirements of the education system were met (Den'gi, den'gi ..., 1995, p. 16). In general, then, this is a bleak outlook, whose nature has been complicated by the process of regionalising responsibility for finances. Indeed, the problems have been so acute that they have brought into question not only the fate of the reforms but, I would suggest, the very survival of the school itself as a viable social institution, as it struggles with, among other things:

- the social and psychological problems of the pupils, part of the fall-out from broader societal crises in Russia (e.g. increasing criminal activity among the young, the rise in substance abuse as well as malnutrition and destitution) (Education for all?, 1998)
- difficulties in obtaining adequate supplies of teaching and learning resources, needed to introduce curricular innovation
- a shortage of teaching staff, to the order of some 34 000 personnel across Russia, with rural schools worst hit, and with the largest shortages overall among teachers of the sciences, foreign languages and Russian language (Osnovnye napravleniia ..., 1998, p. 11)

It is clear, then, that although the school system may be showing signs of internal stabilisation and development, such progress will be of little long-term value if the external problems associated with the school's relations with society are not resolved. As will be shown in the next, concluding, section, however, the experience of the schools since 1991 gives relatively little encouragement in this matter. (Some further information on the Russian school system is provided in Box 9.6)

СПРАВКА 9.6   **Facts and figures about the Russian school system**

In the school system of the Russian Federation there are:

- 67 200 schools (12.9 per cent overall, and 23 per cent of village schools have no heating system; 6.3 per cent of school buildings are in a dangerous state of repair)
- 21.4 million pupils (some 2.8 million children of school age, however, are not in education)
- 1.7 million teachers (in 1997 some 10 per cent of them, however, were of pensionable age, a sign of the difficulties encountered in recruiting and retaining younger staff, as a protest against the worsening material position of teachers, who, in some cases, did not receive their miserly salary for months on end, an increasing amount of strike action was seen in the 1990s: there was strong support from teachers, for instance, for the All-Russian day of protest organised by the unions on 9 April 1998, with over 1.8 million teachers taking part (Ne khotim rabotat besplatno, 1985, p. 5))

Source: if not otherwise indicated, Osnovnye napravleniia ... (1998)

The social contexts of the Russian school

The propaganda of the Soviet regime, which boasted of the achievements of its education system, could not but wear off on the population, with many Russians still retaining (to an extent justifiably) positive perceptions of the capacity of the Soviet–Russian school system. The stark reality is that this foundation, for all its inherent weaknesses exposed and vilified by the reformers, has been eroded in the post-Soviet era by the neglect of the needs of the system described in the previous section, with little sign that Russian society is either fully aware of, or able or willing to do much about, this state of affairs or the drastic consequences which it might entail. In this concluding section I will briefly draw the reader's attention to some of the areas of concern and their possible implications.

A disintegrating safety net

School systems are fragile social institutions, and, in order to survive the ravages of economic constraints, criticism of falling standards and blame for a country's economic performance or moral climate, they need the support of strong and effective relations with society, which will serve as a safety net to protect them from such external 'threats' and to maintain a constructive, if highly contested, debate over the role that schools are to play in society. In Russia these ties have been strained in recent years, as the various crises in other aspects of life have consumed the thoughts and activities of the ordinary population and of the politicians and policy-makers. In the mass media, for instance, while education issues can, occasionally, make the front-page headlines and do receive a good deal of coverage, the majority of attention, understandably, is devoted to the never-ending political upheaval and economic turmoil, leaving little time or energy, it seems, to deal with the issue of education. Further, owing to various reasons outlined elsewhere in this volume, the degree to which the population at large feels willing or able to take an active stance on issues of this kind, even if they and their dependants are directly affected, is relatively low in Russia, another legacy of the Soviet period, and a symptom of civic life in contemporary Russia. There is only a low level of collective activity among parents, for instance, with few parents' groups to speak of, and while the teachers' unions have been engaged in a long battle to extract salary concessions from the authorities, they have been less concerned with the protection of the fabric of the school system itself. Meanwhile, the commerce and industry sectors have been too preoccupied with their own problems to spare that much attention to education. As a result, the school finds itself neglected, protected only by a weak and fragmenting safety net.

Selection and exclusion as a feature of the new Russia

Although the Law on Education of 1992 stated in its opening paragraphs that 'The right of receiving education is one of the fundamental and inalienable constitutional rights of citizens of the Russian Federation' (The Law on Education of the Russian Federation, 1993, p. 117), developments in the schools since 1991 have steered towards a more exclusive approach, in which the selection of certain pupils – and, thus, the rejection of others – has become an increasingly prevalent feature of the system. By 1995, for instance, in a study of 77 Moscow schools, some 44 either had already introduced or intended to introduce competitive selection of pupils. Since the criteria for selection were (ostensibly) based on academic ability and/or (less openly) on the ability to pay, increasing numbers of children of 'below-average' ability or poorer economic backgrounds began to find themselves with decreased opportunities to receive education, to the point that many children of school age found themselves denied a place at school altogether. By 1997, it was estimated that some 2.7 million children who should have been at school were, in fact, outside the school walls (information passed to the author by Russian researchers, using information obtained from official sources in the Ministry of General and Professional Education of the Russian Federation). A proportion of these may well have chosen this option for themselves, it is true, but investigations by journalists and researchers demonstrated clearly that a good number of children were being forced out of education against their will (see, for example, Gleizer, 1996).

   This trend of selection developed at the level of individual schools, which pursued their own aims in choosing which children they did and did not want to teach, but it took place as part of a broader shift away from the principle of universal education which the Soviet system was supposed to have promoted, and it should thus be seen as another example of the reaction against the Soviet legacy referred to earlier. The momentum received official endorsement in the

1992 Law on Education, which stated that free education would only be guaranteed until the age of 15, rather than the previous limit of 17, a decision which was confirmed in Article 43 of the 1993 Russian constitution. While the drop of two years may not seem that dramatic, with the upper-age mark of 15 not too far off the range found in many countries, it was the symbolic statement that the introduction of this article seemed to make which aroused the concerns of some in Russian society (although it should be noted that a good proportion of the population, and even the teaching profession, seemed indifferent to, or even supported, this move). Eventually, Yeltsin saw fit, in the summer of 1994, to issue a decree reversing the decision announced in Article 43, although the practice of selection and rejection of pupils continued (an indication of the dichotomy which exists in Russia between the existence of legislation and the ability of the authorities to enforce it).

Building a democratic, market-based future for Russia?

Such examples point to the presence of a strong element of conflict in post-Soviet Russian education, i.e. the clash of interests between various social groups, competing for what has proved to be a contracting resource. While some are able to continue to gain access to education, through financial means or by dint of academic ability, others are denied such opportunities. Is this really the kind of basis on which Russia can build a future for itself, in which democratic values are able to thrive, and the necessary skills and knowledge are available for the development of a strong, market-based economy? These are, after all, the aims declared by the Russian political leadership since 1991.

Surely it will not be possible to talk of a democratic future if this process does not include the vast majority of Russian citizens – and surely those children who find themselves rejected by society at the age of 15 or less (some cases of exclusion have occurred among children as young as nine) are not likely to feel that they are, in fact, included. Also, if educational provision continues to be cut (not just at primary and secondary, but also at pre-school, tertiary and higher-education levels as well), if an increasing number of vocational colleges are being closed in order to sell them off to private companies for use as offices, and if the material and personnel crises of the education system continue to worsen, will Russia really be able to talk seriously of developing long-term economic growth, and of becoming a true international competitor on world markets? It seems rather doubtful.

References

Bolotov V 1994 The Challenge of Educational Reform in Russia, *ISRE Newsletter*, Vol. 3, Nos. 1 and 2, pp. 3–7.

Bolotov V 1997 The Reform of Education in New Russia: A Background Report for the OECD Review of Russian Education, *ISRE Newsletter*, Vol. 6, No. 1, p. 9.

Coons J 1993 The New Russian Education Law: An Appreciation and Some Precautions, in De Groof J (ed.), *Comments on the Law on Education of the Russian Federation*, Acco, Leuven, pp. 87–94.

Den'gi, den'gi. Nichego, krome deneg 1996 *Uchitel'skaia gazeta*, Vol. 27, 6 June, pp. 16–17.

Dneprov E 1994 *Chetvertaia shkolnaia reforma v Rossii*, Interfaks, Moscow.

Education for All? 1998 UNESCO Florence.

Finansy v Rossii: Statisticheskii sbornik 1996 Gokomstat Rossii, Moscow.

Frumin I 1997 The Festival of the Russian Association of Innovative Schools, *ISRE Newsletter*, Vol. 6, No. 1, pp. 23–4.

Gleizer G 1996 Vash rebenok 'ne sootvetsvuet shkole'?, *Narodnoe obrazovanie*, Vol. 8, pp. 12–15.

Gorbachev M 1989 Youth: A Creative Force for Revolutionary Renewal, *Soviet Education*, Vol. 31, No. 3, pp. 3–4 (translated from *Uchitel'skaia gazeta*, 18 April 1987, pp. 1–2).

Johnson M 1996 Russian Education Reform in the 1990s, *The Harriman Review*, Vol. 9, No. 4, pp. 36–45.

Jones A, Connor W and Powell D (eds) 1991 *Soviet Social Problems*, Westview, Boulder, Co.

Kohli W 1991 Humanising Education in the Soviet Union: A Plea for Caution in These Postmodern Times, *Studies in Philosophy and Education*, Vol. 11, No. 2, pp. 51–63.

The Law on Education of the Russian Federation 1993 in De Groof J (ed.), *Comments on the Law on Education of the Russian Federation*, Acco, Leuven, pp. 117–60.

Louis K and Miles M 1990 *Improving the Urban High School: What Works and Why*, Teachers' College Press, New York.

Löwenhardt J 1995 *The Reincarnation of Russia: Struggling with the Legacy of Communism 1990–1994*, Longman, Harlow.

Ob itogakh raboty Ministerstva obrazovaniia Rossiiskoi Federatsii v 1994 godu i osnovnykh zadachakh razvitiia obrazovaniia na 1995 god 1995 *Vestnik obrazovaniia*, Vol. 6, pp. 4–82.

Osnovnye napravleniia i itogi deiatel'nosti Ministerstva obshchego i professional'nogo obrazovaniia Rossiiskoi Federatsii v 1997 godu I pervoocherednye zadiachi na 1998 god 1998 *Uchitel'skaia gazeta*, No. 11, 24 March, p. 11.

Russia: Education in the Transition 1995 World Bank, Washington, DC.

Sobkin V and Pisarskii P 1992 *Sotsiokul'turnyi analiz obrazovatel'noi situatsii v megapolise*, Respublikanksii tsentr sotsiologii obrazovaniia, Moscow.

Webber S 1996 Demand and Supply: Meeting the Need for Teachers in the 'New' Russian School, *Journal of Education for Teaching*, Vol. 22, No. 1, pp. 9–26.

Webber S 1997 Mechanisms of Cohesion and Support: Teacher Appraisal and School Inspection in Russia, *Education in Russia, the Independent States and Eastern Europe*, Vol. 15, No. 2, pp. 59–75.

Webber S and Webber T 1994 Issues in Teacher Education, in Jones A (ed.), *Education and Society in the New Russia*, M E Sharpe, Armonk, NY, pp. 231–59.

Williams C 1996 Economic Reform and Political Change in Russia, 1991–1996, in Williams C, Chuprov V and Staroverov V (eds), *Russian Society in Transition*, Dartmouth, Aldershot.

Yeltsin B 1989 School Reform: Ways to Accelerate It, *Soviet Education*, Vol. 31, No. 2, pp. 76–90 (translated from *Uchitel'skaia gazeta*, 3 July 1986, pp. 1–2).

Further reading

Webber S 1999 *School, Society and Reform in the New Russia*, Macmillan, Basingstoke.

10 Religion and politics in Russia

Edwin Bacon

Introduction

It is something of a truism to state that religion has played an increasing role in Russian political life over the past decade. Given the history of church–state relations in Russia, this is not telling us much. The Soviet state, to varying degrees between 1917 and 1987, sought the destruction of religion hand in hand with the building of communism. The two were connected. Marx and Marxists – and many more besides – adhered to the view of secularisation as an inevitable adjunct to modernisation. Modernity and rationalism came together. Religion was ancient superstition and a source of refuge for the uneducated masses from the harsh realities of late nineteenth-century life. The ordering and management of all spheres of life by the people in the interests of the people would remove the need for such a refuge, and fulfilment would be found in the material here and now.

Consequently, during the Soviet era the party line was that, just as communism would be built, so religion would be destroyed. Within each of these broad assertions, however, lies a variety of specific policies. The building of communism took different forms. At times it was super-activist: war communism's sweeping nationalisation in the immediate post-revolutionary period, Stalin's collectivisation of agriculture and rapid industrialisation programme in the early 1930s, the 'export of revolution' as a pretext for war against Poland in 1920 and the continued occupation of Eastern Europe after the Second World War.

At other times, however, communism was to be built more slowly. According to the ideology of the Communist Party of the Soviet Union, it was a scientific fact that communism would supersede capitalism as it represented a superior form of socio-economic organisation. Consequently, there were those who advocated a more gradual approach to the building of communism. In the 1920s the leading party theoretician Bukharin, in opposition to those arguing for rapid and forced collectivisation, spoke of progressing 'at the speed of a peasant nag'. Nikita Khrushchev made a widely misinterpreted statement to Western diplomats, translated everywhere as 'we will bury you' and presumed to be a threatening boast about inevitable military victory in any future superpower conflict. In fact a better translation would have been 'we will be there at your funeral', suggesting something rather different from military conflict – that the long-term steady success of Soviet socialism would outlive the declining capitalist system, without the necessity of war.

Similarly, the destruction of religion was alternatively carried out actively or more passively allowed to happen with little more encouragement than that given by anti-religious propaganda. Super-activism in this regard, however, did not always follow the same cycle as did super-activism in regard to building communism. The first burst of post-revolutionary Bolshevik enthusiasm which saw the radical policies of war communism also saw the separation of church and state, the arrests and execution or imprisonment of thousands of clergymen and believers and the deprivation of religious groups of their status as 'legal persons'. In this period the Russian Orthodox Church, suffering for its close links with the Tsarist regime, was the focus of persecution. In the late 1920s and early 1930s, a renewed wave of religious persecution saw both the promulgation of the Law on Religious Associations of 1929, which strengthened the state's control of religious groups, and the rapid growth of the League of Militant Atheists, formed in 1926.

Subsequently, however, the Orthodox Church was allowed a degree of rehabilitation – albeit under strict state control – during the latter years of the Stalin era, and the greatest post-war onslaught on religion came under Khrushchev whose anti-religious campaign of 1960–64 resulted in the wholesale closure of churches and arrests of believers. Religious persecution in the Brezhnev years was less by comparison, but nonetheless persistent, and even Mikhail Gorbachev began his years in office calling for an end to religious belief before his ideological *volte face* of 1987 onwards abandoned this and other previously sacrosanct elements of the Marxist–Leninist canon.

Therefore, to recognise the increased role of religion in Russian politics since the collapse of Soviet communism, given the history of religion in twentieth-century Russia, reveals little more than the fact that between 1992 and 1997 religious freedom was once again allowed in the Russian Federation. According to opinion polls churches are widely trusted and regularly attended by between 5 and 7 per cent of the population. They therefore represent one of the stronger elements of a weak civil society, and consequently politicians in a nascent democracy have sought to gain the support of those who adhere in one way or another to religious belief.

In order to understand better the interaction between religion and politics in Russia, this chapter will consider the various elements which make up the politico-religious interface. The first, and underlying a number of subsequent analytical factors, is the quantification of religious belief in Russia, primarily through a consideration of opinion poll data. Second, how has the level of religious belief affected two key areas of the post-Soviet polity – electoral politics and ideology? The third is religion and the law in Russia. The 1993 Constitution guarantees a secular state and freedom of religion, with all religious groups being equal before the law. The 1997 law on religious associations contradicts these fundamentals, and the passage of this law was unusual in post-Soviet Russian politics as the parliament insisted on its passage despite an initial presidential veto. Fourth, the particular role of the Russian Orthodox Church, seemingly the main beneficiary of the new law, and rapidly seen to be taking on the accoutrements of being a state church in all but name, is considered. Finally, this chapter seeks a theoretical understanding of the relationship between state and religion in Russia. It will argue the particular relevance of the 'civil religion' explanation of the development of this relationship, and further seek to go beyond the previously dominant rational-modernity school of thought to consider whether a post-modernist approach to religion and political culture has any relevance in the Russian context.

Quantification of belief

To quantify accurately the extent of religious belief, definitions are vital. The two definitions used here are 'self-identified believers' and 'regular attenders'. Religion can be a matter of birth or belief, and the former definition will produce a larger number of adherents than the latter. In other words, an ethnic Russian citizen of the Russian Federation might identify themself as a Christian indicating that they are not a Muslim or a Jew. They might further identify themselves as a Russian Orthodox Christian as a statement of nationality. Despite such identifying statements, however, that citizen might never attend church nor have a grasp of, let alone belief in, the doctrines of Christianity in general or Russian Orthodoxy in particular.

Using the criteria of self-identification, opinion polls in Russia in the 1990s show that around 50 per cent of the Russian population would call themselves believers. Despite the decades of state-sponsored atheism under the Soviet regime, nominal adherence to religion has far from died out. Nonetheless, taking a narrower definition of believers produces different results. The same opinion polls which tell us that half of the Russian population consider themselves religious believers also reveal that only between 5 and 7 per cent of the population regularly (once a month or more) attend a place of worship. This definition of believer comes closer to identifying active belief rather than cultural identity. The wider definition – that of self-identified believers – suggests more an identification with elements of nationalism and tradition than a daily faith. According to opinion polls of the early 1990s, those who identify themselves as believers are more likely to hold conservative views and to be less tolerant of minorities (Wyman, 1997, p. 114).

During the Soviet era, anti-religious propaganda liked to give the impression that religious belief in the Soviet Union was confined to 'survivals' of the pre-revolutionary era, primarily old women in the countryside. Surveys in the 1990s do indeed show that the incidence of religious belief among the elderly female rural population is above average. The full picture, however, is not quite so straightforward. In socio-demographic terms a dual typology of believers, using the narrower definition of 'regular attenders', can be constructed. Regular attendance is more common among women than among men. Age-wise both the over 55s and the under 24s are more likely to attend church, and in terms of place of residence the levels of attendance are higher in the countryside and in the 'capital' cities, meaning Moscow and St Petersburg.

This dual typology of old and young, rural and big city, is not simply a post-Soviet phenomenon. Soviet studies of the early 1980s showed increasing numbers of the educated urban population joining the Russian Orthodox Church in adulthood (Anderson, 1994, p. 87) and a marked propensity for non-Orthodox congregations, such as those of the Baptists and Pentecostals, to contain a large proportion of young educated urban believers (Anderson, 1994, p. 77). According to a study carried out under the auspices of the Academy of Sciences among city dwellers in 1990 and 1991, belief in God was highest in the under 20s and the over 60s (Filatov and Furman, 1992). Such a dual typology has also been found to be the case in recent research among Muslims in the five Islamic autonomous republics of Russia, according to a survey carried out in 1993 (Lehman, 1997).

In the 1990s Russia much has been made by politicians across the political spectrum of the centrality of Russian Orthodoxy as a unifying factor in Russian society (Chinyaeva, 1997). Excluding the obvious exceptions of Russia's five Islamic republics and one Buddhist republic, can the Russian Federation be described as a Russian Orthodox country? In terms of the widest definition of self-identified believers then the answer is yes, with the figures cited above meaning that over 72 million people identify themselves as Russian Orthodox. Using the narrower definition of regular attenders, however, produces a far less clear-cut picture. If we accept a figure of 5 per cent of the population for those who attend a place of worship at least once a month, this amounts to some seven and a half million believers. Estimates of Christian denominations outside of the official Russian Orthodox Church in Russia (Pentecostals, Baptists, Lutherans, Adventists, Catholics and Old Believers) put their total at some 3.3 million and growing in 1993 (Johnstone, 1993, p. 467). Making the plausible assumption that those who actually choose a denomination other than the national church are very likely to be regular attenders, then under this definition almost half of the practising Christians in Russia today are not Russian Orthodox. This becomes significant when considering, as we shall do later, the implementation of a law on religious associations which privileges the Russian Orthodox Church.

Electoral politics and ideology

Opinion polls consistently show the Russian Orthodox Church to be the most trusted public body in post-Soviet Russia. The New Russian Barometer III Survey in 1994 provided a list of 16 'public institutions' including the presidency, government, parliament, army, media, trade unions and political parties. The Church outscored them all as a recipient of trust (White *et al.*, 1997, p. 52). A survey conducted at the time of the summer 1996 presidential election similarly indicated that a very high proportion of respondents, some 41 per cent, 'fully trusted' the Orthodox Church, and only 9 per cent did not trust it at all (Dubin, 1996, p. 15). This level of trust and respect contrasts markedly with attitudes towards political parties, the institutions of government, and politicians in general. It is scarcely surprising therefore that politicians have sought to transfer some of the respect for the Church into their own sphere of activity, particularly at election times.

The interaction of religion and politics in Russia's parliamentary and presidential elections has not generally come at the most obvious substantive level of religious parties or key religious voting issues. Instead religion has been a fairly ubiquitous tool in electoral campaigning to symbolise a general stance of morality, tradition, and 'Russian-ness'. In Russia's parliamentary election of December 1995 there were 43 parties on the ballot paper contesting the party list side of the election, which accounts for half of the members of the lower house of parliament, the Duma. Out of these 43 parties there were only two specifically religious parties, namely the All-Russian Muslim Social Movement and the Christian Democratic Union/Christians of Russia bloc. These two groups achieved respectively 0.57 and 0.28 per cent of the vote on the party list ballot, a vote comparable with the 0.35 per cent received by the Association of Russian Lawyers, and below the 0.62 per cent garnered by the Beer Lovers' Party.

It is clear that there was no great mobilisation of a religious vote by avowedly religious candidates in the 1995 parliamentary election. Nonetheless, religion in some form played a part in the campaign strategies of leading candidates for the Duma elections of 1995 and, more particularly, the presidential elections in June 1996. In December 1995, for example, representatives from 17 parties attended a conference hosted by the leader of the Russian Orthodox Church Patriarch Aleksi II at the Danilovsky Monastery. Those present included the Communist leader – and subsequent 'runner up' in the presidential election six months later – Gennadi Zyuganov, Vladimir Zhirinovsky, leader of the ultra-nationalist Liberal Democratic Party of Russia which had topped the party list ballot in the 1993 parliamentary election, and the then Prime Minister and leader of the pro-government 'Russia Is Our Home' Party, Viktor Chernomyrdin. The opportunity to be seen with the head of the Church represented the chance to appeal by association to a large electorate.

This strategy of the use of religion in campaigning became even more marked in the 1996 presidential election. Often engagement with the Church came in the form of symbolism. In a campaign where scarcely a candidate departed from overt adherence to some form of Russian national patriotism, and pride in the traditions of the great Russian nation, then almost the ideal photo-opportunity – except in ethnically non-Russian areas – was of the candidate with an Orthodox priest. Both of the second-round candidates, Boris Yeltsin and Gennadi Zyuganov, went frequently to be seen at church during the campaign. Both talked favourably of the influence of the Orthodox Church in Russia and denounced the persecution of the Church during the Soviet era. Both made specific appeals to the Muslim population of Russia (Bacon, 1997, p. 258), and each used the Church to attack the other (see Box 10.1).

In terms of specific policies, however, religion was again not a great issue for policy debate during the campaign. When the policy platforms of various candidates did mention religion there was little difference between them. Candidates generally claimed to be in favour of religious freedom, and often particularly emphasised the 'traditional religions' of Russia, notably Orthodoxy and Islam, with the occasional reference to Buddhism and Judaism. In terms of the policies of the two candidates who progressed to the second-round run-off, Yeltsin and Zyuganov, their stated policies on religion and use of it during the campaign virtually coincided. Both promised religious freedom at the same time as proposing to act against religious groups from the West.

If candidates sought to draw on widespread support for Orthodoxy and other traditional religions during the presidential election campaign, then how

СПРАВКА 10.1   **A prayer in favour of the Communist Zyuganov in the 1996 Russian presidential election, published in the nationalist paper *Zavtra***

Lord Jesus Christ, Son of God, do not deal with us according to our sins, but rather deal with us according to Your great mercy. And deliver our Motherland from her great misfortune, and us from the destroyer of our innermost beings, from Boris Yeltsin, the destroyer of the great Russian power, who gave her in chains to the enemy and in disgrace to the devil, having deprived the people of their victuals, having condemned us to despondency of heart and seduction of the mind. Sweet Jesus, light up Russia with the sun of Your love and Heavenly Grace. Take away from us the ruination given to us for our sins.

Source: *Zavtra*, No. 16, 1996

did the leaders of these religions react? Although religious organisations across the board encouraged participation in the elections, few actually took a stance in favour of a particular candidate.

The Russian Orthodox Church, at the highest level, declined to offer overt support for any particular candidate, with the Patriarch declaring in May 1996 that 'the Church does not take part in political battles because it must remain open to everyone' (Bacon, 1997, p. 260). Nonetheless, splits within the Orthodox Church meant that by no means all of the hierarchy remained content with a neutral line, and even Patriarch Aleksi made the occasional partisan statement. The Patriarch's comments in relation to the election campaign often referred to the need for stability and the dangers of returning to repression. In themselves these themes can be read as support for the incumbent president Yeltsin and a warning against voting for the communist leader Zyuganov. When abroad in Tbilisi during the election campaign, Aleksi went further than usual in specifically mentioning Yeltsin positively and warning of the horrors of the old regime returning to power (Babasyan, 1996, p. 43).

At the height of the campaign, Communist leader Zyuganov sought an audience with the Patriarch, who reluctantly agreed on the condition that no photographers be present. One of the reasons for the Patriarch's apparent reluctance to grant an audience to Zyuganov may be that the latter's connections and supporters in the Russian Orthodox Church came from the wing of the Church somewhat estranged from Aleksi. Zyuganov shared much common ground with the late Metropolitan Ioann of St Petersburg and Ladoga, a nationalist with reputedly anti-semitic leanings. This split within the hierarchy of the Church was present throughout campaigning, with many priests from the nationalist, anti-Western wing of Russian Orthodoxy supporting Zyuganov, while others supported Yeltsin.

The ideological message being sent out by candidates' eagerness to be seen with priests was broadly, as has been noted above, one of support for Russia, her traditions and her uniqueness. Such a stance stood well alongside a national mood which was less pro-Western than that of the immediate post-Soviet period of the early 1990s. Not only had democratisation of the polity and marketisation of the economy failed to deliver the prosperity perhaps naively expected in the early years of the decade, but there was also a substantial body of opinion which deplored other elements of westernisation. The values of the market were seen to centre around a 'me first' individualism, characterised by the *nouveau riche* 'New Russians' but at odds with Russian communitarian tradition. Many saw traditional Russian culture as under threat, shallow Western thrillers and detective novels taking over from the spiritual writings of a Dostoevsky or a Tolstoy on the book stalls, and Latin American soap operas attracting huge television audiences. Specifically in the area of religion, there was a perception that 'Western' creeds were proving more attractive than the supposedly deeper spirituality of Orthodoxy.

All of these concerns could and did fill in the background to a range of different political stances. The reformers, among whom Boris Yeltsin counted himself, sought to make their declared commitment to liberal democracy and a market economy more attractive by emphasising too their commitment to a Russia-first stance, showing that their preference for reformist policies did not equate with kow-towing to all the demands of the West. The symbolism of Russian Orthodoxy helped to demonstrate this. For the opposition forces, headed by the Communist Zyuganov, the nationalist elements of Orthodoxy came to the fore. He attacked the Yeltsin regime for allowing the influx of all things Western and spoke in emotive terms of the 'cultural genocide' of the Russian people.

Religion and the law in Russia

According to Article 14 of the Russian Constitution of 1993, the Russian Federation is a secular state. This article further states that all religious associations are equal before the law. Article 28 guarantees freedom of religion, including the right to profess and disseminate any religion, and Article 13 states that there should be no national ideology in Russia. Despite this constitutional basis, however, a law 'On Freedom of Conscience and Religious Associations', was passed in September 1997 which created two different categories of religious association and favoured particular faiths, foremost among them being Russian Orthodoxy, above others.

Russia's constitutional commitment to freedom of religion placed the Russian Federation firmly in the liberal tradition, in contradistinction to the close control over religion exercised by the communist regime in the Soviet era. Russia was, in this area as in many others, seen to be rejoining the global community. Such a view, although is has truth in it, was always too simplistic. For a start, there had never been a great tradition of religious freedom in Russia. Even before the 1917 revolution, the Tsarist regime had been linked with the Orthodox Church in opposition to 'foreign sects' bringing their own brand of Christianity into the

Empire. There existed, if you like, a tradition of persecution of 'non-traditional' religions.

During the Soviet era no religion had actually benefited from the state-sponsored persecution, but certainly the treatment of Orthodox and non-Orthodox differed at times. In the immediate post-revolution years, the Bolsheviks showed a particular determination to remove the entrenched Orthodox Church from public life, and so, in comparison, groups such as the Baptists and the newly arisen Pentecostals seemed to suffer less harassment. The Stalin years saw separate state bodies overseeing religious groups, one monitoring the Russian Orthodox Church, the other monitoring 'cults'. During the state–Church rapprochement of the Second World War years, it was primarily the Orthodox Church which received minor concessions. In the post-Stalin years, and particularly under Brezhnev, there existed to some extent an awareness of common suffering among Christians of all denominations, although the distinction between those who were deemed to have compromised with the state and those who had not remained. Both the Baptists and the Pentecostals divided into groups which registered according to Soviet regulations and groups which refused to do so. Many of the Orthodox hierarchy were suspected of having close links with the organs of state, particularly the KGB.

After the collapse of the communist regime in 1991 Russia became open to missionaries from abroad. Freedom of speech and the right to believe facilitated the growth of all forms of religious belief, Christian and non-Christian, and – within the framework of Christian belief – Orthodox and non-Orthodox. As the last Soviet leader Mikhail Gorbachev had found when promoting his policy of *glasnost* (openness), with freedom comes risk. The freedom to believe in post-Soviet Russia allowed the whole range of spiritual and pseudo-spiritual beliefs to spread, albeit relatively thinly in relation to the size of the population. In addition, the influx of missionaries, largely from the West, presented an easy target for nationalists. This target was made easier by the lack of cultural sensitivity inevitably identified among some non-Russian missionaries. Add to this mix scare stories of 'doomsday cults' and their alleged bizarre or dangerous activities, however minor their impact compared with the growth of other groups, and the arguments to be used in favour of a backlash against religious freedom were clear.

The fear of 'cultish' activity was used to tar many globally accepted expressions of Christianity and other faiths. For those who sought to limit religious freedom, the primary measure of acceptability of a faith came to be the length of time which that particular religion or denomination had existed in Russia. Many conservative Russian Orthodox Christians were therefore, for example, keener on supporting the rights of Islamic believers than of fellow Christian groups.

Fairly shortly after the collapse of the Soviet Union there were attempts to pass a law in Russia limiting the newly instituted freedom of 'non-traditional' religious groups. The Supreme Soviet even passed such a law in 1993, shortly before its forcible dissolution by President Yeltsin later in September.

Limitations on religious activities in post-Soviet Russia then continued to be enacted at a regional level. From 1994 onwards, local laws were passed restricting in various ways the activities of different religious groups. By 1997 over a quarter of the 89 regions which make up the Russian Federation had passed some form of local law on religion. These laws were not uniform, designed as they were for local conditions and sensitivities. Nonetheless common elements recurred, and later became part of the national law of September 1997.

First, these laws regularly made a distinction between 'traditional' and 'non-traditional' religions. Those commonly named as traditional were Orthodoxy, Islam, Buddhism and – less commonly but still named – Judaism. Russian Orthodoxy is unique in this list as it alone is not a religion in itself, but rather a denomination within the Christian religion. A second common feature of the local laws on religion was the requirement that groups receive official recognition by means of registration, as had been the case in the Soviet era. In this way local authorities could monitor the activities of groups and deny registration to those of which they did not approve.

Third, many local laws sought to prohibit specific activities, such as healing or active attempts to attract new members. Such laws ran the risk of a *de jure*, if not *de facto*, contradiction with their support for Orthodoxy as both healing and evangelism are central to traditional Christian, including Russian Orthodox, doctrine and practice. A fourth common factor in the local laws on religion promulgated between 1994 and 1997 was the prevention, rather than prohibition, of the activities of certain groups. This was achieved by administrative means, usually involving the removal of the right to hire public buildings for meetings. In Russia most buildings suitable for the holding of worship services remain under civic ownership.

The proliferation of local laws on religion led by 1996 to attempts in the State Duma to pass a national law on religion. The first reading of the religion law was passed in July 1996. After much debate in the committee stage the bill was finally passed in June 1997, only to be vetoed by President Yeltsin under pressure from Western governments, particularly that of the United States, who objected to its content. All of the features of the local laws noted above found their way into the law vetoed by Yeltsin in July 1997, and he sent the bill back to parliament asking that it be re-drafted. The revised version of the law 'On Freedom of Conscience and Religious Associations' was passed by parliament and accepted by the President in September 1997, and came into force on 1 October. The revised version was scarcely more liberal than its predecessor; indeed, some commentators thought it to be even harsher.

According to Lawrence Uzzell the Russian law on religious associations of September 1997 represents 'the first systematic roll-back of fundamental freedoms since the collapse of the USSR' (Uzzell, 1997). At the time of writing it is too soon to say whether a further rolling-back of freedoms in other areas is to follow. However, it is clear that thus far both the content and application of the law on religious associations match this description. It is also the case, however, that the Russian constitution of 1993 remains in force as the fundamental law of the Russian Federation. There are elements of the 1997 law which are exactly in line with the constitution, and indeed the law explicitly repeats the rights guaranteed by the constitution. There are other elements of the law, however, which appear to contradict both the constitution and earlier articles of the law, the most obvious example being the contradiction of the constitutional

СПРАВКА 10.2   Rights granted to religious organisations and denied to religious groups under the 1997 law 'On Freedom of Conscience and Religious Association'

The right to:

- own property
- establish and maintain buildings
- employ people
- conduct services in hospitals, prisons, homes for the elderly, children's homes, and prisons, at the request of citizens in them
- produce and distribute literature
- conduct charity work
- establish and maintain international communication and contact and issue invitations to foreign citizens

provision Article 14/2, repeated in Article 4/1 of the 1997 law, which states that 'religious associations are separated from the state and are equal before the law'. Article 6/2 of the law on religious associations, however, demonstrates the somewhat Orwellian nature of such equality, as some religious associations are more equal than others. It states that 'religious associations may be formed as religious groups and religious organisations'. This apparently directly contradicts the earlier statement and constitutional provision that religious associations are equal before the law, as the distinction between 'groups' and 'organisations' is the pivot on which the 1997 law turns and the basis for allegations that religious freedom has been seriously curtailed. The majority of the text of the law is devoted to the differing rights granted to religious groups and religious organisations.

The complexity of the 1997 law requires deeper analysis than the present chapter allows. Nonetheless, the main features of the law can be identified. Religious organisations are officially registered associations. They receive a number of rights along with their registration. In order to register these associations must provide documentary evidence, certified by the local authority, that they have been in existence for at least 15 years on the territory in question. Therefore, from the promulgation of the law in 1997 this 15 year rule extends back into the Soviet period when the atheist state persecuted religious believers and many religious groups either existed in secret or simply refused to register with the very state that oppressed them. Under the 1997 law, a non-registered religious association is termed a 'religious group' and simply has the right to exist, to conduct its activities in premises provided by its members and to teach its own adherents. The benefits of registration are a whole raft of rights granted to religious organisations and not to religious groups (see Box 10.2).

The role of the Russian Orthodox Church

According to its constitution, the Russian Federation is a secular state which allows no state religion or state ideology. This constitutional provision, however, is a declaration made in the face of a long history of state religion and state ideology in Russia. Before the revolution of 1917 the Russian Orthodox Church had been on one level virtually a department of the state since the reign of Peter the Great, 1672–1725, and was governed by a secular bureaucracy appointed by the Tsar. After the revolution of 1917, the separation of Church and state was decreed, persecution followed, and Marxism–Leninism became the ideology of the state.

With a number of the constitutional provisions of 1993, the burden of tradition weighs heavily on their application in contemporary life. For example, it is one thing to declare the existence of a democratic political system, as Article 1 of the Constitution does, and quite another thing to create the cultural and behavioural transformations necessary for democracy to function. Similarly, the declaration of a state free of official religion or ideology was not immediately followed by the implementation of this declaration. Indeed, the 1990s have seen the cultivation of ever closer contacts between the Russian Orthodox Church and the state. The Patriarch has taken a central part in numerous state occasions at the highest level, such as the signing of a 'treaty of union' between Belarus and the Russian Federation in April 1996 and the inauguration of President Yeltsin for his second term in office in 1996.

At lower levels, the armed forces look to the Orthodox Church for pastoral support: it is far from uncommon for major construction projects – from shopping centres to MiG fighters – to receive a blessing from a priest on completion (Lloyd, 1998); a central element of Moscow's physical regeneration under Mayor Luzhkov in the late 1990s has been the rebuilding of the Cathedral of Christ the Saviour, whose external structure at least was completed in time for President Yeltsin to attend a service conducted by the Patriarch on Easter Sunday 1996.

Nor are Church–state links merely symbolic. The state has granted to the Russian Orthodox Church tax concessions in the trading of lucrative goods, notably oil, cigarettes and alcohol. Such fiscal benefits enrich the Church by up to an estimated $40 million per annum (Scott, 1997) and create further ties between Church and state. These *de facto* links form the background to the *de jure* declaration of 'the special role of Orthodoxy in the history of Russia and in the establishment and development of its spirituality and culture' which makes up part of the preamble to the 'Law on Freedom of Conscience and Religious Associations'. Orthodoxy is therefore singled out above all other religious creeds in the law of the Russian Federation. At a local level in particular the application of the law on religious associations has often led to Orthodox priests exercising a great influence over the religious life of an area. Local officials charged with assessing the suitability of different religious associations for registration have in a number of cases sought the advice of Orthodox clergy.

Given the strong links between the Church and the state which have become increasingly apparent in the 1990s, is it fair to say that Russia has returned to a

СПРАВКА 10.3   **Patriarch Aleksi II, March 1998**

I am convinced that the Church must be separate from the state, but it must not be separate from society. The Church must have the right to evaluate from ethical positions what is happening in the country, and sometimes this evaluation will not agree with the state's.

Source: *Pravoslavie v Rossii*, 18 March 1998

situation where the state authorities dominate a subservient Orthodox Church? The short answer is no. First, the Russian Orthodox Church defends its official separation from the state. Mutual interests, and perhaps to some extent financial benefits, mean that the Church–state relationship is close. However, the means by which the authorities can 'lean on' the Orthodox hierarchy at the end of the twentieth century differ vastly of course from the brutal tactics and administrative control of previous eras. The Orthodox Church is self-governing and conscious of the advantages of this independence as well as of good relations with the state. Patriarch Aleksi spelt out the position in March 1998 (Box 10.3) and cited the Chechen War of 1994–96 as an example of Church–state disagreement, noting that the Church had frequently spoken out against military action over this period. The Russian Orthodox Church is not simply a mouthpiece for the state.

Second, it is difficult to talk of the Church as being subservient to the state for the simple reason that neither of these two entities is a monolithic body with a single point of view. The Russian Orthodox Church contains a liberal wing in both the political and the theological senses. There are traditionalist and reformist parishes, and there are political differences among the hierarchy which were evident in the presidential election of 1996 (Bacon, 1997). In relation to the law on religious associations, the Orthodox Church officially supports the law and was involved in its drafting, but elements within the Church have opposed it. Similarly, and more obviously, 'the state' contains a wide range of opinions. Even within the powerful presidential administration views about the religion law differed markedly, and President Yeltsin vetoed a version of the law in July not radically dissimilar from the one he passed in September.

Theoretical context

We have considered the role of religion in Russian political life by means of a quantification of belief, an assessment of the impact of religion on electoral politics, a survey of legal developments and a consideration of Church–state relations in the 1990s. This last section seeks to conceptualise the largely empirical study which has preceded it. How do we best understand the role of religion in Russian politics today? As was noted above, for much of the past two centuries, the secularisation theory held sway. However, events of the last quarter of the twentieth century in particular have put this hypothesis to flight across the globe. Instead of secularisation we have seen what has been termed 'the world-wide resurgence of religion in politics' (Westerlund, 1996). We must be careful not to over-state this phenomenon in Russia; as is evident from the analysis of this chapter, religion has not taken a dominant role in political activity which remains institutionally and to a large extent ideologically secular. Nonetheless, religion has increased its presence in the Russian polity and society.

Two approaches, not mutually exclusive, which illuminate developments in post-cold war Russia focus on the socio-political role of religion. First is the concept of civil religion. Civil religion is created when a state seeks to adopt, often in rather general terms, an appropriate religious underpinning to its political behaviour. The most commonly cited example of civil religion is the United States of America where the state (or more specifically its political actors) recognises and reflects the widespread Christian beliefs of the populace, without becoming sufficiently specific to be denominationally partisan (Fowler and Hertzke, 1995, p. 244). According to Jeff Haynes, 'the development of civil religion in a polity is a strategy to avoid social conflicts and promote national co-ordination, especially in countries with serious religious or ideological divisions' (Haynes, 1998, p. 6).

The Russian polity of the 1990s has demonstrated deep ideological divisions, and President Yeltsin, a populist politician *par excellence*, has sought a unifying national idea, with Orthodoxy as an obvious central element. Furthermore, the complex politicking surrounding the adoption of the law on religious associations in September 1997, following its presidential veto a couple of months earlier, suggests that to some extent the president agreed to the law as a sop to parliamentary opponents whose political ideology is at odds with his own in what might be seen as more substantive politico-economic areas.

The second concept which illuminates our understanding of the interaction between religion and politics in contemporary Russia is that of a 'culture war'. It can be convincingly argued that the central political cleavage in post-cold war Russia remains the East–West division (Truscott, 1997). This being the case then the political importance of the Russian Orthodox Church arguably has increased as it symbolises and contains key elements of Russia's cultural identity. Adherence to Orthodoxy by political conservatives in particular can be seen in terms of cultural defence in an era of globalisation. The post-modern argument would maintain that the rejection of Marxism–Leninism in Russia fits a global trend which has seen the rejection of meta-narratives, that is, belief systems with a claim to absolute truth. In the area of religion this trend does not necessarily mean a decline in belief, as post-modernism projects an inherently more 'spiritual' than 'rational' modernity. Post-modern trends in religion, however, have been seen to present a threat to centralised institutional creeds, with the growth of less hierarchical church groupings in the West and a focus on inner spirituality above ritual. The growth of non-Orthodox religious groups in 1990s Russia combines elements of globalisation and post-modernism, both of which can be seen as threatening to the Russian Orthodox Church and to substantial elements in the Russian polity and society.

References

Anderson J 1994 *Religion, State and Politics in the Soviet Union and Successor States*, Cambridge University Press, Cambridge.

Babasyan N 1996 Bog v pomoshch, *Novoe vremia*, No. 29.

Bacon, E 1997 The Church and Politics in Russia, *Religion, State and Society*, Vol. 25, No. 3.

Chiniaeva E 1997 The Search for the 'Russian Idea', *Transitions*, Vol. 4 No. 1.

Dubin B V 1996 Pravoslavie v sotsial'nom kontekste, *Ekonomicheskie i sotsial'nye peremeny: monitoring obshchestvennogo mneniia*, No. 6.

Filatov S B and Furma D E 1992 Religiia i politika v massovom soznanii, *Sotsiologicheskie issledovaniia*, Vol. 7, pp. 3–12.

Fowler R B and Hertzke A D 1995 *Religion and Politics in America: Faith, Culture, and Strategic Choices*, Westview, Oxford.

Haynes J 1998 *Religion in Global Politics*, Longman, London.

Johnstone P 1993 *Operation World*, OM Publishing, Carlisle.

Lehman S G 1997 Islam and Ethnicity in the Republics of Russia, *Post-Soviet Affairs*, Vol. 13, No. 1, pp. 78–103.

Lloyd J 1998 *The Times* (London), 16 January.

Scott C 1997 Army–Church Charities In Russia: Who Benefits?, *Keston News Service*, 25 July.

Truscott P 1997 *Russia First: Breaking with the West*, I B Tauris, London.

Uzzell L A 1997 A Show Of Bad Faith, *The Washington Post*, 2 November.

Westerlund D (ed.) 1996 *Questioning the Secular State: The World-wide Resurgence of Religion in Politics*, Hurst, London.

White S, Rose R and McAllister I 1997 *How Russia Votes*, Chatham House Publishers, New Jersey.

Wyman M 1997 *Public Opinion in Post Communist Russia*, Macmillan, London.

Further reading

Anderson J 1994 *Religion, State and Politics in the Soviet Union and Successor States*, Cambridge University Press, Cambridge.

Bacon E 1997 The Church and Politics in Russia, *Religion, State and Society*, Vol. 25, No. 3.

There are also two very useful web sites which provide up-to-date assessments of current religious developments in the Russian Federation:
http://www.stetson.edu/~psteeves/relnews/
http://www.keston.org/

11 Russian nationalism and democratic development

Richard Sakwa

Introduction

Nationalism in Russia is a rather weak concept which has often changed its meaning over time. In this respect it is not unlike its English counterpart (Anderson, 1983, p. 12). Both were subsumed into larger entities; English nationalism into the larger idea of Britain (Colley, 1992), and Russian identity became the core of an imperial project (Hosking, 1997). The ambiguous and multifaceted relationship of these two 'nationalisms' to its other is the key problem in the study of the nationalism of these countries. Nationalism as such, moreover, is only part of a much larger 'identity' (although here, too, the word identity is misleading in suggesting a complete view whereas in practice identity is – like the nationalism which it selectively reflects – part of a larger set of shifting relationships) (Rajchman, 1995). Nationalism and national identity are two very distinct phenomena (Smith, 1986, 1991a), with the latter providing the cultural matrix and symbols for the former, which represents the politicisation of a community's culture (Schöpflin, 1991).

Only at the end of the twentieth century did both English and Russian nationalism begin to emerge from the detritus of the dissolution of the larger imperial missions and take on autonomous forms. They did so at a time when what we might call 'classical nationalism' was itself, while apparently triumphant after the disintegration of the colonial empires and the dissolution of communist universalism, being hollowed out by processes of liberal globalisation and universalisation. Marxism and liberalism may well have been right that nationalism would gradually die out; they were only out by about 150 years.

Approaches to nationalism

The distinction between political nationalism and ethnic nationalism should be stressed. While the nationalism of the nation-state is on the wane, the nationalism of ethnic groups is at an unprecedentedly high level. Ethno-nationalism, as the latter is called, seeks to strengthen the identity, language and culture of a particular ethnic group, and usually to achieve some sort of administrative autonomy for it, whereas the political nationalism of the state is constrained by the growing web of globalising and universalising processes. These two nationalisms operate in different ways and at different levels, as can be seen in the following issues.

Nation-state in West and East

It is customary to distinguish the West European evolution of the nation-state from developments in the East. In the continental West European countries the civic-territorial model predominated; the early modern monarchies incorporated the peripheral regions (Wales, Brittany) into a single system of sovereignty marked by common laws and taxation systems. The distinction between nation and state was eroded, and in practice the latter predominated over the former. With the French revolution the ideas of popular and national sovereignty fused in a common citizenhood. The East European model, outlined by Hans Kohn (1967) and John Armstrong (1982), suggested a radical disjunction between the state and nation. This had been precipitated by the region's failure to maintain its independence: both the so-called *historic* nations such as the Poles, the Czechs and the Magyars as well as the *non-historic* ones such as the Serbs, Bulgars and Romanians fell under foreign domination of Russians, Prussians or Ottomans from early modern times. Habsburg rule was rather different but until at least 1867 it allowed only the slimmest scope for independent national development. A further factor was the relative economic backwardness of the region. In the post-communist period this provoked numerous variations in the pattern of nation-state building to the point that, for example, in Belarus the national idea is weak almost to the point of invisibility.

Russia falls into a third category, reminiscent in an inverted way of the British pattern. Russia has traditionally had a strong state, a weak society and an underdeveloped sense of nation. The imperial idea substituted for nationalism, and thus Russia remained rooted in nineteenth-century ideas of national grandeur, but failed fully to enter the era of mass nationalism. Today, however, it would be misleading simply to say that Russia has a weak state and a weak nation: in fact, the country has not a strong nation-state, but a vigorous nation-society, a strong cultural sense of its own identity. In this respect both political nationalism and ethno-nationalism are relatively weak, while cultural nationalism (perhaps better defined as civilisational identity) is extremely strong. As in so many other areas, terms and definitions that are appropriate for the rest of Europe have to be modified when applied to Russia.

Primordialist vs modernist approaches to nationalism – and beyond

The literature is divided between two broad approaches to modern national identity. The first is the 'primordialist' view, arguing that identity arises out of permanent features like religion, language and customs. The corollary for primordialists is the tendency identified by Carlton Hayes, namely the aspiration to fulfil the principle of 'one nation, one state' (Hayes, 1949, Chapter VI). The second 'modernist' view insists that nationalism is primarily a modern phenomenon, 'the pathology of modern developmental history' as Tom Nairn (1977, p. 359) put it. Ernest Gellner (1983) has argued that it is created by modernisation and the broadening of politics to encompass a mass element and acts to integrate societies challenged by the passage into modernity. While nationalism can be interpreted as a response to the traumas and stresses provoked by the industrial revolution, it can also represent a reaction to the fears and stresses engendered by the transition from traditional to modern life. The modernist position, however, underestimates traditional forms of collective identity. Anthony Smith (1991b) has stressed that although nationalism is a modern phenomenon, it relies on pre-modern historical traditions and identity-formation.

At the core of Ernest Gellner's modernist definition of nationalism is the desire to achieve congruence between state and nation, between state borders and cultural frontiers. For the exponents of idealist nationalism, the state in addition represented a civilisational idea as much as a corporeal reality. For the Herderesque German romantic nationalists who rejected the universalism of the Enlightenment in favour of cultural particularity, moreover, this was embodied in an exclusive ethnic group, a view that gave rise to integral nationalism. The core of both primordial and modernist nationalism (although by different routes) is that each nation (defined by cultural identity or ethnic affiliation) is to have its own sovereign state, and that 'no state should forcefully yoke different nationalities together' (Leerssen, 1993, p. 3). None of this applies directly to Russia in that, while ethnic Russians may informally be regarded as the core of the post-communist state, neither the 1993 constitution nor any subsequent legislation privileges any particular ethnic group. Russia is defined as a civic state in which ethnic affiliation does not register politically.

The central principle of the 1993 Russian constitution is that individuals, not communities, are the supreme legal entity in the country. There is no scope for national rights here, and laws in principle apply with equal force throughout the country. The USSR had been shockingly negligent in establishing a national identity, perpetuating separate ethnicised identities through the notorious fifth point in the passports issued from 1932. Russia also seemed to be taking this path, with debates continuing over the symbols of statehood, the flag and hymn, and with the old Soviet passports still in circulation. However, from 1997 Russia began to issue new passports. Ethnicity is no longer stated on the new passports, provoking a storm of protest in Tatarstan, Dagestan and some other ethno-federal republics. President Mintimer Shaimiev in Tatarstan, for example, feared that the officially recorded existence of non-Russian majorities at local level, in effect the source of ethnocratic power, was being deliberately undermined. The end of the formal registration of nationality could lead to the identity of minority ethnic groups becoming lost in the amorphous mass of a denationalised citizenry. It appeared to be the first step towards the gubernification of Russia (that is, its transformation into a unitary state) long advocated by Alexander Solzhenitsyn and Vladimir Zhirinovsky. Even Jews, long discriminated against on the basis of their passport identification, were hesitant about the measure. However, Valeri Tishkov (director of the Institute of Ethnography and an adviser to the government), insisted that the abolition of point five was a major advance, removing one of the most divisive forms of totalitarian control, and allowing the emergence of a civic national identity.

The institutionalist approach to nationalism

Mancur Olson notes that 'Nationalism, moreover, is often not a pre-existing primitive belief to which other forces adapt – it is often a consequence rather than a first cause of political outcomes. As often as not, it is governments that create nationalisms rather than nationalisms that create nation-states'. In an argument prefiguring that of Rogers Brubaker (see below), Olson goes on to argue that '...we get nationalism and a sense that a given set of human beings are a "people" or a "nation" mainly because the accidents of history have given us governments with a certain domain. The people in this domain are then given a common set of experiences by this government and an indoctrination in a nationalism that is convenient for the government in question. Even a language is, as the saying goes, usually a dialect backed by an army' (Olson, 1990, p. 23). Rebellious collective action in the former Soviet republics was possible, according to Olson, because there were already selective incentives promoting it, above all, people staffing an embryonic state. The key element, Olson (1990, pp. 25–6) insists, is not so much the preferences of the people themselves but the regime itself, and in particular its civil and military officials.

Brubaker's (1994, 1996) central notion is that of 'nationalising states', regimes that have a state and then seek to paint it the colour of the ruling nation. This is misleading in that it assumes a stark distinction between civic and ethnic models of nation building, whereas most lie at different points along a continuum. Ukraine, for example, is certainly involved in a complex process of nation building in the territory it inherited from the Soviet Union, and although there is a strong 'Ukrainising' process at work, this does not necessarily threaten the quarter of the population that are not ethnically Ukrainian. Any reasonably effective nation-building process requires a national element, but this does not necessarily have to take nationalistic, let alone 'nationalising', forms. It was the Soviet Union's failure seriously even to begin the process of creating a nation that provoked its disintegration in 1991, but this would not have mattered all that much if the state itself had been viable and flourishing. It was the combination of failures that provoked the Soviet Union's disintegration, not any one single factor, and any attempt to prioritise one element over all the others risks seriously distorting the true picture.

Post-communism and nationalism

We can identify yet another model that we can call 'post-communist nationalism'. While still committed to the establishment of sovereign nation-states, post-communist nationalism has to take into account the erosion of state sovereignty that has taken place both from above and from below. Post-communist international relations are characterised by two types of internationalisation. Globalisation is the process whereby the global economy is increasingly independent of state borders, where capital is mobile and can set the terms for investment (low inflation, rising productivity, flexible labour, secure legal framework for the repatriation of profits), and where local branches of a transnational corporation can negotiate directly with the state. Universalisation, however, refers more directly to the generalisation of certain political norms and the way that states are increasingly embedded in a dense network of intergovernmental and supranational agencies, from the European Union (EU) to the Council of Europe to the United Nations. The currency of sovereignty is being increasingly devalued by the pressures of globalisation (primarily economic) and universalisation (political). Eric Hobsbawm (1990) advanced a similar view in arguing that nationalism was above all a feature of early modernity that gave way to other (often transnational) forms of popular allegiance in the later, more internationalised, forms of modernity.

In this context, post-communist nationalism has lost much of the fire typical of earlier versions. Political nationalism is on the wane (although with some notable exceptions), while ethnic nationalism is inhibited (although by no means denied) by the globalising and universalising processes at work today. Romania's aspirations, for example, to join the EU and NATO prompted it to sign a friendship treaty with Hungary, while Russia's bid to join international economic and political bodies has so far restrained national revanchism. If this argument sounds familiar, it is of course the one advanced by liberals over the last hundred years or so. Economic liberalism was always associated with pacifism. As Carlton Hayes put it, 'Material economic conditions, they asserted, were far more decisive than mere political action; they were bound, in the new age, to assure the success of economic liberalism, to guarantee peace throughout the world, and to get rid of the excesses of nationalism' (Hayes, 1949, p. 244). Economic liberalism of the Jeremy Bentham sort, however, was never anti-nationalist; from the beginning it was associated with liberal nationalism – that is, a political nationalism that exerted itself mainly in expanding the sphere of trade and constitutionalism.

Democracy on its own, moreover, is by no means the antithesis of nationalism; indeed, the opposite is often the case. The introduction of democratic proceduralism can act to empower nationalist mobilisation, as took place in the former Yugoslavia. As Zakaria notes, 'without a background in constitutional liberalism, the introduction of democracy in divided societies has actually fomented nationalism, ethnic conflict, and even war' (Zakaria, 1997, p. 35). Drawing on Michael Doyle's view, lately restated in his *Ways of War and Peace* (1997), Zakaria argues that it is not so much democratic states that do not go to war with each other but states marked by constitutional liberalism: 'In countries not grounded in constitutional liberalism, the rise of democracy often brings with it hyper-nationalism and war-mongering' (Zakaria, 1997, p. 38). This is an important corrective in the post-communist context where too often there has been excessive emphasis on abstract principles and processes of 'democratisation' at the expense of framing constitutional orders appropriate to distinctive national conditions (Eckstein, 1998, pp. 26–9).

The Soviet legacy

The theory of path dependency suggests that earlier institutional choices (institutions here being defined in broad terms as the organisation of social relations) limit and define later actions. This is nowhere more true that in the area

Table 11.1 Independent states of the former Soviet Union

State	Territory square miles (square, kilometres)	%	Population Number	%
Russian Federation	6 592 692 (17 075 400)	76.65	149 299 000	51.12
Kazakhstan	1 049 039 (2 717 300)	12.17	16 947 000	5.80
Ukraine	233 206 (603 700)	2.71	52 103 000	17.84
Turkmenistan	188 418 (488 100)	2.19	3 856 000	1.32
Uzbekistan	172 588 (447 400)	2.00	21 301 000	7.29
Belarus	80 154 (207 600)	0.93	10 263 000	3.51
Kyrgyzstan	76 834 (198 500)	0.89	4 506 000	1.54
Tajikistan	55 213 (143 100)	0.64	5 272 000	1.80
Azerbaijan	33 591 (86 600)	0.39	7 146 000	2.45
Georgia	27 027 (69 700)	0.31	5 476 000	1.87
Lithuania	25 174 (65 200)	0.29	3 736 000	1.28
Latvia	24 942 (64 500)	0.29	2 702 000	0.92
Estonia	17 413 (45 100)	0.20	1 581 000	0.54
Moldova	13 127 (33 700)	0.15	4 372 000	1.50
Armenia	11 583 (29 800)	0.13	3 504 000	1.20
Totals	8 601 001 (22 400 000)		292 064 000	

of nationality relations, where the development of a distinctive form of ethno-federalism severely circumscribed post-communist Russia's institutional choices.

Historical context: from empire to nation-state

The largest single national group in the USSR was the Russians, with a population in 1989 of 149 million representing 51 per cent of the Soviet population (Table 11.1). The declining birthrate in Russia from 1960 meant that Russians became an ever smaller proportion of the total Soviet population, and already by 1979 the ethnic Russian part of the population was less than half if the number of mixed marriages and children opting to have Russian as the nationality placed into their passports is taken into consideration. This represented a major psychological turning point and emphasised even more clearly the multi-national character of the Soviet Union.

Russian nationalism in the Soviet era took many forms and ranged from orthodoxy into unorthodoxy. Stalinism was imbued with a sense of militant nationalism, but Mussolini was mistaken when he argued that Bolshevism had disappeared in Russia and in its place a Slav form of fascism had emerged. Soviet nationalism on the whole had little in common with the fascist type since it was not based on the militant projection of one ethnic group at the expense of others. The Russification that did occur was more of an administrative process than an attempt to glorify Russia proper. Soviet nationalism certainly projected its Russian credentials, but at the same time forms of Russian patriotism that deviated from the Soviet path were as persecuted as much as any other national deviancy. Russian nationalism was coloured by the paradox that while the Soviet state ensured Russian political pre-eminence, in economic terms Russia was far from being the most prosperous.

Unorthodox Russian nationalists condemned the persecution of the Russian Orthodox Church, the excessive internationalism whose burden fell disproportionately on Russian shoulders, the distortion of Russian history and the imposition of socialist realism in place of Russian romanticism. National Bolshevism was condemned by more religious nationalists for espousing a Russian patriotism without a Christian foundation, based purely on the great power status of the Russian part of the Soviet Union – communism with a national face. Religious patriots stressed that Soviet nationalism was in fact antithetical to genuine Russian traditions; the Russian patriotism incorporated into Soviet nationalism, they insisted, served to buttress the power system but had little to do with genuine national traditions. Solzhenitsyn (1974a, 1974b) argued that Russians should be permitted to pursue their destiny freed from the burden of empire. Liberal nationalists like him argued for the conversion of Russia from a military superpower to a spiritual great power, which they insisted would pose no threat to non-Russians or the outside world. Russian patriots of this sort were contemptuous of Western democracy but merciless in their condemnation of Soviet totalitarianism. The authoritarian implications of such views derive from their sense of moral absolutism; the attempt once again to remove politics from society and instead to impose an organic theocratic government of justice and order.

The debate over whether the USSR was an empire or not continues to this day (Beissinger, 1995; Lieven, 1995). For the subjugated peoples of the Baltic, Western Ukraine and some other places there is little to be discussed: the Soviet regime perpetuated (and indeed intensified) Russian imperial dominance. For the rest, however, the question is not so clear cut; while repressing overt forms of nationalism, the Soviet ethno-federal system sustained, and in some cases engendered, nationhood. The USSR certainly differed from the Austro-Hungarian or even the British empires, which were based on very different dynamics. A geographically compact 'empire' such as the Soviet Union, with a high proportion of the core ethnic group living in the other territorial units, is usually called a multi-ethnic country (Hough, 1997, p. 373). As Simonia argues, 'Soviet imperialism was a rather unusual phenomenon . . . The new, rather specific "metropolitan country" finally took shape as a central bureaucratic party and state machinery (establishment), with the military–industrial complex as its mainstay. All the republics, including the Russian Republic, found themselves in the position of one big colony exploited by this metropolitan country' (Simonia, 1995, pp. 20–1). This is the theory of the Soviet party-state as a hypothetical sixteenth republic; the empire of ideology, lacking national roots or a national identity but subjugating all the other republics equally – albeit in different ways.

Neither the Russian empire nor the USSR, of course, had been nation-states in the conventional sense, but neither were they, according to the patriots, empires in the colonialist sense. Beissinger stresses the ambiguity in the distinction between states and empires, with the Tsarist empire in particular representing 'a confused mix of empire and state-building' (Beissinger, 1995, p. 158). Russia did not have an empire; it was an empire, although towards the end it became more classically a colonial power in both internal and external aspects. The USSR had been an empire-state, like the Bismarckian Second Reich and the Habsburg empire, based not on the colonial model of a subjugated people but rather a system in which all came under the tutelage of an abstract principle incarnated in the guise of the collective emperor, the Communist Party. While Russians were over-represented in all-union institutions, giving the Soviet Union the appearance of a Russian empire, the ethno-federal system had, as it were, become increasingly ethnicised but not federalised by the advancement of national elites to positions of power in their respective republics.

Since the death of Stalin in 1953 it was not clear whether protest against the system used the language of nationalism or whether nationalist movements in the old regime had no other option but to become movements against the system itself. In the last years of *perestroika* the rise of nationalism was used as a battering ram against the communist system and, perhaps unavoidably, the old state as well. It should be stressed, however, that it was not nationalism as such that was responsible for the disintegration of the USSR: the failure was above all political, the inability to transform the 'sixteenth republic' into a viable polity rooted in a national community. Only in the wake of the disintegration did the various republics seek to root their (sometimes enforced) state building in a national (but not necessarily nationalist) discourse. Indigenous elites (commonly former party functionaries) grasped at the symbolic power of nationalism to consolidate their own regimes.

Although Soviet leaders 'had long identified themselves with Russian nationalism, it was a superpower nationalism and not an ethnically centred one' (Hough, 1997, p. 238). Russians themselves as a nation, irrespective of where they lived, retained an 'all-union' concept of territory. As the Soviet ethnographer Yuri Arutyuniyan put it, 'Wherever they lived they actively used their own language and almost always clung to their own culture' (Arutyuniyan, 1991, p. 21). In most parts of the USSR Russians behaved as if they were at home and failed to learn the local language, assuming that the local peoples should learn Russian, whereas most other peoples remained loyal to a distinct homeland. It was this generalised 'imperial' attitude that made it more difficult for Russians after 1991 to identify with the Russian Federation as a separate homeland. The challenge now was for them to become *Rossiyane* (citizens of the Russian republic) rather than ethnically defined *Russkie*.

To this day 'imperial' themes are strong in Russian policy and debates. Sergei Baburin, the leader of the nationalist Russian All-People's Union (ROS), in 1991 forcefully made the argument that 'the restriction of Russia to "the RSFSR" . . . is the ideological inheritance of Lenin, Stalin, and Khrushchev' (*Rossiiskaya gazeta*, 20 September 1991, p. 2). Patriots and nationalists argue that the destruction of the USSR does not necessarily mean the end of some sort of multi-national state, but while patriots hope for the voluntary reconstitution of some sort of supranational union (above all bringing together the Slavic peoples of Ukraine, Belarus and North Kazakhstan), nationalists use the language of threats and sanctions to create an entity which privileges Russians as the core of an imperial identity. Both agree that the borders bequeathed by the Soviet regime are arbitrary; the many administrative changes in territories reflected political expediency rather than ethnic, historical or linguistic realities. This argument, reminiscent of the revisionists in Weimar Germany who were intent on revising the Treaty of Versailles, however, has been taken up neither at the official level nor by the mass of the citizenry. While the present borders cut across communities they are no more arbitrary than any other, and broadly speaking they reflect historical realities.

The passage from empire to nation-state entails not only the institutionalisation of new political forms but also the recasting of fundamental political categories. As Khazanov notes, 'Many Russians conceive the nation as an ontological category and/or confuse nation with ethnicity' (Khazanov, 1994, p. 164). In Russian, he notes, the word 'nation' ('*natsiya*') means 'ethnic group', a 'people', 'but not an aggregate of all citizens of a given state'. The notion of Russia as a nation is only beginning to emerge and is to a large degree a product of the geopolitical realities that came into being in 1991.

Political context: ethno-federalism

The creation of ethno-federal units in the Soviet Union was already a concession to a part of the population identified by its ethnic characteristics, introducing an ingredient into the process of Soviet state building that would ultimately destroy it. Article 15 of the 1936 Soviet constitution stated that the union republics were 'sovereign' with the right of secession from the Union. Early drafts of the 1977 constitution deleted references to sovereignty, but it was restored precisely to differentiate them from Russia's autonomous republics, autonomous oblasts and national districts. Article 76.1 stated: 'A union republic is a sovereign Soviet socialist republic that has united with other Soviet republics in the Union of Soviet Socialist Republics'.

The Russian word *soyuz* here means 'alliance' rather than the English meaning of 'union'. The USSR was in theory an alliance of sovereign states – but Russia's own sovereignty was institutionally less developed than in the other republics, lacking its own party organisation, academy of sciences, KGB and other bodies that were to be found in the other fourteen. Russia was a superfluous link between the regions and the union centre. As long as it was weak its existence as a union republic did not matter all that much, but a strong Russia would inevitably be an uncomfortable partner for the all-union government. During *perestroika* the latent belief that Russia had been exploited by the centre as much as any other republic burst into prominence, and Yeltsin used these perceptions to fuel his bid for power. It appears that Gorbachev came to accept Solzhenitsyn's argument that Soviet leaders had sacrificed Russia on the pyre of world revolution and ideology, and this fatally undermined his self-confidence in the final struggle with Yeltsin and the resurgent Russia (Chernyaev, 1993, pp. 277–9).

Russia itself is a federation consisting of a number of different units: 21 republics, 57 ordinary regions (oblasts and krais plus two cities, Moscow and St Petersburg, with the rights of oblasts), 10 autonomous okrugs and the Jewish Autonomous Oblast, a total of 89 so-called 'subjects of the federation'. A Federation Treaty of 31 March 1992 sought to regulate relations between the various units and the centre, but it was only with the adoption of the new constitution in December 1993 that, formally at least, all the subjects of federation became equal in status. The new constitution did not recognise the various declarations of sovereignty adopted by some republics, yet the signing of bilateral treaties between the federal authorities and the subjects of federation, beginning with the one signed with Tatarstan in February 1994, formalised 'asymmetry' in Russian federal relations. Russian federalism, like the USSR earlier, institutionalises ethnicity in the form of the ethno-federal republics, autonomous okrugs and the Jewish oblast. Nations in Russia are therefore defined in both political and ethno-cultural forms. It was the tension between the two that provoked the disintegration of the USSR, yet the Russian Federation in the immediate term is unlikely to suffer the same fate on a global scale. While a republic such as Chechnya may well be successful in its bid to secede, few others are likely to follow.

The differences can be summarised as follows: (1) the preponderance of ethnic Russians, making up at least 81 per cent of the Russian Federation (see Table 11.2), compared to only about half of the USSR; (2) the beginning of the development of a genuinely federal system, granting the subjects of federation some of the genuine attributes of sovereignty in content if not in name; (3) while there has been some fiscal federalism, resources are still overwhelmingly concentrated in the centre, and most regions are financially dependent on the centre; (4) a genuinely national market for goods and resources is beginning to emerge in which the whole country is enmeshed in a myriad mutually beneficial economic interactions; (5) the logistics of independence for areas in the interior of the country, such as Tatarstan (while far from insurmountable), would prove enormously costly in terms of transport, delivery of resources and finances; (6) the war in Chechnya transformed the way that elites and peoples framed national agendas, reinforcing peaceful and procedural forms of collective action; (7) relatively democratic procedures and institutions have been established through which regions and republics are integrated into the national political community (for example, the Federation Council), thus most problems can be dealt with politically rather than provoking insurmountable crises; (8) the Russian state, however weak, does guarantee protection from external threats, whether in the form of demographic overspill, armed intervention or irredentist claims; (9) membership in the Russian (*Rossiisski*) community confers a certain cultural status and membership in one of the world's great civilisations, including its cultural, linguistic and scientific traditions; far from least, (10) the intermingling of populations, including a high proportion of 'mixed'

Table 11.2 National composition of Russian federation in 1989

Ethnic group	Total number	Percentage of RF population	Living on the territory of their own ethno-federal unit	
			Number	Percentage of the national group
Total population	147 021 869	100		
of whom:				
Russians:	119 865 946	81.53		
living outside ethno-federal areas	108 063 409	73.50		
living in others' ethno-federal areas	11 802 537	8.03		
Tatars	5 521 096	3.75	1 765 404	31.97
Ukrainians	4 362 872	2.96		
Chuvash	1 773 645	1.21	906 922	51.10
Bashkirs	1 345 273	0.91	863 808	64.21
Belarusians	1 206 222	0.82		
Mordvinians	1 072 939	0.72	313 420	29.21
Chechens	898 999	0.61	734 501	81.71
Germans	842 000	0.57		
Udmurts	714 833	0.49	496 522	69.46
Maris	643 698	0.44	324 349	50.39
Kazakhs	635 865	0.43		
Avars	544 016	0.37	496 077	91.19
Jews	536 846	0.36	8 887	1.65
Armenians	532 390	0.36		
Buryats	417 425	0.28	341 185	81.74
Ossets	402 275	0.27	334 876	83.24
Kabards	386 055	0.26	363 492	94.15
Yakuts	380 242	0.26	365 236	96.05
Dargins	353 348	0.24	280 431	79.36
Azerbaijanis	335 889	0.23		
Komis	336 309	0.23	291 542	86.69
Kumyks	277 163	0.19	231 805	83.63
Lezgins	257 270	0.17	204 370	79.43
Ingush	215 068	0.15	163 762	76.14
Tuvans	206 160	0.14	198 448	96.26
Peoples of the North	182 000	0.12		
Moldovans	172 671	0.12		
Kalmyks	165 821	0.11	146 316	88.28
Gypsies	153 000	0.10		
Karachais	150 332	0.10	129 449	86.11
Komi-Permyaks	147 269	0.09	95 215	64.65
Georgians	130 688	0.09		
Uzbeks	126 899	0.09		
Karelians	124 921	0.08	78 928	63.18

Source: Modified from *RSFSR v tsifrakh v 1989g*, Financy i statistika, Moscow, 1990, pp. 23–5

(interethnic) marriages, means that no area is entirely homogeneous, and in only a few ethno-federal republics is the titular nationality in a majority.

Any fragmentation that does occur is as likely to take place on simple regional grounds as on the basis of ethno-federal separatism. The Urals and Siberia, for example, have very strong regional identities. The conditions outlined above, it must be stressed, will only apply as long as Russia remains on the path of democratisation. Any attempt at an overtly authoritarian solution to Russia's myriad problems, like the August 1991 coup earlier, would provoke the result that it seeks to avoid, namely the fragmentation of Russia. Above all, the multiplicity of post-communist identities must be stressed. On the level of nationality politics this means that one might *simultaneously* consider oneself a Russian, a Tatar and, residually, a Soviet person, while politically favouring democracy *and* the restoration of closer links between the former republics of the Soviet Union. It is for this reason that Tishkov has argued for the development of a multi-cultural nation on the basis of a 'dual and not mutually exclusive identity (cultural-ethnic and state-civic)', a formula that proposes a strategy of 'the gradual de-ethnicisation of statehood and the de-étatisation of ethnicity' (Tishkov, 1995, p. 9).

Nationalism and democratisation in Russia: transforming tradition

The focus here will be less on 'the Russian idea' than 'the idea of Russia'. It is clear that the emergence of the scaled-down Russian state in 1991 did not settle the definition of 'Russianness', and to a degree exacerbated it. The idea of Russia as an enduring culture and historical entity has played a cohesive role, but it has in most respects been a 'weak force' in giving meaning to the reborn Russian state. Johnson formulates the problem well: 'In an age of disenchantment and rationalization, all forms of legitimation based upon appeals to faith, a teleological conception of human nature, or the inherent sanctity of tradition lose their power to persuade' (Johnson, 1996, p. 42).

Transforming tradition

Russia has always been a distinctive combination of received European cultural influences and its own social traditions. 'The incommensurability between cultural and political borders is two-fold. First, political borders are precise, whereas cultural borders are fuzzy; second, political borders are volatile whereas cultural borders are (relatively) stable' (Leerssen, 1993, p. 10). Cultural space itself is constantly changing, but it is the difference in time-scale between political and cultural change that provokes conflict. The cultural identity of Austrians as a separate nation only really took root after the Second World War. It must be stressed that there is no simple contrast between tradition and modernity: tradition is transformed and sustains modernisation, and a modernisation process that radically negates tradition is liable to be fragile. The Iranian revolution of 1979 is the classic case of a reaction not so much against modernisation but against Westernising modernisation that failed to find a native idiom in which to conduct the transformation of the country. The ayatollahs are no less committed to the modernisation of the country than the Shah but seek to root it in traditional forms.

In Russia, too, post-communist modernisation has taken dangerously Western-centric forms and the failure to root the transition in a native idiom might

БИОГРАФИЯ 11.1 **Yuri Luzhkov (born 1936)**

Luzhkov first entered politics full-time in the era of *perestroika*. In June 1991, he was elected deputy mayor of Moscow, and he played a leading role in resisting the coup the following August. He became mayor of Moscow in June 1992 and has been highly influential in the city ever since. He was close to Yeltsin throughout the period, although after the August 1998 economic crisis he joined the chorus of those calling on Yeltsin to reconsider his position as Russian President. In October 1998, Luzhkov came to Britain to attend the Labour Party conference in Blackpool. Afterwards, he told a Russian journalist that he considered himself a Blairite and agreed with the British Prime Minister on most of the important political issues of the day (*Londonskii kurier*, No. 82, 8–21 October 1998). He is second only to Alexander Lebed in the betting to become Yeltsin's successor.

provoke a reaction. This is counter-balanced, however, by the sheer fragmentation of political space in Russia, and in the regions governors have vigorously revived local traditions. A case in point would be governor Mikhail Prusak in Novgorod who has explicitly rooted development in the region's history, even to the point of calling the representative assembly the Veche, the name used for the area's relatively democratic 'parliament' destroyed by Ivan the Terrible in the 1580s. In Moscow mayor Yuri Luzhkov has espoused a form of populist nationalism, rebuilding the church of Christ the Saviour, blown up by Stalin in the early 1930s, rebuilding the Voskresensky gates at the entrance to Red Square and everywhere identifying himself as a Russian patriot.

Anthony Giddens has written much about the role of tradition in the modern world, arguing that we are indeed living in a 'post-traditional' world: although tradition endures in society, it no longer has its old privileged status over other points of view and instead has to justify itself like any other. In a post-traditional society everything is 'constructed' while the givenness of social practices gives way to choices over every aspect of one's life, from religion, profession to sexual identity. He has recently argued that 'Fundamentalism is not just received tradition: it is traditional identity actively reconstructed and fought for. It is created by globalisation, but stands in opposition to it. It is the chief cultural threat to the expansion of cosmopolitan democracy' (*New Statesman*, 23 January 1998, p. 45). It might have been expected that nationalism would become a way of escaping from the burden of transition, and in a sense support for Zhirinovsky was precisely this, but as a mass movement fundamentalist nationalism has been a failure – so far.

Nationalist fundamentalism has been a relatively minor political phenomenon. Perhaps more important is the escape from tradition, from the burden of messianic interpretations of Russian national destiny in either the traditional imperialist or communist forms. This is equally true in many of Russia's own

СПРАВКА 11.1 **Wahabism**

Wahabism is a puritanical Saudi Islamic sect founded by Muhammad ibn Abd-al-Wahab (1703–92). It regards all other sects to be heretical. By the early twentieth century, Wahabism had spread throughout the Arabian peninsula. It still remains the official ideology of the Saudi Arabian kingdom.

national republics. In Dagestan, for example, Wahabism (Box 11.1) is a way of escaping from the burden of tradition, from the elaborate (and extremely expensive) rituals that have traditionally attended all stages of a person's life in the country. Wahabism is a pared down reading of Islamic tradition.

Analogously, it might be argued, post-communist democratisation for Russia is a way of escaping from the burden of the past, and allowing a re-interpretation of tradition that brings to the fore the democratic elements in Russian political culture (Petro, 1995). Nationalism is a set of competing symbols over which elites struggle. The concept of tradition in the hands of national communists, for example, has become an ideology in its own right; a trap that liberals and other modernisers have sought to escape. History no longer provides a mandate to establish links either with territory or a specific cultural tradition.

The status of nationalism

'Nationalism' as such is alien to the Russian tradition, where the focus has historically been on maintaining the state. Igor Klyamkin noted that 'Nationalism has not taken root in the Russian mentality, and contrary to the West, is perceived by Russians with suspicion' (*Ogonek*, Vol. 47 (1995), p. 19). Patriots in the Slavophile tradition consider nationalism yet another Western invention, like Marxism, imposed on long-suffering Russia. Pozdnyakov (1994, p. 61) insists that patriotism, love of the motherland and one's people, has nothing in common with nationalism. In his view 'Nationalism is the last stage of communism, the last attempt of an outdated ideology to find in society support for dictatorship' (Pozdnyakov, 1994, p. 74).

Rather than imposing the notion of nationalism, it might be better to speak of the Russian national movement, associated with the development of the Russian national idea. A burgeoning literature has emerged around these two themes. The main problem for the post-communist Russian national movement is that it is perceived as having been born out of failure. Whereas the Ukrainian national movement in the twentieth century can point to two major successes in the twentieth century, the establishment of a distinct territorial state identity between 1917 and 1923 that was recognised by the communist regime in the form of a separate Ukrainian Soviet Socialist Republic and the emergence of an independent state between 1987 and 1992, the Russian national movement has been forced to negotiate the passage from expansive 'empire-state' to a reduced notion of the nation-state.

Varieties of post-communist nationalism

The tension that was apparent throughout the Soviet era, and which divided the 'dissident' Russian national movement in the Brezhnev years, continues to this day. On the one hand, the *gosudarstvenniki* (statists) argue that a strong Russian state is the central feature of the very existence of the Russian people, and thus 'national Bolsheviks' from the 1920s made their peace with the Soviet system as the re-creator of the Russian empire. Today this tradition is reflected most vigorously in the pages of Alexander Prokhanov's paper *Zavtra* (before October 1993 *Den'*), arguing that for centuries the Russian multi-national state has been engaged in a struggle to defend 'the Russian idea' against cosmopolitanism, freemasonry and Zionism, and, as Dostoevsky had suggested earlier, Russia should turn its back on the decadent and insidious West and seek its destiny in the East (the Eurasian option). On the other hand, the *vozrozhdentsy* (a term that can loosely be translated as 'revivalists') condemned the Soviet state and Marxist ideology for having subverted the true nature of Russian statehood and culture, and insist that only the cultural and moral revival of the Russian people, based on the values of Orthodoxy, can save Russia. Solzhenitsyn is firmly in this tradition, insisting unequivocally: 'The time has come for an uncompromising *choice* between an empire of which we ourselves are the primary victims, and the spiritual and physical salvation of our own people' (Solzhenitsyn, 1991, p. 15).

The distinction between patriots and nationalists is one drawn by patriots themselves. Patriots draw on the 'soil-bound' (*pochvennik*) tradition of Slavophilism and stress the existence of a historically constituted supra-national community on the Eurasian land mass in which all the various peoples have broadly been able to pursue their own destinies even when incorporated into the Russian empire (see Box 11.2). While Russians might be an 'elder brother' to some of the peoples, with a particularly rich culture and destiny, all the various cultures had an equal right to their development. This 'imperial' approach is supra-national and stresses the rights of individuals and communities rather than nations. The nationalists, however, stress precisely the development of state structures exalting the ethnic Russian nation and defend a type of colonialist relationship with other peoples and its neighbours. Nationalists consider the Soviet regime, with its crude 'Russification' policies and its power politics, in a more favourable light than the patriots, and hence are more willing to ally with Soviet nationalists and rejectionists.

Following his victory in the July 1996 presidential elections Yeltsin suddenly discovered the need to find an ideological basis to the new Russian state and sponsored a form of *state-sponsored nationalism*. As the presidential statement put it: 'In Russian history of the twentieth century there were various periods: monarchy, totalitarianism, *perestroika*, and finally a democratic path of development. Each stage had its ideology; we have none' (ITAR-TASS, 12 July 1996). The presidential apparatus was called upon to devise a new national ideology within a year, to be ready for the next presidential elections in the year 2000, and soon after a national competition was launched for the best summary of Russian national purpose. This appeared to run counter to Article 13 of the 1993 constitution, which specifically prohibits the imposition of a state ideology,

СПРАВКА 11.2 **Pan-slavism**

Pan-slavism was a movement to unite all slavs for common political, economic and cultural purposes. It gained strength in the nineteenth century, but only took off in Russia in the 1860s. The rise of pan-slavism was due to a number of factors, including the Crimean War (which led to Russia believing that all of Europe was against her) and the unification of Germany. Two of the main writers in this tradition were Mikhail Pogodin (1800–75) who wanted a slavic buffer between Russia and Europe, and later Nikolai Danilevsky (1822–85) who believed the differences between Russia and the rest of Europe would inevitably lead to conflict. However, there has been little unity in the slavic world in practice. The Russian vision tended to see Russia as the centre of the pan-slavic world, a vision which has always been resisted by many of the other slavic nations. The experience of the Soviet years only served to reinforce this view among the Poles, Ukrainians and Yugoslavs.

Source: M. T. Florinsky (ed.), *McGraw-Hill Encyclopedia of Russia and the Soviet Union*, McGraw-Hill, New York and London, 1961, pp. 408–10

although later it was stated that what was desired was not a state ideology as such but a national idea around which the people could rally.

The aim, clearly, was to seize the ideological high ground from Yeltsin's opponents, who could mobilise a range of traditional collectivist and spiritual themes (ranging from *sobornost* to *derzhavnost*), whereas all that Yeltsin had was 'democracy', 'civilisation' and the ambiguous 'return to Europe'. Just as Yeltsin's typical tactic was to co-opt individuals from the opposition, now he sought the wholesale co-optation of its vocabulary. It is easy to ridicule Yeltsin's attempts to find an 'ideology' of the Russian state. However, the attempt has a long and honourable tradition in political philosophy. Positive political authority has dissolved in Russia, and all that remains is what might be called residual political authority. Above all, the key point is that no new national 'idea' emerged or was formulated, and the constitution was used as the reference point to prevent the establishment of a national ideology.

Less satisfactory from the constitutional point of view was the law passed in September 1997 restricting the rights of 'non-traditional' religions (excluding Orthodoxy, Islam, Judaism and Buddhism), those with a track record of less than 15 years in Russia. The law infringed several articles of the constitution and appeared to represent a capitulation to the Orthodox hierarchy, fearful of the growing influence of external Orthodox congregations, the militant evangelisation of Russia by American Protestant churches and sectarian new age cults such as the Japanese doomsday cult Aum Shinrikyo. Metropolitan Yoann in 1992 considered that this amounted to 'spiritual aggression' against Orthodoxy. This law would suggest that the 'universalisation' of Russian politics is only partial (see Chapter 10). Many have argued that membership of the Council of Europe, which Russia joined in 1996, was premature. On a number of issues, including the use of the death penalty, prison conditions and human rights in general, Russia has infringed if not outright violated standards established by the Council's European Convention on Human Rights. However, excessive Western pressure can be counter-productive, as it was over the law on non-traditional religions, provoking national sensibilities and hardening anti-Western attitudes. Engagement, rather than confrontation, appeared to be the most fruitful policy. In February 1998 the State Duma ratified the European Convention on Human Rights, allowing Russian citizens to appeal to the European Court.

A distinctive *national liberal* tendency began to take shape joined by such figures as Oleg Rumyantsev, Vladimir Lukin, Sergei Stankevich, Boris Fedorov (who served as Finance Minister during 1992–94) and many more. Fedorov's party, 'Forward, Russia!', was the only liberal party to advance the idea of patriotism, although of an inclusive and non-ethnic sort. The new patriots insisted that they could provide an alternative to the 'vulgarised version of the "Russian idea"', which stressed the cult of the state and of Russia as a great power, and which associated the idea of empire and state. They insisted that 'only a democratic Russia could be great', a greatness which lay 'not in force but in truth, not in material power but in nobility of spirit'. The growth of chauvinism would only provoke the persecution of Russians in other CIS states, and then turn back on Russia itself in the form of refugees and migration (Vladimir Ilyushenko, *Literaturnaya gazeta*, 19 February 1992, p. 11). National liberals tried to prove that not all manifestations of Russian identity were right-wing and sought to retrieve the national idea from the domination of the nationalist rejectionists, with their inability to understand the aspirations of the peoples of Russia for elements of sovereignty, their crude threats to the other former Soviet republics and their hankering for the restoration of the old USSR. One of the most interesting recent exponents of the national liberal idea is Boris Nemtsov. One of his advisers was Viktor Aksyuchits, the leader of the 'enlightened patriots' of the Russian Christian Democratic Movement. In numerous interviews and speeches he stressed the need to strengthen the state.

Traditionalist patriots represent one of the weakest tendencies of all. This is reflected in Solzhenitsyn's declining popularity. It was also revealed in the rather disappointing performance of the Congress of Russian Communities in the December 1995 Duma elections, failing to surmount the 5 per cent representation threshold (see Chapter 3). A number of opposition politicians have also campaigned under 'state-minded' principles, representing an *authoritarian statist* tendency. This is clearly the pose of Moscow mayor Luzhkov and of Alexander Lebed. One of the key themes is re-unification with diaspora Russians. As Neil Melvin puts it, 'With only a weak sense of national identity, the boundaries constituted by history, culture, language and kin emerged as powerful alternative definitions of the Russian nation to the one provided by existing political borders' (Melvin, 1995, p. 5). There remains a tension between the *political* definition of statehood (defended by the democrats) and the *social* definition, insisting that the diaspora Russians are part of the Russian state. For them, the Russian nation is larger than the present Russian state, and thus there are rich grounds for irredentist and revisionist claims. There is, moreover, an *historical* argument for a larger Russia, a view espoused by Luzhkov with Sevastopol in the Crimea. The All-Russia Movement for the Support of the Army headed by Lev Rokhlin represented an attempt to co-opt the disgruntled military to advance statist slogans.

In the transition from communism, two main exit paths were available for the Communist Party: social democratisation or Russification. The Communist Party of the Russian Federation (CPRF) under the leadership of Gennadi Zyuganov took the latter and became the leading exponents of *national communism*. This placed them in direct competition with other nationalistic groupings and meant that they were also essentially fighting for the same political terrain as the authoritarian statists. The CPRF tried to broaden its appeal to the patriotic opposition, fighting the 1996 presidential elections under the umbrella of a broad patriotic alliance. The establishment of the Popular-Patriotic Union of Russia on 7 August 1996 sought to give the opposition permanent organisational form by cementing the alliance of leftist and nationalist groups that had supported Zyuganov's presidential bid. Zyuganov described this as the emergence of a two-party political system: the 'party of power' and the 'popular-patriotic bloc' centred on the CPRF. Zyuganov sought to redress what he perceived as the imbalance in ethnic relations, allegedly favouring minorities at the expense of ethnic Russians. He insisted that a nationalities policy that focused on reviving the ethnic Russian nation was the only 'serious answer' to separatism in the Russian Federation (*Sovetskaya Rossiya*, 12 February 1998).

The Zhirinovskyites are a tendency very much associated with Zhirinovsky's own eccentric style of politics, even though formally organised in the Liberal Democratic Party of Russia (LDPR). In his best-known work *The Last Push to the South*, Zhirinovsky argued that Russia's geopolitical problems (and the world's) would be resolved by a Russian advance to the Indian Ocean that would bring Turkey, Iran and Afghanistan under Moscow's control. His thinking is imperial rather than nationalistic, although he clearly privileges ethnic Russians over all others as the core of empire. It was the LDPR's success in the December 1993 Duma elections that brought attention to focus on them, winning 22.9 per cent of the party list vote and a total of 64 seats to parliament. It has never been satisfactorily demonstrated whether this vote was a positive endorsement of Zhirinovsky's policies or whether it was merely a protest vote reflecting disillusionment with the West and disgust at Yeltsin's dissolution of the old Supreme Soviet. In the December 1995 elections, moreover, the LDPR vote halved to 11.2 per cent of the proportional vote, and they won only one single member seat (see Chapter 3).

The *right-wing (left conservative) nationalists* have much in common with the last few categories and the next, but it is worth separating them out. This tendency includes Alexander Prokhanov, Igor Shafarevich, Lev Gumilev (who died in 1992), Sergei Kurginyan and Alexander Dugin, called the Russian new right by Thomas Parland (1993). A mere mention of the names above, however, shows the enormous variety in rightist thinking. Prokhanov was obsessed by empire and, in a Russia once again torn between the Slavophile and Westerniser traditions, he was a Slavophile who insisted on a 'sovereign path for Russia'. 'Russia', he insisted, 'will keep producing for the world, and particularly the Western world, the idea of a subtle irrationalism, of a universal love, of pan-humanity' (*Transitions*, August 1997, p. 76). He showed little of this universal love towards what he called the Occidentalists: 'Today's Westernisers in Russia are the liberals and radicals. They are criminals; they are destroying Russia' (*Transitions*, August 1997, p. 77). Dugin's vast historiosophic discussions returned to the ideas of conservative Russian nationalists of the late nineteenth century, who opposed the liberalism of the West and bureaucratic absolutism in favour of a popular authoritarianism based on the unity of the Tsar and the people. Lev Gumilev brilliantly but eccentrically expounded on the birth of nations (ethnogenesis) and Russia's Eurasian destiny. Kurginyan's brilliant formulations added up to less than the parts. Sharafevich's denunciation of Russophobia was in part sound and in part unsound. It is for this reason that Parland's simple description of them as 'right-wing' is inadequate: the 'left-wing' component needs to be recognised, and the fact that right-wing thinking veers into fascism at one extreme and moderates into democratic conservatism at the other.

It is on the basis of this group that Alexander Yanov (1995) compares contemporary Russia with Weimar Germany, and, although marred by sweeping generalisations and the failure to define terms, some of his points are valid. He insists that the transition to capitalism by no means denotes the triumph of democracy and that the failure of democracy in Russia would have enormous international security implications and asserts that the West in the early 1990s focused too narrowly on economic reform and failed to support the broader democratisation process.

As for *fascists and neo-fascists*, during perestroika the rise of the extreme right, above all the various tendencies of *Pamyat*, attracted much attention, yet when faced by the test of the ballot box they attracted few votes. Today there are numerous extreme rightist organisations, yet none can be portrayed as a genuine mass movement.

No discussion of the trends in Russian nationalism would be complete without mention of popular attitudes. A recent survey by the St Petersburg Institute for Complex Sociological Research (NIKSI) suggests that, among young people at least, 'state-mindedness' is not a slogan that would attract their votes. A majority of respondents rejected the use of military force for the sake of statehood, with statehood as such valued by no more than a third of them. As for patriotism, while 59.7 per cent are proud of being born in Russia, 'serving Russia' is a priority only for 2.7 per cent, appearing last on a list of priorities (*The New Federalist*, 26 May 1997). Other survey evidence suggests little support for imperial policies, although cultural nationalism remains strong. Like China and other modernising societies, Russia is torn between globalising pressures and nativising reactions. In China this was reflected in a best-selling book entitled *China Can Say No*, published in June 1996, and its sequels, that reflected a new assertiveness that has not yet found its popular counterpart in Russia.

Conclusion

As an exercise in state building the USSR proved a failure. The Bolsheviks tried to transform an empire into a state, and failed. Some parts were simply unassimilable, especially when Stalin's greed re-incorporated parts, such as the Baltic republics and Galicia (Western Ukraine around Lvov), that would later lead the struggle that destroyed the Soviet empire-state. The creation of 15 post-Soviet states can be seen as the completion of the process of national emancipation that had taken shape in the nineteenth century, yet the problems associated with national liberation have still not been resolved. It was the fusion of federalism with its vision of shared sovereignty and nationality issues that proved fatal for the Soviet Union and which introduces an element in post-communist politics that is unique. Federalism is a political principle regulating the separation of power between the centre and the locality, whereas ethnicity is an absolute that as a matter of principle is non-negotiable. In post-communist Russia these two elements fused to create qualitatively new problems. The USSR in theory was a multi-sovereign state, and Russia is now faced with the challenge of finding a political form to fulfil this promise. How can demands for sovereignty by some of its components be made compatible with the Russian state's own claims to sovereignty? Alternatively, put more directly for our purposes: how can the nationalism of the non-Russian ethnic groups be rendered compatible with the continued existence of the Russian Federation? (See Chapter 4.)

The effects of the dissolution of the Austro-Hungarian and Ottoman empires have still not been entirely worked out, and there is no reason to suspect that the impact of the Soviet disintegration will be resolved any quicker. The end of the cold war has indeed seen the 'return of history', not only in the sense that East European countries have had their destinies returned to them, but also in the resurgence of 'the old business of history, nineteenth-century style, replete with national self-assertiveness and ethnic separatism' (Ekedahl and Goodman, 1997, p. 181). Russia's post-cold-war national identity is still in the early stages of formation. The process is distorted by a range of distinctive factors: the legacy of empire; the presence of some 25 million Russians in the former Soviet republics; the existence of ethno-federal republics within the borders of its formally sovereign republic; the humiliation of the geopolitical collapse at the end of the cold war; the unprecedented scale of economic collapse and social polarisation. At the same time, a number of salutary features reinforce a sense of national cohesion: the Russian Orthodox Church; cultural traditions that transcend ethnic divisions; a growing civic sense of national identity. The main problem today is to give this a coherent political form. While Russian nationalism in the late nineteenth century might have begun to reach the 'mass movement' phase (Hroch, 1985), its history for most of the twentieth century has taken a very different trajectory. There is now little evidence that post-communist mass Russian nationalism has been mobilised to pursue a more aggressive or irredentist foreign policy, even though there is a broad consensus among the elites that Russia must remain a great power. At home, the primordialist view of 'one state – one nation' has not taken root.

While Russians did not become Soviets in quite the same way that the English became British, the challenge facing Russia (and Britain and France earlier), was to achieve self-liberation from imperial ambitions and messianism. The question is often posed: will Russia become a nation-state or restore its imperial status? While the existence of Russia in its present borders is questioned, the population is gradually becoming reconciled with the 'smaller Russia'. The *political* definition is understood to be the only viable one at the present time. Ethnicity is *not* becoming political identity. The Russian nation is *not* substituting for the Russian state.

References

Anderson B 1983 *Imagined Communities: Reflections on the Origin and Spread of Nationalism*, Verso, London.

Armstrong J A 1982 *Nations Before Nationalism*, Chapel Hill.

Arutyuniyan Yu 1991 Changing Values of Russians from Brezhnev to Gorbachev, *Journal of Soviet Nationalities*, No. 2.

Beissinger M 1995 The Persisting Ambiguity of Empire, *Post-Soviet Affairs*, Vol. 11, No. 2, pp. 149–84.

Brubaker R 1994 Nationhood and the National Question in the Soviet Union and Post-Soviet Eurasia: An Institutionalist Account, *Theory and Society*, Vol. 23, pp. 47–78.

Brubaker R 1996 *Nationalism Reframed: Nationhood and the National Question in the New Europe*, Cambridge University Press, Cambridge.

Chernyaev A S 1993 *Shest' let s Gorbachevym*, Progress, Moscow.

Colley L 1992 *Britons: Forging the Nation, 1707–1837*, Yale University Press, New Haven, CT.

Eckstein H 1998 Congruence Theory Explained, in Eckstein H, Fleron F J Jr, Hoffmann E P and Reissinger W M, *Can Democracy Take Root in Post-Soviet Russia? Explorations in State–Society Relations*, Rowman & Littlefield, Lanham, MD.

Ekedahl C M and Goodman M A 1997 *The Wars of Eduard Shevardnadze*, Pennsylvania State University Press, University Park, PA.

Gellner E 1983 *Nations and Nationalism: New Perspectives on the Past*, Basil Blackwell, Oxford.

Hayes C J 1949 *The Historical Evolution of Modern Nationalism*, Macmillan, London.

Hobsbawm E 1990 *Nations and Nationalism Since 1870: Programme, Myth, Reality*, 2nd edition, Cambridge University Press, Cambridge.

Hosking G 1997 *People and Empire, 1552–1917*, Harper Collins, London.

Hough J F 1997 *Democratization and Revolution in the USSR, 1985–1991*, Brookings Institution Press, Washington, DC.

Hroch M 1985 *Social Preconditions of National Revival in Europe*, Cambridge University Press, Cambridge.

Johnson G R 1996 Modernity and Postmodernity in the Thought of José Merquior, in Gellner E and Cansino C (eds), *Liberalism in Modern Times: Essays in Honour of José G Merquior*, Central European University Press, Budapest.

Khazanov A 1994 The Collapse of the Soviet Union: Nationalism During Perestroika and Afterwards, *Nationalities Papers*, Vol. 22, No. 1.

Kohn H 1967 *The Idea of Nationalism: A Study in its Origins and Background*, New York.

Leerssen J 1993 Europe as a Set of Borders, *Yearbook of European Studies*, No. 6.

Lieven D 1995 The Russian Empire and the Soviet Union as Imperial Polities, *Journal of Contemporary History*, Vol. 30, pp. 607–36.

Melvin N 1995 *Russians Beyond Russia: The Politics of National Identity*, Royal Institute of International Affairs, London.

Nairn T 1977 *The Break-up of Britain*, New Left Books, London.

Olson O 1990 The Logic of Collective Action in Soviet-type Societies, *Journal of Soviet Nationalities*, No. 1.

Parland T 1993 *The Rejection in Russia of Totalitarian Socialism and Liberal Democracy: A Study of the Russian New Right*, Societas Scientarium Fennica, Helsinki.

Petro N 1995 *The Rebirth of Russian Democracy: An Interpretation of Political Culture*, Harvard University Press, Cambridge, MA.

Pozdniakov E A 1994 *Natsiia, natsionalizm, natsional'nye interesy*, Progress-kultura, Moscow.

Rajchman J (ed.) 1995 *The Identity in Question*, Routledge, London.

Schöpflin G 1991 Nationalism and National Minorities in East and Central Europe, *Journal of International Affairs*, Vol. 45, No. 1, pp. 51–66.

Simonia N A 1995 Priorities of Russian Foreign Policy and the Way it Works, in Dawisha A and Dawisha K (eds), *The Making of Foreign Policy in Russia and the New States of Eurasia*, M E Sharpe, New York.

Smith A D 1986 *The Ethnic Origins of Nations*, Blackwell, Oxford.

Smith A D 1991a *Ethnic Identity*, Penguin, Harmondsworth.

Smith A D 1991b *Theories of Nationalism*, Duckworth, London.

Solzhenitsyn A (ed.) 1974a *From Under the Rubble*, Fontana, London.

Solzhenitsyn A 1974b *Letter to the Soviet Leaders*, Collins/Harvill, London.

Solzhenitsyn A 1991 *Rebuilding Russia: Reflections and Tentative Proposals*, Harvill Press, London.

Tishkov V A 1995 Chto est' Rossiia? (perspektivy natsie-stroitel'stva)', *Voprosy filosofii*, No. 2.

Yanov A 1995 *Weimar Russia, and What we Can do About it*, Slovo/Word Publishing House, New York.

Zakaria F 1997 The Rise of Illiberal Democracy, *Foreign Affairs*, Vol. 76, No. 6.

Further reading

Bremmer I and Taras R (eds) 1996 *New States, New Politics: Building the Post-Soviet Nations*, 2nd edition, Cambridge University Press, Cambridge.

Petro N 1995 *The Rebirth of Russian Democracy: An Interpretation of Political Culture*, Harvard University Press, Cambridge, MA.

Suny R G 1996 *The Revenge of the Past: Nationalism, Revolution and the Collapse of the Soviet Union*, Stanford University Press, Stanford, CA.

Tishkov V 1996 *Ethnicity, Nationalism and Conflict in and After the Soviet Union: The Mind Aflame*, Sage, London.

12

Russian military forces and reform

Christoph Bluth

Introduction

The most tangible symbol of the change in Russia's standing in the world since 1991, other than the disintegration of the Soviet Union itself, is the dramatic collapse of the Soviet military machine. From the position of having been a first-rate military power believed to be capable of occupying the whole of Europe, Russia's military has been reduced to a position where it has difficulty keeping internal order and cannot be relied upon to defend the country against a large-scale external attack without recourse to nuclear weapons. More importantly, the sorry state of the Russian military, which has been affected by the socio-economic dislocation in the entire country, poses a potentially enormous threat for the stability and security of Russia itself (Defence and Foreign Ministers are listed in Box 12.1).

Military doctrine and policy

Russia inherited a substantial portion of the Soviet armed forces which were largely designed to engage in high-intensity warfare with the West or China. The general staff in Moscow, however, lost control over substantial military assets that had been forward deployed in other republics. The task for the Russian military leadership was to restructure the country's military forces on the basis of this inheritance in a radically different geopolitical environment. The political instability, administrative chaos and economic weakness of the

---

СПРАВКА 12.1 Russian Defence and Foreign Ministers

Foreign Ministers	Defence Ministers
Andrei Kozyrev (1990–95)	Pavel Grachev (1992–96)
Yevgeni Primakov (1996–98)	Igor Rodionov (1996–97)
Igor Ivanov (1998–)	Igor Sergeev (1997–)

Russian state, furthermore, put severe constraints on the resources available to the military.

During the Soviet period, 'military doctrine' expressed the view of the state on the political objectives of war and the military–technical aspects of military policy. The armed forces of the Russian Federation were created in May 1992, but it proved difficult to establish agreement on a military doctrine. A document entitled 'Principal Guidance on the Military Doctrine of the Russian Federation' was approved by the Security Council on 2 November 1993 (see *Izvestiya*, 18 November 1993; Arbatov, 1998). Even then, President Boris Yeltsin made it clear that it was only part of a general security doctrine (see Dick, 1994b; Bluth, 1992, pp. 83–123). It remained unclear throughout the period what this general security doctrine was, although some of the elements were presumably contained in Yuri Skokov's 'The Basic Provisions of a Foreign Policy Concept', which was endorsed by Yeltsin himself although it was never published (see Baev, 1996, p. 31).

After the dissolution of the Soviet Union, the traditional perceptions of the international security environment that dominated the cold war period were abandoned surprisingly quickly by the political elite. The military was somewhat slow to follow along a similar path. By mid-1992 the relevance of the 'defence of the Western Perimeter was seriously questioned' (Baev, 1996, p. 28), but traditional thinking still pervaded the debate until well into 1993. By the time a new military doctrine was approved in November 1993, a radical re-evaluation of the security threats facing Russia had been adopted by the Russian military (*Izvestiya*, 18 November 1993). The military and arms control policies of Russia under Yeltsin since then reflect the perceptions of the security environment after the cold war. There is widespread acceptance among the military leadership and the political elite that there is no threat to Russia from the United States and that the principal military threats come from the southern periphery of the Russian Federation and from Third World countries that are acquiring weapons of mass destruction and ballistic missiles. In line with a general restructuring of the Russian military to rapid reaction and crisis intervention roles, there is a fundamental change in thinking about the role of nuclear weapons to meet the new range of threats. The utility of strategic nuclear weapons in this environment is perceived to have declined fundamentally. Russian military research and development efforts are now almost exclusively focused on high-technology conventional weapons. Tactical nuclear weapons were withdrawn from Eastern Europe and the non-Russian newly independent states.

It is a paradox that in a security environment where the only plausible threats arise from localised civil conflicts the main focus of security policy has become the reliance on nuclear weapons (Arbatov, 1998). The aim of the Russian Federation's policy in the sphere of nuclear weapons is to eliminate the danger of nuclear war by deterring any aggression against the Russian Federation and its allies (*Voennaya Mysl*, 1992, p. 5).[1] This commits Russia to a policy of

---

1 Note that only a description of the basic provisions of the military doctrine of the Russian Federation has been published. Any reference to the military doctrine in this chapter is to that description as published in *Voennaya mysl*, Special Issue, May 1992, pp. 3–23.

extended deterrence against threats to the security of its (unspecified) allies. There is a policy of no nuclear use against non-nuclear states that have acceded to the Non-Proliferation Treaty, but there is no longer such a policy *vis-à-vis* nuclear weapons states or non-nuclear states which enjoy a nuclear guarantee from nuclear weapons states. This constitutes an abandonment of the pledge not to use nuclear weapons first, which some commentators have found alarming. However, it should be pointed out that the 'no first use' pledge was made in the context of the confrontation in Central Europe, where the Soviet Union was determined to avoid escalation to the nuclear level in any conflict. The new doctrine is more in line with the notion of a deterrent as a last resort in the kinds of conflicts for which Russia is now preparing. It could also be interpreted as a warning to Turkey against any involvement in the conflict between Armenia and Azerbaijan, or to Ukraine as it considers the fate of nuclear weapons on its territory (Dick, 1994a). However, as the capabilities of the Russian armed forces decline, it was possible to detect from interviews in Moscow in April 1996, an increasing emphasis on nuclear forces to compensate for weakness at the conventional level.

The use of the armed forces in international peacekeeping operations, their deployment outside the national territory, and the conduct of peacekeeping operations on the territories of the former Soviet republics together perhaps constitute the most important new element in Russian military doctrine. The doctrine also states that the units of the armed forces can be used in *internal* conflicts to support the forces of the Interior Ministry of the Russian Federation to localise and blockade the conflict region, to suppress armed clashes and to separate the conflicting parties as well as to defend the strategically important objects (*Voennaya Mysl*, 1992, p. 16). This part of the military doctrine is in conflict with the law on defence, which prohibits the use of regular armed forces inside the Russian Federation.

The military doctrine asserts that Russia does not consider 'any state as its enemy' and will not use its armed forces or other armed formations against any state for any purposes other than individual or collective self-defence in the case of an armed attack on the Russian Federation, its citizens, territory, armed forces or the other Russian armed formations, or its allies (*Voennaya Mysl*, 1992, p. 4).

The potential sources of a military threat against the Russians from outside include, according the military doctrine:

- territorial claims to the Russian Federation from the other post-Soviet states;

- existing and potential sources of local wars and armed conflicts, primarily those in direct proximity to the Russian borders;

- proliferation of nuclear and other weapons of mass destruction, the means of delivery and modern military technologies;

- the oppression of the rights, freedoms and legitimate interests of the citizens of the Russian Federation abroad;

- the enlargement of military blocs and alliances (e.g. NATO) in such a way as to violate the military security interests of the Russian Federation.

According to the document, the greatest threat to Russia arises from armed conflicts caused by aggressive nationalism and religious intolerance.

The main objective of the organisational development of the Russian Federation armed forces and other troops is to create and develop forces capable of defending the independence, sovereignty and territorial integrity of the country, the security of the citizens, and the other vitally important interests of society and state in line with the military–political and strategic situation in the world (*Voennaya Mysl*, 1992, p. 16). However, in view of the absence of an agreed concept of the national security of Russia, it is unclear what the vital interests of the Russian Federation are. Such statements in the military doctrine therefore remain open to interpretation.

The military part of Russia's new military doctrine sets out a view of the possible character of future conflicts. Under conditions in which the danger of global war (both nuclear and conventional) is reduced substantially although it is not eliminated completely, local wars and armed conflicts represent the main threat to stability and peace. Their probability in some regions is increasing (*Voennaya Mysl*, 1992, p. 12).

Local wars and armed conflicts are perceived as the most likely source of military threats to Russia. The military doctrine assumes that a wide variety of forces can be engaged in these operations, from a small number of armed units up to operational-strategic groups of forces, along with the use of all types of weapons, from small arms to modern precision-guided 'smart' weapons. The priority is the development of the Russian Federation armed forces and other troops intended for deterrence against aggression, as well as the mobile forces of the Russian Federation armed forces and other troops able to re-deploy within a short period and to mount and conduct manoeuvre operations in any sector (region) where a threat to the security of the Russian Federation may arise (*Voennaya Mysl*, 1992, pp. 17–18). Furthermore, Russian armed forces can be deployed outside the national territory to safeguard the security of either the Russian Federation or other former Soviet republics (*Voennaya Mysl*, 1992, p. 18).

The document on military doctrine reflects a basic contradiction in the way in which force requirements are defined. On the one hand, local wars and armed conflicts are clearly presented as the principal security threat. On the other hand, the operational strategic concepts and the remarks on practical implementation have the appearance of a guide for the preparation for military operations around the globe, based on the acquisition of sea and airlift capabilities on a global scale. This is also in contradiction to the intention asserted by the Soviet Union in the period of 'new political thinking' of liquidating the capabilities to launch surprise attacks or large-scale offensive operations. The emphasis on the defensive nature of the military–technical aspects of military doctrine thus appears to have been lost.

Although five years have passed since the 'new military doctrine' was formulated, there has been no significant refinement of doctrine since then. This is partly due to the inability of the government to move ahead with well-defined and sensible sets of measures of military reform and to the failure to get agreement on a radical restructuring of the armed forces in line with the contemporary security environment.

Force levels and military reform

The Soviet legacy and Russia's dilemma

When the Commonwealth of Independent States was formed at the meeting in Minsk in December 1991, to be followed soon thereafter by the dissolution of the USSR, there was concern, both at the highest political levels in Russia and in the former Soviet military high command, that the integrity of the Soviet armed forces should be preserved and that the former Soviet Union (except for the Baltic states) should form a common security space. However, it became apparent very quickly that this was incompatible with the requirements of state-building in the CIS, of which the establishment of independent armed forces and the neutralisation of former Soviet forces formed a critical element. The principal consequence of these developments was that the integrity of the Soviet military system could not be preserved and a major proportion of the military assets of the former Soviet Union was lost to the general staff in Moscow. For this reason, the then Russian Defence Minister Pavel Grachev stated that the Russian armed forces had to be built up from scratch (*Izvestiya*, 1 June 1992).

Russia inherited armed forces comprising 2.8 million troops and large quantities of tanks, armoured vehicles, helicopters, aircraft, artillery and other types of military equipment. Dealing with this legacy in conformity with the security requirements of the post-Soviet state is itself a major task. However, as we have seen, the military doctrine is in many respects rather vague and general. Furthermore, it contains ambiguities which result from the fact that while the Russian military leadership clearly wants to develop the forces and capabilities required to meet the security threats as it perceives them, it would also like to retain as much as possible of the former Soviet capabilities for large-scale, high-intensity conventional warfare. While the military leadership recognises that the armed forces must be reduced in size, it is unwilling to accept reductions of such a scale as to bring the armed forces to a more sustainable level, at which they could be properly trained, equipped and deployed to meet Russia's security requirements. This recalcitrance is motivated at least in part by a perception of the unacceptable social consequences of decommissioning a large number of Russian officers who would have a hard time finding alternative means of support.

Whatever the ambitions of the military leadership may be, they are subject to some important constraints. One is the Conventional Forces in Europe (CFE) Treaty, which imposes upper limits on the military equipment Russia can maintain. Another is the limit on the resources available for the military from the state. Political attempts to set and maintain a lower ceiling on force numbers as a way of controlling the military's demand for resources have met with limited success. In December 1992 the law on defence set a ceiling on the armed forces of 1 per cent of the population, which means 1.5 million troops, to be achieved by the end of 1995. By 1994 the authorized number of personnel was 2.2 million; in 1995 it was reduced to 1.9 million, against strenuous objections from Defence Minister Grachev. The state budget for 1995 included a target of 1.5 million for the armed forces by the end of 1995, in line with the law on defence, although this reduction was not fully achieved.

Financial aspects of military reform

On 16 May 1996, at the height of the presidential election campaign in Russia, President Yeltsin announced an end to military conscription. He signed a decree according to which the Russian armed forces would, by April 2000, consist entirely of professional officers and contract soldiers. With one stroke of the pen he thereby seemed to have resolved a controversy over the future of the Russian armed forces. It is a testimony to the unpopularity of military service and the low status of the once revered armed forces that Yeltsin believed this measure would add a major impetus to his campaign. The disastrous intervention in Chechnya has done much to deepen popular disdain for the military and has further reduced the public acceptability of military service. Military affairs continued to be subordinated to the requirements of electoral politics.

It is clear that Yeltsin made these commitments without any clear concept of how the armed forces are to be restructured and how the various demands of force requirements and budgetary constraints are to be reconciled. The principal reason why Yeltsin announced the move to a professional army is evidently the unpopularity of conscription. However, the financial constraints that will apply for the foreseeable future mean that the implementation of the measure will require serious choices to be made as regards the mission and overall size of the armed forces.

The overall GDP of the Russian Federation can be taken as a measure of the resource base that limits the options for the development of the armed forces. When the Soviet Union was dissolved, Russia accounted for 61 per cent of the GDP of the former Soviet Union. This has fallen precipitously, and by the end of 1995 Russian GDP amounted to only 36 per cent of the last figure for the Soviet Union. By 1997 the total decline of Russia's GDP since the Soviet era amounted to 50 per cent. The maintenance of military forces and capabilities on anything approaching the scale of those of the former Soviet Union on such a reduced and falling resource base is clearly an untenable position (Trenin, 1995). In August 1998, the collapse of the ruble and the financial and political meltdown in Russia has shattered the hopes of the Russian military that a more stable economy and incremental economic growth might provide the resources needed for military reform and the revitalization of the Russian armed forces.

There have been vigorous internal debates in Russia about the appropriate share of resources for the military so that it can adequately provide for the security of the state. Defence Minister Pavel Grachev and his deputy Andrei Kokoshin fought hard to maximise the resources allocated to the military. Two concerns were uppermost in their minds. One was that although the defence industrial base clearly has to contract, it should not be allowed to wither away. Russia must remain at the leading edge of military technology. There must also be sufficient funds to permit the maintenance of military hardware. Military industries are a major employer, and the social consequences of their closure must also be considered. The other concern was that the personnel of the armed forces should have proper living conditions and that military infrastructure and weapons should be properly maintained to retain their operational capability. If the living conditions and the pay of personnel in the armed services were allowed

| СПРАВКА 12.2 | **Safety concerns in the nuclear arms industry** |

The despair in the Russian submarine fleet has produced a disturbing increase in incidents. On 11 September 1998, a sailor went berserk on a modern Akula-class nuclear submarine and killed eight people before shooting himself. Six days earlier, three people were taken hostage at a nuclear test site at Novaya Zemlya in the Arctic. Two weeks ago, two people were killed in an incident on board a Russian submarine in the Black Sea and an interior guard at Mayak in Siberia killed three colleagues.

But the utter lack of confidence in safety standards was revealed in May 1998 when there was an explosion on board a submarine loaded with 16 nuclear warheads in the Barents Sea after water leaked into the missile compartment. As the submarine limped towards Severomorsk, near Murmansk, the headquarters of the northern fleet, wild rumours spread. The city fathers fled to the hills. Kindergartens were evacuated. Police started taking iodine pills. Norwegian intelligence noted that after the incident no Russian missile submarine put to sea for three months.

Source: I. Mather, Tension Primes Nuclear Timebomb in the Russian Arctic, *The European*, 12–18 October 1998, p. 10

to deteriorate even further, control over substantial portions of the armed forces might be lost. At a minimum, their combat-readiness would seriously decline. See also Box 12.2.

On the whole, it must be said that Grachev and Kokoshin were not very successful. Despite very vigorous lobbying of parliament, almost to the point of blackmail, military spending has steadily declined as a percentage of GDP. According to IMF estimates, Russian defence expenditure in 1992–95 amounted to between 4.4 and 5 per cent (compared with at least 15 per cent for the Soviet era). It is quite clear that there has been a consensus in the legislature since 1992 that military spending should not exceed 5 per cent of GDP – despite the predominance of Communists and nationalists in the Duma.

This can be explained by the competing political influences on government spending. The defence budget is drawn up by the Ministry of Defence, but has to be approved by the government in the first instance. It is evident that the Ministry of Finance has the backing of the President and the Prime Minister in imposing severe limits on all government spending, including military expenditures, in order to keep inflation in check and to satisfy the IMF that Russia is moving towards a sound financial policy. The draft state budget is subsequently submitted to parliament. The Duma imposes a limit on the overall budget deficit, thereby further reducing the scope for lobbying by special interests. Moreover, the military industry has to compete with other important interest groups, such as the gas and oil industries and the agricultural lobby.

Another important aspect of Russian budgetary politics is the underfulfilment of public spending plans. Even when the military can persuade the Duma to agree to a higher military budget, this does not mean that the monies authorised will also be available. The persistent shortfall between projected tax receipts and actual revenues means that military expenditure tends to be a good deal less than is budgeted for. This shortfall is added to the arrears from previous years, which spills over into the next federal budget. As a consequence the government debt to the armed services and defence industries increases, while actual expenditures amount to only about half the amount that the military leadership considers to be the bare minimum. Indeed, at the end of the year the Duma typically makes additional emergency appropriations of the order of 2–3 trillion rubles to prevent mass starvation in the armed forces (*Obshchaya gazeta*, 31 October 1996).

The defence budget for 1996 reflected the priorities of the political elite. Defence spending was reduced from 21.3 per cent to 17.0 per cent of the federal budget. This implied a reduction from 5.5 per cent to 3.8 per cent of GDP. Social costs (salaries, pensions, housing, etc.) accounted for most of the budget; a mere 10 per cent was to be spent on procurement. In view of the large sums required by the Ministry of Defence to pay off its debts to military enterprises, this meant that actual procurement was virtually reduced to zero.

For the 1997 budget, the military had to go around the same loop again. The request for minimum sufficient financing exceeded the government draft figure by 40–50 per cent. The 1997 federal budget submitted by the government allocated about 104.3 trillion rubles for the item 'national defence'. This amounts to 19 per cent of the entire federal budget for 1997, or 3.7 per cent of the forecast GDP of Russia. This total amount represents an increase over the 1996 allocation equal to the rate of inflation. However, again it can be assumed that not all of these funds will actually become available, and moreover substantial sums are owed to banks and military enterprises. A closer analysis of the defence budget (as close as the limited information published permits) shows that again most of it goes on the maintenance of the armed forces. Procurement of weapons and military equipment and, even more importantly, research and development are to get even fewer resources than in the previous year. Alexei Arbatov has calculated that (prior to the collapse of the ruble) Russia's defence budget had shrunk to $25–30 billion, compared with $300 billion per annum during the Soviet period (Arbatov, 1998, pp. 95–7). As a consequence, he has painted a vision of the Russian army in ten years' time, facing new military threats on Russia's geostrategic borders without a modern military, without state-of-the-art weapons. This raises the question of how Russia should plan for its armed forces on the basis of the available resources. Analysts in the General Staff concluded that there are three alternatives:

- a well-equipped army of at most 650 000–750 000 troops;
- a poorly equipped army of 1.5 million troops;
- a substantial increase in the military share of national income.

However, this was based on assumptions about the level of Russian GDP in the year 2000 which were optimistic at best and since August 1998 seem hopelessly unrealistic. Furthermore, the current levels of training and equipment are much lower than assumed. The military would quite clearly prefer option 3 and remains unwilling to contemplate option 1, with the result that, so far, option 2 is the actual policy being implemented.

The Russian debate about the size and structure of the armed forces is hampered by a lack of consensus on its future role and missions. The military doctrine does not identify a potential adversary and remains vague on the threats or security risks that Russian armed forces are likely to face. The question as to whether the armed forces are purely to serve the territorial defence of the Russian Federation, whether they are also to provide for the security of all signatories to the Tashkent collective security agreement or the entire Commonwealth of Independent States or whether they are to be used as an instrument to sustain geopolitical objectives further afield has not been resolved or even openly debated. Nevertheless, it is critical to the issue of force planning.

In view of the end of the cold war and partial normalisation of relations with the West, some prominent analysts, including military leaders, have argued that the size of Russia's armed forces should be assessed according to criteria applicable to a 'normal' civilised state. A comparison with other OSCE countries would lead to the conclusion that, taking into account Russia's territory and population, the size of its armed forces should be about 0.9 million troops. The majority view in the general staff, however, seems to be that Russia has special problems and that such criteria are not applicable.

There is a wide range of views among the opposition parties. Vladimir Zhirinovsky's Liberal Democratic Party, which has very ambitious views about Russia as a regional and global power, advocates a minimum target of 3 million troops, of which 1 million should be officers. This is obviously completely unrealistic. The most detailed proposals have been put forward by the Yabloko coalition. They advocate a target of between 1 million and 1.2 million troops. This is based on the view that Russia is not going to be embroiled in a regional conflict with another major power in the near future. Russia will not attempt to play the role of a great military power; however, it will be responsible for the security of Russia and the signatories to the Tashkent collective security agreement. A vital part of this programme is the formation of a number of elite forces which are fully manned and equipped and combat ready. Support for the most important branches of military industry is also considered essential. The emphasis is on focusing resources so that at least some parts of the armed forces are capable of realistically implementing their tasks. The Yabloko programme is perhaps the most thorough attempt yet made in Russia to deal with the implications of the reduced resource base for military policy and to match requirements with capabilities.[2]

Yeltsin decided, after much internal debate, that the nominal level of the armed forces should be 1.7 million by the end of 1995 and 1.5 million by the end of 1996. This objective has now been postponed until 1998. However, it is also quite clear that even before the financial collapse Yeltsin wanted to reduce the armed forces further.

Military reform appears to have received more high-level attention since the presidential elections in 1996. Grachev's successor as Defence Minister, Igor

---

2 See Rodin I, *Nezavisimaya gazeta*, supplement, 14 December 1995, for an overview of the attitudes of different political groupings with regard to military reform and military policy.

Rodionov, made frequent speeches emphasising the need for military reform and for a solution to be found to the problem of the chronic underfunding of the armed forces. He went so far as to say that the projected 1997 defence budget covered only a third of the necessary expenses on the armed forces and added that, if it were not corrected, Russia might finally lose the armed forces as an integral and capable state structure (Interfax, 25 October 1996, cited from FBIS-SOV-96-208).

Plans for military reform continue to be hampered by a lack of clear direction at the highest level about Russia's security interests and force requirements. In order to provide a more unified approach to policy on the armed forces, a Defence Council (an institution which previously existed in the Soviet Union) was established with Yuri Baturin as secretary. During its first session on 4 October 1996, Prime Minister Viktor Chernomyrdin described the four aims of restructuring the armed forces as (Interfax, 4 October 1996, cited from FBIS-SOV-96-195):

- adjusting the composition, structure and size of the armed forces to the existing political and military situation and the economic possibilities of the situation;

- developing a core of technically well-equipped and well-trained armed forces capable of removing threats emerging in key strategic directions;

- the full and unconditional provision of the armed forces and other troops with funding, armaments, combat and other hardware, material and technical means;

- keeping troops in high readiness for defence.

However, Chernomyrdin gave no indication of how these objectives were to be achieved. It soon emerged that Baturin had views on military reform which were at odds with those in the military establishment. Having been tasked with monitoring implementation of the presidential edict 'On Measures to Ensure Military Organizational Development in the Russian Federation', he began to advocate the concept that military reform should to be started now, using existing resources, while simultaneously cutting the country's power structures by an average of 30 per cent (*Rossiiskaya gazeta*, 17 January 1997).

On 7 February 1997, Rodionov and Baturin gave a press conference designed to dampen press speculation about disagreements between the Ministry of Defence and the Defence Council on military reform. Rodionov affirmed his support for a three-stage programme advocated by Baturin. The first phase, until 2000, would consist in a reduction in the size of the armed forces; the second phase (2001–05) would deal with qualitative problems; the third phase (after 2005) would involve large-scale rearmament. According to Rodionov, the size of the armed forces was to be reduced by 200 000 to 1.5 million (OMRI Daily Brief I, 10 February 1997).

However, it was clear that Rodionov and Baturin disagreed quite fundamentally about the future of military reform.[3] The disagreement focused around three

3 The following section is in part based on a paper by Dov Lynch, 'A New Era in Russian Civil–Military Relations and Military Reform', forthcoming.

different issues. The first was the role and very existence of the Defence Council, which increased civilian influence over military policy, an area in which the General Staff continued to claim unique expertise and competence. Although Rodionov had initially supported its creation, he gradually became increasingly vocal against such an alternative locus of decison-making on military affairs. The second was the financial allocation to the military. Rodionov forcefully advanced the view that the military needed to be financed properly and moreover, that substantial resources needed to be made available to implement military reform. The defence allocations for the 1997 budget amounted to only 104.3 billion (old) rubles, even though the military had asked for 160 300 billion rubles. In February 1997, Rodionov went as far as to raise questions about the safety and secure control over the Russian strategic nuclear arsenal, thereby breaking a major taboo, in order to highlight the desperate need for more funds for the military. Moreover, as Rodionov also pointed out on various occasions alongside other military experts, there are also structural problems about implementing military reform. A reduction in the number of officers does not save money immediately if the social obligations (redundancy payments, pensions, housing, etc.) are taken into account. Some analysts believe that savings will not become significant until five years have passed. Indeed, the initial costs of military reform have been another obstacle to prevent this issue from being dealt with in a rational and decisive manner.

The Secretary of the Defence Council on the other hand clearly maintained the position that there was no possibility of increasing the proportion of the federal budget allocated to the military. Indeed, in February 1997, when Rodionov made a desperate plea for more funds, Baturin stated bluntly that there could be no increase in the military budget (*Nezavisimaya gazeta*, 8 February 1997) and, given the problems of achieving the tax income targets on which the budget was based, further reductions in allocations were likely. Armed forces planning and military reform would have to be carried out within the financial constraints of the budget.

The third area of disagreement related to military doctrine. In November 1996, Yuri Baturin called for a revision of Russia's military doctrine in view of the changes in its economic and geopolitical situation. Rodionov's response was to reaffirm the military doctrine adopted in November 1993, only to publish an outline for a new doctrine shortly thereafter, presumably in order to pre-empt a revision of military doctrine by the Defence Council (see Lynch, forthcoming; *Nezavisimoe voennoe obozrenie*, 28 November 1996).

Clearly there was a power struggle between the Ministry of Defence and the Defence Council. In the absence of clear guidance from the President, no progress was made on any of these issues and indeed in the first five months of 1997 the Defence Council did not meet.

When Yeltsin had seemingly recovered sufficiently from the consequences of his multiple heart by-pass operation and other medical problems, a meeting of the Defence Council was held on 22 May 1997. Two days before Rodionov submitted a report to the President which projected constant military expenditures at 160 000 billion rubles for the next 10 years. This apparent unwillingness to take on board the fiscal realities, and moreover the failure to make any progress

СПРАВКА 12.3   Sergeev's appointment

In May 1997, Yeltsin went to a televised meeting of the Defence Council and declared himself 'indignant' over the state of the Russian military. He said there was a vital need for defence cuts, but the military establishment continued to oppose them. Yeltsin was dismissive of the views of the military, declaring that 'the soldiers get thinner and the generals get fatter' (*Keesings Record of World Events*, 1997, p. 41658). Rodionov was dismissed as Defence Minister and replaced by Igor Sergeev (born 1938). Sergeev has spent his life in the military (with the rocket forces since the 1960s), but he is obviously expected to force arms cuts through despite the opposition of his former colleagues.

with regards to military reform as well as the criticism of the decision to establish the Defence Council as an institution, angered Yeltsin. At the meeting of the Defence Council on 22 May 1997, Yeltsin berated the high military command and Rodionov personally for their obstructive behaviour. He expressed the view that military expenditure at a level of 5 per cent of GDP was unsustainable and higher than the military expenditure anywhere in the 'civilised word'. He set a target of 3–3.5 per cent of GDP for defence expenditure in the future (Lynch, forthcoming). Yeltsin's intent to bring the leadership of the armed forces into line was dramatically demonstrated by the dismissal of both Rodionov and Chief of the General Staff Viktor Samsonov from their posts. Igor Sergeev (Box 12.3), commander of the Strategic Rocket Forces, was named Defence Minister, and Anatoli Kvashinin, commander of the North Caucasus military district was appointed Acting Chief of the General Staff (*Nezavisimaya gazeta*, 23 May 1997).

The consequence of these developments is that, with regard to the arguments about military reform, the political leadership has firmly come down on the side of the Defence Council and the reformers against the military leadership. Moreover, a certain degree of momentum has been injected into a process of pushing the reforms forward. Ironically, the architect of this process, Yuri Baturin, was dismissed (later to become an astronaut on the MIR space station) and Andrei Kokoshin took control over the process. However, it remains unclear to what extent there is political will to face the hard issues. In 1997, the cost of just implementing the mandated reduction of the armed forces by 200 000 was estimated at 10 trillion rubles (*Obshchaya gazeta*, 29 May 1997). Moreover, the armed forces has a huge payment arrears crisis of about 44 trillion (old) rubles for food and salaries (not counting arrears to the military industry). Thus, while the military high command has been unwilling to face reality, the civilian reformers likewise face contradictions which may prove impossible to resolve (Perera, 1997, p. 69). This dilemma has been sharpened by the financial crisis of 1998.

СПРАВКА 12.4   **Life for the conscript soldier**

'Conscript life was a mixture of the tedious, humiliating and dangerous – with the danger coming from older recruits who treated the entrants abominably. Estimates made in the Russian army of this "hazing" pointed to four out of five recruits suffering physical brutality, of whom one in three had to be hospitalised and one in twenty was a victim of homosexual rape. Food, accommodation and medical care was so bad that one in five left the army chronically ill.'

Source: J. Lloyd, *Rebirth of a Nation: An Anatomy of Russia*, Michael Joseph, London, 1998, p. 119

The future of conscription in Russia

The problem becomes more complicated if conscription (see Box 12.4) is entirely abolished. There has been a steady professionalisation of the army, which continued until the Finance Ministry declared in 1995 that the limits of the afford- able had been reached. The military leadership is also opposed to the concept of a smaller professional army, even though Grachev himself at one stage advo- cated an all-volunteer army of 1 million troops as the ultimate goal of military reform (ITAR-TASS World Service, 7 May 1993, cited in SU/1684 C1/2). After that point, attitudes changed; the military leadership took steps to increase the number of conscripts by removing many exemptions from military service and lengthening the period of the draft from 18 months to two years. This, how- ever, is bound to increase the personnel costs of the forces, and, without con- comitant increases in the military budget, the consequence is likely to be a further deterioration in the living conditions of troops and an even greater squeeze on funds available for procurement. If action is taken to implement Yeltsin's elec- tion promise to abolish conscription, then the direction of policy is going to be reversed once again.

As the preceding discussion makes clear, such a move can only be contem- plated if accompanied by a very substantial reduction in the level of forces. A professional army of more than 600 000 troops cannot be sustained at present levels of military expenditure. Even this may be an overestimate. A professional army is currently not sustainable because of the severe shortage of junior officers and the large number of officers reaching retirement age. It is quite clear that unless service conditions and remuneration are substantially improved, it will be impossible to recruit sufficient personnel of adequate qual- ity to create a viable professional army.

At the same time, conscription itself is becoming less tenable. For one thing, popular resistance to conscription means that President Yeltsin will find it difficult not to live up to his election promise to abolish it. More important are the demographic trends which indicate a sharp reduction in the pool of available conscripts. Despite the measures taken to extend the period of conscription from 18 to 24 months, most units of the armed forces are far below nominal strength because of a lack of conscripts. The airborne forces, which are the best-organised elite force in the Russian military, have only 85 per cent of their nominal authorised level of troops. At the same time, Russian military expert Dmitri Trenin (1995) reckons that only one-third of the troops can be relied on in an emergency. The strategic rocket forces, another elite force which has a far higher ratio of officers to enlisted troops than other forces, is also experiencing a serious shortfall in personnel because of declining numbers of conscripts and a large number of junior officers leaving the service. Missile crews are generally staffed at only 50–60 per cent of their required level. This raises problems of security, safety and combat readiness. The situation is generally far worse in other branches of the armed forces. Substantial parts of the armed services, especially the Pacific Fleet, but also the ground forces and part of the air force, are subject to material and social decay. Equipment is not properly maintained, there is a shortage of fuel and spare parts and the living conditions of servicemen are often extremely poor. Sixty per cent of pilots receive no systematic flight training because of the lack of fuel. It is estimated that only 250 000 of the Russian armed forces are ready for military action. Modern weapons account only for 30 per cent of the Russian arsenal, whereas in West European armies the figure is typically about 70 per cent. The Russian army is also in danger of losing the traditional advantage of conscript armies of a large pool of reservists, as no call-up has taken place since 1991.

In summary, the only way out of this situation is a determined effort to phase out conscription and to reduce the size of the armed forces very considerably, to about 500 000, and to make the appropriate investments in social infrastructure, training and military procurement. However, the most likely outcome at present is that the situation will be allowed to continue to drift on, thereby increasing the cost of military reform in the future.

The other forces

One aspect of this debate which confuses the situation further is the exclusion of many important items from the military budget. Funding to maintain the 25 closed cities and towns under the jurisdiction of the Ministry of Defence and the Ministry of Atomic Energy is not included. Troops and civilian staff of the Interior Ministry, the federal security service and the border guards (otherwise known as 'the other forces') are also excluded. The costs of the Chechnya operation are likewise not included in the regular military budget. Thus total military outlays for 1995 were estimated to amount to 7 per cent of GDP.

The most controversial aspect of this is 'the other forces'. Military leaders criticise their expansion while regular forces have been run down. They are better financed and serviced, and personnel are better paid and looked after. Their total numerical strength has reached a level of between 700 000 and 800 000 troops, i.e. about half of the nominal size of the regular armed forces. However, they are not integrated into the operational plans of the regular forces. The consumption of resources by these forces is considered to be partly responsible for the neglect of the regular armed forces. They are not sufficiently regulated by the state, and because of their sheer size constitute a challenge to the regular armed forces (*Krasnaya zvezda*, 30 June 1995).

It is quite clear that there are political reasons why 'the other forces' have become so important. In a country where the principal security threats originate internally, this is not necessarily to be deplored. It is, however, an issue that needs to be addressed when looking at military reform more generally. There are some indications that the Russian government has decided to do this. When Viktor Samsonov replaced Mikhail Kolesnikov as chief of the general staff in October 1996, Defence Minister Rodionov expressed the view that all military units in the country had to be brought under the control of the general staff (ITAR-TASS Moscow, 22 October 1996, cited in FBIS-SOV-96-205). In December 1996 Rodionov resigned his commission to become a civilian Minister of Defence. This was seen as indicative of a package of reforms whereby the Ministry of Defence would be separate from the general staff, and the general staff would be in charge of all military structures. The former secretary of the Security Council, Ivan Rybkin, reaffirmed that this should be the new role for the general staff (*Rossiiskie vesti*, 15 December 1996). How this will be translated into practice remains to be seen.

Conclusion

Russia's military policy reflects the different world-views and institutional interests that inform its foreign and security policy after the cold war. On the one side there is a strong commitment to join the international community, to adhere to international norms and to support arms control and a close partnership with the West. On the other side there is the assertion of national interests, however they may be defined. The latter are often associated with an assertion of Russian dominance in the former Soviet space and cooler relations with the West. In terms of military policy, adaptation to the international environment would require the renunciation of a global role, drastic reductions in nuclear weapons, the downsizing of the armed forces and the development of highly trained, well-equipped and organised mobile forces. However, many in the military establishment see Russia's strategic nuclear forces as the guarantor of the country's great-power status and seek to maintain as much as possible of the former Soviet Union's capabilities for large-scale conventional warfare. The larger ambitions of sections of the political and military elite have blocked a determined and radical approach to military reform, which would also be unpopular as a result of its social consequences. These obstacles have prevented the development of a coherent approach to military policy based on the actual requirements of national security and the nation's ability to provide the resources for its implementation. The severe financial restraints that exist make a deterioration in the situation inevitable. This prospect is fraught with great danger, as the social cohesion of the armed forces may break down to the point where both civil and military control over the armed forces are lost. Moreover, the Russian Federation itself is in some danger of disintegration as the government has become weaker in the course of the August 1998 crisis. There are clearly potential catastrophic outcomes which would have grave ramifications for European security. Military reform in Russia is therefore vital for Russian and European security.

References

Arbatov A G 1998 Military Reform in Russia: Dilemmas, Obstacles and Prospects, *International Security*, Vol. 22, No. 4 (Spring), pp. 83–134.

Baev P K 1996 *The Russian Army in a Time of Troubles*, Sage, London.

Bluth C 1992 *Soviet Strategic Arms Policy Before SALT*, Cambridge University Press, Cambridge.

Dick C J 1994a The Military Doctrine of the Russian Federation, *Jane's Intelligence Review*, Special Report, No. 1, January.

Dick C J 1994b The Military Doctrine of the Russian Federation, *Journal of Slavic Military Studies*, Vol. 7, No. 3 (September), pp. 481–506.

Lynch D, A New Era in Russian Civil–Military Relations and Military Reform, forthcoming.

Perera J 1997 Russian Forces Edge Closer To Financial Ruin, *Jane's Intelligence Review*, No. 2, February.

Trenin D 1995 Russia's Military Resources, paper presented at a BIOst Conference, November.

Further reading

Baev P K 1996 *The Russian Army in a Time of Troubles*, Sage, London.

Galeotti M 1995 *The Age of Anxiety: Security and Politics in Soviet and Post-Soviet Russia*, Longman, Harlow.

Web site on defence and security: http://www.mosinfo.ru:8080/news/ds/index.html

13

Russian policy towards the Soviet successor states

Mark Webber

Introduction: the character of Russia and the successor states

The end of the cold war is seen principally to have been marked by the winding down of the various antagonisms that marked relations between the countries of the West and those grouped around the Soviet Union. This process has been referred to in other chapters and one cannot underestimate its significance in transforming international relations in the last decade of the twentieth century. Yet simultaneous with these events, a parallel process of equally far-reaching change has occurred – the collapse in 1991 of the Soviet Union. This momentous event had a variety of causes, the nature of which has provoked a long-running debate among scholars. Something they all seem to agree on is the fundamental role played in the process of Soviet dissolution by the so-called 'nationalities question', the self-assertion by the Soviet Union's constituent republics against the federal or 'all-Union' authorities located in Moscow. While these protests varied in intensity and degree, the resistance of several republics proved crucial in frustrating Soviet leader Mikhail Gorbachev's efforts at revamping and thereby saving the Union structure. The climax of this process came in the second half of 1991. In September, the three Baltic republics of Estonia, Latvia and Lithuania formally seceded and the following December the leaders of the then Russian, Ukrainian and Belarus republics met and declared the formation of the Commonwealth of Independent States (CIS), a body whose founding declaration proclaimed that the Soviet Union had ceased to exist both as a 'subject of international law and [as] a geopolitical reality'.

The CIS subsequently came to embrace 12 of the 15 former Soviet republics, only the three Baltic states remained outside it (see Figure 13.1). It should be noted, however, that this body was never intended as a successor to the Soviet Union itself. Indeed, its formation was soon after accompanied by the entry of all 15 of the former Soviet republics into the international community as legally constituted independent states. However, what the CIS did reflect, at least at the time of its formation, was the obvious fact that having once been part of the same country, these former Soviet republics (or 'successor states' as they became known) remained closely interconnected – by virtue of ethnic and linguistic ties, geographic contiguity and all manner of military and economic interdependences. These linkages, however, did not bear down equally. A defining quality of the international relations of the successor states has been the dominant position occupied by Russia. Notwithstanding the fact that this position has been

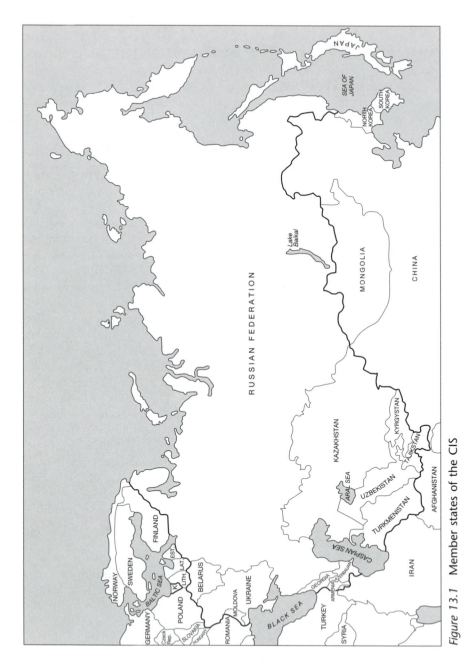

Figure 13.1 Member states of the CIS

Source: R. Sakwa, *Russian Politics and Society*, 2nd edition, Routledge, London, 1993, p. 327

Table 13.1 Russia and the successor states – a comparison

	Territorial size (square kilometres)	Population (1989 census)	GDP in 1995 (million $)
Russia	17 075 400	147 022 000	344 711
East European			
Belarus	207 600	10 149 248	20 561
Moldova	33 700	4 322 363	3 518
Ukraine	603 700	51 449 479	80 127
Baltics			
Estonia	45 100	1 565 662	4 007
Latvia	64 500	2 666 567	6 034
Lithuania	65 200	3 673 362	7 089
Transcaucasus			
Armenia	29 800	3 304 353	2 052
Azerbaijan	86 600	7 019 739	3 475
Georgia	69 700	5 395 841	2 325
Central Asia			
Kazakhstan	2 717 000	16 463 115	21 413
Kyrgyzstan	198 500	4 257 755	3 028
Tajikistan	143 000	5 089 593	2 520*
Turkmenistan	488 100	3 512 190	5 156*
Uzbekistan	447 400	19 808 077	21 590

Sources: The World Bank (1997), pp. 236–7; Dieter (1996, p. 374)
Note: * GNP in 1993

compromised in various ways (as we shall see below) it remains indisputable that by almost any measurement Russia was, and remains, truly the 'first among equals' on the territory of the former Soviet Union (FSU) (see Table 13.1). In practice this has meant that Yeltsin and his colleagues have held a distinctive set of assumptions about their country's regional role and that they have been able to take advantage of a tool kit of foreign policy instruments unavailable to their neighbours.

Russian objectives towards the successor states

The assumptions that the Russian leadership have brought to bear upon its foreign policy have been the subject of much attention and debate, both within Russia and beyond. Early on these debates reflected an initial uncertainty in foreign policy that stemmed from Russia's sudden emergence onto the world stage at the end of 1991 and its entry into an entirely new regional system of international relations constituted by the FSU (Zviagelskaia, 1995, p. 3). What constitutes the central features of a distinctive foreign policy outlook at the leadership level, however, has become clearer the longer the Yeltsin presidency has endured. This 'official line' may not enjoy a consensus throughout Russian society (as indeed is the case in almost any state), and in its particulars may not attract the agreement of even all those in the government (again, Russia is not unlike

БИОГРАФИЯ 13.1   Andrei Kozyrev (born 1952)

Kozyrev was born into a Russian family in Brussels, Belgium. Not surprisingly, given his background, he was always keen to become involved in some area of foreign policy or diplomacy. He studied at the Institute for International Relations and wrote a doctorate on the UN and détente. Kozyrev was appointed Russian Foreign Minister in 1990 and became a leading reformer and Westerniser in the Yeltsin government. However, he came under increasing attack from parliament and he finally resigned after being elected to the Duma himself in the December 1995 elections.

many other states in this respect); it may also be accompanied by an abundance of ambiguity and at times even contradiction. What matters is that Russian foreign policy has assumed a tangible quality (even if a good deal of interpretation is still required in discerning it) and this has persisted over time.

At what point can we speak of the emergence of such a foreign policy line? On this question observers of the Russian scene are pretty much in agreement in pinpointing the latter half of 1993 as of crucial importance. Insofar as policy towards the successor states is concerned that year marked a significant U-turn. Prior to this the policy pursued by Yeltsin and his then Foreign Minister, Andrei Kozyrev, was largely passive in nature. This reflected at least three considerations: first, the priority then accorded to improved relations with the West and the parallel objective of what the Russian President dubbed Russia's entry into the 'civilised community' of states; second, a preoccupation with domestic economic reform, itself a driving force behind the Western orientation; third, a belief that the successor states would gravitate naturally towards Russia (something the CIS was intended to facilitate) as a consequence of their shared military and economic interdependencies and common experience of post-communist transition. This, it was assumed, would create, in Kozyrev's words, a 'region of neighbourliness and partnership' embracing Russia and its neighbours (Webber, 1997, pp. 6–7).

The reality of relations, however, departed markedly from Kozyrev's optimistic scenario. Rather than the development of partnership, during 1992 and early 1993 Russia found itself challenged by the successor states in several ways. It also had to contend with the escalation of a clutch of civil wars around its borders, in Tajikistan, Moldova, Georgia and Azerbaijan (see Box 13.1).

If these twin processes were not enough, Yeltsin was also embattled at home, and his alleged neglect of the successor states provided a route by which his nationalist opponents both in parliament and within the armed forces could criticise him freely. It was in response to these pressures that the Yeltsin–Kozyrev line shifted from 1993, away from passivity towards a greater assertiveness (Lough, 1993, pp. 53–60). In the remainder of this section we will outline some

СПРАВКА 13.1 Russian policy challenges from the successor states during 1992–93

Nuclear weapons. At the time of the Soviet Union's dissolution, strategic and tactical nuclear weapons were distributed among several of the successor states as well as in Russia. It was agreed at the time of the formation of the CIS that Belarus, Kazakhstan and Ukraine would transfer these weapons to Russia and in return would enjoy a form of joint command under CIS auspices. The handing over of tactical weapons was completed by the middle of 1992. Strategic weapons, however, presented numerous problems. These were most trying in the case of Ukraine, when then President Leonid Kravchuk alluded that his country might seek retention of some weapons and lodged various demands relating to compensatory financial and security guarantees, and the right to exercise direct control over the launching of weapons on Ukranian territory.

National armed forces. As well as nuclear weapons, the fate of the Soviet armed forces as a whole was called into question by the collapse of the Soviet Union. At the end of 1991, CIS agreements outlined an intention to retain their integrity through the maintenance of CIS joint armed forces. This position was solidly backed by Yeltsin. It was undermined, however, by the efforts of several of the successor states to create national armed forces based on former Soviet weaponry and infrastructure located on their territories. In response, Russia set about the creation of its own armed forces during 1992, in the process unilaterally assuming control of many assets outside its borders. This again brought it into conflict with Ukraine, in this instance over rival claims to ownership of the Black Sea Fleet, the vast bulk of which was headquartered on Ukrainian territory.

Conflicts in the successor states. During 1992, open warfare flared up in a number of states near to Russia – in Tajikistan, Georgia, Moldova and Azerbaijan (the conflict there had in fact been in train since 1989, but escalated considerably during 1991–92). The duration and intensity of the conflict varied from case to case, as did Russia's particular interests and policy responses. Taken as a whole, however, they raised some alarm within the Russian leadership. The military doctrine signed into law by President Yeltsin in November 1993 referred to local wars and armed conflicts as the 'main danger' to Russian security.

Economic issues. The costs of post-Soviet economic co-ordination became painfully apparent to Russia during 1992. The use of the old Soviet ruble as a common currency among CIS member states and the provision of cheap fuel supplies both proved to be unsustainable burdens on Russia's troubled economy (fuel subsidisation alone was estimated to have cost Russia the equivalent of 14 per cent of its GDP in 1992).

general and specific themes that have characterised the formulation of Russian policy objectives since this point.

General objectives of Russian policy towards the successor states

If one is to regard the development of the Soviet Union as in some senses a continuation of the process of steady territorial expansion Russia has engaged in since the fifteenth century, then the Soviet collapse of 1991 marked a decisive break in Russian history. The 'loss' of the Soviet republics means that present-day Russia occupies a territory equivalent to that of the Russian empire upon the death of Peter the Great in 1725. The scale and suddenness of this territorial dismemberment have raised the question of whether the Russian political elite is capable of adjusting to a post-imperial environment. Richard Pipes, for one, has argued that the legacy of continuous expansion has created a 'patrimonial mentality embedded in the Russian psyche, which holds that anything inherited from the past is inalienable property' and thus, by implication, must be restored if lost (Pipes, 1997, p. 71). The presence of over 20 million ethnic Russians in the successor states, the close cultural bonds that exist between Russia and some of its neighbours (especially strong in the cases of Ukraine and Belarus) and the claims of the Russian Orthodox Church to uphold authority over all Orthodox Christians in the FSU all, it is argued, serve to reinforce this compulsion. What is more, some very visible political forces exist in Russia that are seemingly prepared to act upon it, whether this be in the guise of a revamped Soviet Union (a course favoured by the Communist Party of the Russian Federation) or an enlarged Russia (as advocated by Vladimir Zhirinovsky's Liberal Democratic Party).

Others, by contrast, have argued that there is nothing inevitable about imperial thinking in Russia. According to this view, the very suddenness of the Soviet collapse is seen as having had a cathartic effect. Rather than generating revanchist feelings it has instead led to intense preoccupations closer to home (economic regeneration, state-building and the management of Russia's own internal ethnic issues). It has also generated the opportunity for an appreciation of certain benefits of a smaller Russia, namely, a more compact and homogenous nation-state as a basis for national identity and an avoidance of the economic 'gigantism' and over-stretch of the Soviet period (Mendras, 1997, pp. 90–103).

Whatever the merits of these arguments, what concerns us here is how these processes of adjustment have been reflected in the attitudes of the Yeltsin leadership. What can be said with some certainty is that Moscow has shunned any public claim to the restoration of the Soviet Union (indeed, Yeltsin himself was a prime mover in that state's collapse). Under Yeltsin it has also claimed to have ended any imperial ambition towards its neighbours. What does survive, however, is a presumption that Russia has a right of interference and oversight in the FSU. This is, in part, a simple product of the clear asymmetries of power in the region, but it reflects also a lingering mentality that is rooted in centuries of presumed Russian political, economic and cultural ascendancy (Tolz, 1993, pp. 41–3). As Kozyrev was to remark in early 1994 '[t]he countries of the CIS and the Baltics . . . [constitute] a region where the vital interests of Russia are concentrated . . . We should not withdraw from those regions which have been the sphere of Russia's interests for centuries' (cited in Webber, 1996, p. 100). This does not mean a policy of imperial reconquest, but rather an ambition to preserve positions of influence and to establish Russia's credentials as a leading regional power.

Moscow's self-perception of its regional weight is, in turn, informed by a wider claim to great power status. This has become a central dogma of Russian foreign policy. Ironically, it is a claim made amidst fairly conclusive evidence to the contrary. The objective underpinnings of status, specifically economic resources and military prowess, have eroded significantly. However, what matters just as much is the subjective basis of the claim, one based on Russia's (for which read, in part, the Soviet Union's) historical achievements, its contribution to world culture and its spiritual traditions. Yet how to pursue a foreign policy commensurate with this claim has proven an enduring predicament for Moscow. As other chapters in this book have suggested, Russia has lost much of the international influence once enjoyed by the Soviet Union and crucially can no longer regard itself as an equal of the USA (other than in the single sphere of nuclear defence) or even by some indices of China either. In this disappointing context for Moscow, what compensation can be found lies among the successor states. Here Russia is a regional leader and is able to give expression to the duties and responsibilities which help to demonstrate status, hence the oft-repeated injunction, proclaimed by Yeltsin and others, that it falls to Russia to uphold peace and stability in the region and hence also the claim beloved of Kozyrev's successor, Yevgeni Primakov, that Russia should, through the consolidation of ties with its neighbours, seek to establish itself 'as one of the influential centres of a multipolar world' (Primakov, 1997, p. 4).

Specific objectives of Russian policy towards the successor states

Russia's desire to play a leading role among its neighbours manifests itself in several specific policy objectives. The first of these is a public commitment to furthering the development of the CIS. Since its formation this body has, in fact, proven less than successful in preserving the links that formerly bound the successor states. As we saw in Box 13.1, CIS armed forces and the ruble zone were effectively abandoned in 1992–93. Subsequent military and economic co-operation has been piecemeal and, as Table 13.2 suggests, has not always enjoyed the full support of all CIS member states.

However, despite its problems, Russia remains committed to the development of the organisation as 'the most important mechanism for strengthening the integration processes (among the successor states)' (Yeltsin, 1997). There appears to be a degree of wishful thinking here; however, what matters in this connection is not so much the actual level of recent or current CIS integration but what is perceived as its long-term potential. The CIS may well be in a condition of torpor but so long as it survives it presents at least the possibility for Russia of breathing life into post-Soviet inter-state co-operation. It should also be noted that, even at a low level of operationalisation, the CIS also grants to Russia certain specific benefits. It acts as a means of institutionalising Russian influence

Table 13.2 Participation in CIS agreements

	Treaty on Collective Security (May 1992)†	Collective Security Concept (May 1995)	Treaty on Joint Border Protection (May 1995)	Treaty on Joint Air Defence (February 1995)	Statute on Collective Peace-keeping forces (January 1996)	Economic Union (September 1993)	Payments Union (October 1994)	Customs Union (March 1996)‡
Armenia	+	+	+	+	+	+	+	
Azerbaijan						+	+	
Georgia		+	+	+	+	+	+	
Russia	+	+	+	+	+	+	+	+
Kazakhstan	+	+	+	+		+	+	+
Kyrgyzstan	+	+	+	+	+	+	+	+
Tajikistan	+	+	+	+	+	+	+	+
Turkmenistan				+		+	+	
Uzbekistan	+			+	+	+	+	
Ukraine				+		*	+	
Moldova						+	+	
Belarus	+	+	+	+	+	+	+	+

Key: +, signatory; *, associate member

† Azerbaijan, Georgia and Uzbekistan signed the Treaty on Collective Security in May 1992 but withdrew in April 1999.

‡ Tajikistan signed the Customs Union in February 1999

(its personnel dominate CIS structures of military and economic co-operation), as a device for legitimising Russia's external presence (peacekeeping in Tajikastan and in the Abkhazian region of Georgia has occurred under mandates granted by the CIS) and as a route of communication with the leaderships in the successor states.

That Russia should seek to preserve the CIS at all, of course, suggests the rather obvious point that it has identifiable interests among the CIS member states. Taking the military and security spheres, these interests include the following:

- access to facilities of the former Soviet armed forces, many of which (for instance, air defence facilities) are considered germane to the defence of Russia
- the sealing of outer borders that would otherwise go unprotected (hence the willingness of Russia to patrol Armenia's borders with Iran and Turkey, Tajikistan's border with Afghanistan and so on)
- the resolution of local conflicts owing, in part, to feared de-stabilisation in Russia itself in the form of refugee flows and the exacerbation of tensions in the north Caucasus
- the containment of Islamic fundamentalism in Central Asia.

As listed here, such interests have an essentially defensive quality and seem rooted in the practical security realities of the post-Soviet military–security environment. As such, their practical pursuit need not require that Russia achieve a hegemonic position among its neighbours. That it has chosen to do so reflects, rather, a dominant viewpoint in Moscow that conceives Russia's security interests in the region in competitive terms and which consequently desires to limit perceived encroachments upon its self-defined sphere of interests. The application of this position has, however, differed on a case-by-case basis. Moscow has expressed very little anxiety at the economic initiatives of the European Union or the political activities (e.g. election monitoring) of the Council of Europe and the Organisation for Security and Co-operation in Europe (OSCE). Indeed, it has often regarded these as being to its benefit insofar as they have helped to publicise Russian concerns (as in the case of the rights of Russian-speakers in the Baltic states). Russia has also been fairly permissive towards the activities of international organisations such as the UN and the OSCE in conflict resolution efforts in Nagorno-Karabakh (Azerbaijan) and Tajikistan. Where it has had a major problem, however, is in cases where external initiatives are seemingly aimed at the establishment of some lasting influence that might usurp its own predominance. Arguably, such concerns have been over-stated, in that they tend not to match the actual ambitions of outside powers such as Turkey and Iran, which are the targets of Russian criticism. Nonetheless, they cannot simply be rejected as the products of misperception or propaganda. Take, for instance, Russia's hostile attitude to NATO enlargement. However remote may be the prospect of NATO actually accepting any of the successor states into its fold (only the three Baltic states have voiced a serious case for inclusion), the enlargement issue does generate significant worries for Russia. Also, such concerns are not simply of a military character. As well as its obvious defence implications, NATO enlargement would be of momentous political significance entrenching, seemingly in perpetuity, a Western orientation among its new members. Should this occur in the successor states (that is, not just in East–Central Europe) and in the face of Moscow's opposition it would clearly give the lie to Russia's claims to great power status and regional leadership.

As well as military and security issues, Russia also has some clear policy objectives in the economic sphere. These stem, in part, from the legacy of interdependence left by the disintegration of the Soviet economy. Having once been an integrated whole, the economies of the successor states were at the point of the Soviet Union's dissolution still connected by a multitude of ties. In many instances, these have subsequently been rent asunder either through simple neglect owing to the common experience of economic decline and difficulties brought about by legal and political wrangles over rights of access, ownership, maintenance and so on, or because the successor states have sought external diversification (trade among the successor states, for instance, has declined markedly since 1991). Russia was, in fact, among the better placed of the successor states in dealing with this disruption. This reflected not simply the relative size of its economy but also the fact that it was already well oriented to trading with the outside world and that its economic output was already fairly diverse (it departed, in other words, from the high degree of specialisation found in some republics which was to prove an impediment in the development of post-Soviet economic viability). It should also be noted that during the Soviet period Russia was a net subsidiser to the other republics; it consequently had much to gain from the end of this form of redistribution (van Selm, 1997, p. 22). However, even while Russia was cushioned in some senses, the break-up of the Soviet economy has exerted some harmful effects. It has proven disruptive to those parts of Russian industry which rely on raw materials and equipment derived from the other successor states and has confronted Russian exporters with transportation problems in that many railway and pipeline routes leaving the country are required to transit other successor states before they reach their end destinations. It is because of such problems that Russia has promoted various schemes of econ-omic integration within the CIS framework (the Customs Union, the Economic Union, the Payments Union etc. – see Table 13.2) and, given the problematic nature of these initiatives, has also instituted parallel bilateral arrangements (free trade agreements, debt for equity swaps, long-term programmes of inter-state co-operation etc.).

What informs these economic aims is Russia's desire not simply to satisfy specific economic needs but also to preserve, and indeed to enhance, its position as the leading economy among the successor states. In order to achieve this, however, Russia has had to operate in an increasingly competitive environment. This applies both to trade (Russian exporters are no longer guaranteed a ready market for their goods in the successor states) and also, importantly, to issues of access. The exploitation and transportation of gas and oil resources in several of the successor states (Azerbaijan, Kazakhstan, Turkmenistan and Uzbekistan) while coveted by Russian energy conglomerates have also been the subject of intense interest to European and American companies. In this context, Russian policy has increasingly been informed by 'geo-economic' ways of thinking.

The constraints on Russian policy

The analysis so far, while hinting at some circumspection on Russia's part, has nonetheless emphasised the more robust aspects of Russian policy. In this sec-tion we will qualify this picture by pointing out that this policy does, in fact, have to take into account certain very real constraints. These act both to tem-per Russian ambition and to circumscribe its pursuit of policy objectives.

The first constraint lies in the very complexity and variety of the successor states themselves. The sheer scale and diversity of the region has required on Russia's part some ordering of priorities and a consequent recognition that it cannot pursue effectively its interests in all simultaneously. This, in turn, has interacted with the manner in which Russia is regarded among the successor states themselves. Armenia, Tajikistan and Belarus have welcomed close ties to Moscow; indeed, the latter went so far as to sign a treaty in April 1997 on the establishment of a union with Russia. Kazakhstan and Kyrgyzstan have also main-tained strong ties, apparent from their membership (along with Russia and Belarus) of the so-called Community of Integrated States centred around the CIS Customs Union. Turkmenistan and Uzbekistan have been less forthcoming but have nonetheless pursued selective military and economic co-operation with Russia on pragmatic grounds. Georgia, Ukraine, Azerbaijan and Moldova have been much less inclined towards Russia. Indeed, these states have since the summer of 1997 organised themselves into an informal grouping known as 'GUAM'. Least interested of all are the Baltic states, all three of whom have eschewed mem-bership of the CIS and have signalled their desire for full integration into the Euro-Atlantic structures of NATO and the EU.

In these circumstances, Russia has been compelled to pursue a selective engage-ment. This has manifested itself in Russia's differentiation of the successor states in terms of their attitudes towards post-Soviet co-operation. Recognising the impossibility of achieving a consensus among all the successor states, Russia has since the policy turn of 1993 increasingly advocated a process of what Primakov has dubbed 'multi-level, multi-rate integration' (see Webber, 1997, p. 67). This involves a tolerance of different levels of participation within the CIS and a willingness on Russia's part to pursue initiatives with smaller groups (a policy exemplified by the Russian–Belarus Union and the Community of Integrated States). Russia has also been discerning in its ranking of policy preferences. Certain continuities have been evident throughout the post-Soviet period, and some issues have been of constant concern to Moscow. Nonetheless, how Russia has ordered its priorities has tended to vary with time, region and issue. Ukraine was the main concern of Russian policy in 1992–93 (a consequence of the disputes concerning nuclear weapons and the Black Sea Fleet outlined in Box 13.1). During 1993–95, attention shifted to the Transcaucasus owing to regional wars and the proximity of the region to Russia's own internal conflict in Chechnya. In 1996 Belarus moved to the top of the agenda, policy being galvanised on this occasion by the intense debates over NATO enlargement (a Russian–Belarus military alliance was posited as one possible response) and the domestic political capital Yeltsin hoped to earn from an appearance of activism in an election year (an initial agreement on a Russian–Belarus Community was reached in April, just two months before the vote for the presidency). Since 1997 Russian policy has placed some emphasis on a stabilisation of relations with Ukraine and, in light of the onward development of energy exploitation initiatives in the successor states, on trade and energy issues in the Caspian and Central Asian regions.

Conditions within Russia have also been important. As chapters elsewhere in this volume have described in some detail, Russia has, during the 1990s, experienced a profound economic restructuring. In the period 1991–96 this meant a substantial decline in economic output and a consequent shrinking of the Russian economy. According to the World Bank (1997, pp. 221, 237), in 1995 Russia was, in GDP terms, the world's fourteenth largest economy, similar in size to India and Brazil. Measured in terms of GNP per capita its ranking was for less flattering – seventy-eighth, a position just behind Namibia, Columbia and Tunisia. The Third World status of the Russian economy means that it lacks the wherewithal to act as an engine of integration among the successor states. Russia cannot afford a state strategy of massive subsidisation as a means of courting its neighbours (since 1993 it has consequently limited state credits to a few select cases, notably Armenia, Belarus, Tajikistan and Kyrgyzstan). In the absence of a vibrant economy, neither can it act as a magnetic pole of attraction (when given the choice, most of the successor states have preferred to diversify their external economic relations away from Russia and towards Europe, North America, China and the Far East). Also, while an economic revival in Russia may alter this state of affairs, such a development seems at present a long way off. The Russian economy did register a slight upturn in 1997, but even allowing for optimistic projections for further growth, it has been estimated that it will take some 15–20 years for Russia to restore its GDP to the level of 1990 (Rogov, 1997, p. 7). Moreover, even if growth does occur at a significant rate this need not mean that the government in Moscow will enjoy the means to pursue assertive policies among neighbouring states. Indeed, these resources may well be diverted by claims within Russia itself, for as Pavel Baev (1997, p. 188) has argued, the ongoing political trend in Russia towards a strengthening of the regions will mean 'the absolute amount of resources available to and controlled by the "centre" is going to shrink . . . and, accordingly, power projection (outside Russian borders) . . . will become even less feasible than it is now'.

Russia's military capability is also a poor basis for policy in the successor states. As we shall note below, Russia has established a military presence of sorts among its neighbours. However, the ongoing process of downsizing and restructuring of the Russian armed forces (with all the attendant problems of low morale, poor training and under-preparedness) means that the limits have probably been reached concerning their use as a tool of external influence beyond the country's borders. Russia is simply unable to mount new military operations in its periphery (Garnett, 1995, p. 40). Indeed, if anything the pressure is on to withdraw from places such as Tajikistan where Russian-commanded troops have faced intransigent opposition. Such pressures have, of course, been intensified by the military lessons of the war in Chechnya (Allison, 1998, p. 125). Similarly, Russia also now lacks the capability to undertake anything more than a holding operation with regard to the development of multilateral CIS military structures. The creation of national armed forces (see Box 13.1) had led in June 1993 to the disbanding of the CIS High Command, thereby ending efforts towards the creation of joint armed forces. Since then the CIS's military remit has been concerned with selective developments in the field of peacekeeping, border protection and air defence. Russia has been the determining influence in these efforts, and their success has depended in large measure on Russian commitment and resources. These resources, however, are finite, and are in any case spread extremely thin by virtue of the tight limits of the Russian military budget. Furthermore, Russia's military reforms have had organisational consequences that run counter to the evolution of the CIS. To take just one example, the disbanding of Russia's Air Defence Forces and its merger with the Air Force will, according to one respected Russian military analyst, result in the dislocation not just of Russian air defence but in the disruption of the putative air defence system of the entire CIS (Felgengauer, 1997, pp. 4–5).

As well as lacking the capability for an ambitious policy towards the successor states, one might also question the level of desire for such a course in Russia. We have already noted above the contours of the Russian debate and two further points are worth noting here. First, public opinion in Russia is ambivalent on how far the country should go in seeking influence among the successor states. One recent poll taken in January 1998, for example, suggested that 80 per cent of the 1500 Russians asked favoured a strengthening of the CIS and thus, by extension, were sympathetic to an institutionalised Russian role in the FSU. When asked whether Russia should bear the cost of CIS integration, however, only 18 per cent answered in the affirmative. There was, moreover, a clear delimitation of preferred Russian priorities among the successor states. Only Ukraine, Belarus and Kazakhstan emerged as clear favourites for a strengthening of cooperation (Interfax, 1998). A similar ambivalence may also be noted at the elite level. Notwithstanding the tentative consensus on the need for Russian leadership among the successor states, there appears to be some division regarding how far Russia ought to go in promoting this aim within the context of limited resources. A very important presidential document issued in 1995 entitled 'The Strategic Course of Russia towards the member States of the Commonwealth of Independent States' outlined all manner of Russian ambitions in terms of the military, economic and political development of the CIS with seemingly little appreciation of the possible costs of such a policy (Webber, 1997, pp. 14–15). This document although signed by Yeltsin reflected the influence of Primakov (1994, pp. 1–5), then Director of the Foreign Intelligence Service and author of a 1994 report that advocated an active drive towards Russian-led integration. Others within the Yeltsin leadership, by contrast, have been more equivocal. Erstwhile Prime Minister Viktor Chernomyrdin (1996, p. 2), for one, has argued that Moscow should be discerning in its commitments and prioritise those policies 'that will benefit above all Russia and Russian citizens'. Such an attitude also informs later foreign policy documents – notably Yeltsin's 1996 national security memorandum, with its emphasis on the dangers of over-commitment and the complexities of CIS integration (Webber, 1997, pp. 15–16), and the 1997 'National Security Concept' which emphasises the priority of internal reconstruction and the weakness of Russia's international position.

Case studies of Russian policies towards the successor states

By now it should be apparent that the Russian approach towards the successor states is far from straightforward. Its interests are seemingly clear, yet at the same time qualified. There is also a clear gap between the expressed ends and means of policy. In this section we will illustrate how such ambivalence has fed through to specific policies – Moscow, it appears, has struck an uneasy and sometimes contradictory balance between assertiveness and forbearance.

Assertiveness

One area in which Russian policy has been consistent, indeed insistent, is that of nuclear weapons. The challenge posed by proliferation noted in Box 13.2 has been met by Moscow in a determined manner; it has demanded, without exception, that all weapons be transferred to its territory. In this regard, its claims have been met. The transfer of these weapons, it is true, has owed much to factors other than simply Russian persuasion. The US, in particular, has played a vital role, notably in the Ukrainian case, by offering financial compensation and non-specific security guarantees. It should also be noted that the retention of nuclear weapons was of only marginal benefit to Belarus, Kazakhstan and Ukraine. With the partial exception of the latter, all three lacked a credible strategic rationale for their use and were bereft also of the facilities and expertise required for their safe storage (Webber, 1996, pp. 158–63). However, Russian demands have also had an impact. Again, it is Ukraine which is instructive. Its decision in 1994 to sign the Nuclear Non-Proliferation Treaty as a non-nuclear state marked a symbolic close to its ambiguous stance on nuclear possession and came on the heels of threats from Moscow to abandon weapons maintenance arrangements and to impose economic sanctions should Kiev eschew nuclear disarmament. In May 1996, the final warheads were transferred from Ukraine to Russia.

More conventional military issues elsewhere have also called forth a firm Russian response. The desire for military presence, for instance, has been actively pursued. Given the fragile nature of CIS mechanisms, Russia has set some store by bilateral routes to military co-operation with its neighbours. In the cases of Belarus, Armenia, Kazakhstan, Kyrgyzstan and Tajikistan this has been fairly comprehensive and, moreover, largely welcomed by the host government. In three other cases, however, Russian access has been achieved in less welcoming circumstances.

First, in Georgia, agreements concerning the lease of bases, Russian defence of the Georgian–Turkish border and the maintenance of a CIS (but Russian-staffed) peacekeeping force in Abkhazia have materialised only as a consequence of the multiple domestic threats the regime of Eduard Shevardnadze has faced since coming to power in 1992. It is a moot point whether Russia has in fact cultivated these threats; it has, however, certainly taken advantage of them as a means of convincing Shevardnadze of the benefits of a Russian military presence (Morris, 1995, pp. 90–3). What is more, this presence has been maintained in the face of growing local resistance. The Georgian parliament has refused to endorse the agreement on Russian military bases and Shevardnadze has since 1994 actively sought a UN peacekeeping force as an alternative to that provided by Russia.

In Moldova, secondly, Russia has persistently obstructed requests to remove its troops (the bulk of these date back to the Soviet period and fell under Russian command in 1992). An agreement was signed in October 1994 that provided for a three-year withdrawal period. The Russian parliament, however, has thus far refused to ratify the document, while the Yeltsin administration has effectively ignored it by linking any withdrawal to a settlement of the conflict in the Dniester region that has since 1992 pitted ethnic Russian separatists against the Moldovan government.

Turning to Ukraine, thirdly, here Russia has doggedly sought an advantageous resolution of the Black Sea Fleet issue, one which would allow it unfettered access to facilities on Ukrainian territory and the lion's share of the ships and other assets of the fleet itself. In pursuing these demands, Moscow has put pressure on Kiev by linking them to the resolution of other political and economic disputes. The utility of this approach was obvious from documents signed in May 1997. While granting Ukraine seemingly significant benefits relating to debt, trade and the recognition of its territorial integrity, these at the same time effectively handed Russia a near total control over the fleet and its infrastructure (Sherr, 1997, pp. 33–50).

What of economic issues? Above, it was noted that a distinct geo-economic flavour had become apparent in Russian policy, notably in regard to energy issues in the successor states. In terms of specifics this has manifested itself in at least three ways (Holoboff, 1997, pp. 123–7). A first policy has been to dispute the legal rights of the successor states to energy resources. This has been a tactic employed with regard to Azerbaijan's claims to oil reserves in the Caspian Sea.

By suggesting that the Caspian is, in fact, a lake rather than a sea, the Russian Foreign Ministry has argued that all the littoral states have equal rights of access, thus boosting what would otherwise be a minor Russian share by virtue of its small coastline. This position has not been shared by Azerbaijan and Kazakhstan, both of whom have argued that the Caspian is more rightly a sea and that its waters and seabed ought, therefore, to be divided along territorial lines. The Russian position on this issue has, in fact, proven to be largely irrelevant, if not counter-productive – it has not prevented the leasing out of Caspian fields to foreign firms and it has damaged relations with otherwise friendly Kazakhstan. In January 1998, Moscow seemingly conceded the principle of national seabed sectors, although it remains wedded to joint management of sea waters and wishes the entire issue to be put before a Caspian summit of all littoral states (Anonymous, 1998, p. 92).

Russia has been somewhat more persistent in the way in which it has exploited its controlling position at the heart of the former Soviet oil and gas pipeline network. At present it enjoys a near monopoly over routes connected to international energy markets, something that has afforded it the opportunity to interfere with the passage of oil and gas from Azerbaijan, Kazakhstan and Turkmenistan both for political and for commercial purposes. In the long term this advantage could be undermined through the construction of routes that would bypass Russia (a Turkmenistan–Iran pipeline opened in December 1997, an Azeri–Georgian route is scheduled for opening in late 1998 and the construction of an ambitious Kazak–Chinese route is also planned). Given this possibility, Moscow has also pursued a third policy, lending its support to the efforts of Russian companies aimed at obtaining access to energy resources at source. Although the inevitability of involvement by American and European concerns has also been conceded, these companies have nonetheless elbowed their way into projects undertaken by international oil consortia or, as in the case of Turkmenistan's gas, have formed a joint stock company with the local state monopoly.

Forbearance

Although Russia possesses clear interests among the successor states and is seemingly intent upon achieving a position of regional leadership, it has, nonetheless, pursued its policies largely in conformity with the established norms of inter-state behaviour (MccGwire, 1998, p. 32). It has, for instance, honoured the requests of the Baltic states for the removal of Russian troops (contrast this with its stance on Moldova) and has relied on negotiations rather than force to obtain concessions relating to the political status of the large Russian minorities in two countries of the region, Estonia and Latvia.

Even more significant, the Yeltsin leadership has made no formal claims relating to the territorial dispensation of Soviet dissolution. The principle by which the administrative borders of the Soviet republics have been recognised as the inviolable frontiers of the successor states (Russia included) has gone unchallenged. It formed a corner stone of the agreements signed by Russia and the majority of the successor states in 1991 establishing the CIS and is reaffirmed in the 1993 CIS Charter. In more general terms, the legality of the post-Soviet order was confirmed still further by Yeltsin in 1996, this time in a rather dramatic fashion. In March of that year the State Duma, the lower chamber of the Russian parliament, passed a communist-sponsored motion revoking a December 1991 resolution of the Supreme Soviet that had ratified the founding accords of the CIS. It also resolved that a referendum of March 1991 that had voted to maintain a 'renewed' USSR should remain legally valid. These resolutions implied that the USSR still existed and suggested, in turn, that the independent existence of the successor states had no basis in law. They were, however, forcefully criticised in the other CIS states, gathered little support among the Russian public (less than a third supported them) and were soundly rejected by Yeltsin himself.

Russia's position on the territorial issue is, in part, defensive. The upholding of established borders while denying Russia the opportunity to make claims upon its neighbours does, by the same token, preclude infringements of its own territorial integrity. This is important on several counts: first, because certain successor states (Estonia and Latvia) have questioned the legality of their borders with Russia, second, because other states too (China, Japan and Finland) have pretensions towards Russian territory, and, third, because it undermines causes based on demands for secession, germane in view of Chechen calls for an exit from the Russian Federation.

This has meant a restraint on Russia's part even in circumstances where it could quite easily have made a revisionist case. Take, for instance, the example of Kazakhstan. At the end of 1991 some 40 per cent of the population, was concentrated in the northern part of the country abutting the border with Russia itself. Amidst the uncertainty of Soviet dissolution it would have been a straightforward action on Russia's part simply to annex this territory; one, moreover, that Kazakhstan would have been largely powerless to resist. Similar restraint has also been evident with regard to Ukraine. Here, Moscow's approach towards the Crimea is particularly instructive. This territory has, in fact, strong connections to Russia. It had constituted part of Russia itself from the end of the eighteenth century (something that accounts for the fact that Russians constitute a majority of its population) and was only transferred to Ukrainian administration in 1954 under Soviet rule. However, despite the dubious legality of Ukrainian possession and occasional demands by the Russian parliament for the transfer of the region to Russian jurisdiction, the Yeltsin administration has both rejected the notion of a territorial alteration and kept its distance from the strongly pro-Russian regional government in the Crimea (MccGwire, 1998, p. 32).

Conclusion

Analysis of Russian foreign policy is often informed by the notion that Russia is bent incorrigibly upon an expansionist course. That Moscow has so far refrained from full-blooded *Sturm und Drang* among the successor states is seen implicitly as a temporary aberration, something that will be eliminated once the leaders in the Kremlin revert truly to type (Pipes, 1997, pp. 71–4). The actuality

БИОГРАФИЯ 13.2   Boris Nemtsov (born 1959)

Nemtsov was a researcher in radio-physics until he entered politics. Good-looking and known as an intellectual, he made his name as governor in Nizhni Novgorod oblast in the 1990s. Seen by many as a future President of Russia, he became a leading member of the government when he was appointed First Deputy Prime Minister in 1997. This was viewed positively at the time by reformers in Russia because of his reputation as a liberal and innovative thinker. However, Nemtsov resigned his post in the Yeltsin administration in August 1998. Nevertheless, this could work out to Nemtsov's advantage since everyone in Russia is currently seeking to distance themselves from Yeltsin. It might also leave him with more time to pursue his many hobbies, which include tennis, fishing and windsurfing.

of Russian policy to date, however, has departed markedly from this stereo-type. True, elements of assertiveness have been apparent, but these have been accompanied by equally telling examples of caution and restraint. While Russia is alert to particular interests in the successor states and does aspire to regional leadership, these are causes it has pursued through selective engagement and occasional intervention rather than imperial reconsolidation. In this sense, Russia's position among the successor states is more akin to American actions in Central America and the Caribbean than it is to Tsarist empire building or Soviet territorial annexations (MccGwire, 1998, p. 32).

The trends in Russian policy outlined in this chapter are likely to prove long-lasting, for the following reasons. First, even though policy thus far has been associated only with the Yeltsin administration, certain of the candidates for future presidential office (Grigori Yavlinsky, Boris Nemtsov) share a similar foreign policy outlook. Others, of course, differ. However, while a more bellicose president (for example, Alexander Lebed or the leader of the Russian Communist Party, Gennadi Zyuganov) would certainly approach the successor states with more activist and interventionist intentions, such a figure would still have to contend with the inescapable economic, military and political constraints upon policy noted above.

Second, in the eventuality that Russia experiences positive internal transformation involving economic and military revival and political stability, something that might increase its weight and confidence among its neighbours, there will still remain disincentives for aggressive action. This is because at the same time that Russia revives, so may some of its neighbours and, in the case of the energy-rich successor states, at a faster rate. Coupled with a sense of confidence accumulated from the experience of independent statehood and self-government this will produce an increased ability on their part to resist unwanted outside interference, in the process raising the costs to Moscow of any attempts to pursue policy by coercive means.

Third, one needs to take account of the broader international context within which Russia and the successor states are situated. In terms of the broader themes suggested by this volume, it is worth noting here the growing diversity of ties that link Russia and the successor states to the world beyond the region of the FSU. A deepening involvement in these extra-regional economic, political and, in some cases, military and security relations not only pulls the successor states away from Russia but pulls Russia away from the successor states. Membership of the World Trade Organisation may well be more important for Russia than the preservation of the CIS Customs Union, an association with the European Union more of a priority than the implementation of the CIS Economic Union, and the realisation of an OSCE-based European Security Charter more meaningful to it than the CIS Collective Security Treaty. Indeed, even allowing for the immediacy of Russian interests, Moscow's concentration on the successor states is, in part, only a mirror image of exclusion elsewhere. Logically, therefore, the development of proper and equitable relationships further afield (through NATO, the EU, the OSCE, the Council of Europe and the 'G8', and with the US and regional powers such as Germany, China, India, Iran) will preclude any preoccupation with the region as a fixed and permanent feature of Russian foreign policy.

References

Allison R 1998 The Chechenia Conflict: Military and Security Policy Implications, in Allison R and Bluth C (eds), *Security Dilemmas in Russia and Eurasia*, The Royal Institute of International Affairs, London, pp. 241–80.

Anonymous 1998 Caspian Carve-up, *The Economist*, 7 March, p. 92.

Baev P 1997 Russia's Departure from Empire: Self-assertiveness and a New Retreat, in Tunander O, Baev P and Einagel V I (eds), *Geopolitics in Post-Wall Europe. Security, Territory and Identity*, International Peace Research Institute, Oslo, and Sage Publications, London, pp. 174–95.

Chernomyrdin V 1996 Russia: Chernomyrdin on Russia's Concerns in the CIS, Foreign Broadcast Information Service, Central Eurasia, 30 July, p. 2.

Dieter H 1996 Regional Integration in Central Asia: Current Economic Position and Prospects, *Central Asian Survey*, Vol. 15, No. 3/4, pp. 369–86.

Felgengauer P 1997 A Manilov-style Reorganisation of the Army, *Sevodnya*, 21 July, translated in *The Current Digest of the Post-Soviet Press*, Vol. XLIX, No. 29, pp. 4–5.

Garnett S 1995 The Integrationist Temptation, *The Washington Quarterly*, Vol. 18, No. 2, pp. 35–44.

Holoboff E 1997 Russia's Strategic Pipelines, *Brassey's Defence Yearbook*, Brassey's, London and Washington, DC, pp. 117–37.

Interfax 1998 80 per cent of Russians Support Strengthening of CIS, reprinted in *Johnson's Russian List*, 10 February.

Lough J 1993 Defining Russia's Relations with Neighbouring States, *RFE/RL Research Report*, Vol. 2, No. 20, pp. 53–60.

MccGwire M 1998 NATO expansion: 'a Policy Error of Historic Importance', *Review of International Studies*, Vol. 24, No. 1, pp. 23–42.

Mendras M 1997 Towards a Post-imperial Identity, in Baranovsky V (ed.), *Russia and Europe. The Emerging Security Identity*, Oxford University Press, Oxford, pp. 90–103.

Morris H 1995 Ethnicity and International Relations: Russian Involvement in the Conflict in Georgia, *Slovo*, Vol. 8, No. 1, pp. 80–101.

Pipes R 1997 Is Russia Still an Enemy?, *Foreign Affairs*, Vol. 76, No. 5, pp. 65–78.

Primakov Y 1994 Russia and the CIS: Does the West's Position Need Adjustment?, *Rossiiskaya gazeta*, 22 September, reprinted in *The Current Digest of the Post-Soviet Press*, Vol. XLVI, No. 38, pp. 1–5.

Primakov Y 1997 Yevgeniy Primakov's Year (Interview with Primakov in *Rossiiskaya gazeta*, January 10), reprinted in *The Current Digest of the Post-Soviet Press*, Vol. XLIX, No. 2, pp. 4–5.

Rogov S 1997 *Military Reform and the Defence Budget of the Russian Federation*, Centre for Naval Analyses, Alexandria, VA.

van Selm B 1997 *The Economics of Soviet Break-up*, Routledge, London and New York.

Sherr J 1997 Russia–Ukraine *Rapprochement?*: The Black Sea Fleet Accords, *Survival*, Vol. 39, No. 3, pp. 33–50.

Tolz V 1993 The Burden of the Imperial Legacy, *RFE/RL Research Report*, Vol. 2, No. 20, pp. 41–6.

Webber M 1996 *The International Politics of Russia and the Successor States*, Manchester University Press, Manchester and New York.

Webber M 1997 *CIS Integration Trends: Russia and the Former Soviet South* (Former Soviet South Key Paper), Royal Institute of International Affairs, London.

World Bank 1997 *World Development Report*, Oxford University Press, Oxford.

Yeltsin B 1997 Yeltsin Praises CIS in Message to Heads of Member States, BBC, *Summary of World Broadcasts*, SU/3106 B/7, 19 December.

Zviagelskaia I 1995 *The Russian Policy Debate on Central Asia* (Former Soviet South Key Paper), Royal Institute of International Affairs, London.

Further reading

Webber M 1997 *CIS Integration Trends: Russia and the Former Soviet South*, RIIA, London.

14 From the cold war to strategic partnership? US–Russian relations since the end of the USSR

Michael Cox

Introduction

For the better part of 40 years the United States and the Soviet Union were engaged in a bitter rivalry that seemed to brook no compromise or offer a great deal of hope to those who yearned for peace. The reasons for this antagonism were neither accidental nor contingent but flowed from certain core assumptions. Thus the USSR, for its part, regarded the US as a determined enemy whose ultimate mission was to undermine the Soviet system by all means short of war. The United States, in turn, saw the Soviet Union as being an equally resolute foe whose long-term ambition was to subvert the West. It is true that at certain critical points – most notably in the 1970s – the two states saw some advantage in managing the relationship somewhat differently. The threat of nuclear annihilation also impelled both to control the conflict with great care and sensitivity. However, neither superpower detente, nor the arms race, challenged the almost irresistible logic of the cold war. In many ways, both were simply different forms which the superpower competition took. Indeed, so intense was that competition, that detente very quickly gave way to the second cold war, while the arms race was viewed by some in the United States as a means of bringing further pressure to bear upon the USSR. So effective was this pressure in fact (at least according to one reading of the more recent past) that it accelerated the downfall of communism and so brought the cold war to a rapid and peaceful end (Cox, 1998).

The most unexpected conclusion of the cold war in 1989, followed two years later by the even more unexpected collapse of the Soviet Union, appeared to some at least to represents a clear victory for the United States. At one level there was much for Washington to celebrate. Its main superpower rival had disappeared in the space of two years; the cause of communism had been seen off; the way had been left open for the further expansion of liberal capitalism – and the world system could now look forward to less dangerous times – or so it was thought at the time. However, as more sober voices warned, the abrupt (and to some) unwelcome implosion of the last remaining European empire posed enormous problems – different in kind perhaps to those which had existed in the cold war, but genuine problems nonetheless. Talk of a new world order might have sounded fine in public, but as both Presidents Bush and Clinton reasoned, there was little chance of realising such a dream without the careful management of what remained of the former USSR in general and post-communist Russia in particular. As Secretary of State James Baker pointed out in 1992, America's old rival – and hopefully new-found friend – remained 'the greatest challenge' facing the US in the last decade of the twentieth century (Baker, 1992, p. 8). The cold war might have been won, but as former President Nixon observed just before his death, there was no way of 'winning the peace' without integrating Russia into the international system (Talbott, 1994).

In this chapter, my main aim is to explore the evolution of US–Russian relations since the fall of the Soviet empire in 1991 (Cox, 1994, pp. 635–58). My first job will be to explain why the United States decided to devote so much attention to post-communist Russia, even after the USSR had disintegrated. I shall then go on to explain why it has found it so difficult to achieve its larger goal in Russia. As I will attempt to show, while this failure can in part be ascribed to what Stephen Cohen has termed America's over-ambitious missionary zeal, the larger problem always facing the US was the almost impossible task of building a market democracy in a country where neither democracy nor the market had ever been practised for any extended period of time (Cohen, 1993, pp. 453–79). In this sense, the underlying obstacle standing in the way of Washington realising its dream of capitalism in Russia was Russia itself. However, as I shall also argue, the impasse in Russia does not necessarily have to lead to a new cold war or to a breakdown in relations with the United States. To this extent the film of history need not run backwards. On the other hand, the nature of the relationship has changed over time. Constructed in the first instance in the hope that Russia could successfully build a market economy, a few years later US policy-makers saw the importance of a partnership less in terms of building a new liberal order in Russia – although the vague hope remained that Russia might one day become a 'normal' country – and more as a way of ensuring that Russian decline did not have a disturbing effect on the rest of the world. Thus what began life as an optimistic American adventure, a few years later looked more like a desperate holding operation to prevent the disintegration of Russia impacting on the larger international system.

Towards a 'strategic alliance' with Russian reform

The conclusion of the cold war and the implosion of the USSR constituted two of the most important moments – if not the most important moment – of the post-war era, and one of the results was to provide the United States with a breathing space within which it could re-define its priorities. Whether it really did so remains a moot point, but boiled down to essentials the US basically set itself four broad goals for the post-communist era:

- to maintain its own hegemony in a stable global order
- to control the spread of nuclear weapons

- to promote the benefits of democracy and human rights to others
- to extend market capitalism to those countries attempting to make the transition out of planning and economic autarchy

Taken together, these formed the 'core' of America's strategic mission in the 1990s (Cox, 1995).

There was, however, a crucial connection between the achievement of these larger goals and developments in Russia. Without a strong, vibrant and outward-looking America, there was little chance (or so it was thought by US policy-makers) of Russia escaping its past and rejoining the community of nations. Conversely, if reform in Russia failed, this would make it much more difficult for America to achieve its larger objectives (Clinton, 1993a). Certainly, if Russian democracy collapsed, or the transition from one economic system to another did not take place, then the US would face a very insecure future with the strong possibility – according to one very senior official – of 'a renewed nuclear threat, higher defense budgets, spreading instability, the loss of new markets and a devastating setback for the wordwide democratic movement' (Christopher, 1993). Engaging with reform therefore was not just in Russia's interest, but in America's too.

The success or failure of Russian reform was thus a first-order concern for the United States. However, merely supporting or endorsing change was not enough. The United States, in effect, had to construct what President Clinton and his main adviser on Russian affairs (Strobe Talbott) came to characterise as a 'strategic alliance' or a 'new democratic partnership' with a reforming Russia (Clinton, 1993b). There were a number of reasons for it doing so.

The first had to do with the process of economic reform. In this, the United States saw itself playing a decisive role. Indeed, if it remained a bystander, then according to Washington, the reform process could easily fail. There were many things the United States could do – some would say had to do, if economic reform was to be successful. Most obviously, it could mobilise international support behind the reforms, using its considerable influence and power within the IMF (see Box 14.1 below) in particular to keep the reformist train on the rails. It could, in addition, help by attempting to create a more congenial global environment by persuading major lending institutions to be more sympathetic to Russia's needs and getting the European Union to be more open to Russian goods. Finally, it could get engaged itself in the new Russian economy. In this endeavour, US business was likely to play second fiddle to the Europeans in general and Germany in particular. Nonetheless, there were huge profits awaiting the adventurous in the financial sector, in oil and in food exports, and these simply could not be passed up. Indeed, as the champion of American business, Clinton was especially keen to ensure that US capital played its part in building the new Russia.

If one reason for becoming more seriously engaged with Russia was to give a major boost to the market, another was to help to manage the potentially explosive transition from empire to self-determining nations. Although the break-up of the USSR had been welcomed by some in the United States, there was still grave concern about its consequences. Rhetoric apart, the Clinton administration – very much like its predecessor – was acutely aware of the fact that the fall

СПРАВКА 14.1 The IMF

The International Monetary Fund (or IMF) was set up in 1944 alongside the International Bank for Reconstruction and Development (more commonly known as the World Bank). The World Bank gave out loans to West European countries to rebuild their economies after World War II, while the IMF was concerned more with the issue of exchange rates and stable currencies. The postwar international economic system based around these two institutions as well as the strong US dollar was very successful in helping to quickly revive the economies of Western Europe. As attention shifted more to the third world from the 1960s and to the post-communist states of Eastern Europe in the 1990s, the role of the IMF and World Bank has become more controversial. The main criticism has been that they have promoted free market principles as a universal panacea with little regard either for the social cost or the very different cultures and histories of these target countries.

of the Soviet Union had opened up a Pandora's box containing all sorts of unpleasant problems. Devising a coherent strategy to deal with these was therefore a priority. This was no easy job; yet the United States could hardly wash its hands of the situation. It thus aimed through a combination of economic inducement, political mediation and reassurance to encourage the development of what Washington hoped would one day become strong bilateral relations between the new independent states. If it could succeed, then it would have made a major contribution to international stability. If it could not, then it might be facing another Yugoslavia; with nuclear weapons thrown in for good measure (USGPO, 1993).

This brings us logically to the question of nuclear weapons. Having shaped the course of the cold war, it was inevitable that they would continue to impact upon Russian–American relations after 1991; possibly more so than ever under conditions of political and economic uncertainty. What made the situation even more dangerous, of course, was the break-up of the USSR and the attendant threat of nuclear proliferation. Dealing with this problem (one official defined 'non-proliferation' as '*the* arms control priority of the post-cold war world') quite literally impelled the United States to develop close ties to Russia and the other republics (Davis, 1994, p. 49): partly because the fall of the USSR threatened the reliability of Moscow's centralised command and control over nuclear systems, partly because near-bankrupt nations such as Russia and Ukraine might try to sell nuclear equipment and material in the international marketplace and partly because there were tens of thousands of poor or unemployed nuclear scientists and engineers in the former Soviet Union who might be tempted to sell their services abroad. Offering their knowledge to the West was one thing: however, there was a very real danger, according to the CIA, that 'some may be tempted to sell their expertise to Third World countries' – a possibility that was quite unacceptable and had to be controlled (Gates, 1992, pp. 17–18).

The problem of proliferation was in turn related to the wider issue of world order and America's post-cold-war role in world affairs. By the time Clinton entered the White House, the traditional Soviet threat had evaporated. Russia, however, by virtue of its size, geographic location, continuing membership of the nuclear club, position on the UN Security Council and still significant diplomatic resources, remained a force in international relations and could not be ignored. Moreover, its ability to influence world events (for good or ill) made it a particularly attractive partner for the United States. For although its assets were less – and its global reach much reduced – it continued to have the capacity to disturb the international peace. Also, in an era when America was becoming increasingly reluctant to pay any price or to go anywhere to preserve the peace, Washington had good reason to seek a new partnership with Moscow. Indeed, in Clinton's version of the new world order, in which the United States was likely to play a far more selective role, a secure and integrated Russia closely tied to the US had a number of things to recommend it: as barrier to the potential ambitions of (usually unspecified) nations in the Eurasian 'heartland', as secular dam to the spread of Islamic fundamentalism and as stabiliser in an uncertain world which the United States could no longer manage on the basis of its own resources.

Finally, the Clinton administration in particular sought a deal with Moscow not just for global but for domestic reasons as well. Indeed, according to one commentator, the success or failure of the Clinton presidency depended in large part upon events in Russia, or more precisely upon Russia's orderly transition to free market democracy. Clinton therefore desperately needed a solid and stable relationship with Moscow: first, because he feared that any increase in tensions would play into the hands of his conservative opponents at home; second, because a new 'cold war' would make it more difficult for him to realise his economic goal of getting military spending down; finally, because without a quiescent international scene he would be unable to focus his attention on what he (and the American people) considered to be the nation's top problem, which was, to use the slogan of the day, the 'economy stupid'. If that attention drifted, or more importantly was forced off-course by a major international crisis caused by events in Russia, then his whole domestic programme would be put in jeopardy. Clinton, the 'politician's politician', had no intention of allowing that to happen (Walker, 1994).

Partnership in crisis: 1992–94

Building a partnership with Moscow was thus regarded as a necessity, and after 1992 the US made great play of its new-found friendship with Russia and the Russian President, Boris Yeltsin. Indeed, for a period, it appeared to some critics that the only region in the world in which Clinton had any interest was Russia. Certainly, during his first year in office, he played the 'Russian card' with great regularity. So engaged was he, in fact, that even some of his more ardent political opponents had to concede that on this international question at least (if on no other) he was both decisive and convincing (Fletcher, 1994). Nevertheless,

СПРАВКА 14.2	**Leading figures in foreign policy-making during the Clinton presidency**

President Bill Clinton (1993–)
Vice President Al Gore (1993–)
Secretaries of State: Warren Christopher (1993–6); Madeleine Albright (1997–)
Secretaries of Defense: Les Aspin (1993); William J. Perry (1994–96); William Cohen (1997–)

his apparently coherent strategy contained a number of inherent contradictions obscured at first by the President's clarity of vision, the sheer enthusiasm with which he presented his case and the strong political support he seemed to be receiving at home for his policy. These problems began to manifest themselves at the time of the 'aid to Russia' campaign in spring and early summer of 1993. They became more apparent as the political crisis unfolded in Russia through September and October. They continued during the late autumn as NATO started to contemplate the idea of a 'Partnership for Peace' with the countries of Eastern and Central Europe. They finally reached a critical point when the December elections to the Russian Duma produced the wrong result. Certainly, by the beginning of 1994 – and a long while before the 'great Russian crash' of 1998 – it looked as if Clinton's idea of an alliance with a reforming Russia had run its course, and that either an alternative strategy would have to be devised or a modification would have to be made to his original policy.

Perhaps the most obvious problem with US policy was that it made unwarranted assumptions about both Russia and what Russia needed to make it into a 'normal' country. Assuming that there had been a genuine revolution in 1991 which had cleared the way for a relatively rapid forced march towards the market, policy-makers were somewhat surprised to discover that the obstacles still standing in the way of reform were immense – much greater than they had originally expected (White, 1998, pp. 135–49). Moreover, at no point did they seem ready to match their strong rhetorical endorsement of the market with concrete material support for the reform process itself. Having encouraged (some would even say, pushed) Russia down the path of painful economic restructuring, neither Congress nor the American people were prepared to extend very much material aid. In fact, most of the limited 'aid' that was disbursed was either tied to Russian purchases of American commodities or to programmes designed to make Russian nuclear facilities safer. This hardly constituted a Marshall Plan, nor significantly was Clinton prepared to go to Congress to try to sell one. He did manage to wring a few economic concessions from his allies and the IMF, and as the situation continued to become worse in Russia, he was compelled to do so more and more. However, at the end of the day, these were never enough to give a kick-start to a failing Russian economy (Lloyd, 1993).

The American failure, or refusal to back economic reform with massive injections of US money, had two rather unfortunate consequences. The first and least significant was to expose American rhetoric for what it was; so much hot air without little connection with Russian realities and needs. The second and more serious result, however, was to leave those who had initially backed the reforms inside Russia in an almost impossible position: ridiculed on the one hand by their enemies for not getting the support they had apparently been promised, and on the other for being mere puppets of the United States. To add insult to injury, those hostile to reform were able to exploit the issue most effectively by arguing that the misery now being experienced by the Russian people was all the fault of the Americans and their allies in the IMF. In this way, the political and ideological seeds were sown that first bore fruit in the shape of Vladimir Zhironovsky and his motley band of ill-named Liberal Democrats, and then later in the more credible form of the Russian chauvinist–communist, Gennadi Zyuganov (Reddaway, 1994).

The second problem with US strategy was less economic than political. Although American officials spoke in warm terms of their support for post-Soviet reform in general (Clinton made great play of his administration's support for the principle of self-determination) in reality the main thrust of American policy was directed towards Russia. Naturally, Washington tried to reassure the other republics, arguing that backing for Russia did not imply indifference to, or neglect of, the other new independent states. Warren Christopher, the US Secretary of State, indeed insisted that the United States was totally committed to the integrity of the different republics and would assist in their integration into the world community. However, there was little disguising the fact that in its essentials US policy was taken to mean, and certainly was perceived as being, a 'Russia first' policy. This had a number of negative consequences. The most important perhaps was to fuel non-Russian suspicion of American motives. To most non-Russians, in fact, it now looked as if the United States either favoured some partial reconstruction of the Union or was prepared to turn a blind eye to Russian activities in the so-called 'near abroad'. The other consequence, according to critics, was to encourage greater aggression by Russia itself. Working on the not illogical assumption that Washington had few serious objections to it throwing its weight around, Moscow started to assert itself in its so-called near abroad. In some cases the consequences were merely unfortunate: in Chechnya of course they turned out to be horrendous.

It was not just events within the former USSR that worried US policy-makers, however. It was also Russia's changing attitude towards the outside world as well. Having supported Yeltsin against his many domestic enemies since 1991, the US obviously expected something in return on the international front. Yeltsin was willing to oblige – at least was for a while. However, he was either unwilling or unable to sing all the time from some foreign policy hymn-sheet printed in the United States. Yeltsin, moreover, had to secure himself at home, and the most obvious and effective way of doing this was by wrapping himself up in a Russian flag and asserting Russian interests abroad. This did not lead to anything resembling a major conflict with the West; but within a couple of years of the USSR's disintegration, the brief era of 'Mr Yes', as Sergei Karaganov characterised

Russian foreign policy in the immediate aftermath of the collapse of the USSR, was drawing to a close (Karaganov, 1994). As the Russian Foreign Minister Andrei Kozyrev observed in late 1992, Russia had interests of its own, and these of necessity did not coincide with those of America. Yeltsin apparently agreed. Indeed, he chastised the United States for having displayed a certain 'tendency to dictate its own terms' on international questions, and he added for good measure that, from now on, Russia would no longer be as compliant as it had been before. This declaration of semi-independence was bound to have consequences – and it did: in Bosnia, where Russia took a much tougher stand in support of its Serb allies; at home where there was a marked shift in language towards a new and more militant 'Russia first' rhetoric; most noticeably perhaps in its own 'near abroad', where it now aggressively justified what it was doing (Truscott, 1997).

Russia's new assertiveness posed particular problems for the United States, but Russia's behaviour abroad was not Washington's biggest problem. This was to be found within Russia itself where the situation showed no sign of real improvement after 1992. For a President elected on the promise that he would push Russia more rapidly along the capitalist road, Clinton had little to show for his efforts during his first term in office. One need not blame Clinton personally; but his expert advisers at least should have predicted that the so-called 'transition' in Russia would be more painful than they had originally suggested. Unfortunately, while they continued to talk up the reforms, Russia itself seemed to lurch from one near-fatal crisis to another. Yeltsin managed to negotiate his way through the first of these in April 1993, when he won his referendum. He then navigated the next crisis in October of the same year, but only after having bombed and then closed down the Russian parliament. The third crisis, however, proved far more difficult to resolve, not merely because the December elections in 1993 revealed strong opposition to economic change, but more significantly because those hostile to the market now had a genuine democratic mandate (see Chapters 2 and 3). This was a disaster of the first order that was bound to have serious consequences back in the United States.

Crisis and response

Perhaps one indicator of the seriousness with which the Clinton administration viewed the situation in Russia was its half-hearted public attempts to play down the significance of the December elections and the 'rise' of Vladimir Zhironovsky. The official line at first was to make light of the anti-reform vote, more or less dismissing it as a 'protest' against short-term problems that would evaporate once things improved. This exercise in damage limitation could not hide the administration's concern, however. According to one source, the White House was 'startled and shaken' by the outcome. Vice President Al Gore, it is reliably reported, was 'dazed and speechless' when the results came in.

Thus confusion abounded, and was reflected in certain statements made by leading Clinton officials concerning one of the causes of the Russian crisis. While accepting that the deeper reason for Russia's problems lay within the country itself, first Gore, and then Talbott – in what was seen as a major shift in policy

БИОГРАФИЯ 14.1 **Strobe Talbott and Jeffrey Sachs**

Strobe Talbott (born 1946)

Strobe Talbott worked for many years as writer and then editor-at-large for the American news magazine, *Time*. He wrote a number of books on US foreign policy and edited the English language edition of Khrushchev's memoirs. He entered the Clinton administration as Deputy Secretary of State. He has been a key adviser to President Clinton on Russian and East European affairs.

Jeffrey Sachs (born 1954)

Jeffrey Sachs is professor of economics at Harvard University in the USA. He became adviser on transition economics to a series of governments in Latin America and Eastern Europe. Sachs was a leading proponent of radical and rapid market reform, generally known as shock therapy. Sachs later became critical of Western policy for not providing sufficient economic aid, as he saw it, to Russia.

– attempted to place at least some of the blame on Western economic policies. In Talbott's famous or (infamous) phrase, there had been too much imposed 'shock' and not enough 'therapy' in Russia. Hence it was necessary, or so he implied, both to slow down the reforms and to take account of their negative social consequences. The net result of this intervention was unfortunate, to say the least (*The Economist*, 1993, pp. 27–9).

First, it upset the IMF and the economically more orthodox members of the Clinton team; it also gave the impression that the administration was now split between soft liberals and hard-nosed monetarists. More seriously, it did very real damage to those in Russia who had been advocating radical economic measures. Without consistent backing from their American friends, Russian reformers could hardly be expected to hold to the orthodox line. Talbott's comments, moreover, called forth a wave of criticism from analysts such as Jeffrey Sachs. Sachs, who had for some time been calling upon the US to put far more money into Russia, made the obvious point that, whatever the causes of Russia's problems, they had little or nothing to do with shock therapy. As he among others pointed out, while there had been a good a deal of reformist economic talk, in fact the economic shock had never actually been administered to the patient, except for a brief four-month period back in 1992. To all intents and purposes, there had been no experiment in capitalism: hence there was little point blaming the market for Russia's problems (see Chapter 6).

Once the dust had settled the White House set about picking its way through what looked like the debris of a failed policy. Some modifications would clearly have to be made to the original strategy. However, both Talbott and Clinton were determined to soldier on. The administration was not about to abandon Russia, nor, as one analyst suggested at the time, was it going to move Russia from being 'the most highly favoured of nations beyond the old iron curtain to being only in the second rank'. Clinton himself made this perfectly clear on his visit to Russia in early January 1994. During this, he went out of his way to reassure Russians of America's continuing support and friendship. He also played to Russian *amour propre* by talking (somewhat over-enthusiastically) of the nation's 'greatness' and US recognition of its special place in world affairs. A few days later Talbott followed up on these remarks in an important statement to the House Foreign Affairs Committee. He accepted that Russia was passing through its 'time of troubles' and that 'reformers in Russia were worried and demoralized'. However, this was no reason for America to jump ship. In fact, precisely because 'there was' what he called a 'titanic struggle' going on in Russia, in which the United States had a 'huge stake', it was more important than ever to remain engaged. Moreover, according to Talbott, the situation was more 'mixed' than the pessimists claimed. The democratic process was up and running. Over one-quarter of the labour force was now employed in the private sector. In the 'near abroad' there had been progress, although there were some problems still left to resolve. On the security front, too, things were getting better, with Ukraine just having decided to transfer all its nuclear weapons to Russia, and the United States and Russia having agreed to 'de-target' each other. It was not all doom and gloom, therefore.

Naturally, Talbott accepted that things could still go badly wrong. The 'next two and a half years – between now and the elections scheduled for mid-1996 – would be critical'. However, Russia had not yet passed beyond the point of no return. There was still everything to play for. What the United States should not do, he warned, was base its policy today on 'worst-case assumptions about what tomorrow may bring'. This would not only be foolish, but could lead the United States to 'fall into the trap of the self-fulfilling prophecy'. America had to remain patient and steady, therefore, and continue to work for the integration of Russia rather than begin planning for its containment. The advantages of doing so were self-evident, for 'a Russia integrated rather than contained', he argued, would 'mean fewer tax dollars spent on defence; a reduced threat from weapons of mass destruction; new markets for US products; and a powerful, reliable partner for diplomacy as well as commerce in the 21st century'. There was still a world to be won (Talbott, 1994).

Towards a new realism?

If one result of the December 'wake-up call' was to cause initial confusion fol-lowed by a resolute White House defence of its original strategy, the other was to open a floodgate out of which poured a tide of criticism. A good deal of this, clearly, had as much to do with Republican frustrations and right-wing dislike of the Clintons as it did with the administration's policy on Russia. Clinton's political opponents, moreover, saw his apparent discomfiture over the Russian question as a golden opportunity to erode further his diminishing credibility. However, it would be wrong to conclude that all Clinton's critics were motivated only by political animus. There were genuine questions that needed an answer; about how to deal with a Russia in which communists and nationalists were now in a majority in the new parliament, a Russia that was also continuing to show an alarming tendency to re-assert its prerogatives in the 'near abroad' and a Russia too in which the reformist Yeltsin only seemed able to hold on to power by stealing the rhetorical clothes of his anti-reformist enemies. To many, indeed, it looked in early 1994 as if Clinton's 'love affair' with Yeltsin and his fear of 'losing Russia' was now standing in the way of a more balanced American approach to post-Soviet problems (Krauthammer, 1994).

In good cold war fashion the debate over Russia reached a critical point following the disclosure that a senior CIA official had been working for Moscow for several years, apparently with deadly consequences. As one of Clinton's more vocal opponents noted in late February, 'Americans really did not need a major spy scandal to tell them that the honeymoon with Russia was over. But the arrest of the CIA's Aldrich Ames makes the point with some finality.' (Krauthammer, 1994). With this discovery (coinciding as it did with a particularly tough statement by Yeltsin on Russian foreign policy) the attacks against Clinton intensified. The Republicans' chief spokesman on foreign affairs, Richard Lugar, declared that the US had 'to get over the idea' that it was involved in a 'partnership' with Moscow. 'This is a tough rivalry,' he insisted. Much the same point was made at Talbott's confirmation hearings for the post of Deputy Secretary of State in February 1994. Here the Republicans launched a bitter attack on what one Senator called a policy which endangered 'our national interests'. The Republicans also used the occasion to criticise Clinton's foreign policy more generally. 'If Ambassador Talbott is confirmed by the Senate', argued Senator D'Amato, 'another wrong signal will be sent: that the people who carry out our foreign policy offer nothing but inexperience and naivete' (Dewar, 1994).

The politicisation of the debate obviously made it difficult for the Clinton White House to concede that its policy towards Russia was in trouble. However, there was still a case to be answered. The critics did have a point – several in fact: firstly that Clinton's strategy was based upon an over-optimistic set of assumptions about Russia's potential to become a stable, democratic, capitalist country; that Clinton himself had developed a rather naive faith in Yeltsin and Yeltsin's commitment to political democracy; that while Russia might not at present be a mortal enemy, it was not yet ready to be admitted into partnership, and that although it was reasonable to try to build bridges to Russia, one could not forget the lessons of history, and these taught that Russia was more inclined to authoritarianism and imperialism than to democracy and friendship with its neighbours.

The case against Clinton was thus a powerful one, which logically led some of his more articulate critics – Zbigniew Brzezinski in particular – to some fairly radical conclusions (Brzezinski, 1994, pp. 67–82). Brzezinski was no passive observer of the foreign policy scene, and since the collapse of the USSR had been indulging in what one observer called 'a bit of freelance foreign policy', the primary goal of which was to cultivate links with the non-Russian states of the former Soviet Union, to which he thought 'the American government should have been paying more attention'. Believing that Talbott's 'romantic fascination with Russia' (Russophilia even) was getting in the way of clear strategic thinking, Brzezinski called for a number of changes to US policy. Most importantly, he argued that

БИОГРАФИЯ 14.2 **Zbigniew Brzezinski**

Zbigniew Brzezinski was born in Poland in 1928, but moved to the US and became an American citizen in 1958. He made his name as an academic with a particular interest in the communist countries of Eastern Europe. He was National Security Adviser to President Jimmy Carter from 1977 to 1981. He gained a reputation for favouring a tough stance towards the USSR. He returned to academia in 1981, but has remained a frequent and forthright commentator in the US media on post-communist politics and international affairs.

the countries of Eastern and Central Europe should be invited into NATO sooner rather than later. This was critical. Furthermore, in his view, the US should set as its main objective 'the consolidation of geopolitical pluralism within' the space once occupied by the old Soviet Union. Only in this way could countries such as Ukraine be assured and America achieve a more balanced relationship with the new Europe as a whole. Indeed, according to Brzezinski, the creation of a belt of independent states around Russia, closely allied to the West, not only would serve America's interest but would help Russia as well; for only when its periphery was secured – and when Moscow was no longer tempted to play a spoiling role there – could it become both stable and democratic itself.

Brzezinski's central thesis – that Clinton's call for a partnership with Russian reform was premature – certainly seemed to make a good deal of sense to the administration's critics. It must have made some to a few within the White House itself; for while Clinton and his team continued to talk up the reforms, in private many of them conceded that some of its early optimism had been overdone. Some adjustment to the earlier policy would thus have to be made, without sacrificing basics. This expressed itself in at least four ways.

The first way, quite simply, was at the level of public presentation. Hitherto, the Clinton team had talked quite boldly and optimistically about an alliance with Russia and Russian reform. Now this line was modified somewhat to include a recognition that on certain international issues at least, there were bound to be serious divergences between the two countries. As Defense Secretary William Perry pointed out in March 1994, 'even with the best outcome imaginable in Russia, the new Russia' would have interests different to America's. Nor should the US be particularly concerned about this, for as Perry pointed out (picking his countries ever so carefully) 'even with allies like France and Japan, we have rivalry and competition alongside our partnership', and so it will be with Russia (Gordon, 1994). Following a meeting in Vladivostok between senior Russian and American officials, Warren Christopher made much the same point. Repeating the standard realist line that all great powers come into conflict, he noted that 'large nations with large interests' were bound to have differences. The question facing Washington or Moscow was not to deny their existence, but rather to discuss them 'openly' so as to manage them more effectively.

The first change in policy therefore was to the way in which the US theorised its relationship with Russia: the second was in its attitude towards the non-Russian republics. Sensitive to the charge that it had tilted too far towards Moscow and Yeltsin, Washington now began to make a much greater effort in building stronger relations with countries other than Russia. This pleased not only a number of countries in the former USSR, but Brzezinski too who saw this as exactly the sort of initiative the Clinton administration should have taken much earlier. Whether the White House saw it this way is much less clear; but there was no mistaking the shift in policy. This expressed itself in many ways – both symbolic and practical. Thus during a scheduled visit by the new Ukrainian president to Washington in March 1994 (the first ever undertaken) Clinton re-affirmed 'American support' for Ukrainian independence. Four months later Clinton met with the three leaders of the Baltic republics. Other meetings were held during the course of the year. At the same time, the US issued a series of warnings to Moscow that good relations between Russia and the USA assumed – indeed pre-supposed – better relations with its neighbours.

These various moves were accompanied by perhaps the biggest change of all in US policy: in its attitude towards NATO and NATO expansion. Accepting now that there could be no half-way house for the countries of Central and Eastern Europe, Washington decided during the course of 1994 that it was time to extend the privileges of full NATO membership to Poland, the Czech Republic and Hungary. Having initially been persuaded by Talbott back in 1992 that this was not the way to go (a promise had been made to Moscow that NATO would not be expanded eastwards) after the events in Russia, the US felt it had no altern-ative but to do so. Although in part a move designed to assuage critics both at home and abroad – and to find a new mission for NATO in a post-Soviet world – clearly underlying the move was a growing recognition that Russia's future could not be guaranteed. Once spoken of as only a theoretical possibility, by late 1994 the likelihood of the reform process in Russia going into reverse seemed far less unlikely. Thus there was good reason to hedge one's bets and to secure the peace in Europe now by guarding against a resurgent Russia in the future (Ball, 1998, pp. 43–68).

The final shift in US policy was less dramatic but still significant. Since being elected, President Clinton had promised not only a review of US military object-ives but important cuts in the US military budget as well – and three months before the December elections in Russia he had made good on both promises with the publication of his defence review, suitably entitled the *Bottom Up Review*. Although hardly a radical document it provoked a wave of criticism from conservatives in particular who attacked it, in effect, for undermining American national security by failing to spend enough on the military. For a while, Clinton was able to fend off his opponents. However, with the Zhironovsky 'wake up call' it became increasingly difficult for him to do so. The result was to make him far more cautious on defence matters: partly out of political fear, but partly too because of a genuine concern about developments in Russia. With its future as yet undecided, it would have taken a much bolder American president than Clinton (who felt vulnerable on the issue) to have now argued the case for large cuts in American military spending.

'Steady as she goes'

While the US took what it regarded as sensible measures to guard against any future eventuality, it still did not accept that the situation in Russia was hopeless. As Talbott reminded the Senate in early 1994, although the United States would be acting cautiously, it had no intention of planning for the worse. Quite the reverse in fact, and Clinton (supported by his equally anxious European allies) now embarked on what looked like a diplomatic offensive to draw Russia ever more closely towards the West. Whether this represented one last desperate throw or a coherent strategy was none too clear. The fact remains, however, that within a few months of the crisis of December 1993, some form of equilibrium had been restored to East–West relations. The storm had been weathered; for how long remained an open question.

The administration's determination not to break off its engagement with Russia was first reflected in March 1994, when, after five days of 'tense negotiations', the IMF finally approved a $1.5 billion loan to Moscow. The amount was hardly staggering, and there remained the obvious problem of whether Russia would fulfil its side of the bargain. Nevertheless the deal was of great importance, and was regarded as such by commentators at the time. Most crucially, it provided the West with continued influence over Russian economic affairs, something that was seen as critical if Russia was to remain on the 'right' economic course. It was also seen as a vital signal of support to Yeltsin and to Prime Minister Chernomyrdin, particularly important now when both seemed to be under siege from their enemies at home. Finally, it served as symbolic proof (if nothing else) that Russia had not abandoned the cause of economic reform altogether. Indeed, if the IMF had not gone ahead with the loan, its failure to do so would have amounted to a formal Western abandonment of the reform process. Anders Aslund, the Swedish economist and one-time adviser to the Russian government, was in no doubt about the loan's significance. 'Chernomyrdin and Yeltsin were still on track' he noted, but 'only just'. How much longer they would remain so, however, remained an open question (*Financial Times*, 16 May, 1994).

The IMF deal in March was followed up later in the spring by an equally significant trade agreement between America's economic partners in Europe and Russia. Again this was important less for what it did and more for what it promised Russia in the not-too-distant future, so long as Russia made some progress towards developing a market economy. As Sir Leon Brittan pointed out at the time, 'the agreement' was a 'very ambitious' one: partly because it offered Russia the possibility of a free trade pact with the EU, partly because it marked what he felt was a 'milestone on the road towards greater economic and political stability across the entire continent' of Europe and partly because it was enacted at almost exactly the same time as Russia was moving towards signing the Partnership for Peace. Brittan in fact saw a very real connection between the two agreements. The new trade relationship would, he believed, 'complement Moscow's membership in NATO's Partnership for Peace' and in this way enhance Russia's 'ties to the West' (Buerkle, 1994).

The final act in this rather frenetic three-part play concluded in July 1994, when Russia attended the G7 summit in Naples. Kozyrev, who had been urging the United States to revive what he called the 'lagging partnership', was particularly keen for Russia to participate. Indeed, he hoped – and in fact expected – that the G7 would one day become the G8 (Kozyrev, 1994, pp. 59–71). Others were less impressed. One noted Western sceptic dismissed the whole thing as an irrelevant show. Even the moderate Russian reformer, Shokhin, was not overawed, pointing out that the meeting would do little to solve Russia's economic problems. However, this missed the point of the whole exercise, which had little to do with economics, and more with the United States and its partners reassuring Russia that it deserved a place at the high table. For Russia, it was also important to be there and make plain its disagreements with the West on a number of issues. This not only sent a message to domestic critics that Yeltsin was no mere 'yes-man', but served also to remind the West as well that in spite of its economic problems, no major international question could be resolved without Russia's help. If the 'G8' meeting achieved no more than reminding the US of this fact, then, from the Russian point of view, the Naples summit was a great success (Eyal, 1994).

Partnership in crisis – again: 1994–98

These various attempts to keep Russia on track could not hide the simple fact that the cause of liberal economic reform was already in crisis. Indeed, the more the West felt it had to do, the less it looked as if Russia was moving in the direction it was supposed to be going. Of course this was no reason for the US abandoning Russia. Moreover, optimists could draw some comfort from the fact that important structural changes had occurred in the character of the Russian economy. One such even talked in a most upbeat fashion about Russia's 'economic success story' (Aslund, 1994, pp. 58–71). Overall, however, the United States seemed to have little to cheer about. In December 1994 Yeltsin formally came out against NATO expansion. In the same month, Moscow launched its ill-fated 'invasion' of Chechnya. In early 1995, Russia then sold two light-water nuclear reactors to Iran; in December, the Russian communists did particularly well in elections to the Russian Duma, while parties or political groups which stood for Western-style democracy and an open market were trounced; and, in the race for the Russian presidency in June of the following year, Yeltsin only just managed to win. Although the sound of Washington's relief was audible, the outcome was a very close one indeed. The result, moreover, was less a victory for reform and more the result of Yeltsin's manipulation of the media and his disconcerting ability to steal the nationalist (and populist) thunder of his political opponents in the Russian Communist Party. In fact, at moments during the 1996 election, it was almost impossible to distinguish between the ostensibly pro-Western incumbent Yeltsin and the openly anti-Western challenger, Zyuganov. Certainly, neither had much very good to say about the United States during the course of the campaign (see Chapters 2 and 3).

Worse was yet to come, and as the economic situation continued to deteriorate in Russia (by early 1997 it was calculated that industrial output had fallen by about a third) many began to express deep concerns about the country's future

(*The Economist*, 22 November, 1997). Nearly all of the main indicators pointed to further decline and possible political instability. One rather obvious sign of the times was Yeltsin's somewhat startling decision in March 1998 to sack his entire government; 'good theatre but poor politics' opined one Western source (Lloyd, 1998). Another was the warning then delivered by the new Russian prime minister. According to Sergei Kiriyenko, Russia was living on the 'never never'. The young economist did not mince his words. Russia's foreign debt he noted stood at about $140bn, workers were not being paid and capital continued to leave the country at a far more rapid rate than it was coming in. Also, while the international price of oil continued to fall, living standards for all but the wealthy few continued to decline – at a quite alarming rate. Russia he warned was staring into the abyss. Extremely dangerous days lay ahead (Meek, 1998).

How dangerous only became clear in August when Russia's financial system effectively collapsed. The consequences of this much-predicted crisis were truly appalling – both at home where it wiped out ruble savings overnight and abroad where it totally undermined confidence in the Russian economy. Furthermore, coming when it did (in the midst of a pre-existing global financial crisis) the very real fear was that meltdown in Russia could easily spark a world-wide recession. As the normally staid *Wall Street Journal* pointed out, although the international weight of the Russian economy was small, accounting for only 1 per cent of the world's gross domestic product, any move to default on its large foreign debt could easily precipitate similar actions elsewhere. Equally, if Russia took steps to prevent foreigners from getting their money out, then other 'at-risk' countries might be tempted to do the same. As the newspaper speculated, 'already Malaysia has imposed rigid controls' and there was a genuine worry that, if Russia did the same, then others would follow suit (*The Wall Street Journal Europe*, 1998).

The impact of these momentous events precipitated yet another 'great debate' within the United States. Although similar in tone to that which followed the Duma election of December 1993, the discussion now was far more pessimistic in character. Conservatives in particular wasted no time in advising the administration to give up on Russian reform completely. One such guru of doom was Martin Malia. The American historian who had predicted the failure of *perestroika* a decade earlier now reflected in an equally bleak way about the collapse of the liberal model in post-communist Russia. 'The only certainty in Russia's present crisis' he argued 'is that it marks the end of an era – the Yeltsin years'. However, this was not all. According to Malia, the demise of reformism in Russia also symbolised the 'end of a theory', the one advanced by Francis Fukuyama in the late 1980s which suggested 'that market democracy has triumphed as a universal ideal'. If nothing else, the events in Russia had put paid to that particular pipe-dream (Malia, 1998). George Friedman was even more pessimistic, and whereas Malia simply noted the passing of the liberal western model in Russia, Friedman predicted its replacement by a new form of Stalinism combining economic and geopolitical 'anti-Westernism'. Moreover, there was nothing the West could do about it. 'The new Stalinism' could 'not be stopped' he asserted. This left the United States with only one option: to abandon a strategy which assumed that reform was possible and to adopt a new policy which assumed it was not. The US he concluded had to 'begin defining a post-reform policy towards Russia'. One era had come to an end; a new era had begun, and American policy-makers simply had to come to terms with this unpleasant fact of life (Friedman, 1998).

Gloom about Russia's future was not just the intellectual preserve of Western conservatives, however; the International Monetary Fund was equally downbeat. For the Fund, of course, the crisis in Russia was especially worrying. After all, it was they who had been charged with handling the 'transition' in Russia, and since 1991 had pumped almost $20bn into the country and devoted more staff to managing Russia than any other nation in the world. The August crisis thus represented something close to a catastrophe for them. However, they were in no mood to compromise or backtrack, and instead of interrogating their own past practices, went out of their way to ensure that the proverbial buck did not land on their desks. This became obvious when the IMF gathered to hold a post-mortem meeting on Russia in late November. Everyone agreed that the situation was grim and might even become worse, but instead of assessing their own role, they laid the blame fairly and squarely at the door of Russia's political and economic elites. Significantly, very few of the meeting's participants levelled direct criticism of the Fund itself, perhaps because one of the organisations most vocal critics, Harvard Professor Jeffrey Sachs, was not in attendance. Officials did accept that policies aimed to achieve one set of goals – and which looked right back in 1992 – had turned out by 1998 to have produced unintended and highly undesirable consequences. However, this was about as far as they were prepared to go. Certainly, there was no reason to change course. Indeed, if Russia was to do so now, and abandon the cause of reform entirely, the country was doomed (Rutland, 1998).

US policy at the cross-roads

Confronted with the crisis, US officials charged with Russian policy clearly had an uphill task in front of them. On the one hand, they had to convince both themselves, and the wider American public, that the strategy they had been pursuing since 1992 had borne at least some fruit. On the other, they had to fight off those who were now calling for an abandonment of the policy of engagement. It was no easy job, one that was made all the more difficult by yet another change of government in Russia itself. Although rather less alarming in composition than some commentators assumed (one stressed that Primakov, the new Russian Prime Minister, 'was a former KGB agent, a friend of dictators in Iraq and Serbia, and an enemy of the West' (Safire, 1998)) the new team could hardly be described as reformist. Furthermore, while Primakov himself talked reassuringly about his commitment to the international community and his opposition to strident nationalism, his selection of economic advisers seemed to point backwards to the pre-Yeltsin years rather than forward to the market. As one seasoned observer noted, his choice 'sent strong signals that his approach will be a throwback to another era when economists tried to introduce some free market ideas within a Soviet system'. The return of this 'cast of' Soviet characters according to Celestine Bohlen was 'eerie, even alarming' (Bohlen, 1998).

БИОГРАФИЯ 14.3 **Madeleine Albright**

Madeleine Albright was born in Czechoslovakia in 1937, but only recently discovered she had Jewish blood. She became the first female Secretary of State when appointed to the post in 1997. She is also the highest ranking woman in the Clinton administration. She has a reputation for tough-talking, and was instrumental in pushing for the enlargement of NATO.

American disquiet at the direction now being taken by Russia was expressed most forcefully by Madeleine Albright, the US Secretary of State. In her first comprehensive review of US–Russian relations since Primakov was confirmed as Prime Minister in September, Mrs Albright was in no mood to pour American oil onto Russia's troubled waters. Washington she declared was 'deeply concerned' about the direction in which Russia seemed to be moving. Of particular concern was the apparent shift to the left in economic policy. While praising Primakov as a foreign policy pragmatist, she was highly critical of the new government's economic proposals which included – among other things – plans to print new money, to index wages, to impose price and capital controls and to restore state management of 'parts of the economy'. This was not the way to go. Indeed, she made it abundantly clear that Washington's 'initial reaction to some of the directions' was not 'particularly positive' at all and, if Moscow continued along this particular road, it would raise a major question-mark about the future of the US–Russian relationship. Although the US was keen to maintain the partnership and to 'help Russians help themselves', if the new leadership in Moscow took the country down the path of statism rather than free enterprise, America's ability to support Russia in any way would 'go from being very, very difficult to being absolutely impossible' (Erlanger, 1998).

The view that Russia had reached a cross-roads was stated with equal force by Strobe Talbott – the original architect of American policy. Talbott did his best to defend his original creation. The partnership he argued had been a useful one, and in a short space of time had done much to draw Russia out of its traditional isolation. Russia, moreover, was now playing an increasingly responsible role in a number of major international institutions such as the G8, the Council of Europe and the United Nations. As he observed, Russia had 'gone from being a spoiler to a joiner'. However, there was no hiding the fact that the reform process in Russia had reached an impasse – to such an extent that he argued that Western terms such as 'reform' and the 'market' had gone from 'being part of the vocabulary of triumph and hope, to being, in the ears of many Russians, almost four-letter words'. The situation was thus dire and could become a good deal worse. Nothing could be ruled out. Hence, even though democracy had struck some roots in Russia, it was, in Talbott's opinion, 'too early' to 'proclaim Russian democratisation' to be irreversible; and the 'longer the economic meltdown continued, and the more serious it becomes, the harder it would be for Russia to sustain and consolidate the various institutions and habits of what we call political normalcy'. Furthermore, although Russia had gone a long way to 'joining the European mainstream', there was a very real danger that it could take the wrong turn in the future. Whether it did so would depend on many factors, but the most critical in his view was Russian economic policy. If the country decided to persist with painful reform, then it had a chance of rejoining the international community. If, on the other hand, it began to assert its own economic identity and distance itself from the West, the most likely result would be 'heightened tensions over security and diplomatic issues'. Russia had changed a good deal since the collapse of the USSR in 1991. However, if it formally and finally abandoned Western-style economic reform, then there was a very real chance that the film of history could run backwards. It need not have to happen, but it could (Talbott, 1998).

Conclusion

The crisis of late 1998 was neither the first, nor was it likely to be last in the history of post-Soviet Russia. The result in the short term of a major imbalance in Russia's financial accounts, the events of August were but the most severe expression to date of something far more profound and serious. As observers such as Malia and Friedman correctly noted, the upheavals were not just about the state of Russian banks or the weakness of the ruble as a hard currency, but a symptom of a much deeper malaise. US officials had to agree and, while not drawing the same policy conclusions, did accept that Russia had reached a crossroads. Try as they might to salvage something from the debris, their message seemed to be clear: the reform process in Russia had finally run its course and America had failed in one of its core aims of creating or helping to create a functioning capitalism on the rubble left behind by Soviet communism.

Significantly, however, Albright and Talbott were not yet prepared to give up on Russia altogether, let alone to heed the advice of those who believed that the United States should now start devising an entirely new policy. This they thought was not only unnecessary, but could make things far worse than they already were. Talbott in particular was especially opposed to abandoning Russia. No doubt drawing some lessons from American policy during the cold war – of which he had been highly critical – he firmly believed that, by planning for the worse and isolating Russia, the US could indeed create a worse-case outcome. Moreover, the critics in his opinion did not have an answer about how to manage Russia. The country might not have been *en route* to capitalism, but it still possessed the capacity to disturb the peace and to cause chaos inside and outside of its own borders. Also, one had to deal with the problem, not ignore it. In fact, according to his own logic, the more disturbed Russia became, the more important it was for the United States to remain involved. To abandon the patient now would have been sheer folly – especially as this particular patient had nuclear weapons, continued to be a permanent member of the UN Security Council and occupied the same European space as many of America's closest and most important allies.

The US therefore seemed to be locked into a policy which promised little, but to which there appeared to be no realistic alternative. However, it was not all gloom and doom, and policy-makers could at least console themselves with the fact that even if Russian reform had failed, Russia itself was in such disarray that it simply did not have the capacity to challenge the West (see Chapter 12). As Vaclav Havel rather cynically pointed out, chaos in Russia might have been bad for Russians but for other countries it was perhaps a good thing. As he put it, 'Better an ill Russia than a healthy Soviet Union' (Safire, 1998). Furthermore, although there had been much talk throughout the 1990s about the rise of a new Russian nationalism, the dominant line in Moscow (as opposed to the noisiest) was that there was no longer any point in confrontation with the capitalist world. It was just not in the country's interest (Arbatov, 1994, pp. 55–76). Finally, while most Russians agreed that capitalism was not feasible, few (including Russia's communists) advocated a return to a Soviet-style system (Karatnycky, 1998). This might have been small comfort to US policy-makers as they gazed backwards at their original creation, but it suggested that some form of working relationship – if not partnership – would be possible in the future. This is not exactly what American policy-makers had planned for back in 1992. It certainly represented a lower-level goal than the one the IMF and the White House had in mind when they set out to remake Russia in the wake of the Soviet Union's collapse, but in an imperfect and increasingly unstable world it was perhaps the best they could now hope for.

References

Arbatov A G 1994 Russian National Interest, in Blackwill R D and Karaganov S (eds), *Damage Limitation or Crisis?*, Brasseys, London.

Aslund A 1994 Russia's Success Story, *Foreign Affairs*, Vol. 73 (September–October), p. 5.

Baker J III 1992 *The Future of US Foreign Policy in the Post-Cold War Era*, US Government Printing Office, Washington, DC.

Ball C L 1998 Nattering NATO Negativism? Reasons Why Expansion May Be a Good Thing, *Review of International Studies*. Vol. 24 (January), p. 1.

Bohlen C 1998 Gorbachev's Economists Back at Helm in Russia, *International Herald Tribune*, 16 September.

Brzezinski Z 1994 The Premature Partnership, *Foreign Affairs*, Vol. 73 (March–April), p. 2.

Buerkle T 1994 Trade Accord Widens Russian Access to EU, *International Herald Tribune*, 23 June.

Christopher W 1993 *Securing US Interests While Supporting Russian Reform*, US Department of State Dispatch, 4:13. 29 March.

Clinton W J 1993a *A Strategic Alliance with Russian Reform*, US Department of State Dispatch, 4:14, 5 April.

Clinton W J 1993b *New Democratic Partnership Between the United States and Russia*, US Department of State Dispatch, 4:15, 12 April.

Cohen S 1993 US Policy Towards Post-Communist Russia: Fallacies, Failures, Possibilities, *The Future of US Foreign Policy (Part 1): Regional Issues*, US Government Printing Office, Washington, DC.

Cox M 1994 The Necessary Partnership? The Clinton Presidency and Post-Soviet Russia, *International Affairs*, Vol. 70, No. 4 (October).

Cox M 1995 *US Foreign Policy After the Cold War: Superpower Without a Mission?*, The Royal Institute of International Affairs, London.

Cox M (ed.) 1998 *Rethinking the Soviet Collapse: Sovietology, the Death of Communism and the New Russia*, Pinter, London.

Davis L E 1994 *US Non-Proliferation Policy*, US Government Printing Office, Washington, DC.

Dewar H 1994 Senate backs Talbott for State Department, *Washington Post*, 23 February.

The Economist 1993 Reforming Russia's Economy, 11 December.

The Economist 1997 Russia's Reforms In Trouble, 22 November.

Erlanger S 1998 Economy Shift in Russia, Worries U.S., Albright Says, *The New York Times*, 3 October.

Eyal J 1994 More a Nadir than a Summit, *The Independent*, 7 July.

Financial Times 1994 No Exits on the Road to the Market, 16 May.

Fletcher M 1994 Bush says Clinton has Hurt Image of US Leadership, *The Times*, 29 January.

Friedman G 1998 Russian Economic Failure Invites a New Stalinism, *International Herald Tribune*, 11 September.

Gates R 1992 *Threat Assessment, Military Strategy, and Defense Planning*, Government Printing Office, Washington, DC.

Gordon M R 1994 Perry Says Caution is Vital to Russian Partnership, *The New York Times*, 15 March.

Karaganov S 1994 Russia Finds Independent Foreign Policy, *Financial Times*, 21 March.

Karatnycky A 1998 The Rise of Russia's Third Force – Gorbachevism, *International Herald Tribune*, 15 September.

Kozyrev A 1994 The Lagging Partnership, *Foreign Affairs*, Vol. 73 May–June, p. 3.

Krauthammer C 1994 Honeymoon Over, the Two Powers Go their Own Way, *International Herald Tribune*, 26–27 February.

Lloyd J 1993 Obstacles to Disbursement of Russia Aid Remains, *The Irish Times*, 16 April.

Lloyd J 1998 Yeltsin Leaps Into the Abyss, *The Times*, 24 March.

Malia M 1998 In Russia, the Liberal Western Model Has Failed, *International Herald Tribune*, 5–6 September.

Meek J 1998 Russia Stares Into the Abyss, *The Guardian*, 2 April.

Reddaway P 1994 Visit to a Maelstrom, *The New York Review of Books*, 10 January.

Rutland P 1998 IMF Meeting Weighs Results of Past Seven Years, *Jamestown Foundation Monitor*, 1 December.

Safire W 1998 Primakov is no Short-Termer, *International Herald Tribune*, 18 September.

Talbott S 1994 *America Must Remain Engaged in Russian Reform*, US Department of State Dispatch, 5:5. 31 January.

Talbott S 1998 Dealing With Russia in a Time of Troubles, *The Economist*, 21 November.

Truscott P 1997 *Russia First: Breaking With the West*, I B Tauris, London.

USGPO 1993 *U.S. Nonproliferation Policy*, Washington, DC.

Walker M 1994 Make or Break for Big Daddy, *The Guardian*, 7 January.

The Wall Street Journal Europe 1998 Domino Effect: How a Little Market Like Russia Set Off a Global Chain Reaction, 22 September.

White S 1998 Rethinking the Transition: 1991 and Beyond, in Cox M, *Rethinking the Soviet Collapse: Sovietology, the Death of Communism and the New Russia*, Pinter, London.

Further reading

Cox, M *US Foreign Policy After the Cold War: Superpower Without a Mission?*, RIIA/Pinter, 1995.

Walker M, *Clinton: The President They Deserve,* Vintage London, 1997.

Website: http://www.usia.gov/usis.html

15 The Russian Federation and Central Europe's entry into European institutions

Julie A Lund and Roger E Kanet

Introduction

Since the end of the cold war a major concern of the former communist countries of East–Central and Eastern Europe, including the Russian Federation, has been the search for a new security regime in the region.[1] This regime is generally defined much more broadly than in the past to include domestic stability and economic well-being and the strengthening of economic relationships with the West. However, there is no necessary agreement among the states involved on the nature of that regime or of those relationships, especially between Russia and most of the other states of Central and Eastern Europe. From the very emergence in 1989–91 of the countries of the region from decades of Soviet dominance the new political and economic leaderships made clear their full commitment to major institutional reorganisation, including re-integration into the broader Europe. This was evident in their refusal to consider modifications in the old Soviet-dominated institutions of the Warsaw Pact and the Council for Mutual Economic Assistance. Both organisations, which had formed the institutional base of Soviet dominance in Central and Eastern Europe since the 1950s, died in 1991 for lack of continued support (Birgerson and Kanet, 1995; Kanet and Souders, 1993). That the peoples of the region would look to the West for guidance seemed to be a certainty. In fact, efforts to re-define the identity of the region were already under way that emphasised the historical European orientation and ties of the various cultures and countries (see Alamir and Pradetto, 1998; Millard, 1998). Since the concept of 'the West' has implied development, economic advance, wealth and liberty, it represents the goal to which the peoples of East–Central Europe aspire. However, membership in

---

1 For purposes of this article, 'Central Europe' refers to the Visegrad states: the Czech Republic, Hungary, Poland and Slovenia. Normally Slovakia, the other successor state of Czechoslovakia, would be included in this group. However, since internal political developments in Slovakia precluded its being considered for membership in Western institutions, it is not included in the term. 'Eastern Europe' also includes the Baltic states (Estonia, Latvia, and Lithuania) and the Balkan states (Albania, Bulgaria, Romania, and the successor states of former Yugoslavia, except Slovenia). 'East–Central Europe' is used as a shorthand expression to include all the former communist states of Central and Eastern Europe. The Visegrad states are so called because they met in Visegrad, Hungary, in 1991 to map out a common approach towards foreign and security policy.

СПРАВКА 15.1 **European institutions**

The European Union

The EU now has fifteen members. It began in 1957 as the EEC when the Rome Treaties were signed by six countries. It was always more than just an economic institution. Its political aims were ambitious – to integrate in order to eliminate nationalism and prevent the re-emergence of war in Europe. However, it has been dismissed by many as an economic giant and a political pygmy. It has a population of 372 million (104 million more than the US), and its GDP is $7.4 trillion, almost the same as America's, yet the EU has had difficulties in uniting around common policies. At Maastricht in 1991, the EU made efforts to create a more integrated institution. The most important innovation was the commitment to introduce a single European currency, the euro, by the year 1999. This step has been controversial in Britain and Germany, but it does not appear to be the end of the drive towards closer integration and a possible European supranational state. The EU has become the leading integrationist institution in the world.

West European Union

The WEU was founded in 1954, but was a largely moribund organisation until the 1980s. It has since become more active as many European states sought to create a military arm for the EU. The Maastricht Treaty called for a Common Foreign and Security Policy but the WEU's exact relationship to the EU and NATO has remained controversial. Officially, the WEU is to develop as a defence component of the EU and as the means to strengthen the European pillar of NATO. Its military roles are collective defence, humanitarian and rescue tasks, peacekeeping and peace enforcement. Twenty-eight states participate in the WEU, but there are only 10 full members. There are 10 associate partners from Central and Eastern Europe, the rest are either associate members or observers. The WEU is important because it has a broader remit than NATO, and because France is a full member, but America is not.

Western institutions has also been viewed as a legitimisation of those portions of the leadership that in the past had been part of the internal opposition to the communist system. Moreover, as Michael Radu (1997) has noted, the largely unspoken motive of fear of a revitalised and newly assertive Russia has also played an underlying, but central role in the desire for membership in NATO and, eventually, in the other West European institutions (see Box 15.1). For many states Russia represents a centuries-old threat to national security, even existence. For others the threat may not be so old, but it is viewed as just as serious. Regular assertions by members of the Russian leadership that imply the possibility of territorial revisionism and a re-assertion of Russian great power interests in the area obviously contribute to security concerns among some of Russia's Western neighbours. For example, the then Foreign Minister Yevgeni Primakov, speaking at the OSCE in September 1996, declared that the borders of the new states that have emerged in Central and Eastern Europe 'are neither fixed nor guaranteed by the Helsinki agreements' (see Goble, 1998). Relations with the Baltic states are generally perceived to be the most important touchstone for possible future Russian behaviour elsewhere (see Krickus, 1998; Shtromas, 1997).

Despite the factors that support and encourage the integration of countries of Central and Eastern Europe into Western institutions, it is in no sense assured that the majority of them (particularly the Balkan states and, for different reasons, the Baltics) will be welcomed soon into the security and economic co-operatives of Western Europe. Although Eastern and Western Europe have significant mutual and overlapping interests in seeing integration come to fruition, the process is likely to be filled with obstacles – not the least important of which is the fact that integration into the West's security institutions has been strongly criticised and opposed by the Russian Federation (Kugler with Kozintseva, 1996). The motives for integration are nonetheless powerful. For East–Central Europe integration into West European institutions means that the political, economic, and social changes under way for the past decade in most countries would probably become 'irreversible' – at least, insofar as such change can be made irreversible. In providing a more reliable security construct, integration is seen as providing a means to escape once and for all the Russian sphere of influence and domination (see Millard, 1998, pp. 161–9). Integration implies permanence for the fledgling democracies and infant constitutional arrangements of these still fragile states. Furthermore, by means of integration the East–Central European countries expect that they will finally recover economically from more than 40 years of mismanagement under Soviet-oriented command economies and from the decade of economic uncertainty ushered in by the collapse of the old command structures in virtually all countries (see Table 15.1).

Bringing Eastern and Central Europe under its wing is hardly a gesture of simple benevolence on the part of Western Europe, since incorporating the East into Western institutions represents an historic opportunity to reformulate security measures across much of the continent for once not in the wake of a major war. For Western Europe integration means extending stability eastward, while simultaneously healing the wounds of the post-World War II partitioning of Europe and establishing the basis for security relations in Europe for countries with vital interests in the region (Grabbe and Hughes, 1997). However, it is in the interests not only of the countries of Western Europe to expand stability eastward, but also of the long-term leadership and security interests of the United States. Moving beyond the security sphere, Western Europe also has an interest in East European economic recovery, for it is expected that an expanded economic network will contribute to social and political stability and

Table 15.1 Economic performance of selected communist states in europe

Country	GDP 1995	Real Change 1996	1989= 100	Per capita GDP EU average = 100 1990	1997
		%			
Czech Rep.	5.9	4.1	97.6	62	57
Hungary	1.5	1.3	90.1	37	37
Poland	7.0	6.1	111.9	27	32
Slovakia	6.8	6.8	94.8	47	42
Slovenia	4.1	3.1	98.3	60	57
ECE-5*	5.7	5.3	103.0		
Bulgaria	2.1	−10.9	62.8	29	19
Romania	7.1	4.1	83.9	26	23
Croatia	5.7	3.5	72.5	31	24
Russia	−4.1	−4.9	57.5	39	23
Ukraine	−11.8	−10.0	37.7	29	11

* ECE is East–Central Europe.
Source: Podkaminer L *et al.* 1998 Transition Countries: 1997 External Deficits Lower Than Feared, Stability Again a Priority, *Research Reports: The Vienna Institute for Comparative Economic Studies*, Vol. 243 (February), pp. 2–19

СПРАВКА 15.2 Scepticism about the need for integration

In a recent article, Timothy Garton Ash (1998, p. 65) argues that, by not focusing strongly enough on expanding the 'liberal order', defined as the renunciation of the use of force and the development of non-hegemonic relationships between states, across the remainder of the continent, the members of the European Union – and Germany in particular – are risking the gains of the past half-century. 'To consolidate Europe's liberal order and to spread it across the whole continent is both a more urgent and, in the light of history, a more realistic goal for Europe at the beginning of the twenty-first century than the vain pursuit of unification in a part of it.'

will also lead to economic profitability and growth for Western Europe (Bauer, 1998). For a sceptical view, see Box 15.2.

For both Eastern and Western Europe integration promises many benefits in terms of both security and economic growth. When the door of Soviet institutional control closed in 1989–91, a Western window opened and the countries of East–Central Europe were granted a singular opportunity to re-align themselves economically and politically. Almost immediately trade patterns shifted, so that Russian trade with the former members of the CMEA, including those in Central Europe, fell between 1989 and 1993 from more than 55 per cent of total trade to less than 15 per cent (Birgerson and Kanet, 1995, p. 31). Although integration into Western institutions is not assured for all the countries formerly enmeshed in the sphere of Soviet domination, it is in the interest of both Eastern and Western Europe to overcome any obstacles that could delay or deter the process. However, some aspects of that integration – particularly in the security sphere – have been viewed in Moscow as a serious threat to the legitimate interests of the Russian Federation, as we will discuss further below (see Eisenhower, 1997; Mandelbaum, 1995).

Integration viewed from Central Europe

Ever since institutions such as the European Union (EU), the Organisation for Security and Co-operation in Europe (OSCE), the Western European Union (WEU), NATO and the Council of Europe (see Box 15.3) began to express an interest in extending membership privileges eastward, most of the former

СПРАВКА 15.3   Organisation of Security and Co-operation in Europe (formerly, the Conference on Security and Co-operation in Europe)

The OSCE is a pan-European security organisation with 55 participating states which span the area from Vancouver to Vladivostok. The OSCE sees itself as the primary instrument in Europe for conflict prevention, crisis management and post-conflict rehabilitation. It began after the Helsinki Final Act was signed in 1975 as a series of meetings and conferences to discuss general matters of security, which included trade and human rights, as well as military affairs. It became a more formal organisation after the Paris summit in 1990 and changed its name from CSCE to OSCE. The OSCE has a number of missions currently in Central and Eastern Europe where it is seeking to mediate in conflicts and areas of tension. It also plays an important role in monitoring democracy in those post-communist countries.

Council of Europe

The Council of Europe is a quite separate institution from the EU. It was set up by 10 countries in 1949. Its main roles are the strengthening of democracy, human rights and the rule of law in Europe. It set up the European Court of Human Rights which allows citizens to bring complaints against their own government for judicial consideration. Until the fall of the Berlin Wall, the Council of Europe was only concerned with Western Europe. Since 1989, however, it has seen its role extended to monitoring democratisation in the former communist states of Central and Eastern Europe. In 1989, the Council of Europe had 23 members; it now has 40, including Russia, which joined in 1996, despite some opposition due to its part in the Chechen war.

communist countries of Central and Eastern Europe have been anxious to prove themselves worthy of inclusion and to demonstrate their readiness they have been scurrying to disassociate themselves from the former Soviet Union and its legacies. The major exceptions have been Belarus, which under President Lukashenko has pursued policies that have increasingly alienated the West, Slovakia, where until his electoral defeat in autumn 1998 President Meciar's brand of nationalism took precedence over integration into Europe, and most of the Yugoslav successor states where locally defined animosities underlie policy.

The Central European countries have a vested interest in the security guarantees that entry into Western institutions are expected to provide. By joining security organisations such as NATO and the WEU, the Central European states expect to remove themselves from the Russian sphere of influence and to eliminate the possibility that they will ever fall under foreign domination from the East again. However, as many in Russia and elsewhere have argued most strongly, the expansion of NATO eastward runs the decided risk of alienating Russia and, in effect, contributing to the emergence of structural hostilities that will, in effect, result in a new form of East–West confrontation in Europe – albeit one that is further east geographically than the old cold war line of confrontation (Davydov, 1997; Kugler with Kozintseva, 1996). Joining the collective security systems of Western Europe is a requisite part of realising peace in that region, Central European leaders have argued (see Clemens, 1997, pp. 109–22; Kerremans, 1997). Furthermore, the uncertainty and instability of governance that characterises the Russian Federation could not then threaten the fledgling democracies of Central and Eastern Europe, if security arrangements with the West are devised. Integration will provide Central and Eastern Europe a safe haven under the umbrella of Western security configurations.

A second presumed benefit to be derived from integration is a strengthening of Central and Eastern European constitutional democracies and liberal economies. Making the transition from a communist command economy to a democratic market economy has been and remains an arduous task (Sharman and Kanet, 1998). Consequently, these new systems of governance and trade are fragile and filled with weaknesses. Integration is expected to provide these countries an opportunity to overcome these defects. Most of the aforementioned Western institutions (NATO, EU, WEU) require stable institutions guaranteeing democracy and the protection of human rights and an open economy as preconditions for membership. Once members, the new states will have to continue to pursue market liberalisation, a multi-party system and a streamlined bureaucracy. Thus, through application for membership and through membership itself, Central and East European states will have to make a concerted effort to protect and promote the new political and economic system. Over time, as the new members become further entrenched in the process of integration with the West, democracy and capitalism will become institutionalised. In effect, integration will make the changes of 1989 irreversible.

From an economic point of view integration with the West is very attractive for Central and Eastern Europe. The Soviet-oriented command economies after World War II neglected the economic infrastructure for decades, making those economies virtually non-competitive in the international arena. It is expected that integration with such powerful economic institutions as the European Union would revitalise the economies of the East – in fact, the expansion of economic involvement with the rest of the world during the 1990s has already had a very positive impact on trade relations and competitiveness in a number of the post-communist states. The Central European countries hope to gain equal access to Western markets as well as to enjoy subsidies from Western institutions. These subsidies, combined with structural funds and loans from Western European banks, would allow the East European countries to invest heavily in infrastructure. In addition, many of the regulations of Western European financial institutions would directly benefit the new member states. For instance, the EU mandates that significant socio-economic gaps across Europe be reduced or equalised (Kerremans, 1997, pp. 48–9; Gabrisch, 1997). Clearly, the former communist states, with their low GNP per capita, stand to gain significantly from this policy. New investments throughout the region promise a lifting of the standard of living for all those countries admitted to the European Union. Moreover, the EU has typically awarded financial compensation for each step made by its member countries towards market liberalisation and economic integration; in the past Italy, Greece, Spain and Portugal, for example, have all been the recipients of this type of assistance (Barbour, 1996). If this continues as the policy of the EU, the Central European countries will be doubly benefited: in terms of both financial compensation and direct economic rewards from a liberalised economy. Finally, membership in the EU virtually means by definition having a competitive market economy. The new member states would have to find their niche in the union and exploit that advantage, finally achieving international competitiveness. Without a doubt, the economies of Central and Eastern Europe would be immeasurably improved in the medium and longer term through integration with Western Europe.

West European perspectives

The motives of Western Europe to join forces with the weaker countries and economies of Central and Eastern Europe are less obvious, but equally compelling. Similarly, to the leaders and peoples of Eastern Europe, those in Western Europe have had security concerns regarding their eastern 'borders'. Advancing Western institutional control eastward would mean extending even further the zone of security created after World War II. For decades the institutions of Western Europe were incapable of providing security on Germany's eastern border (see Carr, 1998; Vogel, 1997). Integrating these 'buffer zone' countries between Germany and Russia into the broader Europe would strengthen Western security through domination of the continent – although the 'border problem' will remain, only pushed further to the east. Clearly, and assuming that there exists no guaranteed method of ensuring that conflict with Russia does not emerge, it is in the interest of the West to transfer the possibility of future conflict with Russia from the highly industrialised Germany to the more vulnerable Poland. Thus, the price of inclusion in the Western security order could be quite high for some of the new states – at least in the longer run. Nevertheless, it is a risk that most Central European countries have been willing to shoulder, in order to gain entrance into Western security organs (Larrabee, 1997).

Besides expanded security for the West, integration with the East would bring about more stability for the region. Integrating the countries of Central Europe would help their governments to solidify democratic reforms and reduce the sources and level of internal conflict. This, in turn, would serve the interests of Western Europe, since the types of power struggles, ethnic battles and nationalistic conflicts that might be precluded have a way of spilling over into neighbouring states. Furthermore, such conflicts typify transitional countries. The combination of these two ingredients makes for a volatile Europe. The West cannot afford to neglect the development of these fledgling countries, since the stability of the whole of Europe is at stake. Integration would contribute to a smoother transition process. Indeed, it might help to heal the wounds of the post-World War II partitioning of Europe.

On the surface, it might appear that inviting Central Europe to join existing Western economic institutions would be more a burden than a blessing. The grants, loans and incentives that would have to be offered to the East in order to bring the economies of these countries into some degree of alignment with their Western counterparts would be very significant. However, West European leaders bank on the possibility that, in the long run, integration will be financially rewarding, despite short-run losses. It is hoped that market liberalisation, which is a prerequisite to integration with the EU, will lead to economies of scale and broad economic growth. However, as Gabrisch (1997, p. 586) and other analysts have argued, the experience of other lesser-developed economies entering European integration organisations indicates that great care must be exercised. Economic transfers can, in fact, exert pressures on exchange rates rather than accelerating economic growth.

If the process of EU expansion operates as is expected, the overall budget of the EU will increase, as net contributions will necessarily go up with more members (current EU members are listed in Box 15.4). Integration will mean a more competitive EU economy where trade and industry lead to profitability and growth for all. At least, that is what is expected by leading economists, if everything proceeds as planned. The reality is, however, that there are many steps to be taken by both Western Europe and East European countries before integration is even feasible. Even successful integration of a number of post-communist states into the structures of the European Union will of necessity change and dilute the nature of integration in the organisation – a development that is not necessarily bad for Europe, if the European security zone is effectively pushed eastwards (Kerremans, 1997; Gabrisch, 1997). Beyond that, there are numerous obstacles to successful integration that may prove insurmountable despite the intentions and desires of East and West alike.

Steps to be undertaken by Eastern Europe

The desire to be a member of an organisation such as the European Union, NATO or Western European Union is not sufficient to make it a reality. There

СПРАВКА 15.4   **Members of the EU in 1999**

Founder members of the EU (1957)

1. Belgium
2. France
3. Germany
4. Italy
5. Luxembourg
6. Netherlands

Joined 1973

7. Denmark
8. Ireland
9. United Kingdom

Joined 1981

10. Greece

Joined 1986

11. Portugal
12. Spain

Joined 1995

13. Austria
14. Finland
15. Sweden

are numerous concrete steps to be undertaken first to establish adequate preparation for membership. To join such an organisation several things must happen. First, an invitation for consideration must be extended to the country in question – such as that issued to the Czech Republic, Hungary and Poland by NATO in summer 1997. Then, the country must prove itself suitable for membership by meeting several criteria. These criteria often include political and economic benchmarks that must have been reached by the applicant prior to consideration. Furthermore, the applicant must prove itself capable and willing to adopt the rules and regulations of the institution in question. To join the EU, for example, a country must demonstrate that it possesses and fosters institutions that guarantee democracy, the rule of law, human rights and the protection of minorities. Furthermore, a country must possess a functioning market economy that is able to cope with competitive pressure from within the Union and from outside market forces (Grabbe and Hughes, 1997).

Once it has met the political and economic criteria, the applicant country must demonstrate its ability to take on the obligations of membership. In the case of the European Union, the applicant will have to take on the *acquis communitaire*, an entire body of legal provisions to which the applicants will have to adapt (Glasmacher and Stern, 1996; Kerremans, 1997, p. 45). While reforming internally, they will simultaneously have to take on the Western rules of competition and trade. They will have to meet high technical and environmental standards, despite their relative developmental disadvantage. They will have to strictly adhere to the aims of the Union as a whole when their domestic agendas may call for some other action.

Overall, the standards for admission are high. This is viewed as essential, however, because once the countries become members their responsibilities and burdens will be significant. The new applicants will fail if they cannot be competitive members upon admission. Therefore, they must be scrutinised beforehand to be certain that they can withstand the pressures of membership. A qualitative judgement must be made by the institutions concerning the applicant's readiness. However, it is important to recognise that political and economic readiness are relative. How much crime is permitted in a system that operates under the rule of law? How much corruption is acceptable in a democratic system of governance? How many human rights violations can be tolerated? How does one judge the ability to withstand competitive pressure? These are values to be determined alone by Western institutions and governments. Their selections will undoubtedly be based on a combination of the evidence demonstrated and the political will of the deciding body. It remains to be seen whether the political will to push integration through will result in ignoring the stringent prerequisites. As two analysts of the expansion process have noted, 'It is critical for the rest of Europe as well as the EU that it gets this enlargement right, not only because of the implications for European security and stability, but because the EU will itself be fundamentally changed by it' (Grabbe and Hughes, 1997, p. 6).

The hurdles that Eastern Europe must negotiate to make integration a reality are many and high. Potential members must demonstrate stable democratic political systems and effectively functioning liberal markets a mere decade after the complete desolation of their old systems. Ironically, it is in part the stability of democratic political and free market economic systems that the applicants are seeking through membership. Political and economic reforms in Eastern Europe are likely to continue regardless of an invitation for membership from Western institutions. Nevertheless, integration would help to secure these reforms, to prevent regression and to hasten the entire process. For these reasons, most of the countries of Central and Eastern Europe will continue to strive to meet the demands of the Western institutions.

Steps to be undertaken by Western Europe

Western Europe will be no less challenged by preparations to integrate with the newly independent states than the countries of the East will be by the

СПРАВКА 15.5 Countries seeking EU membership

Currently, in addition to Malta and Cyprus, 10 other countries are being considered for possible future membership of the EU: Bulgaria, the Czech Republic, Estonia, Hungary, Latvia, Lithuania, Poland, Romania, Slovenia and Slovakia. Of this group, the countries currently being given the most serious consideration in economic terms (in a first wave of new admissions) are the Czech Republic, Estonia, Hungary, Poland, Slovakia and Slovenia. However, Slovakia's sporadic commitment to democracy until late 1998 is likely to result in its being left out of the first group. Latvia's and Lithuania's economic progress has been much slower, while both Romania and Bulgaria have faced serious economic and political problems (For a summary of assessments of the likelihood of successful applications see Grabbe and Hughes, 1997, p. 3).

prerequisites for admission. Western Europe must decide both the nature of the new Europe that is in the process of creation as well as means to accomplish the integration of the East into existing and modified European institutions. This includes matters of enlargement, composition, decision-making procedures and a plethora of other incidentals. The Western security and economic institutions were designed for a much smaller membership and with different objectives in mind. European leaders must now figure out the logistics of expanding – potentially by a factor of two, if all potential candidates (see Box 15.5) are eventually admitted. Expansion is not a simple matter of adding more chairs at the negotiating table; it means modifying the entire framework of membership. A larger institution with more members runs the risk of dilution, in effect becoming a weaker entity (Kerremans, 1997, pp. 49–51; Grabbe and Hughes, 1997, pp. 4–5). It also vastly changes the decision-making process. More votes means a different composition of majority and minority. The members of the EU must decide whether all members will have a vote and whether the current weightings will be retained or modified. For that matter, it remains to be decided what kind of participation the new members will have in the overall decision-making process. Increasing the number of member states in these institutions will not only change minority–majority voting patterns but also increase the overall heterogeneity of the body as a whole. This will make reaching a consensus more difficult, and the institution could become ineffectual (see European Commission, 1997a). It will weaken the decision-making ability of the body as a whole, if the diversity of interests is so vast that no decisions are made. It is quite clear that expansion means that all members will lose some of their power – that is, the extent to which an individual actor can influence the policies of the entire system will be reduced. Each new enlargement will result in a further reduction of representation of the larger member states. Western states that originally began the impetus for expansion will find themselves in the minority after integration is complete (Kerremans, 1997).

Strategies will have to be devised to ensure that enlargement does not undermine the leadership and the authority of the major countries of Western Europe. Western institutions must devise a framework for enlargement that deals with the controversial issues of dilution and decision making. The growing complexity of decision-making procedures will complicate especially efforts to develop a common foreign and security policy for the European Union. Until such time as a comprehensive accession strategy that address all of these issues is developed, real integration will remain on the back burner.

Western Europe has as much work in preparation for integration as does Eastern Europe. They must decide complex issues and devise appropriate accession methods before integration can take place. Issues of decision making and control will not be decided overnight and require a great deal of negotiation. So far, the West has lacked the necessary momentum to propel negotiations along as well as a strategic overview of how to proceed.

Obstacles to integration

While it may seem that the entire preceding discussion consisted of a listing of the obstacles to integration, in actuality it was merely a catalogue of tasks to accomplish prior to the eventuality of integration. By contrast, obstacles are reminders of the very real possibility that integration will be stalled at the gate. First, there are economic obstacles for both Eastern and Western Europe. For Central and Eastern Europe developing competitive economies will not be an easy task. Since these countries began trading seriously with the European Union, the trade balance has been increasingly negative. Exports from the East have been limited to a small range of products including steel, coal and agricultural goods (Kerremans, 1997, p. 45; Šurubović, 1998). If the countries of the region continue to emphasise commodity exchange rather than making competitive other portions of their economies, the prospects for their economic growth will remain dim. Once they become members of the EU, they will find it very difficult to withstand competition from the more technologically advanced West. This is inevitable, despite stringent admission standards. The firms of Western Europe are accustomed to international competition and are more productive than their counterparts in the East. While the East has the advantage of less expensive labour, this comparative advantage does not bode well for long-term growth prospects. From a growth standpoint, it is more profitable to sustain capital-intensive sectors rather than labour-intensive ones. Conversely, if the cheap labour available in Eastern Europe succeeds in attracting investment in that area, unemployment in the West could result. With such grim economic prospects on either side, the incentive to integrate is reduced. Unless efforts are made to ensure that the new economies contain a mixture of all sectors – agricultural, industrial and service – neither the East nor the West will be willing to participate in this venture (Kerremans, 1997).

Another economic constraint affecting negotiations for integration is the reported enormous financial contribution the Western countries must be willing to invest in the weaker members of the European Union in order to make integration a success. The socio-economic differences between the East and the West are so vast that major financial efforts will be necessary to reduce the gap. Although some doubt it (see Martin, 1998, p. 111), extending membership could double the amount of money the EU pays for agricultural funds, for example, if the current rules associated with the Common Agricultural Policy (CAP) continue (Bojnec, 1996; Gabrisch, 1997, p. 585). Moreover, the bulk of the contributions to the budget of the EU comes from a mere handful of states. In addition, the structural funds currently allocated to the southern members of the EU would have to be redistributed to the East, since they are in a vastly worse state in terms of infrastructure than are the current southern EU members. As a result, net recipients of funds from the EU would become net contributors, whether or not their own structural adjustments had been successfully completed. In addition, existing net contributors would have to part with even greater sums of money for minimised returns (Kerremans, 1997).

These projections have caused the advocates of the integration movement some pause. The 'big' states of the Union, including Britain and Germany, are being attacked by their own domestic constituencies for taking on what many consider to be an unduly large portion of the financial burden of the European Union. In addition, more money spent does not necessarily correlate with more influence in the institution; as the Union expands, the power of these states is reduced. It is entirely possible that these net contributors will be unwilling to take on greater financial responsibility, and without the funds integration according to the current *acquis communitaire* is not feasible. Furthermore, the southern states of the European Union have voiced objection to possible expansion. They have no desire to become net contributors to the Union and do not want to give up the structural funds and loans they have been enjoying since accession. The financial burden of integrating with the East may prove insurmountable or unconscionable for Western Europe, thus halting the integration process. However, as former Spanish Prime Minister Felipe Gonzalez (1995) has stated: 'Ten years ago, EU leaders would have gladly paid 1 per cent of GDP to knock down the Berlin Wall, end the separation of Europe, get rid of communism and dictatorships and bring about the prospect of a politically united Europe. Now nobody accepts that it may cost even 0.2 per cent more of GDP. Enlargement will cost money, but much less than is said, and much more if spread out over time . . .'.

In terms of political obstacles, procedures related to decision making in an expanded European Union again take the forefront. In all likelihood the new members of the formerly Western institutions will at the outset have little or no voice in the decisions of the body. Integration means transferring precious and newly acquired state sovereignty to supra-national organisations (von Hagen, 1966, pp. 19–20). It is foreseeable that these new and frequently nationalistic governments will be unwilling to pool their authority with other regional leaders. After decades of foreign domination it seems unlikely that they will voluntarily relinquish their sovereignty; yet that is precisely what entry into the institutions of the European Union requires. By contrast, it is equally unlikely that Western Europe, after making an enormous financial contribution to integration, will allow Eastern Europe to dictate the priorities of the organisation. In sum, the issue of decision-making represents potentially the most serious obstacle that has the potential of bringing the movement towards integration to a standstill.

Integration and the Russian factor

Finally, the greatest political obstacle of all to the full integration of the countries of Central and Eastern Europe into European institutions is, and will probably remain, the Russian Federation. Russia has not been invited to join these multilateral organisations, and it is unlikely that the Russians will be offered anything but an advisory role in the West's economic, political and security institutions in the future. Russia's sheer size and conflicting economic and security interests virtually preclude it from becoming a member of major West European or North Atlantic Organisations. Fortunately, full or even associate membership in these institutions is not a priority for Russia (Zagorski, 1997; Wettig, 1998). What poses a special problem for Russia is the fact that several of the former republics of the USSR are considering and being considered for possible future membership. The post-Soviet sphere is an area that Russians define as essential to their national interest. Russia wants to continue to play a predominant role in the region, and the expansion of Western institutions, especially NATO, is perceived as an attempt to reduce their role in the former Soviet sphere and to isolate them from European affairs (Kozhemiakin and Kanet, 1998; Wenger and Perović, 1998).

Russia objects strenuously to the eastward expansion of Western security co-operatives, particularly NATO. In its original formulation NATO was designed to maintain the balance of power with the Soviet Union and later with the Warsaw Pact. However, as the Russians point out, there is no longer a Warsaw Pact. For that matter, there is no communist empire, no Soviet Union, no cold war and no Soviet troops in Europe (Zagorski, 1997, pp. 532–6). According to the Russians the NATO alliance has lost its mission and by all rights should be dismantled, not expanded! It is the Russian position that expansion of NATO will serve to renew cold war tensions. They believe that the accession of East European countries into NATO will result in a relapse into 'bloc mentality'. Furthermore, they take the move as a direct affront against the Commonwealth of Independent States' collective security arrangements and a questioning of the long-term prospects of democracy in Russia (Allison, 1998). If the former republics join NATO, they will have no need for a security system with Russia. Finally, most members of the Russian security establishment are convinced that this alliance, which claims now to be in the business of peacekeeping and preventing spillover conflicts in Europe, really exists for the primary purpose of keeping a watchful eye on Russia – a policy objective, by the way, that is quite strong in those countries that have petitioned for membership (see Geremek, 1993; Blank, 1998). Indeed, a military alliance oriented against them and perched directly on their borders is completely unacceptable to Russia. Despite the strong criticism of NATO expansion that has characterised the policy of the Russian Federation since at least 1993, evidence exists that Russia is both able and willing to live with expansion. The signing of the Russia–NATO Founding

Act in spring 1997 does in fact minimise the negative consequences for Russia of enlarging the alliance and provides mechanisms to keep relations from deteriorating into a new cold war (see Chapter 16 for an opposing view). The agreements have created new mechanisms that permit all of the governments of Europe to participate in establishing a new security mechanism.

Although Russia has not overtly opposed the expansion of economic unions eastward, it does have some reservations about them. Some Russians fear that admitting the countries of Central and Eastern Europe would establish a barrier between Russia and the rest of Europe that could contribute to the long-term isolation of Russia. Economic collaboration with Western institutions such as the European Union is considered to be vital to the economic welfare of the country. Russia fears that expansion could interfere with its plans for a free trade area with the EU. It wants to avoid the possibility of isolation caused by the integration of Central and East European states into the European Union and simultaneously to maintain its economic relationships with the other former Soviet republics.[2]

Thus, Russia takes exception to the eastward expansion of many Western institutions. This presents a serious obstacle to integration for several reasons. Russia remains in a precarious state, a state of flux caused by the collapse of the old Soviet Union and of the political, economic and security institutions that it had created. As many analysts have noted, Russia could eventually emerge as a hostile state (with nuclear weapons). On the other hand, it could become a co-operative partner for the West, which has a direct interest in seeing the latter situation develop – although it must also be prepared to deal with a hostile Russian Federation. In fact, the very movement to expand NATO has had the unfortunate consequence of uniting opposition in Russia against the West, which, in turn, has led to strong criticism in the West of the expansion of NATO (see Davies, 1997). The commitment to expansion in essence has helped Russian communists, nationalists, and other anti-Western factions, because they have had a common enemy (NATO expansion) against which to rally (Zagorski, 1997). Ironically, as some analysts have noted, Western attempts to expand security measures are in fact making the area less stable. However, this argument is at the heart of the disagreement in the West on NATO expansion as it relates to Russia. While there are those who argue that Western, especially US, policy should focus on the successful inclusion of Russia in a larger Europe, others emphasise the importance of containing the possible aggressive tendencies of Russia. They note that evidence is mounting that Russian perceptions of their interests are increasingly at odds with the interests of neighbours and of the United States. American analyst Stephen Blank argues, for example, that 'Russia seeks equality with the United States at the expense of all other states, an exclusive unchallenged sphere in the CIS, and the demilitarisation of Central and Eastern Europe so that the great powers alone could later revise their status. It aspires to revise regional borders and still seeks to assign the Central and East European states, not to mention the CIS, a diminished sovereignty and legitimacy' (Blank, 1998, p. 16).

2 The formal institutional relations that have evolved in recent years between the EU and Russia are complex and based, in part, on a Partnership and Co-operation Agreement concluded in June 1994. For a discussion of these matters see Zagorski (1997, pp. 527–30).

Regardless of the path that Russia ultimately follows, it will always remain an influential power in the European arena. The West cannot completely ignore the wishes of Russia and press on with expansion without responding to Russia's concerns. If Western Europe wants to keep its very large neighbour to the East happy (and preferably democratic), it will have to consider carefully how expansion can be accomplished without antagonising Russia. Advocates of expansion argue not only that Russia is at present in no position to oppose expansion effectively, but that mechanisms – as yet not fully specified – can be established that will make NATO expansion more palatable for the Russians (see Shtromas, 1997).

Making integration happen

While the integration movement faces serious obstacles, it is also filled with potential solutions to those obstacles. To deal with several of the economic and political issues a multi-speed Europe has been proposed. One prototype for the European Union suggests the creation of a European nucleus, or a small group of key members, which direct and re-inforce the integration process. In the beginning the nucleus would consist of Germany, France, Belgium, Netherlands and Luxembourg. This small group would drive the Union, while the newer inductees could strive to 'catch up' (see Kerremans, 1997, pp. 51–2). This proposal deals with both the decision-making issue and the economic disparities among member nations. A second model was proposed by French Prime Minister Eduard Balladur. His idea revolved around a Europe composed of 'three concentric circles' (see Kerremans, 1997, pp. 51–2). Each circle would consist of different institutions of varying strengths, becoming 'weaker' with each surrounding circle. The outermost circle would include the whole of Europe and its institutions. Ideally, these circles would move closer together over time and eventually comprise a strong union of roughly equal states striving towards a common purpose.

Regarding the obstacle of Russia, opposition might be mitigated, even avoided, if Russia is consulted and invited to participate in all the decisions involving expansion. It is a politically sound idea to involve Russia somehow in this network of institutions. Giving Russia some status in Western institutions could in fact promote the development of democracy in Russia.

In spite of all the obstacles to integration, the trend is gaining momentum and moving ahead. The Czech Republic, Hungary and Poland have already joined NATO, and the EU has begun serious discussions with a number of the Central and East European countries concerning membership. The benefits that could potentially be derived through integration have become so compelling among important groups of decision-makers in both Eastern and Western Europe and North America as to obscure its limitations. For Eastern and Central Europe integrating with Western Europe could bring about economic recovery, political stability and peace for the region. For Western Europe integration will obliterate old divides across the continent and bring a pan-European unity unparalleled across the world. However, all of these benefits will depend on successfully integrating the majority of East–Central European states into Western institutions without simultaneously irrevocably alienating Russia.

References

Alamir F M and Pradetto A 1998 Identitätssuche als Movens der Sicherheitspolitik: Die NATO-Osteweiterungsdebatte im Lichte der Hearausbildung neuer Identitäten im postkommunistischen Ostmitteleuropa und in der Allianz, *Osteuropa*, Vol. 48, No. 2, pp. 134–47.

Allison R 1998 The Network of New Security Policy Relations in Eurasia, in Allison R and Bluth C (eds), *Security Dilemmas in Russia and Eurasia*, Royal Institute of International Affairs, London, pp. 12–32.

Ash T G 1998 Europe's Endangered Liberal Order, *Foreign Affairs*, Vol. 77, No. 2, p. 65.

Barbour P (ed.) 1996 *The European Union Handbook*, Fitzroy Dearborn Publishers, Chicago, IL.

Bauer P 1998 Eastward Enlargement – Benefits and Costs of EU Entry for the Transition Countries, *Intereconomics: International Trade and Development*, Vol. 33, No. 1, pp. 11–18.

Birgerson S M and Kanet R E 1995 East–Central Europe and the Russian Federation, *Problems of Post-Communism*, Vol. 42, No. 4, pp. 29–36.

Blank S 1998 Reflections on Russia and NATO Enlargement, *Heritage Lectures*, The Heritage Foundation, 6 April, No. 607, pp. 9–16.

Bojnec Š 1996 Integration of Central Europe in the Common Agricultural Policy of the European Union, *World Economy*, Vol. 19, pp. 447–64.

Carr F 1998 Security Politics in the New Europe, in Carr F (ed.), *Europe: The Cold Divide*, Macmillan, Houndmills, and St Martin's Press, New York, pp. 51–74.

Clemens C (ed.) 1997 *NATO and the Quest for Post-Cold War Security*, Macmillan, London, and St Martin's Press, New York, pp. 109–22.

Davies R T 1997 Remarks to members of the Senior Seminar Alumni Association of the 40th Seminar, National Foreign Affairs Training Center, Arlington, VA, 17 December; *Johnson's Russia List*, No. 2005, 7 January 1998, <davidjohnson@erols.com>.

Davydov Y 1997 Russian Security and East–Central Europe, in Baranovsky V (ed.), *Russia and Europe: The Emerging Security Agenda*, Oxford University Press, New York, pp. 368–88.

Eisenhower S 1997 Russian Perspectives on the Expansion of NATO, in Clemens C (ed.), *NATO and the Quest for Post-Cold War Security*, Macmillan, London, and St Martin's Press, New York, pp. 137–53.

European Commission 1997a *Agenda 2000: The Challenge of Enlargement*, Commission of the European Communities, Brussels.

Gabrisch H 1997 Eastern Enlargement of the European Union: Macroeconomic Effects in New Member States, *Europe–Asia Studies*, Vol. 49, No. 4, pp. 570–2.

Geremek B 1993 Cited in *Washington Post*, 6 September 1993.

Glasmacher V and Stern N 1996 Round Table on Eastwards Enlargement of the EU: Accession, Transition and the Role of IFIs, *Economics of Transition*, Vol. 4, No. 2, pp. 497–502.

Goble P 1998 Playing the Ethnic Card, *RFE/RL Newsline*, Vol. 2, No. 47 (10 March).

Gonzalez F 1995 Interview in the *Financial Times*, 6 December.

Grabbe H and Hughes K 1997 Redefining the European Union: Eastward Enlargement, *Briefing Paper 36*, The Royal Institute of International Affairs, European Programme, May.

von Hagen J 1966 The Political Economy of Eastern Enlargement of the EU, in Ambrus-Lakatos L and Schaffer M E (eds), *Coming to Terms with Accession*, Forum Report of the Economic Policy Initiative No. 2, Institute for EastWest Studies, Warsaw–New York.

Kanet R E and Souders B V 1993 Russia and Her Western Neighbors: Relations Among Equals or a New Form of Hegemony, *Demokratizatsiya: The Journal of Post-Soviet Democratization*, Vol. 1, No. 3, pp. 33–57.

Kerremans B 1997 Eastward Enlargement and the Dilution of the European Union, *Problems of Post-Communism*, Vol. 44, No. 4, pp. 44–54.

Kozhemiakin A Z and Kanet R E 1998 Russia as a Regional Peacekeeper, in Kanet R E (ed.), *Resolving Regional Conflicts*, University of Illinois Press, Champaign, IL, pp. 225–39.

Krickus R J 1998 The Case for Including the Baltics in NATO, *Problems of Post-Communism*, Vol. 45, No. 1, pp. 3–9.

Kugler R L with Kozintseva M V 1996 *Enlarging NATO: The Russian Factor*, Rand, Santa Monica, CA.

Larrabee S F 1997 East Central Europe: Problems, Prospects and Policy Dilemmas, in Clemens C (ed.), *NATO and the Quest for Post-Cold War Security*, Macmillan, London, and St Martin's Press, New York, pp. 87–108.

Mandelbaum M 1995 Preserving the New Peace: The Case Against NATO Expansion, *Foreign Affairs*, Vol. 74, No. 3, pp. 9–13.

Martin R 1998 Financing EU Cohesion Policy in Central and Eastern Europe: A Budgetary Timebomb?, *Intereconomics: Review of International Trade and Development*, Vol. 33, No. 3, pp. 103–11.

Millard F 1998 Eastern Europe and the 'Return to Europe', in Carr F (ed.), *Europe: The Cold Divide*, Macmillan, Houndmills, and St Martin's Press, New York, pp. 137–69.

Podkaminer L, Boss H, Gligorov V, Hunya G and Viclovic H 1998 Transition Countries: 1997 External Deficits Lower Than Feared, Stability Again a Priority, *Research Reports: The Vienna Institute for Comparative Economic Studies*, No. 243 (February), pp. 2, 19.

Radu M 1997 *Agenda 2000*: Why Eastern and Central Europe Look West, *Orbis*, Vol. 41, No. 1, pp. 40–1.

Sharman J C and Kanet R E 1998 The Challenge of Democratic Consolidation in Postcommunist Europe, *International Politics: A Journal of Transnational Issues and Global Politics*, Vol. 35, pp. 333–51.

Shtromas A 1997 To Expand Beyond Enlargement, *Analysis of Current Events*, The Association for the Study of Nationalities, Vol. 9, No. 12, p. 9.

Šurubović A 1998 Die Wirtschaftsbeziehungen Rußlands mit den Ländern Mittel-und Osteuropa 1992–1995, *Berichte des Bundesinstituts für ostwissenschaftliche und internationale Studien*, No. 13.

Vogel H 1997 Opening NATO: A Co-operative Solution for an Ill-Defined Problem?, *Aussenpolitik*, Vol. 49, No. 1, pp. 22–30.

Wenger W and Perović J 1998 Rußlands Sicherheitspolitik vor der Neubestimmung? Die Herausforderung der NATO-Osterweitung, *Osteuropa*, Vol. 48, No. 5, pp. 451–66.

Wettig G 1998 NATO, Russia and European Security after the cold war, *Aktuelle Analysen, Bundesinstitut für ostwissenschaftliche und internationale Studien*, No. 3.

Zagorski A 1997 Russia and European Institutions, in Baranovsky V (ed.), *Russia and Europe: The Emerging Security Agenda*, Oxford University Press, New York.

Further reading

Ambrus-Lakatos A and Schaffer M E (eds) 1996 *Coming to Terms with Accession*, Forum Report of the Economic Policy Initiative 2, Institute for EastWest Studies, Warsaw, New York.

Grabbe H and Hughes K 1997 Redefining the European Union: Eastward Enlargement', *Briefing Paper 36*, The Royal Institute of International Affairs, European Programme, May.

Kerremans B 1997 Eastward Enlargement and the Dilution of the European Union, *Problems of Post-Communism*, Vol. 44, No. 4, pp. 45–54.

Kugler R L, with Kozinseva M V 1996 *Enlarging NATO: The Russian Factor*, Rand, Santa Monica, CA.

See also the websites for the EU, WEU and OSCE respectively:

http.www.europa.eu.int/index-en.htm

http:www.weu.int/

http.www.osce.prag.cz/

Websites for Central and Eastern Europe are:

http.www.centraleurope.com/ and http://www.rferl.org/

16

Russia and NATO enlargement: the case against

Peter Shearman

Introduction

It might not appear obvious why a volume on *Russia After the Cold War* should have a separate chapter which focuses upon the enlargement of a military alliance which does not include the Russian Federation, and hence some preliminary comments are in order. As this chapter will demonstrate on a number of levels Russia is one of the key factors, both in terms of explaining the decision to extend the alliance to East–Central Europe and with regard to the potential consequences of that decision for political developments inside Russia, and in relation to the future prospects for European and wider global security. The enlargement of the North Atlantic Treaty Organisation is widely perceived as being the most significant policy decision in the realm of international security since the end of the cold war, and the main objective of this chapter is to examine how this decision impacts on Russia. The assumption here is that it is necessary to begin with a consideration of Russia when devising any new architecture for European security, for, because of its current socio-economic circumstances, its unfinished post-cold-war post-Soviet search for identity, its geostrategic position straddling Europe and Asia, its unresolved relationship with its nearest neighbours and the uncertainty surrounding its political development, Russia has the greatest potential of any other state in Europe either to enhance or to disrupt the international security environment. Put simply, my proposition is that what happens inside Russia, what kind of post-Soviet political order finally emerges and what kind of relationship Russia forges with its neighbours will be affected in a major way by the enlargement of NATO, and that this in turn will impact on the international security environment. This chapter examines these issues.

Russia has not been ignored in the debate on NATO enlargement. Indeed, Russia has been central to arguments made both by those who favour the enlargement of NATO (as a means of balancing Russian power) and by those who oppose enlargement (fearing it could lead to a new cold war between Russia and the West). It is interesting to note, also, the unusual political coalitions that formed leading up to the US Senate vote in April 1998 to ratify the decision taken at the NATO summit in Madrid in July 1997 offering membership to Hungary, Poland and the Czech Republic. On both sides of the senate vote (80 in favour, 19 against) were to be found liberal democrats and conservative republicans. Former security and defence officials in the United States and the United Kingdom, former American and British ambassadors to the former Soviet Union and the Russian

Federation, and former senior serving officers of the armed forces in both countries have written letters to the press either pushing for enlargement or warning of its dangers. Academic specialists on foreign and security affairs are also divided. Often these different communities have come together in attempts to add collective weight to their individual arguments. As a result some strange alliances have been established. For example, one open letter calling on President Clinton to postpone NATO enlargement included former ambassadors to the Soviet Union (Jack Matlock and Arthur Hartman), President Reagan's chief arms control negotiator (Paul Nitze) and President Carter's Director of the CIA (Admiral Stansfield Turner), along with Professors Richard Pipes (an adviser on Soviet affairs under Reagan), Marshall Shulman and Michael Mandelbaum (*Washington Times*, 27–29 June 1997). Academic journals dealing with international relations have contained articles arguing against (MccGwire, 1998) and in favour of (Ball, 1998) enlargement (see also Chapter 16 for a further discussion of these issues).

   This chapter will attempt to make sense of these controversies with a more specific and critical evaluation of the Russian question than that offered hitherto. Before proceeding, however, it is instructive to note that while there is disagreement among politicians, security officials and international relations specialists, there is no such disagreement regarding NATO enlargement among a group that one would normally associate with deep divisions over fundamental questions such as this. Here I am referring to historians. This is a point made by John Lewis Gaddis, who notes that among his historian colleagues it is difficult to find one who agrees that enlarging NATO is a good idea: 'Indeed, I can recall no other moment when there was less support in our profession for a government policy'. Gaddis goes on to argue that there has been a '. . . striking gap between those who make grand strategy and those who reflect on it' (Gaddis, 1998). Another historian has written of what he calls '. . . one of the most characteristic and eerie phenomena of the late twentieth century', referring here to '. . . the destruction of the past' (Hobsbawn, 1994, p. 3). What Hobsbawn is suggesting is that at the end of the twentieth century people grow up in '. . . a sort of a permanent present lacking any organic relation to the public past of the times they live in' (Hobsbawn, 1994, p. 3). It is perhaps instructive to remind ourselves that foreign intelligence agencies, diplomats and scholars, and in particular the two separate disciplines of International Relations and Soviet Area Studies, all failed to foresee the collapse of communism in Eastern Europe, the demise of the Soviet empire and the end of the cold war. As this chapter will argue this was in part due to a propensity to ignore history and the lessons it tells us. However, it is also to do with the dominance of structural approaches to international politics which ignore or misrepresent the forces of domestic politics. With Soviet studies, where domestic politics were of course the main focus, the problems included ignoring the fact that the USSR was an empire, discounting the politics of identity, taking too much account of who was where in the Kremlin (hence the term 'Kremlinology') and taking insufficient account of social and economic issues (see Shearman, 1999).

   The recent debates and analyses on the question of NATO enlargement and the Russian question also largely ignore history and have a tendency to reify the state, to treat it as a personified rational actor in pursuit of something called (but never adequately defined) the 'national interest'. While this level of analysis can be useful, providing a picture of some of the international systemic and structural constraints in which states operate, it is ultimately deficient for it ignores the forces of domestic politics and underplays the politics of identity. Below, I separate the analysis into three sections, dealing in turn with the reasons for NATO enlargement, the problems inherent in enlargement and a possible solution to these problems. The stress will be upon the Russian question, demonstrating that Russia is both the problem while simultaneously offering a potential solution to issues of European security and the future of NATO.

Why enlarge?

Military alliances (see Box 16.1 for cold war alliances) are not organic outgrowths of international politics. A threat (or perception of threat) has traditionally been required to produce incentives for states to form military alliances. Similar domestic arrangements, levels of economic development, types of government or political economies have not, traditionally, been relevant factors in alliance formation.

With the demise of the Warsaw Pact and the re-unification of Germany the original threat which gave rise to NATO no longer existed. Furthermore, with the consequent break-up of the Soviet Union and the precipitate decline of Russian power there seemed to be no potential threat anywhere on the horizon to the territorial security of NATO member states in Europe. The cold war was over, and (no matter how that war was defined: whatever mix of ideological, socio-economic, or geo-strategic factors is considered) the end result was a massive defeat for the Soviet Union. One could argue that it was defeat in the cold war that finally led to the collapse of the Russian Soviet empire. What was manifestly evident and uncontroversial by the end of 1991 was that NATO's function was over as the threat for which it was created to counter no longer existed. With the end of the cold war there could be no future for NATO, with realists convinced '. . . that no alliance could hold together in the absence of a clear threat' (Gordon, 1997, p. 1). If there was a potential threat to the United States and Europe in the post-cold-war era then possibly the more complex and fluid power transitions taking place in the Asia-Pacific Region offered the greatest challenge.

However, just a few years after the Berlin Wall fell, NATO has not degenerated (as one would have expected according to the theory and practice of alliances), but is expanding. Also, this expansion (as will be shown below in the next section) further complicates the situation in the Asia-Pacific, increasing the prospects for alliances to develop that will be more hostile to the West than that of the Soviet Union in the cold war. Why should a moribund alliance in the absence of a real and present danger begin to grow?

The decision to offer membership in NATO to former Warsaw Pact states was taken without any serious consideration of the strategic logic nor even based upon an open and inclusive debate among interested parties. It was a decision made at the highest level of the US government for reasons more to do with

СПРАВКА 16.1 Cold war alliances: NATO and the Warsaw Pact

NATO
(established 1949)

Belgium

Canada

Denmark

France (left integrated military command in 1966)

West Germany (joined 1955)

Greece (joined 1952)

Iceland

Italy

Luxembourg

Netherlands

Norway

Portugal

Spain (joined 1982)

Turkey (joined 1952)

United Kingdom

United States

The Warsaw Pact
(established 1955. Dissolved 1991)

Albania (left 1968)

Bulgaria

Czechoslovakia

East Germany

Hungary

Poland

Romania

Union of Soviet Socialist Republics

New Members in the first wave of post-cold war enlargement

Czech Republic (joined 1999)

Hungary (joined 1999)

Poland (joined 1999)

domestic electoral politics than it was based upon any careful calculation of strategy or potential military threats. Bill Clinton in his only foreign policy speech during his re-election campaign set the timetable for NATO's expansion, stating that he wanted new members to join the alliance in 1999, 10 years after the Berlin Wall fell and during the fiftieth anniversary of the establishment of the alliance. The key timetable here, arguably, was the forthcoming presidential election in the United States. There is a large constituency (20 million citizens) in the United States with origins in Central and Eastern Europe, spread most heavily in 14 states that together account for a large proportion of electoral votes. Jeremy D. Rosner notes that together these states carry in fact 194 electoral votes, which was more than two-thirds those required for a majority in the presidential election (Rosner, 1997, p. 25). Apparently it was Richard Holbrooke,

СПРАВКА 16.2   Who has pushed the hardest for NATO enlargement?

- The Clinton Administration (in part for electoral politics)
- East Central European leaders (in part due to perceptions of a possible Russian threat)
- NATO itself, for existential reasons: enlarge or risk death

former US ambassador in Bonn, who persuaded Clinton that enlarging the alliance to Central and Eastern Europe was a good idea, stating the case '... in the only language the President really understood: votes' (Haslam, 1998, p. 124).

In addition to enhancing Clinton's re-election bid, NATO enlargement also, clearly, enhances the prospects for US arms manufacturers to increase their profits. This has not been lost on the Russians, who themselves rely upon arms sales for a large proportion of foreign trade. A report in *Izvestiya* noted the lobbying conducted by Boeing and other large corporations in the corridors of Washington which were pushing for NATO enlargement for their own instrumental 'financial interests' (25 March 1998). New members will be obliged to standardise their military equipment with those of existing members, and hence be forced to buy arms that they can ill afford as part of the entry fee, where the only winners '... would be US arms merchants for which enlargement would be the boon of the decade' (Rubinstein, 1998, p. 40). In addition to bureaucratic and other domestic pressures pushing for enlargement of NATO in the United States the bureaucratic structures of the alliance itself would naturally be seeking a new role for NATO to ensure its very survival. As Christopher Bertram has put it, following the collapse of the Soviet bloc NATO has required a new cohesive purpose, hence (in the absence of a clear and present danger) enlargement has become 'existential' for NATO itself (Bertram, 1997). See Box 16.2.

It is understandable why elites in Poland and other former Warsaw Pact states would advocate joining NATO, given the history of their relations with the former Soviet Union. Similarly, one recognises the concerns of those American voters with origins in these states and appreciates why they too would support NATO enlargement. It is all too easy to appreciate the instrumental gains that will accrue to US arms manufactures emanating from this policy. However, the decision to enlarge a military alliance in the absence of an obvious threat should not be made on the basis of short-term electoral gains, emotions or economic profit, yet this is arguably what has occurred. Having set the timetable for enlargement in the midst of an election campaign it became incumbent upon the Clinton Administration (and other NATO members' governments) to present arguments to support this policy. That the policy had not been well thought out is, perhaps, evident in the different and sometimes conflicting arguments offered to justify it. Again this reflects in part the requirements of domestic politics, for what is said in support of the policy differs depending upon which audience is being addressed. Polish voters in the US (and officials representing the Polish state) are told a different story to that offered to Russian state officials. NATO enlargement is at the same time said to deter a resurgence of Russian power while simultaneously facilitating democratic development in the former Soviet bloc. In seeking to placate different groups contradictions abound, both in terms of proposed policy objectives and in terms of the theoretical assumptions upon which the arguments are based. Russia cannot at the same time be deterred by an expanding military alliance while being a 'partner' with it. Realism as the theoretical underpinning for balancing the power of Russia clashes with the neo-liberal assumptions of expanding the democratic security community. Another problem is that the arguments supporting the decision have only come *after* the decision had already been taken in principle. I will turn now to an examination of some of the problems inherent in the enlargement of NATO where the weaknesses of both the realist and neo-liberal arguments will be revealed.

Problems with enlargement

Problems relating to the democratic development thesis

The idea that NATO is a cause for democracy is a new one – one invented as part of the contemporary search for a new mission for the alliance (see Box 16.3). NATO was not originally designed to foster democracy – this was already largely in place in Western Europe when NATO was formed – but to deter the perceived threat from the Soviet Union. The prerequisites for democratic development are linked to social and economic factors, not common membership of military alliances (Shearman, 1996). This was recognised by the United States in the immediate aftermath of the Second World War and was reflected in the Marshall Plan, which provided massive economic assistance to European states to help rebuild their economies. In support of this policy George C. Marshall noted in his famous Harvard Address in June 1947 that the principle problem for European (and global) security was the return of economic health to the region '. . . without which there can be no political stability, no assured peace' (Marshall, 1947, p. 161). The revival of a working economy Marshall argued was necessary '. . . to permit the emergence of political and social conditions in which free institutions can exist' (Marshall, 1947, p. 161). NATO was only born some two years later, as a war-fighting machine to deter external powers from

---

СПРАВКА 16.3   **Some official objectives behind NATO enlargement**

- Helps to spread democracy to East Central Europe
- Ends the artificial division between 'East' and 'West'
- Extends the Euro-Atlantic Security Community
- Deters any future territorial ambitions that might come from Russia
- Maintains a stable balance of power

challenging the territorial status quo in Europe. Why then, some 50 years later, at the end of another war (albeit a 'cold' one) should the United States be arguing that increasing the membership of a military alliance, rather than making provisions for a new Marshall Plan, is the key to fostering democracy?

The theoretical basis rests on the neo-liberal assumption that democracies do not go to war against one another, and hence policies that help expand the zone of democracy increase the prospects for peace (see Russett, 1993). Whatever merits this theory has, and there are a number of problems with it (see, for example, Cohen, 1994), it is inapplicable in this instance. The consolidation of democracy is linked to domestic developments, not common membership of a military alliance. Theories of democracy demonstrate that socio-economic and political factors, political culture and the role of elites are instrumental in developing democracy (Putnam, 1993, pp. 9–11). It is unclear how membership of a military alliance can help to create the economic or political prerequisites for democratic development. Indeed, obliging states suffering from economic dislocation in the midst of an economic transition to the market to increase their defence expenditure is hardly conducive to ensuring the socio-economic conditions necessary for political stability and democracy. It has been pointed out, for example, that, although Belgium and Hungary each have a population of about 10 million, Belgium (a NATO member) spends six times more than Hungary on defence, and as a price of entry to NATO Hungary will need to fill this gap (Clemens, 1997, p. 355).

Insofar as external forces can help internal democratisation a much more sensible strategy for the West would be to employ some form of economic assistance package to help construct the infrastructure for the capitalist market, with the Marshall Plan as a rough model. It is not a military infrastructure (command and control, communications networks, military bases) that is required, but an economic infrastructure (restructured enterprises, legal mechanisms and tax systems). Hence, even within the Visegrad states themselves one can reasonably argue that the costs of NATO enlargement actually undermine rather than reinforce democratic development. However – and this is the crux of my argument here – the main problem relating to the neo-liberal thesis is that enlarging NATO actually threatens the much more tenuous process of democratisation in the Russian Federation.

Why is it that only Hungary, Poland and the Czech Republic (at this first stage of enlargement) are deserving of assistance in this particular manner, and not other states in the region who are also in the process of democratic transition? The argument is apparently that they are the three states furthest along this path! If this is so then surely there is a much stronger case to invite other states that require more help to join the alliance (such as Romania, Slovakia, Slovenia or even Russia, a question I take up in detail below). By extending the alliance to only the three East–Central European states NATO risks undermining the already shaky democracy in Russia, and hence threatening the very stability that the policy is designed to enhance. While there is nothing in democratic theory to support the assumptions of NATO enlargers, there is a great deal of historical (and contemporary empirical) evidence that highlights the dangers that their actions could bring. Russia is clearly the most important state of the former communist bloc, and whatever foreign and security policies Russia pursues will have a fundamental impact on European (and global) security. If there is any credence to the neo-liberal theory it is that established democracies do indeed seem much less likely to fight one another. Hence, given the importance of Russia, and the plight it has been in since the collapse of the Soviet Union in 1991, it is surely in the best interests of NATO member states to give priority to assisting democratic development there. Democratic development in Poland or other former communist states is not dependent upon membership of a military alliance, but on levels of economic growth, and the maturation of civil society linked not to defence policies but to those relating to health, education and welfare. The limited enlargement of NATO agreed to in Madrid could make democratic development even more difficult than it already is.

It has been argued that, even if democracies are less likely to wage war, authoritarian states in the *process of democratisation* are much more likely to go on the war path than even authoritarian states (Mansfield and Snyder, 1995). We know from history that transitions to democracy, especially in states beset with serious economic problems, can be very fragile. This problem is exacerbated in states that have lost wars and/or empires. Hitler and Mussolini gained power through democratic elections. As Robert D. Kaplan has put it 'Democracies do not always make societies more civil – but they do always mercilessly expose the health of the societies in which they operate' (Kaplan, 1997, p. 56). The argument is simple: if the society is not in good health, then democracy will find it difficult to flourish. No one can argue that contemporary Russian society is in good health – rather the Russian Federation demonstrates the classic symptoms conducive to the rise of the far right and fascism (Shearman and Cox, 1998). Since the collapse of the Soviet empire life expectancy in Russia has declined, infant mortality rates have risen, crime has increased and, while a small proportion of the population has become conspicuously rich, a much large proportion lives in poverty. The key to security in Europe lies in dealing with these socio-economic issues, not enlarging a military alliance. If there is any credence to the theory that democracies do not fight each other then the priority should surely be in assisting the development of democracy in the former Soviet bloc's largest and most important state: Russia. The idea that offering membership to East–Central European states is designed to foster democracy will be as difficult to comprehend for NATO military commanders as it is for Russian foreign policy and security elites.

Problems of credibility

By pushing for NATO enlargement the United States is theoretically committing itself to the possibility of serious risks to ensure the territorial integrity of East–Central European states. There is a huge problem of credibility in the idea that the United States, as the strongest member of the alliance, will risk its own security in the event that the Czech Republic or Hungary should be threatened by external forces, a commitment that is enshrined in Article 5 of the NATO Treaty. Part of the agreement made with Russia in Paris in 1997, written into the Founding Act (Box 16.4), states that NATO has 'no desire, no need, nor

СПРАВКА 16.4 **Founding Act on Mutual Relations, Co-operation and Security between NATO and the Russian Federation signed 27 May 1997**

There are four key sections in the Founding Act

1. Section I details the principles on which the NATO–Russia partnership will be based. These include commitments to norms of international behaviour as reflected in the UN Charter and OSCE documents, as well as more explicit commitments such as respecting states' sovereignty, independence and right to choose the means to ensure their security, and the peaceful settlement of disputes.

2. Section II creates a new forum: the NATO–Russia Permanent Joint Council (PJC). This will be the venue for consultations, co-operation and – wherever possible – consensus building between the Alliance and Russia. The PJC will:

   - hold regular consultations on a broad range of political or security-related matters;

   - based on these consultations, develop joint initiatives on which NATO and Russia would agree to speak or act in parallel;

   - once consensus has been reached, make joint decisions, if appropriate, and take joint action on a case-by-case basis.

3. Section III details a broad range of topics on which NATO and Russia can consult and perhaps co-operate, including preventing and settling conflicts, peacekeeping, preventing proliferation of weapons of mass destruction and exchanging information on security and defence policies and forces.

4. Section IV covers military issues. In this section, the members of NATO reiterate their statement of 10 December 1996 that they have no intention, no plan and no reason to deploy nuclear weapons on the territory of new members, nor any need to change any aspect of NATO's nuclear posture or nuclear policy – and do not foresee any future need to do so.

any foreseeable plans' to station new NATO/US forces or nuclear weapons on the territory of the new member states (*Founding Act*, 1997). A NATO guarantee with no US military bases or nuclear weapons deployments to give it real meaning does not provide a concrete deterrent. For alliances to operate effectively a resolute guarantee system is required to secure each member state from any potential attack. US troops stationed on the Western side of the Oder offer a trip-wire and hence a real sense of security for NATO members in Western Europe, something which is missing in the case of the new East–Central European member states. Thus, as in 1939, so in 1999 the Poles and Czechs will have their security guaranteed by scraps of paper with questionable operative

СПРАВКА 16.5   **NACC/EAPC and PfP**

NACC/EAPC

NACC, the North Atlantic Co-operation Council, was succeeded by the Euro-Atlantic Partnership Council in 1997. This is a body with 44 member countries which meets regularly to discuss security issues. Security still includes the more traditional issues, such as the situation in Kosovo and Bosnia, but nowadays the concept has been broadened to also include international terrorism, the environment and the proliferation of weapons of mass destruction.

Source: *NATO Review*, Vol. 3, 1998, p. 3

PfP

The Partnership for Peace programme was set up in 1994. It was an attempt to go beyond discussion to practical security co-operation between the countries of Europe, the former Soviet Union and North America. Each country has a bilateral agreement with NATO so that it can strengthen its relations with the Alliance in accordance with their own interests and capabilities. These individual agreements are co-ordinated through the EAPC. Currently, there are 27 members of the PfP programme: Albania, Armenia, Austria, Azerbaijan, Belarus, Bulgaria, Czech Republic, Estonia, Finland, Georgia, Hungary, Kazakhstan, Kyrgyzstan, Latvia, Lithuania, Malta, Moldova, Poland, Romania, Russia, Slovakia, Slovenia, Sweden, the former Yugoslav Republic of Macedonia, Turkmenistan, Ukraine and Uzbekistan.

Source: *NATO at a Glance*, NATO Office of Informationa and Press, Brussels, 1996, pp. 31–2

use in the event of a real crisis to their territorial integrity. A balance of power and security guarantees are not simply based upon power relativities but also, critically, on a balance of resolve to employ that power when necessary. There needs to be a balance of resolve demonstrating a clear willingness to use power under clear circumstances.

Henry Kissinger is surely correct when he argued that the *manner* in which NATO is expanding is actually undermining its very ability to act (Kissinger, 1997). At the same time that the NATO Council is being expanded it is simultaneously being diluted by competing NATO-plus forums, including Partnerships for Peace, the North Atlantic Co-operation Council (see Box 16.5) and the NATO–Russian Permanent Council, the last of these established as part of the Founding Act. One problem here relates to Russia. There was (and still is) a general consensus in the Russian political establishment that expanding NATO to East–Central European states is a very bad idea, and the argument that Russia has come to accept expansion, signified in the Founding Act, is to misread the situation seriously. The Russian government could not (although it did try to) prevent the alliance from expanding, and the agreement to sign the Founding Act was indicative of getting what was considered the best possible outcome for Russia from what is widely considered to be a generally dangerous and negative process. By definition Russia is left on the outside of what is the single most powerful military alliance in the Euro-Atlantic area, but at least the Founding Act provides Russia with a voice (if not a veto) in NATO's decision-making structure. Rather than providing the basis for ongoing co-operative relations between NATO and Russia, the NATO–Russia Permanent Council could well, in the event of a real security crisis in Europe, act as an institutional device for Russia to try to play off NATO allies against one another. In the event of a crisis the reformed and enlarged NATO risks becoming less cohesive, if not impotent, owing to the new dividing lines it is establishing across Europe which leaves Russia on the outside, while seeking to mollify it by giving it access on the fringes. It is difficult to see how this enhances the credibility of the alliance.

It should also be pointed out in terms of credibility that never has an alliance added to its own strength and resolution in the event of crisis by enlarging to include new members that are 'weak, dependent, resource poor, geographically vulnerable . . . , none of which is in immediate or foreseeable danger of attack by any power' (Rubinstein, 1998, p. 40). NATO has already demonstrated its inability to act decisively and coherently in responding to the war in Bosnia, and it is difficult indeed to see how the proposed limited enlargement can in any way serve to improve the alliance's ability to act more decisively.

Problems relating to the balance of power

For many the concept of the balance of power, commonly associated with realist assumptions of world politics, is a moribund and dangerous concept in the post-cold-war era. Nevertheless, no matter what arguments are put forward in the academic community on this topic, it is still surely true to say that most political leaders and foreign and defence ministry officials across the globe perceive the world in terms of power and influence. After all the (often unstated but implicit) logic of NATO enlargement is linked to ideas relating to the balance of power, threat perceptions and traditional security issues, whether in the corridors of power in Washington or Warsaw. However, whether one considers the balance of power as a useful guide to policy or as an outmoded and dangerous notion that has no relevance in a globalising age in which information technologies and economic issues are paramount, NATO expansion is bad policy in terms of power relations. If the balance of power is a guide to action (based upon the idea of maintaining security through a system of competing alliances) then it is arguably an error of historic proportions to enlarge NATO to include the East–Central European states.

During the course of the present century the United States has three times demonstrated that its fundamental security interests have resided in maintaining a balance of power on the European continent. In two hot wars against Germany and a long cold war against the former Soviet Union the US ensured that no single, hegemonic power could dominate Europe. With the end of the cold war and the collapse of the Soviet Union the balance of power at the century's end is so clearly favourable to the United States that endeavouring to enlarge NATO could actually undermine rather than enhance the US position – at least this is likely given the present limited expansion of the alliance that is planned.

In balance of power terms perhaps a far more dangerous area that requires more attention by the US as the world's primary political, military and economic power is the Asia-Pacific region. It is here that many perceive the continued relevance of realism, for the Asia-Pacific region has a large number of emerging powers with uncertain relations, authoritarian or quasi-democratic forms of government, and numerous unresolved territorial disputes. It is also an area recently beset with economic crises, with a potential for further financial woes. Potential problems include a resurgence of a post-communist nationalist China reasserting itself, challenges to the status quo from Pakistan and India, nuclear proliferation and arms races and conflicts over Taiwan and the two Koreas. Another real potential problem relates to Russia, which straddles Europe and Asia. It is, then, not only a question of the wrong focus, expending energy and money on the Atlantic alliance while giving insufficient attention to China and the Asia-Pacific – but also the unforeseen but possible consequence of an alliance between Russia and China. By pushing NATO further to the East and excluding Russia the outcome could be to push Russia to the East, resulting in a major shift in the global balance of power to the detriment of the Western democracies (Shearman, 1997).

A Russian–Chinese strategic alliance might seem like a far-fetched idea at this juncture in world politics, and most specialists tend to dismiss it as such. However, we should recall that the re-unification of Germany, the collapse of communism and the disintegration of the Soviet Union were all seen as far-fetched ideas even as those events were about to unfold. Although it is indeed the case that Russia and China have seemingly very little in the way of immediate mutual interests that could stimulate an anti-US or anti-NATO military alliance, it is not inconceivable that both China and Russia will in the future have crises in their relationship with the US and the West that could motivate closer strategic ties. NATO will be celebrating its fiftieth anniversary on the eve of the next (scheduled) Russian presidential election, which is the same year that Macau, the last outpost of European imperialism in Asia, reverts once more to China's control. With new members being welcomed into NATO at that time, and the possibility of increasing claims from a more nationalist and assertive Beijing for sovereignty over Taiwan, domestic politics in both Russia and China, stimulated by NATO expansion to the East–Central European states and American support for the government in Taiwan, could well lead to growing anti-Western sentiments in both countries. Increasing levels of Sino-Russian co-operation in the military sphere during recent years could further add to an impetus to forge a closer strategic alliance.

Although at the moment perhaps very unlikely, the prospects for such an alliance should not be dismissed lightly. Gennadi Zyuganov, leader of the Communist Party of the Russian Federation (CPRF), has proposed such an alliance; former Defence Minister Andrei Grachev hinted at the possiblity; Sergei Rogov, head of the Institute for the Study of the USA and Canada in Moscow, sees it as a possible response to NATO enlargement; former Foreign Minister Primakov

СПРАВКА 16.6	**Potential problems with NATO enlargement**

- Could undermine democracy in Russia
- Could draw a new dividing line between 'East' and 'West'
- Could undermine the cohesiveness and credibility of the alliance
- Could strengthen hyper-anti-western nationalism in Russia, stirring militarist ambitions
- Could undermine the balance of power by fostering a Sino-Russian alliance

consistently spoken of the need for Russia to foster a careful 'balance' in its foreign relations between the United States and China (Shearman, 1998). Both Russian and Chinese government leaders have referred often to the need to prevent any single state from gaining hegemony in global politics, specifically calling for co-operation in preventing unipolarity and ensuring that the world remains multipolar. Both sides utilise a similar (realist) discourse in terms of ensuring a balance of power that does not give the US a predominant role. If domestic politics in the United States pushes human rights onto the forefront of the agenda of US policy towards China, then this could lead to increasing domestic pressures on the Chinese authorities to take a hostile approach in dealings with Washington. An alliance between China and Russia is not something that is beyond the realm of possibility, and limited NATO enlargement serves to make it more likely.

As Bruce Russett and Allan Stam remind us, when faced with a potentially hostile alliance, the combined strength of which is equal to, or stronger than, a particular state's own strength, then that state can do one of three things. It can *hide*, withdrawing into 'heavily armed isolation', where nationalist forces gain the upper hand as they seek to construct policies of autarchy rather than being dependent upon potential adversaries for the state's well-being, or it can *bandwagon*, by joining the alliance that would otherwise threaten it, or it can *balance*, by forging a counter-alliance to deter the potential threat (Russett and Stam, 1997). Given the process of globalisation and the integrated nature of the world capitalist economy, autarchy is not a feasible choice for Russia in the current setting as a response to NATO enlargement, so hiding is not an option. Russia has not been invited to join the alliance, and it has been clear during the discussions of NATO enlargement that it would not be offered a place as a full member had it submitted an application, so to bandwagon has not been a real choice. This then leaves balancing as the only available response to NATO's decision to enlarge, and the only realistic partner (in global balance of power terms) for Russia is China. Although this is not a foregone conclusion, in the event of serious crises between Russia and the West this outcome in the long term is not unlikely (Russett and Stam, 1997; Shearman, 1997), and it surely would be the worst possible post-cold war outcome for the United States and other Western democratic states (Potential problems with enlargement are summarised in Box 16.6).

Problems relating to issues of identity

As NATO enlarges to incorporate the Visegrad states, then possibly later the Baltic states, Slovenia and Croatia, it will as a consequence become (or be perceived to have become) more *Western*. Although not wishing to give any credence to Samuel Huntington's 'civilizational thesis'(Huntington, 1996a) – indeed, like most specialists on World Politics I do not find it at all convincing – we should not ignore the saliency of the politics of identity, particularly perhaps in this instance given the complex and turbulent domestic controversies in Russia, going back centuries, concerning Russia's relationship with the West. Russia's political elites have been torn between conceptions of Russia as part of the West or as something unique and different to the West, based upon specific Russian, Slavic features. Here we could also note that each new member of NATO will have a veto over the inclusion of any future new applicants, and hence Czechs could keep out Slovaks, Hungarians could veto Romanians, Croatians, Bosnians, and so forth. As unlikely as this might seem at the time of writing one should not ignore the potency of ethnicity and nationalism since the collapse of communism across the whole of the Euro-Asian landmass. Huntington himself refers to a possible *contraction* of NATO with, for example, Turkey, feeling increasingly isolated and frustrated in having its application to join the European Union constantly dismissed and ultimately deciding to pull out of NATO (Huntington, 1996b, p. 45).

It could be argued (and it is certainly seen this way by many in the Russian Federation) that NATO is setting itself the task of defining Europe's borders, with Russia (and Turkey) being pushed to the margins. Grigori Yavlinsky, leader and presidential hopeful of Yabloko, the party representing the liberal, Western-oriented faction in Russian politics, has recently stated that 'the most important message of NATO expansion for Russians . . . is that the political leaders of Western Europe and the United States do not believe that Russia can become a real western-style democracy' (Yavlinsky, 1998, p. 77). Sergei Rogov has argued that NATO enlargement without Russia is the single most serious danger to international stability, for it seeks to exclude Moscow from the mechanism of decision making on key issues of global security, and to isolate Russia from the West (Rogov, 1997). Sergei Kortunov has similarly argued that the concept of 'universal security' and the end of divisions between 'East' and 'West' would be dealt a deadly blow by NATO enlargement (Kortunov, 1997). During the late-Soviet period Mikhail Gorbachev, as part of the new political thinking in Soviet foreign policy, developed the concept of a 'Common European Home'. The idea here was that security was indivisible and that the iron curtain dividing Europe was anachronistic, the priority in global politics now being the '. . . interests common to all humanity', rather than narrow class-based interests (Gorbachev, 1987). New thinking on foreign relations marked an end to the ideological confrontation between East and West, between communism and capitalism – but more specifically in terms of identity it marked a shift among Russia's political elite towards accepting Russia as part of the 'West'. Although Gorbachev's political rhetoric at this time contained many ideas relating to 'global consciousness' and 'interdependency', in terms of specific identity politics the

Soviet leadership was seeking to reformulate Russia's political and cultural position firmly as part of Europe. The Soviet leadership argued that it was wrong and
dangerous to divide Europe between East and West. As Gorbachev put it, 'Russia's
trade, cultural and political links with other European nations and states have
deep roots in history. We are Europeans. Old Russia was united with Europe by
Christianity . . . The history of Russia is an organic part of the great European
history' (Gorbachev, 1987, p. 191). Later, when Gorbachev reluctantly agreed
to German unification he did so only after receiving an assurance that NATO
would not extend its zone of operations to the East. He stated at that time to
the Bush Administration in the United States that any 'policy of enlarging NATO
will be considered in Russia an attempt to isolate it' (Gorbachev, 1996, p. 675).

Since the break-up of the Communist bloc Poland, Hungary and other
East–Central European states have also been re-defining their identities – seeing
themselves as integral parts of the West and of Europe. By including these
states in the alliance, NATO is drawing new lines, not just in military/territorial
terms relating to the balance of power, but also in terms of identity. A common
European home is indeed being constructed, but without the inclusion of
Russia. Excluded from full participation as an equal member of the key security community in Europe, Russia by definition is left outside, hence giving rise
to sentiments of isolation. NATO enlargement runs the danger of strengthening those hyper-nationalist forces inside Russia that argue that the West is deliberately seeking to weaken Russia, thereby undermining the Westernizing forces
that had sought, during the past decade, to integrate Russia into the European
family of democratic nations. It has already been noted that democratisation as
a process, especially in societies undergoing economic stress, can result in militarism and hyper-nationalism. NATO enlargement simply enhances these
prospects, as a consequence risking the very creation of the security threat that
it is supposedly designed to deter.

In order to understand better contemporary Russian perceptions on the issue
of NATO enlargement it might be useful to engage in a little counterfactual history, and to turn the tables around, re-imagining a different end to the cold
war. Imagine for a moment that the United States and the 'West' had lost the
cold war. Not only did the United States lose the cold war but it emerged in
the post-war period in a state of economic, social and political crisis as it was
forced to re-conceptualise its identity and role in world politics. NATO was dis-
banded, but the Warsaw Pact survived to include Western Germany as part of
a unified German Democratic Republic. In order to gain agreement for the
unification of Germany and its membership of the Warsaw Pact, Gorbachev gave
assurances to the United States that the Soviet Union would not seek to expand
the alliance. However, later, in response to requests to join the alliance from
sovereign independent states both close to the United States (say Cuba and
Mexico) and in Europe (say Italy and France and the United Kingdom),
Gorbachev announces during a Communist Party Congress that the Warsaw Pact
will indeed be enlarged. Gorbachev states that this is in the best interests of international security, and in particular to security in the Western hemisphere, and
especially for the new member countries given their previous difficult relations
with the United States (although this last point is not articulated explicitly). The

United States voices its opposition to Warsaw Pact enlargement, and in order to appease this opposition Gorbachev agrees to sign a Founding Act which give the United States a 'voice', but not a veto, in the security arrangements in Europe and the Americas. It is surely obvious, the Soviets keep on arguing, that enlargement of the Warsaw Pact is actually in the national interests of the United States, and any Americans who might not see this are suffering from misperceptions, but will eventually be persuaded of the logic of the argument.

It is not difficult to imagine the national humiliation in the United States that would have resulted from such a scenario. For example, it would surely have led to an increase in nationalist sentiments, possibly leading to hyper-nationalism and militarism. These domestic forces would play themselves out in elections, and elections to Congress and the White House coinciding with Warsaw Pact official celebrations marking the ascension of new members to the alliance would provide an environment for an American equivalent of Zhirinovosky to compete for the Presidency. This is of course all far fetched, and the Clinton Administration's argument when discussing Russian concerns about NATO enlargement is that these concerns are based upon a misperception that it will be detrimental to Russia's security and its position in Europe. However, the point to be made here is that perceptions are very important. By not giving adequate attention to the perceptions that many Russians have about enlargement NATO runs the risk of a self-fulfilling prophecy by helping to create the very threat that it is designed to deter. The dangers of misperceptions and their consequences in world politics have been amply demonstrated in a number of works, many of them linking misperceptions to the outbreak of war (Jervis, 1976; Stoessinger, 1985).

Conclusion: potential solution to the problems of NATO enlargement

There are other serious problems linked to NATO enlargement, consideration of which space does not allow here (for example, questions relating to cost, see Box 16.7, the states left outside NATO, nuclear proliferation and environmental security). However, when it comes to finding a solution to the potential problems emanating from NATO expansion, there is perhaps only one that would deal with each and all of them together. This solution also requires some imagination and creative thinking, but given that there is no going back on the decision to enlarge it is one that is worthy of consideration. I am referring to Russia itself being invited to join the alliance. The logic of the argument set above is that NATO should not be expanding at all, but given that it is in the process of expanding then it should be further expanded to incorporate Russia. Russia on the outside could give rise to problems relating to democratisation, credibility, the balance of power and cultural conflicts. Russia on the inside could assist the process of democratisation, foster a stable balance of power and expand a zone of peace across Eurasia that would detract from disputes over cultural (or civilisational) identities and provide a credible institutional structure for keeping the peace.

СПРАВКА 16.7   **'The Cost of NATO Expansion? Washington is Aiming Very Low':
Joseph Fitchett**

The United States plans only minimal extra spending when NATO expands into Central Europe – a message that Secretary of State Madeleine Albright will take to Moscow as tangible evidence that enlargement of the alliance poses no security threat to Russia. In its first official cost estimate, the Clinton administration has concluded that plans to take in new members would probably cost the United States only about $150 million to $200 million a year for the next fifteen years.

The low level of financing – 'peanuts' in military spending, a Defense Department official commented – offers the clearest indication yet that NATO's blueprint does not include any significant shift of forces or new military infrastructure on the territory of the main candidates for membership: Poland, Hungary and the Czech Republic. The planned US expenditure implies only modest, gradual improvements in new member states' armed forces, mainly in the form of improved communications so that their command centers, aircraft and ground troops can cooperate effectively with NATO operations. The proposed spending levels appeared to confirm US statements that the alliance does not plan to construct major headquarters or garrisons for allied forces on new member states' territories – investments that would have moved the old NATO front line eastward.

. . . The US figures are an indicator of broad military thinking among Western governments, and they imply an overall outlay by the alliance, including current members and new ones, of roughly $20 billion in the coming decade.

Source: *International Herald Tribune*, Saturday–Sunday 15–16 February 1997, p. 2

With institutional linkages with 'Western' organisations Russia would be encouraged to develop further economic and political pluralism, the market and democracy. On its own, as noted above, being included in a military alliance cannot serve the interests of democracy. However, in Russia's case, being excluded could serve to undermine democratic development. Bringing Russia in would therefore reduce this possibility. With full Russian participation NATO could also develop a more credible and effective organisational structure for dealing with new threats to European security, such as nuclear leakage, terrorism, international drug trafficking, environmental and resource problems, and issues relating to ethnic conflicts. Again, inside the alliance Russia would have a much greater incentive to co-operate in dealing with these and other common threats to international security. In terms of the balance of power limited NATO expansion that excludes Russia is likely to make a potential enemy of Russia, but with Russia included it could expand a zone of peace and a 'security community' which, while balancing the power of any challengers to the status quo (perhaps principally China), actually moves beyond the old outworn ideas of power politics. In the psychological domain including Russia in NATO would strengthen the domestic influence of those pushing for Russia's integration into the 'West' (and again, thereby, assisting democracy). Left on the outside

Russia's hyper-nationalist forces would portray the 'West' as the dangerous 'other', reawakening an anti-West cold war mentality that lurks below the surface of much of Russian society.

There is a number of arguments that one can make against offering membership to Russia. First, some would argue, you simply cannot trust the Russians, especially given the history of relations with its neighbours and tendency towards imperial expansion. Although there are some who (as with France and Britain earlier this century) decry the loss of empire, it is not a realistic possibility that Russia would (or could in present circumstances) try to regain forcefully an extended empire. Also, any influence of those that might wish to would only be enhanced by being excluded from an expanding alliance that was originally designed to counter Soviet power. However, even if there were genuine reasons for mistrust, then this is again an argument to include, and not to exclude, Russia from NATO membership. It was after all because of a mistrust of the Germans after 1945 that West Germany was incorporated into NATO; better to be able to keep check on any resurgent hyper-nationalist forces in German society. The same logic should apply to Russia for those asserting the 'cannot trust the Russians' argument.

Another argument against including Russia in the alliance is that this would certainly upset China. However, why should the West refuse to admit a democratising Russia from joining an expanded democratic security community to appease an authoritarian China? This is a point made by Russett and Stam (1997) who state that Russia would be better to bandwagon with NATO than to hide or balance with China. With Russia left out of NATO then the alliance could make an enemy out of both China and Russia in a counter-alliance that the two states might be encouraged to establish. Again, it would be better to have the Russians in than out.

Incorporating Russia into an expanded NATO would of course bring with it a different set of problems. US leadership would be reduced; there would be possible historically derived disputes between Russia and some of the other new member states; decision-making could be hampered in some cases or agreement and compromise difficult to reach (for example, over conflicts involving the Serbs); then, where do you stop, if Russia is allowed to join? Although I do not have the space to deal with these issues, they are not, in my view, irresolvable, and nor do they represent as serious a problem as that linked to the isolation of Russia that NATO expansion threatens. NATO has an opportunity to transform itself into a new type of security institution which would institutionalise some of the ideas of indivisible security articulated in Gorbachev's new thinking. This is only possible, however, with the inclusion of Russia. With Russia outside the alliance the old, dangerous balance of power mindset will prevail in an era made all the more dangerous by the rising tide of ethnic and cultural cleavages.

References

Ball C 1998 Nattering NATO Negativism? Reasons Why Expansion May be a Good Thing, *Review of International Studies*, Vol. 24, No. 1, pp. 43–67.

Bertram C 1997 Why NATO Must Enlarge, *NATO Review*, March.

Cohen R 1994 Pacific Unions: A Reappraisal of the Theory that 'Democracies do not Go to War with Each Other', *Review of International Studies*, Vol. 20, No. 3, pp. 207–24.

Clemens W C Jr 1997 An Alternative to NATO Expansion, *International Journal*, Spring, pp. 342–65.

Founding Act on Mutual Relations, Co-operation and Security Between NATO and the Russian Federation 1997 United States Information Service, Washington DC.

Gaddis J L 1998 *New York Times*, 27 April.

Gorbachev M 1987 *Perestroika: New Thinking for Our Country and the World*, Collins, London.

Gorbachev M 1996 *Memoirs*, Doubleday, London.

Gordon P H 1997 Introduction, in Gordon P H (ed.), *NATO's Transformation: The Changing Shape of the Atlantic Alliance*, Rowman & Littlefield, London, pp. 1–10.

Haslam J 1998 Russia's Seat at the Table: A Place Denied or a Place Delayed?, *International Affairs*, Vol. 74, No. 1, pp. 119–30.

Hobsbawn E 1994 *Age of Extremes. The Short Twentieth Century, 1914–1991*, Michael Joseph, London.

Huntington S P 1996a *The Clash of Civilizations and the Remaking of World Order*, Simon and Schuster, New York.

Huntington S P 1996b The West Unique, Not Universal, *Foreign Affairs*, Vol. 75, No. 6, pp. 28–46.

Jervis R 1976 *Perception and Misperception in International Politics*, Princeton University Press, Princeton, NJ.

Kaplan R D 1997 Was Democracy Just a Moment?, *The Atlantic Monthly*, Vol. 280, No. 6, pp. 55–80.

Kissinger H 1997 *Washington Post*, 30 March.

Kortunov S 1997 *Nezavisimaya gazeta*, 13 February.

Mansfield E and Snyder J 1995 Democratisation and the Danger of War, *International Security*, Vol. 20, No. 1, pp. 5–37.

Marshall G C 1947 Against Hunger, Poverty, Desperation and Chaos (the Harvard Address), reprinted in *Foreign Affairs*, Vol. 76, No. 3 (1997), pp. 160–1.

MccGwire M 1998 NATO Expansion: 'A Policy Error of Historic Proportions', *Review of International Studies*, Vol. 24, No. 1, pp. 23–42.

Putnam R D 1993 *Making Democracy Work*, Princeton University Press, Princeton, NJ.

Rogov S 1997 *Nezavisimaya gazeta*, 20 March.

Rosner J D 1997 The American Public, Congress and NATO Enlargement, *NATO Review*, Vol. 45, No. 1, pp. 12–14 (Web edition).

Rubinstein A Z 1998 NATO Enlargement vs American Interests, *Orbis*, Winter, pp. 37–48.

Russett B 1993 *Grasping the Democratic Peace: Principles for a Post-Cold War World*, Princeton University Press, Princeton, NJ.

Russett B and Stam A 1997 Russia, NATO, and the Future of US–Chinese Relations, unpublished paper appearing on the world wide web: http://www.fas.org/man/nato/ceern./nato-final_vs.1997htm

Shearman P 1996 Russia and Democracy, *Russian and Euro-Asian Bulletin*, Vol. 5, No. 11, pp. 1–9.

Shearman P 1997 Russia's Push to the East, *Discussion Paper*, Organization Committee for International Symposium on Russia–Japanese Relations, Tokyo.

Shearman P 1999 Russia and NATO Expansion, in Patman R (ed.), *International Security after the Cold War*, Macmillan, London.

Shearman P 1999 The Collapse of Communism in the USSR, the End of the cold war, Nationalism and the State, in Owen S (ed.) *The State and Identity Construction in International Relations*, Macmillan, London.

Shearman P and Cox M 1999 The Russian Far Right, in Hainsworth P (ed.), *The Extreme Right in Europe and the USA*, 2nd edition, Pinter, London.

Stoessinger J G 1985 *Why Nations Go to War*, 4th edition, Macmillan, London.

Yavlinsky G 1998 Russia's Phoney Capitalism, *Foreign Affairs*, Vol. 77, No. 3, pp. 67–79.

Further reading

Patman R (ed.) 1998 *International Security after the Cold War*, Macmillan, London.

Baranovsky V (ed.) 1997 *Russia and Europe: The Emerging Security Agenda*, Oxford University Press, Oxford.

Gordon P H (ed.) 1997 *NATO's Transformation, The Changing Shape of the Atlantic Alliance*, Rowman and Littlefield Publishers, London.

The NATO website is: http//www.nato.int/

17

Russia's relations with China and Japan: the balance of power in the Asia-Pacific region

Andy Patmore

Introduction: the historical background

At the beginning of a new millennium Russia has an old problem: how to translate its potential into performance in the Asia-Pacific region (see Figure 17.1) in order to help to create a secure environment for itself, and to maximize the economic opportunities that a co-operative international environment could provide for a country desperately needing finance, technology, trade and jobs. In order to bring this necessary external and internal change to fruition Russia will need to pay great attention to its relations with both China and Japan, the most important and powerful neighbours in North-East Asia, and to the way the sole superpower, the United States, interacts with the politics of the region. The weight of these nations is likely to be the decisive core of the Asia-Pacific in the future.

Unfortunately for Russia, its relations with China and Japan over the past 100 years or so have rarely been good. This has not been exclusively the fault of Russian and Soviet policy during that time, although their contributions have been weighty, but reflects the structure of international and regional politics as well. It is worth considering the baggage of history in order to explain the reasons for some of Russia's difficulties in dealing with the present, and the wariness of neighbours such as China and Japan in North-East Asia. We also need to consider whether the structure of international relations has changed and is likely to provide an environment conducive to peace and prosperity.

Spheres of influence

The second half of the nineteenth century saw the interests of Russia, China and Japan come into conflict in North-East Asia. Up until this time Russia had been expanding across northern Asia for centuries, the Chinese empire had entered a period of decline and Japan had been operating a self-imposed policy in isolation for two centuries. The international politics of that time were characterized by imperialism and by the perceived need for control of territory for reasons of both military strategy and economic exploitation. Where control

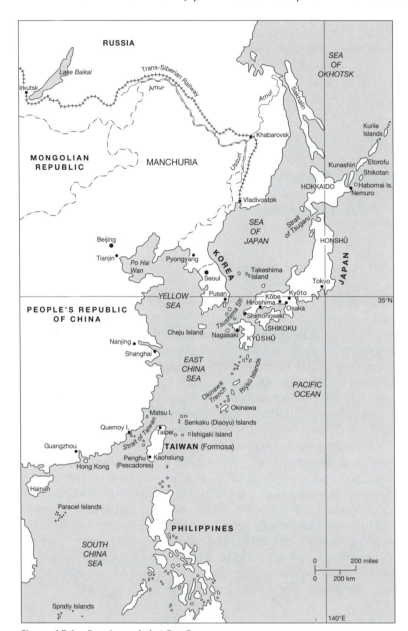

Figure 17.1   Russia and the Far East

Source: W. Mendl, *Japan's Asia Policy, Routledge*, London, 1995, p. xvi, who sourced it from *Issues in Japan's China Policy*, Macmillan for the Royal Institute of International Affairs, 1978, London, and who reproduced it with minor alterations by permission of The Royal Institute of International Affairs and Macmillan Press Limited

was not direct, spheres of influence could be constructed to protect against potentially hostile competitors and to promote one's own interests against such competitors. The idea of a crude balance of power lay behind this state of affairs, as did a sense of nationalism, the idea being that war was a result of clashes of interests and nations, with the stronger taking the prize. Russia and Japan joined the European imperial powers in looking for economic advantage in a declining Chinese empire. The problem was that Russia and Japan were geographically close to each other and to China in North-East Asia, and problems of security between them rose from the late nineteenth century onwards. This became very much the case after Japan defeated China in 1894–95 and began to assert its influence in Korea and Manchuria. This expansion of Japanese authority was seen as a threat to Russian interests in the Far East and led on to the Russo-Japanese War of 1904–5 which brought defeat for Russia, and a realisation of the power of Japan in regional terms, along with a sense of vulnerability on the part of Russia.

At this time of Japanese expansion the idea of balancing power by forming closer relations with China came to nothing for Russia because of the generalised scramble for concessions in the decaying Chinese Empire by the colonial powers. Japan then used the preoccupation of the European powers with the First World War to pressure China for even more commercial and territorial concessions, while Russia imploded in the 1917 Bolshevik Revolution. This introduced a further element of conflict into Russia's relations with the region, as communist ideology was rapidly identified as a potential threat by imperial Japan and the nations of Europe and the United States. From 1918 to 1922 Japan had large-scale troop contingents involved in fighting in the Soviet Far East, which brought home to the new communist regime just how great a security problem they had in North-East Asia, and the lengths to which Japan was prepared to go. At this time Soviet interest in China's fledgling communist movement began to increase.

The period between the First and Second World Wars was characterised by increasing Japanese pressure on China and the increasing response of China's Nationalists under Chiang Kai Shek. This can be seen in the Manchurian Incident of 1931 and the outbreak of more general war in 1937. During this period the Soviet Union was internally preoccupied as Stalin concentrated on 'socialism in one country' and on European affairs where the rise of Hitler took priority. This is shown by the Soviet–Japanese Non-Aggression Pact of April 1941 which allowed Stalin to focus on the threat from the West and the Japanese to nullify the threat to the North while turning south to attack European colonialists in Asia and the US at Pearl Harbour (see Box 17.1). Meanwhile the Soviet Union tried to use its influence in China to bring the communists and nationalists together to combat Japanese influence, not often to great effect.

The Second World War and its outcome changed the face of the Asia-Pacific region. Removed was Japan's militarised attempt to dominate East and South-East Asia and fatally wounded were the colonial powers of Europe, their credibility destroyed by Japan's wartime successes. The great beneficiary of the vacuum of power, so blindingly obvious after the dropping of the atom bombs on Hiroshima and Nagasaki, was the United States, the only nation with increased

СПРАВКА 17.1   Soviet and Japanese relations in the inter-war period

The armed forces of the Soviet Union and Japan were involved in clashes along the borders of Manchuria in northern China, on the Korean–Soviet border, and on the Mongolian–Soviet border, between 1937 and 1939. The first clash, instigated by the Japanese army, is thought to have been to test Soviet resolve as Japan prepared for large-scale operations to the south in China in 1937. The larger operations at Changkufeng in 1938 and at Nomonhan in 1939, which resulted in defeat for the Japanese forces, may well have influenced Japanese leaders to think in terms of strategic defence in North-East Asia, while attacking to the south. This policy developed so that by April 1941, Japan and the Soviet Union signed a Non-Aggression Pact, while in December 1941 Japan attacked the United States at Pearl Harbor and in the Philippines, and the forces of the European powers across South-East Asia.

СПРАВКА 17.2   Japan and the USSR in World War II

The Soviet Union declared war on Japan on 8 August 1945. This has often been presented as 'a stab in the back' in the Japanese literature, as the Japanese were clearly on the brink of defeat, and also as a violation of the 1941 Non-Aggression Pact. In essence, Soviet actions were perceived as opportunist in wanting to share in the spoils of Allied victory in the Far East, a theatre in which they had not been actively involved.

Adding to this resentment was the fact that Soviet forces took prisoner over 600 000 Japanese, military personnel and civilians, as they invaded Manchuria, Korea and the Kurile Islands. Transported to Siberian labour camps, perhaps 100 000 died. Many survivors were not returned to Japan until the formal re-opening of diplomatic channels between Moscow and Tokyo in 1956.

military, political and economic power and a global reach. Across the Eurasian continent the military power of the Soviet Union also affected the balance of power. As agreed at the Yalta Conference in February 1945 the Soviet Union joined the war against Japan in August that year, a week before Japan's surrender. This created more resentment in Japan than the defeat orchestrated by the Americans. No doubt the cynical impression given by late Soviet entry against Japan caused this, along with the taking of hundreds of thousands of prisoners of war, and the seizure of the Kurile Islands, this last having been agreed at Yalta (see Box 17.2).

Cold war

At this stage of history we can see that Russo/Soviet–Japanese relations had been basically hostile and uncomfortable, while Russo/Soviet policy towards China had been partly a function of that hostility towards Japan's attempt to dominate. Soviet support for the Chinese Communists was often less than one would expect for ideological friends as Stalin had to take into consideration the US support for the Chinese Nationalists.

With the development of the cold war in Asia in the late 1940s we see that the competitive relations of the Soviet Union, Japan and China were for a time subsumed by the growth of a global confrontation between the US and the Soviet Union which combined strategic and ideological pillars and pressurized lesser states into following the lead of the two superpowers. This was true of Japan, which was turned into an ally of the United States linked to it by a security treaty and US bases in Japan, and of China whose Communist Leader Mao Zedong signed the Sino-Soviet Treaty of Friendship and appeared to accept Moscow's lead following Mao's victory in the Chinese civil war in 1949.

The Korean War (1950–53) indicated that North-East Asia was a strategically important area in the cold war just as it had been in the previous era. The security of the superpowers as well as China and Japan were all involved in this buffer zone, and the continued division of the peninsula confirmed the stand-off between rival camps at the height of the cold war. With the advantage of hindsight we can see that this was the high water-mark of the cold war as a fiercely polarised system of international relations. Japan began to carve itself a new future by concentrating on economic development under an American secur-ity umbrella which allowed for Japan to keep its constitutional commitment not to employ force in settling disputes. China, increasingly under Mao Zedong's leadership, began to question Soviet leadership of world communism until a split between the two nations over ideology and national interests became clearly visible in the 1960s. These developments taken together meant that the strength of both Japan and China had to be taken into consideration by the superpowers in Asia, and for the Soviet Union these developments were most unwelcome. Not only did Japan remain within the US orbit but its growing wealth allowed it to play a greater role in the economic developments of the Asia-Pacific region. As for China, the disputes over ideology, historic border delineations and atti-tudes towards the West brought about a new security concern along the Sino-Soviet border, and reinforced an older Russian/Soviet fear of encirclement in both east and west. So hostile did the relationship become with the outbreak of fighting on the border in 1969, that China turned to the US in order to balance against the Soviets, as is shown by the Nixon–Mao summit of February 1972. This accelerated the long-desired Sino-Japanese process of normalisation consummated in a treaty between these old rivals in 1978, and led to the general polarisation of the Asia-Pacific region against the Soviet Union and its perceived clients in Vietnam and North Korea.

This general posture in the region remained true until the end of the cold war and was re-inforced by the trend towards economic development across many of the states of East Asia. It was further bolstered by the perception that the

Soviet Union had little to offer the region in economic terms in the 1970s and 1980s as its own economy performed poorly and by the perception that the only field in which the Soviets could compete was the military one. Therefore, a common priority for China, Japan, the US and much of the region was to exclude the Soviet Union as far as possible from the politics of the region.

In a very real sense the Soviet Union, despite its vast military power that had continued to build as part of the cold war competition with the US, and then China, was in a worse position than Russia had been in the nineteenth century. All around its borders were states hostile to it, or afraid of it, and in the Asian region this was compounded by the fact that it was excluded from the economic opportunities that were becoming apparent. Its ideology was, furthermore, becoming viewed as irrelevant to the futures of the politically different states that began to talk about the possibilities, both political and economic, of a more co-operatively based Asia-Pacific region from the early 1980s onward.

The international politics of North-East Asia in the 1990s

It would be naive to assume that with the end of the cold war everything changed. For example, it is possible to suggest that the idea of a general balance of power still exists, and that behaviour among the core powers in the region, China, Japan, Russia, the US, indicates this. Is the territorial imperative of earlier eras over? It may well be less generally applicable in an expansionist sense, now that global finance, technology and trade are such vital components of power. However, territorial issues still remain to be solved. Economic matters have increased in importance as growth and social improvement are legitimising factors for governments irrespective of political coloration. In this environment foreign policy needs to create a secure environment in order that the economic imperative can be worked upon. It is here that foreign and domestic policies are part of the same continuum. Do the international relations of the Asia-Pacific conform to this picture in the modern era?

The transformation in Soviet foreign policy thinking begun by Gorbachev in the mid-1980s, and responded to in time by both China and Japan, was originally intended to revitalise the Soviet position in international affairs, and although the Soviet Union itself passed from the scene in 1991, this transformation set the scene for later developments.

Sino-Soviet normalisation

Gorbachev began by addressing the most pressing problem in Asia, namely relations with China, in a speech in Vladivostok in July 1986. He began to address several security issues that had bedevilled relations for some time, including proposals for negotiating an end to the Afghan conflict, a troop withdrawal from Mongolia, a reduction of troops on the Sino-Soviet border and recognition of the problems in Chinese relations with the Soviet client in Vietnam (Garthoff, 1994, p. 652). The selection of China as the main target for an initial improvement in relations was influenced by the counter-productive policies of previous Soviet administrations which had alienated China (Kimura, 1987). The concessions Gorbachev hinted at indicated a willingness to see security matters as more than a zero-sum game, which would mean a recognition that China had important interests. In addition, the fact that China had, since Deng Xiaoping's policy of modernising the economy began in 1978, shown dramatic economic growth in a communist country was of interest. Not least, any improvement in relations would mean that Japan and the US would have to reassess their hostility to the Soviets in Asia to take account of any improvement in Sino-Soviet relations.

Writing in 1988 Japanese analyst Tsuyoshi Hasegawa suggested, 'It is hard to believe, therefore, that Gorbachev's objective is to establish a Sino-Soviet alliance that will draw China away from the Western orbit into the Soviet sphere of influence. What he can realistically aim to accomplish is to restore normal neighbourly relations, reduce bilateral tensions, and draw Beijing away from the anti-Soviet entente formed in the late 1970s . . . I would suggest that Sino-Soviet rapprochement has already gone far enough to change the dynamics of international relations in Asia' (Hasegawa, 1988). This was proved accurate with the normalisation of relations between the Soviet Union and China in May 1989 on the occasion of Gorbachev's visit to Deng Xiaoping during the upheavals in Beijing that culminated in the Tiananmen Square massacre. Hasegawa's assessment could also be used to cover the general development of Russian relations with China in the 1990s, as we shall see.

Meanwhile the prominence of China in regional affairs, already growing through its increasing economic interdependence with Japan and the US, received a great boost from the normalisation process with the Soviets as a strategic threat was greatly ameliorated. Additionally, it meant that previously conflicting security concerns over other regional issues, such as the competition for influence in divided Korea, or in Indochina, could be addressed in a less intense fashion than had been possible during the cold war.

In addition to this the American reaction to Sino-Soviet normalisation was relatively relaxed, partly because of the ongoing superpower detente that indicated the seriousness of Gorbachev's foreign policy reassessment, and partly because it was realised that China would still need American and Japanese involvement in its modernisation process. Therefore the Bush administration refused to isolate China after the human rights abuses of Tiananmen, and balanced sanctions with secret discussions to preserve the US relationship with China (Foot, 1997, p. 245). Again, the presumption here was that both sides gained from their relationship, and both were now operating in a system where mutually improving relationships could be achieved as the rigidities of the cold war began to dissolve. The trick would be not to move back to the competing system of powers in Asia that operated before the cold war.

Gradual improvement, historical impediments with Japan

The slowest to respond to Gorbachev's initiatives and the consequent changes in the strategic environment in the region was Japan. Several reasons contributed

СПРАВКА 17.3   **The Kurile Islands dispute**

The Kuriles are made up of four islands which Moscow seized from Japan as part of the war-time Yalta agreement with the US and Great Britain. The islands served as an important military and naval base in the Pacific and were economically important for fishing and minerals. Since Japan never signed the Yalta agreement, the Soviet occupation of the islands was always perceived in Tokyo to be illegal.

When Gorbachev came to power in 1985, he indicated a willingness to break the diplomatic log-jam which had soured Russian–Japanese relations for so long. He seemed ready to revive a plan first discussed by Khrushchev in the 1950s which involved Moscow giving back two of the islands – Shikotan and the Habomai archipelago. However, Tokyo wanted all four islands back and initially rejected the offer. By the time that Tokyo had reconsidered, Gorbachev (and later Yeltsin) felt constrained from following through on the plan owing to the rise of nationalism in Russia.

to this relative immobility. Despite Gorbachev's recognition of Japan's economic power in the Vladivostok speech and more emphatically at Krasnoyarsk in 1988, several factors impeded progress. Firstly, there was Japan's alliance with the United States, which had defined Japan's security policy for the whole of the cold war. This alliance had been predicated upon a Soviet threat, which in terms of weaponry and proximity the Japanese still perceived as existing (Defence of Japan, 1989, p. 3). Japanese politicians were much slower to accept that Gorbachev represented serious change because they worried that such an admission could remove the main rationale behind the security alliance with the US. This was then seen as leading on to the possible remilitarisation of Japan and the likelihood of increasing competition with a suspicious China, holding a strong memory of Japanese militarism in the period up to 1945, and with the Soviet Union itself, also possessed of a strong historical memory of problems with Japan.

The US alliance was also seen as the cornerstone of Japan's economic success during the cold war, as American markets were open, and American involvement in Asia was seen as providing the security influence needed to ensure a stable regional environment where Japan and other indigenous states could continue to achieve economic benefit.

Finally, there was the bilateral issue of the 'northern territories', or Kurile Islands, which had been taken by the Soviets at the end of World War II (Box 17.3). This issue had become a particular favourite of the domestic right-wing in Japan, with megaphone-laden trucks driven by members of gangster organisations daily driving through Tokyo to bellow abuse outside the Soviet Embassy. This was quite amusing for passers-by, but less so for Japanese domestic politics where the links between these gangsters and the ruling Liberal Democratic Party were widely assumed. The lock that the LDP had on electoral politics until 1993 precluded any Japanese concessions on the idea of sovereignty over the Kurile Islands and meant that Gorbachev would have to come up with a gift to Japan of the islands in order to appease the Japanese governments.

By the time the Japanese governments came around to accepting that Gorbachev was interested in moving the agenda forward, the Soviet leader was coming under fierce domestic pressure from hardliners and resurgent nationalists who felt that concessions by the Soviet Union to all and sundry were going too far. Gorbachev's strength was waning domestically and his prestige would have needed to be at its height in order to concede sovereignty in this long-running territorial dispute. As the Japanese were not willing to provide aid and investment in the Soviet Far East without a settlement of the territorial issue, it appeared that this cold war legacy remained in place. Japan's belated offers of a staged reversion on sovereignty, a softening of its position, in early 1991 came too late to produce results at the time of Gorbachev's visit to Tokyo in April that year, the first by a Soviet leader (Saito, 1993, pp. 287–8).

Apart from recognising the territorial problem, Gorbachev could give no commitments to Japan on the islands and the sense of let-down in Tokyo was palpable (*The Japan Economic Review*, 15 May 1991, p. 2). It was agreed to try to accelerate efforts towards a formal peace treaty, something held in abeyance by the cold war, and to continue consultations, but the relations between Moscow and Tokyo were clearly not responding in the same way that other bilateral relationships were.

As Gorbachev's position crumbled along with the Soviet Union itself, Japan began to place its hopes for a resolution of the territorial issue on Boris Yeltsin who had been associated with some apparently more liberal views on the transfer of sovereignty over the Kurile Islands. After initial optimism, however, the cancellation of Yeltsin's visit to Japan in September 1992 showed that the new Russian president was subject to the same conservative and nationalist forces at home which equated territory with status and 'face' in international affairs. As a result, Russo-Japanese relations remained cool, and this influenced Japanese decisions concerning investment and aid and dampened enthusiasm for accepting the new Russia as a full participant in the affairs of the Asia-Pacific region. Tokyo had too much at stake in its long-standing relationship with the US, in its attempts to overcome the burdens of history by being a significant contributor to the economic growth of China, and in its role as economic and diplomatic partner for the rest of the increasingly prosperous Asia-Pacific region, to concentrate on the dubious benefits that Russia might provide. With the cold war clearly over and the relations of the major states with interests in the region improving in varying degrees, one observer described North-East Asia as looking 'like a zone of rival great powers with cross-cutting levels of co-operation and conflict' (Segal, 1991, p. 760).

Competition and co-operation

This was clearly different from the ideological and strategic dividing lines that had characterised the cold war, although some of the problems of that era remained to be solved. Did this represent a return to the late nineteenth century and early twentieth-century system of balance of power in a region where concentration on territorial issues and spheres of influence, and resultant war, predominated? The answer to this question was a fairly clear, no. Although this period in the early 1990s was one of uncertainty in a changed and changing environment, all the participants in the region were aware of their own vulnerabilities both domestic and international, and of their strengths and the strengths of others. They also appeared to be aware of potential problem areas between them, and because the overwhelming sense of threat had been removed as the cold war wound down, a more flexible political and diplomatic environment was made possible. This would be consistent with the idea of a zone of rival, but not necessarily hostile, powers and a mixture of conflict and co-operation between them. A period of transition then, with a theme of both competitive and co-operative coexistence running through it, is a realistic way of looking at the current affairs of the region. Let us consider the two elements that made this a period of transition and the factors which constrained the major states in the region both domestic and international, before moving on to recent developments and some prospects for the future.

The domestic economic and political weaknesses of Russia under Yeltsin have been described elsewhere in this volume. This situation has remained a factor until the present day and has undercut the legitimacy of the government in Russia in as much as the people, broadly speaking, see it as incompetent and corrupt. The weak economic base, which still offers overseas customers little except raw materials, and the overseas investor little except great difficulties, is exposing the weakness of the free market strategy as applied to Russia. Given this, it has been difficult for Russia to interest other nations in supplying the kind of investment needed to develop the infrastructure of a modern state. Something of a vicious circle operates here; no investment, no infrastructure, no infrastructure, no involvement. When corruption is added, the mix is quite unattractive.

This, and the decaying utility of much of the Russian armed forces, would suggest that Moscow would concentrate on economics (see Box 17.4) and be unlikely to become involved in hostilities with powerful, or better-armed, neighbours. The factor which runs against this acceptance of a limited foreign policy agenda is the rise of nationalist thinking, combined with a resentment about the decline that the Soviet Union/Russia has experienced. So while Russia is not in a position to exploit others in the region, it would be as well for other states to limit the concessions they expect to see Russia make. Certainly, Yeltsin was unwilling to concede to Japanese pressure over the Kuriles when his summit in Tokyo took place in October 1993, because of domestic nationalist opposition. The relative weakness of Russia, however, suggests that it will utilise whatever political, diplomatic and military strategies it can in order to try to rebuild its position as a power that others in the Asia-Pacific take seriously again (Miller, 1995, p. 152).

For Japan, the 1990s have been a shock (Smith, 1998, p. 127). It has been described as a country 'rocked loose from its moorings'. This is true to a certain extent in both its domestic and external affairs. As the 1990s progressed it became clear that Japan was experiencing its worst economic slowdown and

СПРАВКА 17.4	**The prospects of Russian economic integration in the Asia-Pacific region**

Interest in Russian resources, particularly oil and natural gas reserves, is growing once again. States in the Asia-Pacific region would like to diversify their sources of energy, which are seen as vulnerable to the instability in the Middle East. As the states of the region are likely to need access to more energy sources in the longer term, future investment in, and development of, Russian natural resources is a strong possibility. The presence of oil and gas in Sakhalin and in various locations across Siberia could lead to pipelines connecting to China, Korea, Japan and beyond. The processes of economic integration beloved of global capital would be pushed forward, bringing Russia much closer to the heart of Asia-Pacific affairs. Internal stability in Russia and outside investment would have to combine, something not yet achieved on a large scale.

recession since the immediate post-war period. As this followed the unprecedented prosperity of the 1980s and Japan's achievement of economic superpower status and the growth of confidence that went with it, Japanese society began to question, albeit hesitantly, the political relationships that had underpinned the country's success since the Second World War.

In the firing line were the leaders of the Liberal Democratic Party, in office for nearly 40 years, and involved in a symbiotic relationship with big business and the bureaucracy – the three legs of the tripod that had established Japan as an economic power. The inability of the ruling elite to deal with the prolonged recession and to suggest new policies has led to a series of weak governments, party splits and re-alignments, which looks set to continue. The relative weakness of the economy has thrown into doubt Japan's ability to act as an engine of growth for the region, which had been the case for a quarter of a century, and the crisis of the financial system threatens to affect investment abroad upon which the Asia-Pacific has to a great degree depended.

At the same time the foreign policy of following the United States has been questioned since the end of the cold war as trade friction with the US has been a constant, and concern has developed as to how far the US is committed to its security alliance with Japan now that the cold war threat is over. In addition, recession or not, Japan is clearly a power of great note in economic terms, and the widespread feeling is that the relationship with the US should cater for Japanese political and diplomatic positions, and not just those promoted by Washington. This is not the nationalism of territorial acquisition of pre-war Japan, but the nationalism of status and recognition as an equal, something historically lacking during the cold war. It would manifest itself in the taking of different political positions at times from the US on issues, such as how to deal with an emergent China, on accommodation with Russia, on the way forward for Asia-Pacific bodies which Japan sees as an avenue for Japanese diplomatic approaches, while recognising that in broad security terms US involvement is still the best guarantee of a stable region. As Japan does not want to re-militarise and cause a panic in the region, and as the instability on the Korean peninsula represents an important security problem involving the interests of all the powers, one could expect Japanese diplomacy to be characterised by caution and attention to its primary alliance. As has been written, 'Tokyo seeks to reduce its dependence on Washington, to channel Beijing's rise toward co-operation rather than confrontation, and to focus its assistance to Russia on the Russian Far East, while influencing Moscow's path in entering North East Asia and the Asia-Pacific region' (Rozman, 1998, p. 15).

The United States regards itself as the primary factor in the security structure of the region despite the end of the cold war threat. Concerns about US withdrawal are overblown as the Clinton administration's policy of 'Deep Engagement' has shown (Nye, 1995). By remaining involved the US can prevent the region from becoming dominated by any one power in the future, something that has always been inimical to both the security and the economic interests of the United States. There has, however, been a recognition that the nations of the region need to be fully involved in the process, and this has lain behind efforts to push the Japanese to share more of the security burden for themselves as they are net gainers from the structure. The US sees its presence as likely to help to shape the emergence of China in a co-operative direction, while its relationship with Japan allays Chinese worries over Japanese re-militarisation. At the same time the economic importance of the region is well known in Washington and is seen as a factor that can promote peaceful co-operation and security, hence the importance of the first Asia-Pacific Economic Co-operation (APEC) summit in Seattle in 1993, and its annual successors, at which leaders from politically diverse regional states can discuss the issues of the day.

The problem for the US is that it cannot be seen to be moving too close to one regional state, for fear that it will be perceived as ignoring the positions of another. Even as first among equals, and as the only superpower, a policy of dramatic shifts should not be expected, but more an attention to incremental movements in its relationships with the powers in the region.

For China the 1990s has been a period of relative success. Sino-Soviet normalisation removed a strategic threat, and relations with Japan and the US despite fluctuations, notably over Beijing's claim to Taiwan, have continued to provide trade, commerce, investment and export opportunities. This has allowed the communist government to preside over rapid growth and industrialisation in their effort to modernise the country. Communist ideology has taken a back seat to nationalist exhortations to the people to work for growth and a more powerful China. Outsiders want to share in the business opportunities that a developing China provides, while some strategists worry about the effects that a more powerful China might have on the region in the long term. Will it want to dominate the region? Will it use force to reclaim Taiwan? Will it upset the balance of power in the process? These questions about intentions in the long term are notoriously difficult to answer, but a look at the United States suggests that powers with the requisite military and economic capabilities usually want a big say in political arrangements. China's present situation, however, is much less

Table 17.1 The Great Powers: Indices of Power in 1997

	US	Russia	EU	China	Japan
Population (millions)	268	150	372	1200	125
Size (million square kilometres)	9.5	17.0	3.2	9.5	0.4
GDP (trillion $)	7.6	1.1	7.4	0.6*	4.6
Growth rate (%)	2.4	−2.8	1.6	9.0	3.6
Defence outlays (billion $)	267	32–71	187	38	44
Armed forces (millions)	1.5	1.2	1.4	2.8	0.25
Long-range nuclear missiles	1012	1329	120	85	0
Long-range bombers	174	66	0	0	0
Combat aircraft	5000	2200	3673	3740	368
Aircraft carriers**	12	1	7	0	0
Combat ships***	143	60	185	54	58
Submarines****	93	128	90	0	16
Main battle tanks	8239	15 500	10 050	8500	1110

* Estimates vary by a factor of four; the Russian number is similarly soft
** US carriers are far larger than those of the EU and carry up to seven times as many planes
*** Frigates and larger
**** Most US submarines are nuclear powered and thus superior in range and noise suppression
Source: Josef Joffe, *The Future of the Great Powers*, Phoenix, London, 1998, p. 9, from International Institute of Strategic Studies, *The Military Balance, 1997/98*, IISS, London, 1997, and EUROSTAT

powerful. It needs the co-operation of other nations in its own development, and it is not militarily strong enough to challenge the US (see Table 17.1). It is, however, vitally interested in regional developments, including Taiwan and the future of Korea, and in making sure that no hostile power, or combination of powers, poses a threat to its path to modernisation and status.

Once again, this mixture of factors leads to the supposition that China at present has no interest in policies that would dramatically alter the regional situation but will pursue its agenda with competitive and co-operative elements running side by side.

This look at the general conditions pertaining for the major states of the region in the 1990s suggests that none wish in the short term to overthrow regional stability, even if they may wish for changes in relative balance. All are concerned with their economic positions and are searching for greater benefits, but all are aware that sudden and dramatic challenges to the regional system could be counter-productive. Let us see whether recent behaviour conforms to this picture of caution.

Summitry

Certainly Russo-Chinese relations have been marked by summitry between Yeltsin and Jiang Zemin on a number of occasions. By 1996 the two nations could see each other as potential strategic counter-weights to American superpower predominance. This could be seen in Chinese purchases of Russian weaponry and in the Russian desire to supply oil and gas to China. Both were signalling that they had alternatives and should not be taken for granted (*Guardian*,

22 April 1996). This followed shortly after the Clinton administration had sent naval forces to the Taiwan area in response to China's war games which were designed to remind Taiwan of China's claim to the island. While a warming of Russo-Chinese relations is intended as a signal and as an alternative it is not widely seen as changing the strategic balance as both still require US involvement in improving stability in Asia (*Guardian*, 23 April 1996).

By the time of Yeltsin and Jiang's next summit in Moscow in April 1997, they were talking of partnership and calling for a 'multipolar' system to address problems. The incentives for such calculations stemmed from China's continuing worry that the US might be trying to contain China's political influence in Asia, impeding Beijing's agenda over Taiwan and hectoring China about human rights abuses. Yeltsin was responding to NATO expansion and the domestic problems caused by the adoption of free market mechanisms and democracy supported by the West and international institutions such as the IMF. As a result the Chinese model of authoritarian rule and market economics was looking more appealing to those in Russia of a more nationalist bent. These policy movements were attributed to the then Foreign Minister Yevgeni Primakov who was thought to be intent on improving Russia's relations with a variety of states in order to counteract over-dependence on the US (*Times*, 24 April 1997).

Despite the appearance of closeness and talk of strategic partnerships, there are various impediments to Russo-Chinese relations. Rhetoric aside, there are concerns in Russia over demographic pressure in border areas, thinly populated on the Russian side, heavily so on the Chinese. The levels of economic interaction are low, with both sides preferring goods of higher quality from alternative suppliers. This makes really close co-operation look rather hollow, especially since China and Russia, in reality, are not strategic partners but, as a Russian journalist pointed out, rivals for foreign investment (*New Times*, January 1998, p. 30).

In any event, Russia's diplomacy with Japan would, in recent times, not suggest attempts to re-polarise the region by moving closer exclusively to China. After years of relative coolness, Russo-Japanese relations received the stimulus of the so-called 'sauna summit'. This event, bringing Yeltsin together with Japanese Prime Minister Ryutaro Hashimoto at Khabarovsk in Siberia in November 1997, included a trip to a bath house where relaxation, good food and, as ITAR-TASS put it, 'naked contact' encouraged a good and friendly atmosphere (*Financial Times*, 1–2 November 1997).

The issue of the Kurile Islands and a general peace treaty was addressed with both leaders talking of making 'maximum efforts' to conclude a deal by the year 2000. While this is unlikely because of the domestic constraints of nationalists in both countries, it appears that Hashimoto may have changed Japan's policy by talking of the need for mutual trust and the benefit of long-term vision. This would allow for Japanese investment to precede territorial and sovereignty questions, thus satisfying Japanese business interests who want to participate in Russia's Far East, while not overly alarming nationalists in Russia's Pacific and Siberian provinces (Fukui and Fukai, 1998, p. 32). The economic possibilities were taken further at a follow-up summit in Japan in April 1998. If a compromise is reached, both nations could move forward on economic co-operation without losing face on the territorial question, while simultaneously balancing their relations with China.

For Japan this would be useful, as governments in Tokyo have been worried that China's rise would cause potential difficulties for Japan in future, particularly should the US leave the region, or conversely should the US overtly move towards a hostile relationship with Beijing. A priority then for Japan is maintaining good relations with both China and the US, and hoping that these two can coexist as well. The strengthening of the US–Japan alliance in 1996, and the extension of Japan's defence guidelines in 1997 to include support for the US in the vicinity of Taiwan, shows that Japan shares some basic views on regional security with the US, and that at bottom lies concern over China's possible intentions. Hashimoto was quick to reassure China that the alliance was not directed at it during his summit in Beijing in September 1997 (*Times*, 4 September 1997). Meanwhile the Clinton administration began to emphasise the more constructive elements in the US relationship with China in the aftermath of the Taiwan incident in 1996 and the rows over human rights, and agreed at the Beijing Summit in July 1998 to develop a 'constructive, strategic partnership' (*Far Eastern Economic Review*, 9 July 1998). Since Secretary of State Madeleine Albright was telling Tokyo that US–Japan relations were the 'cornerstone of Asia', there was clearly something for everyone in all this balancing behaviour (*Far Eastern Economic Review*, 16 July 1998).

Future problems

The movements in bilateral relationships in the region are consistent with ideas of general balancing of power and of trying to maintain a secure environment in which economic advantage can be gained. No states have taken any dramatic actions which would raise the level of fear in its regional neighbours to the point where a vicious cycle would develop. Crucially, nobody has anything to gain from a more hostile environment. The medium-term prognosis would appear good if we extrapolate from the present.

More likely as causes of instability in the region are problems over which governments have less apparent control than bilateral relationships. We have already noted the Taiwan problem, originating in the early cold war when as a result of the outbreak of war in Korea the US began to protect the island from takeover by the communists on the mainland. The Beijing regime still regards this as unfinished business, while the mood on prosperous Taiwan suggests a reluctance to capitulate to Beijing's agenda. The outbreak of hostilities would pose a fundamental question to the US and Japan about how far they would be prepared to go in maintaining the status quo and in defying China. The possibilities of hostile polarisation are clear.

Another serious strategic problem is Korea, having been so since the second half of the nineteenth century. The division of the peninsula with two rival regimes each allied to rival superpower blocs during the cold war preserved a hostile stand-off with no outside powers seeing it as in their interests to overturn that particular status quo. With the end of the cold war, however, the situation has altered. Both China and Russia now have good connections to South Korea as they see it as a useful economic partner, while their former client in North Korea is viewed as an economic disaster in the grip of an ideologically out-of-date leadership. This leadership appears to be using its nuclear programme in the 1990s to gain recognition from the US and Japan by attempting to threaten to destabilise the region unless it receives aid and recognition in diplomatic terms. It has been partially successful in as much as the US has seen fit to engage North Korea in talks about its nuclear programme. None of the powers wishes to see a nuclear-armed North Korea and this has meant that so far, despite differences in approach, the problem has not seriously divided the powers. However, the potential is indicated by North Korean missile tests overflying Japanese territory in August 1998 and the reaction of the head of the Japanese Defence Agency who stated that Japan had the right to retaliate if attacked by missiles (*Times*, 5 September 1998). Conflict in or around Korea could revive strategic concerns long dormant over influence in the peninsula that were such a factor between Russia, Japan and China in the late nineteenth century.

The problem of competitive influence could be a factor even if the Korean problem takes the course of a collapse of the Kim Jong Il regime in the North and the process of re-unification gets under way. A unified Korea removes the old buffer zones and, therefore, a Korea not aligned specifically to any one of the powers would appear necessary. As the cost of the re-unification process would clearly be beyond the capacity of South Korea alone, if the German case is anything to go by, then the surrounding powers will inevitably have a role to play. Keeping a balance when some of the external powers have more to offer to the re-unification process than others will not be easy.

Finally, there are problems in the economic sphere which could dramatically alter the environment. There has been a presumption in Asia in the 1980s and 1990s that economic growth was an almost natural phenomenon and that the region's future was bright. It may well be, but free markets have a tendency to boom and bust, and the problems in Asia and in Russia which became manifest in 1997 and 1998 deserve to be seen as a crisis, a crisis, moreover, which could be seen as damaging the optimism in the region by removing the growth factor which ameliorates many political tensions (Dibb *et al.*, 1998, pp. 5–6).

Russian domestic collapse, Japanese recession and damage to China's economic programme, all are possible consequences of regional and global financial crises. Governments come under pressure at home, the outside world looks not only competitive but hostile and international affairs can take a different course. It must be hoped that the balancing behaviour we have noted between the powers in the region is strong enough and flexible enough to withstand both domestic and external shocks.

References

Defence of Japan 1989 *The Japan Times*.
Dibb P, Hale D D and Prince P 1998 The Strategic Implications of Asia's Economic Crisis, *Survival*, Summer.

Fukui H and Fukai S N 1998 Japan in 1997, *Asian Survey*, Vol. XXXVIII, No. 1
  (January).
Foot R 1997 *The Practice of Power: U.S. Relations with China Since 1949*, Oxford University
  Press, Oxford.
Garthoff R L 1994 *The Great Transition: American–Soviet Relations and the End of the
  Cold War*, The Brookings Institution, Washington, DC.
Hasegawa T 1988 Soviet Arms Control Policy in Asia and the Japan–U.S. Alliance,
  Japan Review of International Affairs, Vol. 2, No. 2 (Fall/Winter).
Kimura H 1987 Gorbachev's Foreign Policy in Asia and the Pacific, *Japan Review of
  International Affairs*, Vol. 1, No. 1 (Spring/Summer).
Miller R F 1995 Russian Policy Toward Japan, in Shearman P (ed.), *Russian Foreign
  Policy Since 1990*, Westview Press, Boulder, CO.
Nye J 1995 The Case for Deep Engagement, *Foreign Affairs*, Vol. 74, No. 4
  (July/August).
Rozman G 1998 Flawed Regionalism: Reconceptualizing Northeast Asia in the 1990s,
  The Pacific Review, Vol. II, No. 1.
Saito M 1993 Japan's Northward Foreign Policy, in Curtis G L *et al.* (eds), *Japan's
  Foreign Policy After the Cold War: Coping With Change*, M E Sharpe, Armonk, NY, and
  London.
Segal G 1991 North-East Asia: Common Security or a la carte?, *International Affairs*,
  October.
Smith P 1998 Remembering Japan: A Bilateral History, *Washington Quarterly*, Vol. 21,
  No. 1 (Winter).

Further reading

Yahuda M 1996 *The International Politics of the Asia-Pacific, 1945–1995*, Routledge,
  London.
A website on current events in China can be found at:
http://www.insidechina.com/
A Japanese website that looks at policy towards Russia can be found at:
http://www.mofa.go.jp/region/europe/russia/index.html

18 Russian foreign policy: an overview

John Berryman

Introduction: Russia's place in the post-cold-war world

An examination of the foreign policy of the Russian Federation must start with a cold-eyed appreciation of the limits of Russia's much reduced power – a legacy of the collapse of the Soviet position in Central and Eastern Europe (CEE) and the dismemberment of the Soviet Union between 1989 and 1991.

Since January 1992 the shrunken borders of the Russian Federation have contained just 76 per cent of the area and 60 per cent of the population of the former Soviet Union, the new frontiers approximating to those of the Russian empire before Ukraine was incorporated in 1654, wiping out three centuries of imperial expansion under Tsar Alexis, Peter the Great, Catherine, Alexander I and Alexander II. In Europe, thanks to the loss of Soviet control of the states of CEE and the attainment of sovereignty by the European states of the former Soviet Union, Russia has been 'pushed' more than 1000 kilometres east and is now geographically distanced from the centre of European activity (Zagorski, 1993; Baev, 1995).

In military terms, following the collapse of the Soviet Union, more than one-half of the combat aircraft, tanks and armoured vehicles, much of it the best-quality first- and second-echelon equipment, and one-quarter of the warships of the former Soviet Union were located outside Russia's new borders (Lambeth, 1995). Although some of the military equipment was subsequently retrieved by Moscow, by the majority of military indicators the Russian Federation can no longer lay claim to be a military superpower. However, by the end of 1996 all former Soviet nuclear forces located in Belarus, Kazakhstan and Ukraine had been transferred to Russia and Moscow has utilized its status as a strategic nuclear power as part of its claim for great power status.

In economic terms, even in 1992 the Russian Federation accounted for only 40–50 per cent of the GNP of the former Soviet Union, roughly equivalent to 17.2 per cent of that of the United States (Nikolayev, 1993). Since that date, as other chapters in this volume indicate, the economic output of Russia has dropped by roughly a half and by 1997 Russia's GDP was no more than 6 per cent of US GDP. Over these six years foreign direct investment in Russia amounted to less than one-fifth of the international investment in China and prior to the collapse of the Russian banking system in August 1998 interest on Western loans consumed almost half of Russia's export earnings. Even best estimates therefore suggest that Russia is unlikely to restore its GDP to the 1990 level much before 2015 (Gaddy and Ickes, 1998; Adomeit, 1995, p. 56).

Notwithstanding its nuclear capability, the obvious limits which Russia's much reduced geopolitical, military and economic attributes have placed on her international role have raised questions concerning Russia's insistent claims to be recognised as a Great Power. As a Great Power Russia sees herself ranking below the US, the only global superpower, but above other European and Asian powers, laying claim to regional and local spheres of influence in her 'Near Abroad', the Commonwealth of Independent States (CIS). For some Western analysts, although Russia's calls to be treated on equal terms by the West are viewed sympathetically, they are seen to resemble the Soviet Union's one-dimensional claims to be a superpower and are judged to be questionable assertions reflecting illusory ambitions (Adomeit, 1995; Garnett, 1997). Others see a parallel between Russia's claims to be a Great Power in the post-cold-war world, reflecting a sharp reduction in its international position, and the efforts by Charles de Gaulle to assert France's weakened claims to international influence and independence in the post-World War II settlement (Mandelbaum, 1998, p. 7; Aron, 1998, p. 31). Some view such assertions as little more than bombastic threats based on 'self-pity and a wilful disregard of reality' (Blank, 1998, p. 6).

Although the bulk of the Russian political elite share the view that the country should assert its role as a Great Power, reservations have been voiced in Russia. The influential Russian Council on Defence and Foreign Policy has concluded that the new Russia is a middle-sized power, warning that it should not seek to exceed its limited capabilities, while the Russian security analyst Pavel Baev takes the view that Russia's power is broken beyond repair and its days as a Great Power are over (Light, 1996, p. 67; Baev, 1997, p. 188). Another young Russian scholar, Vladislav Zubok, has even suggested that for a limited period Russia's weakness, rather than its strength, argues for a foreign policy strategy based on the 'tyranny of the weak', threatening economic or military collapse to secure Western financial aid and integration in the global economic system (Zubok, 1992).

Notwithstanding such reservations, Russia's claim to be a Great Power forms part of its strategy to construct a multipolar world order and thereby secure the leverage to counter-balance the hegemonic power of the United States (Blacker, 1998, p. 183). As Yevgeni Primakov, Russia's Foreign Minister (January 1996–August 1998), explained to new recruits to the Russian Ministry of Foreign Affairs (MFA) in March 1998, the role of a Great Power was 'not an aim in itself, but a thought-out role for Russia in a difficult zigzag transition to a multipolar world' (Meek, 1998).

Since Russia remains by far the largest state in the world, possesses huge natural resources, a qualified workforce, abundant scientific, technical and cultural potential, and is still the largest conventional military power in Europe and Asia, in the longer term Russia's claim to be a Great Power may not be illusory.

The conduct of Russian foreign policy

As a new and much-reduced actor with borders that are widely regarded as artificial and possibly transient, Russia is struggling to develop a coherent definition of its national identity, statehood and national interests. Fortunately, this struggle

Different foreign policy opinion groups

These groups are by no means fixed. Moreover, figures shift from one group to another, and certain people can be placed in more than one grouping. Yeltsin, for example, has shifted from being a liberal Westerniser to a centrist, while Yavlinsky, the democratic critic of Gaidar's economic reform, can be located as both an international institutionalist and as a state realist.

Reformers: Kozyrev, Gaidar

Liberal Westernisers

Pro-Western group which favoured close relations with the West. This group dominated foreign policy formulation from August 1991 to the middle of 1992.

International institutionalists

A group which put particular emphasis on the benefits for Russia of belonging to international institutions, not only from the perspective of national interest, but also to encourage democracy in Russia, international co-operation and peace. Proponents of this view do not differ greatly from those of the liberal Westernisers, but many centrists (such as Primakov) favour membership of regional and international institutions, they are simply more sceptical that Russia will be allowed to join some of the more important ones – such as, the EU – as a full member.

Centrists: Primakov, Ivanov, Chernomyrdin

State realists

This group favours actively pursuing Russian national interests, even if this means sometimes upsetting the West. Hard bargaining rather than antagonism to the West is the slogan of this group.

Eurasianists

This group wants Russia to act as some kind of bridge between Europe and Asia. More specifically, members prioritise relations with the CIS (and some Asian countries) in preference to the West. This group was founded by Yeltsin's former adviser, Stankevich.

Nationalists: Zyuganov, Zhirinovsky

National patriotic expansionists

There are a wide variety of nationalist groupings in Russia today. Some seek an alliance of slavic states (Solzhenitsyn), others wish to see the revival of the old Soviet Union (Zyuganov); while yet others envisage Russia becoming the centre once more of a great empire (Zhirinovsky).

is being undertaken in a relatively benign post-cold-war international security environment where currently no clear enemies or significant allies (Belarus, Armenia and Tajikistan hardly fit the bill) can yet be identified (Zagorski *et al.*, 1992; Sestanovich, 1994).

In addition to seeking to shape a new foreign policy from such an ill-defined base and in such an uncertain environment, Russia is involved in a 'double-struggle' to develop a new polity, state structure and economy. In these circumstances foreign policy is a contested area, not just subject to the normal clash of domestic politics but also forming the focal point of a wider debate about the very nature, identity and values of the new Russia. This uncertainty as to the identity and place of Russia in the new world order has found expression in the different foreign policy opinion groups (Liberal Westernisers or International Institutionalists; Eurasianists; Geopolitical or State Realists; National-Patriotic Expansionists or Nationalists) (Box 18.1) variously identified by Russian and Western analysts (Arbatov, 1993, 1997; Buszynski, 1996; Tsygankov, 1997).

The volatility and confusion inherent in this situation where policy goals are not clear have been compounded by the institutional fluidity of foreign and security policy-making over the past seven years. The relatively orderly process of policy-making during the late-Soviet period gave way to weak regulatory structures and a haphazard decision-making process under Yeltsin, a consequence of the uncoordinated input of contending political factions and economic and regional interest groups (Malcolm, 1995; Malcolm *et al.*, 1996; Parrish, 1996). Since January 1996 a rough consensus has supported the more assertive foreign policy stance articulated by Yevgenii Primakov, Kozyrev's successor as Foreign Minister, but policy-making remains fragmented. During this period Yeltsin has replaced his foreign minister once and his defence minister and national security adviser twice (Garnett, 1998, pp. 67–8).

Russia and the West

While expectations of financial assistance and Russia's integration within the global economy have fostered Russia's co-operation with the West, resistance to Western demands has encouraged Moscow to assert its prerogatives in the CIS. In either case, the broader context of Russia's relations with the West have helped to shape Moscow's foreign policy agenda and must be examined first (Buszynski, 1996, p. 49).

Thanks to the dominant role which the US plays in the international financial institutions which have provided Russia with financial aid, developing co-operative relations with the US was seen by Moscow to be the priority. Despite widespread doubts as to the efficacy of Western financial aid in easing Russia's transition to a market economy, not to speak of criticisms of the inadequate scale of the assistance and the condescending and insensitive nature of the accompanying Western advice, the strategy was pursued over seven years. Between 1991 and the summer of 1998 Russia received loans totalling $99 billion (Odom, 1998, p. 813). The shortcomings of this strategy were only finally exposed by the financial collapse in Russia on 17 August 1998. Initial payments by the IMF of a

СПРАВКА 18.2   The Near Abroad

This is a term used by some Russians in reference to the former Soviet republics which, like Russia, broke away from the USSR in December 1991. It is not a term the other Soviet successor states much like. It suggests that Russia has still not come to terms with the idea that these countries are now fully independent states.

further long term $22.6 billion loan were suspended but in the absence of any clear alternative strategy, Western (and Russian) policy has for several months been in a state of suspension (see Chapter 14). The way forward remains unclear.

Apart from these financial calculations, which pointed up the need for good relations with the West, the MFA initially looked to the political desirability of the full integration of Russia within the 'civilized international community'. Having absorbed much of the neo-liberal literature of Western international theory in the guise of the 'new political thinking' of the Gorbachev period, the new Yeltsin foreign policy elite adhered broadly to the international institutionalist view that Russia's participation in multilateral economic and security institutions was both desirable and, indeed, unavoidable (Macfarlane, 1994, pp. 241–5; Zubok, 1995, p. 105; Tsygankov, 1997, pp. 249–50). Such participation, it was believed, would help to foster regional and global cultures and contribute to the wider civilising pressures generated by enhanced interdependence. Overcoming its previous ambivalence towards Western multilateral arrangements, Russia accordingly sought membership of or access to a wide range of international institutions (Lucas, 1995; Baranovsky, 1995a; Zagorski, 1997).

To secure this re-integration with the West the first Foreign Minister of the Russian Federation, Andrei Kozyrev, initially pursued an openly Atlanticist strategy, seeking co-operation and a 'strategic partnership' with the West in a manner that critics suggested displayed a humiliating deference to Western priorities – what Vladimir Lukin, the Russian Ambassador to Washington, described as 'romantic masochism'. Thanks to both Western and Russian reservations the shortcomings of this 'partnership' were soon exposed. In the West there was uncertainty as to the permanence of Russia's transition to a market economy and liberal-democratic values and concern over Russia's longer-term intentions and the possible re-emergence of an aggressive anti-Western policy (Pipes, 1997). In Russia, the legacy of cold war suspicions of the West was sharpened by irritation over the marginalisation, not to say the near invisibility, of Russia in global affairs, the West seemingly committed to blocking any possible emergence of the new Russia as a Great Power in the post-cold-war world. Talk in the US of the need to foster regional tensions or 'geopolitical pluralism' within Russia's 'Near Abroad' (Box 18.2) and historic spheres of influence aroused fears in Moscow that its geopolitical dominance over its neighbouring territories, together with the economic ties, might be lost. Speculation by such influential US strategists as Zbigniew Brzezinski as to the possible merits of the geopolitical dismantling of the Russian Federation into Russia, Siberia and the Far Eastern Republic only sharpened Moscow's anxieties (Brzezinski, 1994, 1997; Mikoyan, 1998).

Proposals for the eastward enlargement of NATO which surfaced in 1993 did nothing to dispel such suspicions. In the view of Russian nationalists and Russia's military and intelligence authorities, NATO enlargement was the spearhead of an American global policy of 'neo-containment', no longer directed to contain the ideological threat of communism but to contain Russia as a Great Power, and even as a different sort of civilisation, thereby enabling Washington to establish a US-directed unipolar world order (Kortunov, 1996). These mutual suspicions and the shortfall in the economic returns on the pursuit of 'partnership' with the West, which never matched the exaggerated Russian expectations, generated a shift in foreign policy thinking towards a more assertive *realpolitik* perspective.

Within the 'Key Tenets of the Concept of Foreign Policy of the Russian Federation', approved by the Inter-Departmental Foreign Policy Commission of the Security Council and President Yeltsin in April 1993, Moscow's foreign policy priorities were broadly identified as the following concentric circles of concern:

- Preserving the territorial integrity and state sovereignty of the Russian Federation and its 89 constituent regions.

- Seeking to shape the vast geopolitical space of the former Soviet Union in accordance with Russia's interests. Of special concern for Moscow were the rights of the about 25 million Russian-speakers and Russian citizens living outside the Russian Federation in the other 14 former Soviet republics – after the Chinese the largest diaspora in the world.

- Preventing the emergence of any threats or military–political groupings along the outer borders of the former Soviet Union.

- Advancing Russia's broader international claims to be treated as a Great Power in terms of its potential, its influence on the course of world events and the responsibility it bears as a result of this (Aron, 1994; Baranovsky, 1995a).

Having abandoned 'shallow globalism' and any attempt to maintain a significant Russian role in the affairs of Latin America, Africa or South-East Asia, and finding its influence in much of the Middle East cut back, Moscow has come to perceive Russia's vital interests to lie pre-eminently within those Eurasian regions contiguous with or close to Russia's new borders. Russia's relations with its neighbours to the South and to the East, discussed in other chapters, will be examined only briefly. However, particular attention will be paid to Russia's relations with its neighbours to the West and North-West in Europe since these are not directly treated elsewhere.

Russia and Europe

No region of the world has been more affected by the geopolitical re-alignment and 'shrinkage' of Russia than Europe. Thanks to the emergence of the

European post-Soviet republics, Russia's relations with the core states of Western Europe are now conducted from behind a 'double belt' of independent Central and East European states and states of the former Soviet Union. The transfer of 57 Soviet divisions to Belarus and Ukraine and the peaceful withdrawal over three years of more than 600 000 Soviet troops from CEE and the Baltic states, 'one of the most extensive and least appreciated force withdrawals in modern times', together with the asymmetric reductions in certain categories of offensive military equipment defined by the Conventional Forces in Europe (CFE) Treaty, left Russia confronting a deeply unfavourable 4:1 balance of conventional military forces in Europe by the autumn of 1994 (Litovkin, 1994; Lambeth, 1995, p. 94).

In line with its overall commitment to pursue economic and security multilateralism, the European strategy of the MFA has been directed to the incorporation of Russia within some sort of pan-European security architecture and a Europe-wide free trade zone. Within this ambitious, not to say grandiose, scheme, it is envisaged that Russian–European relations will complement US–European relations within an emerging Euro-Atlantic economic and security community (Baranovsky, 1995b; Berryman, 1996; Danilov and De Spiegeleire, 1998). Apart from playing an active role within the largest pan-European institution, the Organisation for Security and Co-operation in Europe (OSCE), Russia has joined and participated positively in the activities of the newly established Council of Baltic Seas States, the Barents Euro-Arctic Council and the Black Sea Economic Co-operation Council. Russia has also joined the Council of Europe and has been supportive of the enlargement of the European Union (EU). By contrast, Russia has been unwaveringly opposed to the eastward enlargement of NATO. What accounts for Russia's very different reactions to the double enlargement process?

Russia and EU enlargement

Since Gorbachev's advocacy of a 'European Common Home' (Box 18.3), Moscow has taken a positive view of the EU, not least since the EU has become Russia's major economic partner, accounting in the 1990s for over 40 per cent of Russia's trade. The EU therefore constitutes a larger market for Russia than the US (4 per cent), China (6 per cent), Japan (3 per cent) and the states of the Asian-Pacific Economic Co-operation (APEC) (17 per cent) combined. Indeed, Russia's trade with the EU is almost twice the size of its trade with the CIS (22 per cent) and the EU is also Russia's main source of investment, assistance and grants (Ardy and Gower, 1996; Danilov and De Spiegeleire, 1998; Ivanov and Pozdnyakov, 1998).

No objections were raised by Moscow to the accession of Austria, Sweden and Finland to the EU in 1995, thereby obtaining West European Union (WEU) observer status, or to the 1997 Brussels Agenda-2000 timetable for the eventual accession of ten Central and East European states to the EU early in the next century. However, Russian irritation with Brussels over the continued imposition of heavy duties upon its exports to the EU and impatience over the failure

СПРАВКА 18.3   **European Common Home**

The term, European Common Home, was first coined by Brezhnev in 1981, but was used and extended as a concept by Gorbachev. In essence, Gorbachev used the phrase to argue for greater tolerance of ideological difference (see Gorbachev, 1987, pp. 194–5). Gorbachev declared that no social system – neither communism nor capitalism – should seek to impose its ideas on others by force. On that basis, Gorbachev argued that all the peoples of Europe could live together in peace and harmony. Then there would be no need, he said, for political division, the military stand-off or the ruinously expensive and dangerous arms race. In sum, Gorbachev's call for a European Common Home represented an early plea for an end to the Cold War in Europe.

of the EU to recognise Russia as a market economy underpinned Russian Prime Minister Viktor Chernomyrdin's surprise announcement in Brussels in July 1997 of Moscow's serious intention to seek full membership of the EU (Haslam 1998). His remarks were abruptly dismissed by EU officials (Palmer, 1997). Brussels has long taken the view that the accession of a state with a population of 150 million and a land surface five times greater than that of the current EU would seriously unbalance the number of MEPs and votes within the EU political system. The perception of Russia as a Eurasian power has also been seen to distinguish it from other existing and candidate European members (Malcolm, 1994; Ardy and Gower, 1996).

More positively, a new chapter in EU–Russian relations was marked when in January 1998 the Partnership and Co-operation Agreement (PCA) between Russia and the EU, signed at the EU Corfu summit in 1994, came into force and an EU–Russia Co-operation Council was established. A joint PCA Work Programme for 1998 has been agreed which includes consideration of the need to seek a reduction in tariffs as a first step towards the establishment of a free trade area, and the EU has finally removed Russia from the list of countries with non-market economies.

Despite these initiatives there remain clear limits to the Russia–EU dialogue. There are worries that since most of the countries preparing to join the EU currently maintain more favourable trade relations with Russia than the EU, Russia's trade with these countries might become more difficult. The sharp reduction in traditional economic ties between Russia and Finland following the latter's accession to the EU in 1995 has underlined how serious the aftermath of such changes could be (Zagorski, 1998, p. 49). In the longer term, it has been argued that the implications of EU enlargement for the possible integration of the WEU into the EU and for the character of a European Security and Defence Identity may prove to be more intractable issues for Russia than the more limited military–political issues raised by NATO's proposed eastward enlargement (Danilov and De Spiegeleire, 1998).

СПРАВКА 18.4 **Kaliningrad**

Kaliningrad, a Baltic port, was formerly capital of East Prussia. After World War II, East Prussia was divided up between Poland and the USSR with Kaliningrad formally becoming a part of the Russian Republic, despite the fact that it was separated territorially from Russia by the Soviet Republics of Lithuania and Latvia. This separation scarcely mattered while the USSR existed, but, after its break-up, Kaliningrad was left an exposed and isolated part of Russia, cut off from the rest of the federation. Kaliningrad has retained its importance because of the Russian military base on its territory which is perceived by some as a potential threat to its neighbours, Poland, Belarus and the newly independent Baltic states.

Russia and NATO enlargement

Notwithstanding the establishment of the NATO–Russia Permanent Joint Council (PJC) and NATO's Euro-Atlantic Partnership Council (EAPC) to provide consultative frameworks for an enhanced level of dialogue and mutual assurance, the launch of NATO's enlargement at the NATO Madrid Summit in July 1997 marked:

- A humiliating defeat for Russia's policy of sustained opposition to NATO expansion over the preceding four years (Lieven, 1995; Kugler, 1996; Berryman, 1998b).

- A rebuff to Moscow's efforts to construct a pan-European security system of a 'second generation' by raising the powers and profile of the OSCE (Arbatov, 1995, p. 48).

- A further step towards a worsening for Russia of the strategic–military balance in Europe. Despite NATO statements that eastward expansion carried with it no hostile intent towards Russia, Russian military authorities have emphasised that with the accession to NATO of the three Central European states, 15 000 pieces of CFE treaty-limited military equipment will become available to NATO and the zone of NATO's security responsibility will *de facto* have advanced 750 kilometres eastward to the Polish–Kaliningrad District border (see Box 18.4). Not only will Russian forces in the Kaliningrad Special Defence District find themselves in direct proximity to NATO forces in Poland, but Russian cities like Smolensk, Kursk and Bryansk will come within range of NATO dual-capable tactical aircraft operating from NATO's new CEE airfields (Gareev, 1996).

Having failed to block this first step in the enlargement process, Russia has accepted the *fait accompli* and recognised that for the present a stable working relationship with NATO is the only practical strategy. The MFA consequently portrayed the Founding Act which established the PJC as a shared accomplishment and a solid basis for future co-operation (Afanasievskii, 1997). Russia has

СПРАВКА 18.5 **The Concert of Europe**

The Concert of Europe was a system set up in 1815 after the end of the Napoleonic Wars. It was a security system which included the states of Austria, Prussia, Russia and Great Britain. The four allies agreed to hold meetings at fixed periods to discuss their common interests and to take such action as was necessary for the maintenance of peace and stability in Europe (see Cook and Stevenson, 1987, p. 68).

subsequently adopted a 'twin-track' approach in its relations with NATO, seeking to use the PJC to try to influence NATO policy while also looking to build on the mechanisms and procedures for co-operation where a concurrence of interests emerge.

At the time of the signing of the PJC some hard-line Western commentators expressed concern that, notwithstanding President Clinton's insistence that the PJC would provide Moscow with only a 'voice but not a veto', precisely such a use might be made of the PJC (Sicherman, 1997). So far, these fears seem groundless. Working programmes for 1998 and 1999 have been implemented by the PJC and its meetings at Ambassadorial, Foreign Minister and Defence Minister levels have reviewed the situation in Bosnia, including NATO–Russia co-operation in SFOR, and have discussed ways to stabilize the developing crisis in Kosovo – in the latter case without success (NATO–Russia Permanent Joint Council Statements, 1998 and 1999).

Seeking to square the circle of NATO enlargement and Russia's legitimate security concerns, it has sometimes been suggested that Russia might be admitted to NATO. However, Russian membership would imply not only a NATO border with Central Asia and China but a NATO commitment to defend Russia against such Asian powers. Given the improbability of such a development, Russian observers regard such suggestions as patronising and disingenuous (Yost, 1998). Alternative structures for some sort of trans-continental security architecture embracing Russia have therefore been advanced by both Russian and American analysts. A special consultative mechanism within the OSCE procedures, containing Russia and America and several key European powers, and a Council of Greater Europe on the lines of the nineteenth century Concert of Europe (Box 18.5), comprising all the major European powers and America, have been proposed (Brzezinski, 1995, p. 36; Brzezinski, 1997, p. 56; Pierre and Trenin, 1997, pp. 17–18; Odom, 1998, pp. 814–15). While such ideas reflect the broader intellectual enterprise to re-think patterns of regional security management in the post-cold-war world, as yet no concrete proposals have been advanced by the US Government (Lake and Morgan, 1997).

Looking to the medium term, the Russian security analyst Vladimir Baranovsky has identified three options open to Russia with respect to Europe, that is unilateralism, a balance of power strategy and co-operative multilateralism, and argues that Moscow's policy currently contains a fluctuating mix of the three (Baranovsky, 1997, pp. 552–3).

To date, there are no signs that Russia is preparing to retreat into sulky unilateralism. The Russian Mission to NATO and the Senior Russian Military Representative remain in Brussels and Russia continues to participate in the activities of all the pan-European security institutions, including the work of developing a European Security Charter and a European Security Model for the Twenty-First Century, launched at the Budapest OSCE summit in December 1994 and mandated at the Lisbon OSCE summit in December 1996. Moscow has not yet adopted any of the military counter-measures which were threatened to deter or counter-balance the proposed enlargement of NATO, nor has Russia yet concluded a full military alliance with Belarus, established a CIS defence organisation comparable with NATO, thrown out the START II Treaty or withdrawn from the CFE Treaty or from participation in such international institutions as the IMF and the Paris Club. As liberal Russian commentators such as Alexei Pushkov point out, Russia has as much or more interest in participation in such forums as the West (Pushkov, 1997).

In considering a balance of power strategy, suggestions by some of the wilder national-patriotic commentators of a broader re-alignment of Russia against the West with Serbia, Iran, Iraq and China have likewise not yet been taken up by the Russian authorities. At this stage it is recognised that any such 'historical revenge' strategy would be difficult to assemble and would almost certainly jeopardise the maintenance of Russia's economic relations with the West which would not be compensated for by the dubious military and economic assets which such an alignment might bring (Trenin, 1996). Following the financial crash of 17 August 1998, the prospect of an economically weaker Russia adopting such a strategy in the medium term looks even more remote. Whether in the longer term NATO enlargement will trigger some sort of re-alignment of Russia with China to challenge America's global hegemony must, for the moment, remain speculative (see Chapter 16).

Russia and Central and Eastern Europe (CEE)

Looking to the future, the entry of Poland, the Czech Republic and Hungary into NATO in 1999 will demand that close attention be given by NATO to a broad range of security considerations in the western borderlands of Eurasia, a region with which NATO is unfamiliar and in which Russia's presence has historically bulked large (Garnett, 1997, p. 73). How is Moscow responding to the prospect of such developments?

In view of the deep fears within the CEE states of the possibility of Russian re-domination of the region, it was from an early point unlikely that they would be happy to accept Russia's suggestion that their desire to 'return to Europe' be met within the structures of the EU (and the WEU) and the Council of Europe (Radu, 1997; Discussions about NATO, 1996, p. 134). Moscow's proposals in 1994 for a strengthened OSCE were likewise rejected by the CEE states. The OSCE was by common regard perceived to be too large and diffuse to provide the appropriate level of security guarantees, while Russia's suggestions of an OSCE

European Security Council with permanent members, including Russia possessing veto powers, were seen to be self-serving. Subsequent proposals by Moscow for joint Western–Russian security guarantees of the CEE states as a substitute for their participation in NATO only strengthened CEE suspicions that Moscow would be happy with some sort of *droit de regard* if not sphere of influence in the region (Baranovsky, 1995a,b). Indeed, Russia's continued participation in the development by the OSCE of a European Security Model for the Twenty-First Century has only confirmed CEE suspicions that Moscow's strategy is to keep open the shape of European security arrangements in the hope that at some future point Russia's revived military power will enable her to lay claim to a more formal sphere of influence in the region (Blank, 1995, 1998).

For the states of the region, therefore, membership of the EU (and the WEU) is seen to be an important but not sufficient means of securing their future. By contrast, it is precisely NATO's Article 5 security guarantee, underwritten by US nuclear and conventional military power, which has led the states of the region to look to membership of NATO (Larrabee, 1997, pp. 101–6). The retrospective judgement by Alexei Arbatov, Russia's best-known security analyst, that Russia's treatment of its former allies in CEE in 1992–93 represented 'one of the most significant failures of post-Soviet Russia in the international arena, reflecting above all the deficiency in strategic thinking in Moscow', therefore begs the question as to what diplomatic and security initiatives would have met with a positive response in the CEE capitals and headed off the applications for entry to NATO by the states of the region (Arbatov *et al.*, 1997, p. 11).

As to the likely future course of Russia's relations with CEE and the western former Soviet republics, from an early point in the debate concerning NATO's proposed eastward enlargement it was clear to Western observers that it was not the prospect of the Central European states joining NATO that most exercised Moscow. Rather, it was the 'open-ended' nature of the enlargement process which was the primary cause for Moscow's concern since it left open the prospect of NATO membership and NATO facilities encroaching upon the territory of the former Soviet Union which Russia regards as its zone of special responsibility (Lieven, 1995). As early as the summer of 1996 Russian Foreign Minister Yevgeni Primakov signalled that 'at quite a high level, we . . . let NATO people know that we are worried not so much by the simple fact of "extension" but only by the approach of the alliance's infrastructure towards Russia's borders' (Zagorski, 1997, p. 536).

Nor was there any difficulty in identifying which states would become the focus of Moscow's concern. The Russian Council on Defence and Foreign Policy warned in 1995 that if NATO enlargement extended only to the Central European states, the Baltic states and Ukraine would become a 'zone of bitter strategic rivalry between an expanded NATO and a resentful Russia' (Council on Defence and Foreign Policy, 1995, p. 30). However, with the signing of the Ukraine–NATO Charter on a Distinctive Partnership in July 1997, accompanied by the normalisation of Russian–Ukrainian relations as a consequence of the signing of the Treaty of Friendship in May 1997, the prospect of Ukraine's entry to NATO has diminished. The Baltic republics, by contrast, remain fiercely committed to entering both NATO and the EU and the Baltic Sea region has therefore become the primary focus of strategic attention for both NATO and Russia.

Russia and the Baltic

Given the long-established Russian perceptions of the Baltic Sea as the historical gateway to the West and the conviction of the Russian military authorities that the Baltic republics formed part of Russia's strategic space, the withdrawal from the Baltic republics was an especially wrenching process. Although many Russian analysts see Russia's security interests threatened chiefly in the South or the East, analytical centres closely linked to the Russian military authorities have emphasised the challenge which would be posed to Russia's security in North-West Europe should the Baltic republics be admitted to NATO. Their studies have suggested that the prospect of the entry of the Baltic republics into NATO would be as provocative to Russia as the deployment of nuclear missiles in Cuba was to Washington back in 1962, and that in such an eventuality Russian armed forces would be sent into the republics (Coleman, 1997; Berryman, 1998a; Sergounin, 1998a). A former Director of the US National Security Agency has consequently speculated as to the possible international repercussions of a Russian offer to surrender Kaliningrad Oblast to Germany in exchange for German support for a Russian free hand in the Baltics (Odom, 1998, p. 817).

Less dramatically, the double enlargement process now under way in both Central Europe and the Baltic Sea regions, together with the prospects for a change in the purpose and functions of such pan-European institutions, may offer Russia the opportunity within this EU–NATO–Russia triangle to participate in the development of a more distinctive agenda of security co-operation in the Baltic Sea region (Mottola, 1998; Knudsen, 1998). Russia's proposals at the Council of Baltic Seas States summit in Visby in May 1996 for the development of regional security co-operation across a range of 'soft' security issues, her proposals for bilateral and multilateral confidence-building measures put forward between August and October 1997 and President Yeltsin's announcement in Stockholm in December 1997 of 40 per cent troop reductions in North-West Russia, have not gone unnoticed. It is suggested that Russia may be looking to shift the focus of the security dialogue in the Baltic away from 'hard' security concerns towards broader possibilities of subregional and trans-regional co-operation (Baev, 1998).

While there remain serious obstacles to the development of such a comprehensive regional security dialogue, some Russian analysts of Baltic developments see the possibility of Russia and her neighbours in the Baltic Sea area constructing such a co-operative security system. A delay in the extension of NATO to the Baltic republics, coupled with a variety of arms control and confidence-building measures, economic and technical assistance to assist in the diversification of the highly militarised Kaliningrad and St Petersburg regions, and the resolution of the territorial and ethnic disputes between Russia and the Baltic states, it is argued, would encourage Russia to develop a more co-operative range of policies for the region (Sergounin, 1998b). For the moment, at least, NATO membership for the Baltic states is not on the cards and the region appears stable (Kamp, 1998).

Russia and Europe: prospects

Looking to the broader implications of the NATO–EU double enlargement process for Russia's relations with Europe, Russian analysts have suggested that the first step in NATO's enlargement in the spring of 1999 might be followed by the entry of Austria, Romania, Slovenia and, possibly, Slovakia and the Baltic republics, while the Ukraine and certain CIS states might find closer associational links with NATO. In a parallel movement, EU enlargement would embrace Poland, Hungary, the Czech Republic, Cyprus and Estonia. Russia would then find itself confronting the closing of double doors by an enlarged and united Europe, with a powerful nucleus of states linked by close ties with the US and a periphery gravitating towards the nucleus. The critical task in this context, it is argued, would be to secure the partial integration of Russia within these European and Atlantic institutions (Pushkov, 1998, p. 2).

Much will depend on how Russia's relations with Europe are handled in Washington, Brussels and Moscow. Russia has yet to find its proper place in the emerging post-cold-war European security space and, as Andrei Zagorski remarks, 'Russia could become a co-operative partner compatible with European civilization or it could re-emerge, after a period of introspection, as an uneasy European power or a European problem' (Zagorski, 1997, p. 519). If appropriate associational or institutional links between Russia and the new Europe are not found, in the longer term there is the danger that Russia's aspirations to be a Great Power at the centre of a rival regional security complex of CIS states may come to hinder the development of a closer partnership with Europe. Russian commentators, such as Andrei Piontkovsky, Head of the Centre for Strategic Studies in Moscow, therefore urge that the current 'window of opportunity' must be seized by Russia and the West precisely to develop new forms of association to link Russia with the emerging Euro-Atlantic economic and security community (Piontkovsky, 1998).

Russia and the CIS

The CIS was hastily established in December 1991 to facilitate the demand for independence by the former republics of the disintegrating Soviet Union. Despite the reservations of those Russian 'isolationists' who were reluctant to see Russia continue to subsidise the smaller and weaker economies of the former Soviet republics, faced with this enormous geopolitical upheaval Russia quickly sought to use the CIS as a tool to help to preserve the dense network of relations established over the Soviet and pre-Soviet period. As to how Moscow should deal with this sphere of vital interest, the view of the Russian Council on Defence and Foreign Policy that an 'enlightened post-imperial integrationist course' be pursued won widespread support within Russia's policy-making elite. With regard to security considerations, since more than 150 000 Russian military personnel and border troops initially remained on the territory of every member state of the CIS, the somewhat arbitrary inter-republican frontiers established during the Soviet period were regarded as little more than permeable 'inner borders', priority being given to the development of the forward defence perimeter provided by the borders of the former Soviet Union.

However, the difficulties of state-building in the newly independent states were such that by 1993 instability and conflict in Georgia, Tajikistan, Moldova and Azerbaijan threatened to spill over into the Russian Federation. Demands arose that Russia's status as a Great Power should be affirmed by a re-assertion of influence in the 'Near Abroad' rather than by a continuance of Kozyrev's efforts to seek recognition from the West (Saivetz, 1998, p. 26). As one Russian analyst remarked, if 'the Russian Federation does not become leader in its own part of the world, then she will not achieve the status of a real global Great Power for a long time' (Jonson, 1998, p. 94). Moreover, these demands focused on the call to protect the millions of Russian citizens in these states, a rare foreign policy issue of emotive significance for mass public opinion in Russia (Wallander, 1996, p. 209).

In response, Russian forces were despatched to undertake 'peacekeeping' tasks within the CIS, for which Russia sought CSCE and UN legitimisation, while Moscow sought to establish through bilateral negotiations a series of 30 military bases within the CIS to provide a 'zone of stability' to enhance Russia's security and to help protect the rights of the Russian diaspora. To signify the higher priority now attached to advancing Russia's relations with the CIS, in January 1994 a separate Ministry for the CIS was created to replace the Department for CIS Affairs which had been established in the Ministry of Foreign Affairs in the autumn of 1992.

What has been the outcome of Russia's efforts to foster integration within the CIS? Despite numerous summits and hundreds of signed agreements little progress has been made since within the CIS integration is perceived to be an instrument of Russia's efforts to restore its regional geopolitical dominance. Moscow's early expectation of a community of interest of all the republics of the former Soviet Union has consequently given way to a recognition of the growing pressures for decentralisation, diversification and a differentiation and stratification between the regions and sub-regions within CIS. To meet these new demands Russia has sought to combine its initial emphasis on economic and security multilateralism with the development of bilateral agreements with Belarus, Kazakhstan, Armenia and Kyrgyzstan (Bremmer, 1998). Worries that conflict within the Russian Federation (notably the war in Chechnya) would spread to the CIS states has meanwhile focused attention on the need for more effective protection of the Russian Federation's 'inner borders' with the CIS states (Allison, 1998, p. 14).

It has been suggested that, rather than seeking to establish a Russian–Eurasian empire, Moscow should be content to develop a differentiated mix of bilateral and regional associations in which Russia would neither abandon its periphery nor seek to construct complex multilateral integrationist structures but aim for a more flexible mix of political, economic and military interactions with the region (Garnett, 1995, p. 42). However, despite the high economic and political costs Moscow remains committed to creating a unified regional international system in which Russia will have predominant weight. Although Moscow has managed to maintain a well-defined sphere of influence and a distinct regional international system, Russia has not secured the high level of integration it sought. The CIS remains an amorphous, fragile and ineffective multilateral structure. Indeed, such is the shortfall between Russia's ambitions and its capabilities, Moscow's continued commitment to integration within the

CIS is seen as in part symbolic, signifying Russia's longer-term intention to restore Russian great power predominance within the geopolitical space of the former Soviet Union (see Chapter 13; Garnett, 1997, pp. 66–7).

In the longer term, while disintegrative tendencies may not be ruled out it is unlikely that the CIS will fade into irrelevance as the member states consolidate their sovereignty. Russia's singular trans-regional position, huge size and military presence, and numerous historical, cultural, infrastructural and human ties with the CIS states will probably underpin its continued dominant geopolitical position in Eurasia, although the extent of this dominance has not been established. A variety of CIS scenarios can therefore be envisaged. At one extreme, it is possible that following the full assertion of statehood by the former republics a less centralised form of multilateral management might be established. At the other extreme, should Russia find herself permanently excluded from NATO and the EU and economic and political conditions within Russia deteriorate, the possibility cannot be excluded that Russia will seek a way out by means of a coercive re-integration of the CIS (Hopmann *et al.*, 1997). More likely, despite Russia's efforts to check the influence exerted by potentially hostile external powers within the former Soviet space, particularly with respect to control of the oil and gas resources of Transcaucasia and Central Asia, relations within the post-Soviet security complex will become more diverse and variegated as other outside powers such as Turkey, Iran, the US and China play a larger role in its various theatres (see Chapter 13; Roeder, 1997, pp. 240–3).

Russia and North-East Asia

In North-East Asia, a region unaffected by border changes created elsewhere by the collapse of the Soviet Union, the legacy inherited by Yeltsin was clear. While geostrategic and power political considerations had always bulked large in Russian thinking about East Asia, Russia had never been a powerful economic actor in the region. Since 1992 Russia has therefore sought to establish its position as a Pacific power primarily in political and economic terms rather than in a military–strategic sense (Krivtsov, 1993, p. 77). However, in view of Russia's weak and vulnerable position in the region, the maintenance of a stable balance of power remains an important diplomatic priority for Moscow (Arbatov, 1993, p. 36; Trofimenko, 1997, p. 248). A secondary diplomatic objective has been to help to establish a multilateral regional security system which would help to reduce the overhead costs of Russia's involvement in regional security matters (Harada, 1997).

Building on Gorbachev's limited successes, Yeltsin has sought to construct a more durable and substantial relationship with China. Complementary economic interests, especially China's need of Russia's military hardware and a common concern to maintain stability in Central Asia, have been the foundations of the limited 'strategic partnership' proclaimed in 1996 and Russia has become China's biggest arms supplier (Felgengauer, 1997). However, Russia's national security elite cannot ignore the fact that between 1990 and 1995 China's military budget has doubled and that China's future emergence as a first-rate military power will probably require Russia's involvement in a strategy of 'containment' of her huge neighbour (Arbatov, 1994, p. 72; Miasnikov, 1994, pp. 232–3; Harada, 1997, pp. 46–8; Gelman, 1997, pp. 231–5). No such shift in policy is contemplated by Moscow at present. It is recognised that any attempt by Russia to move towards the US or Japan to counter-balance China (or any attempt by China to improve its relations with the US) will threaten the Russo-Chinese *detente.*

It has been suggested that by way of a response to NATO eastward enlargement Russia might seek a still closer alignment with China (see Chapter 16). Like Russia, China confronts a US-dominated unipolar world and seeks to promote the development of a multipolar international order (Harada, 1997, p. 45). To date, however, China has not sought any such arrangement since, like Moscow, Beijing is aware that any such open challenge to Washington would risk jeopardising China's vital trade and investment ties with the West. Aware of Russia's current economic weakness, for the moment China takes a pragmatic and limited view of its partnership with Russia (Anderson, 1997; Gelman, 1997, p. 227). For its part, Moscow has likewise not sought to develop its limited strategic partnership with China into a full-blown alliance. Within the framework of its neo-Gaullist foreign policy strategy Moscow is content merely to use its relations with Beijing as a bargaining chip in its relations with Washington (Aron, 1998, p. 50).

While the development of the Russo-Chinese entente has attracted much attention, a resolution of the Kurile Islands issue and a normalisation of Russo-Japanese relations has, to date, eluded both Gorbachev and Yeltsin. However, it is possible that the Yeltsin–Hashimoto summit in Krasnoyarsk in November 1997 and the visit to Moscow of the Japanese Prime Minister, Keizo Obuchi, in November 1998 may offer the prospects of a partial deal by the time Yeltsin visits Tokyo in the spring or summer of 1999 (Blundy, 1998). Although some Russian analysts have entertained hopes that the US might act as an 'honest broker' to facilitate a settlement of the Kurile Islands issue, it appears that Washington is happy with a stalemate that denies Tokyo the freedom to participate in a balance of power game with Russia and America and maintains Japan as a key US forward base in the North-West Pacific (Trofimenko, 1997, pp. 260–1).

By contrast with Europe, no dense network of multilateral institutions exists within East Asia and Russia has sought to develop a regional security system of the first generation (Arbatov, 1995, pp. 48–9). Russia has participated in the deliberations of the ASEAN Regional Forum and since 1996 Russia, Japan and the US have contributed to a security dialogue within the Trilateral Forum on North Pacific Security which has included joint naval talks and exercises and consideration of the development of confidence-building measures (Trofimenko, 1997, pp. 245–6). However, as in Europe, in handling substantive security matters in East Asia the US has either ignored or deliberately marginalised Moscow. Russian support for the US during the 1994–95 crisis over North Korean nuclear intentions brought no dividends, Russia being excluded from the distribution of commercial contracts for the new nuclear reactors to be built in North Korea and from the four-party talks on the Korean peninsula. Moreover, in the longer term Russia's relative weight in North-East Asia is likely to shrink as Chinese and Japanese military capabilities grow at a faster pace (Betts, 1993–94, p. 51). As elsewhere, Russia's ambitions outstrip its capabilities.

БИОГРАФИЯ 18.1 **Igor Ivanov (born 1945), Foreign Minister from 1998**

Ivanov was born in Moscow and was educated at the Moscow Pedagogical Institute of Foreign Languages. He was a junior researcher at the prestigious Institute for the World Economy and International Relations before entering the diplomatic service in 1973. He has spent considerable time in Spain as a diplomat and briefly served as the Soviet ambassador in Madrid before returning to Moscow to work in the Foreign Ministry. He was made First Deputy Foreign Minister in 1994, and then succeeded Primakov as Foreign Minister in the summer of 1998.

Conclusion

What of Russia's future place in the world? As a 'new kid on the block', which way is Russia heading? Will Russia become a partner or an adversary of the West and its neighbours or something in between?

While much will clearly turn on the policies pursued towards Russia by the United States, its Western allies and Russia's neighbours, nonetheless in a world in which the key determinants of international influence look like being geo-economic as well as geostrategic attributes, the future foreign policy of Russia will in large part be determined by the rate of Russia's economic recovery. The prospects for Russia's economic development will, in turn, be powerfully shaped by the political evolution of Russia in the post-Yeltsin period. Yet whatever new leadership takes up the reins of power the likelihood is that Russia's continued economic weakness will place severe constraints on what can be considered and Russia is likely to be capable of undertaking only relatively limited foreign policy initiatives in the medium term.

For the moment, therefore, the Russian Federation remains 'a very weak regime trying to rule a Russia that has never existed before, the residual centre of a former empire that has yet to define itself politically or territorially' (Odom, 1998, p. 817). In view of the draining of power from the centre to the regions in the past few years, the possibility that the Russian Federation might itself disintegrate cannot be lightly dismissed (Herd, 1998). Although such a development does not look imminent, in such an event consideration of the future character of Russia's foreign policy would become irrelevant.

References

Adomeit H 1995 Russia as a 'great power' in world affairs: images and reality, *International Affairs (London)*, Vol. 71, No. 1, pp. 35–68.

Afanasievskii N 1997 On the NATO-Russia Founding Act, *International Affairs (Moscow)*, Vol. 43, No. 4, pp. 158–63.

Allison R 1998 The network of new security policy relations in Eurasia, in Allison R and Bluth C (eds), *Security Dilemmas in Russia and Eurasia*, Royal Institute of International Affairs, London, pp. 12–29.

Anderson J 1997 *The Limits of Sino-Russian Strategic Partnership*, Adelphi Paper 315, Oxford University Press for The International Institute for Strategic Studies, Oxford.

Arbatov A G 1993 Russia's Foreign Policy Alternatives, *International Security*, Vol. 18, No. 2, pp. 5–43.

Arbatov A G 1994 Russian National Interests, in Blackwill R D and Karaganov S A (eds), *Damage Limitation or Crisis? Russia and the Outside World*, CSIS Studies in International Security, No. 5, Brassey's, London, pp. 55–76.

Arbatov A G 1995 Russia's New Role in World Politics, *New Times (Moscow)*, Vol. 11, pp. 46–9.

Arbatov A G 1997 Russian foreign-policy thinking in transition, in Baranovsky V (ed.), *Russia and Europe: The Emerging Security Agenda*, Oxford University Press for The Stockholm International Peace Research Institute, Oxford pp. 135–59.

Arbatov A G Baranovsky V Hassner P Levgold R Roper J and Rotfeld A D 1997 Introduction, in Baranovsky V (ed.), *Russia and Europe: The Emerging Security Agenda*, Oxford University Press for The Stockholm International Peace Research Institute, Oxford pp. 1–14.

Ardy B and Gower J 1996 *Relations between Russia and the EU*, Post-Soviet Business Forum Briefing No. 10, Royal Institute of International Affairs, London.

Aron L 1994 The Emergent Priorities of Russian Foreign Policy, in Aron L and Jensen K M (eds), *The Emergence of Russian Foreign Policy*, United States Institute of Peace Press Washington, DC, pp. 17–34.

Aron L 1998 The Foreign Policy Doctrine of Postcommunist Russia and Its Domestic Context in Mandelbaum M (ed.), *The New Russian Foreign Policy*, Council on Foreign Relations, New York, pp. 23–63.

Baev P 1995 Drifting Away from Europe, *Transition*, Vol. 1, No. 11, pp. 30–3.

Baev P 1997 Russia's Departure from Empire: Self-Assertiveness and a New Retreat, in Tunander O, Baev P and Einagel V I (eds), *Geopolitics in Post-Wall Europe: Security, Territory and Identity*, Sage for The International Peace Research Institute, Oslo, pp. 174–95.

Baev P 1998 Bear Hug for the Baltic, *The World Today*, Vol. 54, No. 3, pp. 78–9.

Baranovsky V 1995a Russian Foreign Policy Priorities and Euro-Atlantic Multilateral Institutions, *The International Spectator*, Vol. XXX, No. 1, pp. 33–50.

Baranovsky V 1995b Russia and European Security, *EuroBalkans*, Vol. 19 (Summer), pp. 4–17.

Baranovsky V (ed.) 1997 *Russia and Europe: The Emerging Security Agenda*, Oxford University Press for The Stockholm International Peace Research Institute, Oxford.

Berryman J 1996 Author's interviews with officials in the Russian Federation Ministry of Foreign Affairs, Moscow, October.

Berryman J 1998a Russian Security Policy and Northern Europe, in Ferry W E and Kanet R E (eds), *Post-Communist States in the World Community: Papers from the Fifth World Congress of Central and East European States*, Macmillan, Basingstoke, pp. 108–33.

Berryman J 1998b Russia, NATO Enlargement and the West: Fast Lane or Dead End?, in Brett P Dangerfield M Hambrook G and Kostova L (eds), *Europe: Real and Imagined*, PIC, Veliko Turnovo, pp. 141–55.

Betts R K 1993–94 Wealth, Power and Instability: East Asia and the United States after the Cold War, *International Security*, Vol. 18, No. 3, pp. 34–77.

Blacker C D 1998 Russia and the West, in Mandelbaum M (ed.) *The New Russian Foreign Policy*, Council on Foreign Relations, New York, pp. 167–93.

Blackwill R D and Karaganov S A (eds) 1994 *Damage Limitation or Crisis? Russia and the Outside World*, CSIS Studies in International Security, No. 5, Brassey's, London.

Blank S 1995 The Future Security of the Czech Republic, *Jane's Intelligence Review*, Vol. 7, No. 9, pp. 392–3.

Blank S 1998 Who's Minding the Store? The Failure of Russian Security Policy, *Problems of Post-Communism*, Vol. 45, No. 2, pp. 3–11.

Blank S J and Rubinstein A Z (eds) 1997 *Imperial Decline: Russia's Changing Role in Asia*, Duke University Press, Durham and London.

Blundy A 1998 Yeltsin to offer Japan Kurils deal, *The Times*, 12 November.

Bremmer I 1998 Whose Eurasia?, *Analysis of Current Events*, Vol. 10, No. 7–8, pp. 18–19.

Brzezinski Z 1994 The Premature Partnership, *Foreign Affairs*, Vol. 73, No. 2, pp. 67–82.

Brzezinski Z 1995 A Plan for Europe?, *Foreign Affairs*, Vol. 74, No. 1, pp. 26–42.

Brzezinski Z 1997 A Geostrategy for Eurasia, *Foreign Affairs*, Vol. 76, No. 5, pp. 50–64.

Buszynski L 1996 *Russian Foreign Policy after the Cold War*, Praeger, Westport, CT.

Coleman F 1997 The Kaliningrad Scenario: Expanding NATO to the Baltics, *World Policy Journal*, Fall, pp. 71–5.

Cook C and Stevenson J 1987 *The Longman Handbook of Modern European History, 1763–1985*, Longman, London and New York.

Council on Defence and Foreign Policy (1995) No Role for Russia in a Security Order That Includes an Expanded NATO, *Transition*, Vol. 1, No. 23, pp. 27–32.

Danilov D and De Spiegeleire S 1998 *From Decoupling to Recoupling: A New Security Relationship Between Russia and Western Europe?*, (Chaillot Paper 31, Institute for Security Studies, Western European Union, Paris.

Discussions about NATO: Moscow's Arguments are Gaining Weight 1996 *International Affairs* (Moscow), Vol. 42, No. 3, pp. 133–40.

Felgengauer P 1997 An Uneasy Partnership: Sino-Russian Defence Co-operation and Arms Sales, in Pierre A J and Trenin D V (eds), *Russia in the World Arms Trade*, The Carnegie Endowment for International Peace, Washington, DC, pp. 87–103.

Ferry W E and Kanet R E (eds) 1998 *Post-Communist States in the World Community: Papers from the Fifth World Congress of Central and East European States*, Macmillan, Basingstoke.

Gaddy C G and Ickes B W 1998 Russia's Virtual Economy, *Foreign Affairs*, Vol. 77, No. 5, pp. 51–67.

Gareev M 1996 The Expansion of NATO Does Not Solve, but Aggravates Security Issues, *International Affairs*, Vol. 42, No. 3, pp. 141–7.

Garnett S W 1995 The Integrationist Temptation, *The Washington Quarterly*, Vol. 18, No. 2, pp. 35–44.

Garnett S W 1997 Russia's Illusory Ambitions, *Foreign Affairs*, Vol. 76, No. 2, pp. 61–76.

Garnett S W 1998 Europe's Crossroads: Russia and the West in the New Borderlands, in Mandelbaum M (ed.), *The New Russian Foreign Policy*, Council on Foreign Relations, New York, pp. 64–99.

Gelman H 1997 Implications for the United States of Russia's Far East Policy, in Blank S J and Rubinstein A Z (eds), *Imperial Decline: Russia's Changing Role in Asia*, Duke University Press, Durham and London, 213–43.

Gorbachev M S 1987 *Perestroika: New Thinking for Our Country and the World*, Collins, London.

Harada C 1997 *Russia and North-East Asia*, Adelphi Paper 310, Oxford University Press for The International Institute for Strategic Studies, Oxford.

Haslam J 1998 Russia's Seat at the Table: a Place Denied or a Place Delayed?, *International Affairs*, Vol. 74, No. 1, pp. 119–30.

Hedegaard L and Lindstrom B (eds) 1998 *The NEBI Yearbook 1998: Northern European and Baltic Sea Integration*, Springer-Verlag, Berlin.

Herd G 1998 Regional Meltdown, *The World Today*, Vol. 54, No. 10, pp. 251–2.

Hopmann P T, Shenfield S and Arel D 1997 *Integration and Disintegration in the Former Soviet Union: Implications for Regional and Global Security*, Occasional Paper 30, Thomas J Watson Jr Institute for International Studies, Brown University, Providence, RI.

Ivanov O and Pozdnyakov V 1998 Russia and the European Union, *International Affairs (Moscow)*, Vol. 44, No. 3, pp. 49–55.

Jonson L 1998 Russia and European Security: Old Wine in New Bottles, in Ferry W E and Kanet R E (eds), *Post-Communist States in the World Community: Papers from the Fifth World Congress of Central and East European States*, Macmillan, Basingstoke, 87–107.

Kamp K-H 1998 NATO Entrapped. Debating the Next Enlargement Round, *Survival*, Vol. 40, No. 3, pp. 170–86.

Knudsen O 1998 *Co-operative Security in the Baltic Sea Region*, Chaillot Paper 33, Institute for Security Studies, Western European Union, Paris.

Kortunov A 1996 NATO Enlargement and Russia: In Search of An Adequate Response, in Haglund D G (ed.), *Will NATO Go East? The Debate Over Enlarging the Atlantic Alliance* Centre for International Relations, Queen's University, Kingston, Ontario, pp. 69–92.

Krivtsov A 1993 Russia and the Far East, *International Affairs (Moscow)*, Vol. 39, No. 1, pp. 77–84.

Kugler R L 1996 *Enlarging NATO: the Russia Factor*, RAND, Santa Monica, CA.

Lake D A and Morgan P M (eds) 1997 *Regional Orders: Building Security in a New World*, Pennsylvania State University Press, Pennsylvania.

Lambeth B S 1995 Russia's Wounded Military, *Foreign Affairs*, Vol. 74, No. 2, pp. 86–98.

Larrabee F S 1997 East-Central Europe: Problems, Prospects and Policy Dilemmas, in Clemens C (ed.), *NATO and the Quest for Post-Cold War Security*, Macmillan, Basingstoke, pp. 87–108.

Lieven A 1995 Russian Opposition to NATO Expansion, *The World Today*, Vol. 51, No. 10, pp. 196–99.

Light M 1996 Foreign Policy Thinking, in Malcolm N *et al. Internal Factors in Russian Foreign Policy*, Oxford University Press for The Royal Institute of International Affairs, Oxford, pp. 33–100.

Litovkin V 1994 Kak mnogo nas tam bylo, *Izvestia*, 31 August.

Lucas M R 1995 The Search for Security in Greater Europe: the Russian Federation, the CIS and the International Organisations, *Transitions*, Vol. 36, No. 1–2, pp. 165–219.

Macfarlane S N 1994 Russian Conceptions of Europe, *Post-Soviet Affairs*, Vol. 10, No. 3, pp. 234–69.

Malcolm N (ed.) 1994 *Russia and Europe: An End to Confrontation?*, Royal Institute for International Affairs, London.

Malcolm N 1995 Russian Foreign Policy Decision-Making, in Shearman P (ed.), *Russian Foreign Policy Since 1990*, Westview, Boulder, CO, pp. 23–51.

Malcolm N *et al.* 1996 *Internal Factors in Russian Foreign Policy*, Oxford University Press for The Royal Institute of International Affairs, Oxford.

Mandelbaum M (ed.) 1998 *The New Russian Foreign Policy*, Council on Foreign Relations, New York.

Mandelbaum M 1998 Introduction: Russian Foreign Policy in Historical Perspective, in Mandelbaum M(ed.), *The New Russian Foreign Policy*, Council on Foreign Relations, New York, pp. 1–22.

Meek J 1998 Moscow Sees World Through Eastern Eyes, *The Guardian*, 10 March.

Miasnikov V 1994 Russia and China, in Blackwill R D and Karaganov S A (eds), *Damage Limitation or Crisis: Russia and the Outside World*, CSIS Studies in International Security, No. 5, Brassey's, London, pp. 227–40.

Mikoyan S A 1998 Russia, the US and Regional Conflict in Eurasia, *Survival*, Vol. 40, No. 3, pp. 112–26.

Mottola K 1998 Security Around the Baltic Rim: Concepts, Actors and Processes, in Hedegaard L and Lindstrom B (eds), *The NEBI Yearbook 1998: Northern European and Baltic Sea Integration*, Springer-Verlag, Berlin, pp. 363–404.

Mouritzen H (ed.) 1998 *Bordering Russia: Theory and Prospects for Europe's Baltic Rim*, Ashgate, Aldershot.

NATO–Russia Permanent Joint Council Statement 1998 *NATO Review*, Vol. 46, No. 3, p. D6.

NATO–Russia Permanent Joint Council Statement 1999 *NATO Review*, Vol. 47, No. 1, p. 27.

Nikolayev A 1993 Military Aspects of Russia's Security, *International Affairs (Moscow)*, Vol. 39, No. 10, pp. 6–9.

Odom W E 1998 Russia's Several Seats at the Table, *International Affairs*, Vol. 74, No. 4, pp. 809–21.

Palmer J 1997 Russian P M Spells Out E U Hopes, *The Guardian*, 19 July.

Parrish S 1996 Chaos in Foreign Policy Decision-Making, *Transition*, Vol. 2, No. 10, pp. 30–3, 64.

Pierre A J and Trenin D 1997 Developing NATO–Russia Relations, *Survival*, Vol. 39, No. 1, pp. 5–18.

Piontkovsky A 1998 Window of Opportunity: How Russia Might Fit into the International Scheme, *The Jamestown Foundation: Prism*, Vol. 22, No. 2 (11 November).

Pipes R 1997 Is Russia Still an Enemy?, *Foreign Affairs*, Vol. 76, No. 5, pp. 65–78.

Pushkov A 1997 A Compromise with NATO?, *International Affairs (Moscow)*, Vol. 43, No. 3, pp. 13–22.

Pushkov A 1998 'The Primakov Doctrine' and a New European Order, *International Affairs (Moscow)*, Vol. 44, No. 2, pp. 1–15.

Radu M 1997 Why Eastern and Central Europe Look West, *Orbis*, Vol. 41, No. 1, pp. 39–57.

Roeder P G 1997 From Hierarchy to Hegemony: The Post-Soviet Security Complex, in Lake D A and Morgan P M (eds), *Regional Orders: Building Security in a New World*, Pennsylvania State University Press, Pennsylvania, pp. 219–44.

Saivetz C 1998 Post-Soviet Russian Foreign Policy: Domestic Debates, the 'Near Abroad' and the West, in Ferry W E and Kanet R E (eds), *Post-Communist States in the World Community: Papers from the Fifth World Congress of Central and East European States*, Macmillan, Basingstoke, pp. 21–45.

Sergounin A A 1998a The Russian Dimension, in Mouritzen H (ed.), *Bordering Russia: Theory and Prospects for Europe's Baltic Rim*, Ashgato, Aldershot, pp. 15–71.

Sergounin A A 1998b Russia's Security Policies in the Baltic Sea Area, in Hedegaard L and Lindstrom B (eds), *The NEBI Yearbook 1998: Northern European and Baltic Sea Integration*, Springer-Verlag, Berlin, pp. 465–83.

Sestanovich S (ed.) 1994 *Rethinking Russia's National Interests*, Centre for Strategic and International Studies, Washington, DC.

Sicherman H 1997 The Loud Voice of the NATO–Russian Council, *Transition*, Vol. 4, No. 3, pp. 50–55.

Trenin D 1996 Russia and the West. Avoiding Complications, *International Affairs (Moscow)*, Vol. 42, No. 1, pp. 30–8.

Trofimenko H 1997 US–Russian Relations in East Asia: A View From Moscow, in Blank S J and Rubinstein A Z (eds), *Imperial Decline: Russia's Changing Role in Asia*, Duke University Press, Durham and London, pp. 244–71.

Tsygankov A P 1997 From International Institutionalism to Revolutionary Expansionism: The Foreign Policy Discourse of Contemporary Russia, *Mershon International Studies Review*, Vol. 41, No. 2, pp. 247–68.

Wallander C A 1996 Ideas, Interests, and Institutions in Russian Foreign Policy, in Wallander C A (ed.), *The Sources of Russian Foreign Policy After the Cold War*, Westview, Boulder, CO, pp. 207–18.

Yost D S 1998 The New NATO and Collective Security, *Survival*, Vol. 40, No. 2, pp. 135–60.

Zagorski A 1993 Russia and Europe, *International Affairs (Moscow)*, Vol. 39, No. 1, pp. 43–51.

Zagorski A 1997 Russia and European Institutions, in Baranovsky V (ed.), *Russia and Europe: The Emerging Security Agenda*, Oxford University Press for The Stockholm International Peace Research Institute, Oxford, pp. 519–40.

Zagorski A 1998 Consolation Prize from NATO, *New Times (Moscow)*, Vol. 7, pp. 48–9.

Zagorski A, Zlobin A, Solodovnik S and Khrustalev M 1992 Russia in a New World, *International Affairs (Moscow)*, Vol. 38, No. 7, pp. 3–11.

Zubok V 1992 Tyranny of the Weak: Russia's New Foreign Policy, *World Policy Journal*, Vol. IX, No. 2, pp. 191–217.

Zubok V 1995 Russia: Between Peace and Conflict, in Holm H-H and Sorensen G (eds), *Whose World Order? Uneven Globalization and the End of the Cold War*, Westview, Boulder, CO, pp. 103–17.

Further reading

Baranovsky V (ed.) 1997 *Russia and Europe: The Emerging Security Agenda*, Oxford University Press for The Stockholm International Peace Research Institute, Oxford.

Buszynski L 1996 *Russian Foreign Policy after the Cold War*, Praeger, Westport, CT.

Kanet R E and Kozhemiakin A V (eds) 1997 *The Foreign Policy of the Russian Federation*, Macmillan, Basingstoke.

Mandelbaum M (ed.) 1998 *The New Russian Foreign Policy*, Council on Foreign Relations: New York.

Petro N N and Rubinstein A Z 1997 *Russian Foreign Policy: From Empire to Nation-State*, Addison Wesley Longman: Harlow.

Web site for the Russian Foreign Ministry: http//www.diplomat.ru

Index

Note: Pages references in *italics* refer to Boxes